Continued on next page

THE BEACON
HANDBOOK

THE **BEACON HANDBOOK**

FOURTH EDITION

ROBERT PERRIN
Indiana State University

Houghton Mifflin Company   Boston   New York

Address editorial correspondence to:

Houghton Mifflin Company
College Division
222 Berkeley Street
Boston, MA 02116-3764

Senior Sponsoring Editor: Dean Johnson
Senior Project Editor: Rosemary R. Jaffe
Senior Production/Design Coordinator: Jill Haber
Senior Manufacturing Coordinator: Priscilla Bailey
Marketing Manager: Pamela J. Laskey

Cover Design: Mark Caleb
Cover Image: © Richard Cummins. Youghal Lighthouse, County Cork, Ireland

Printed in the U.S.A.

Library of Congress Catalog Card Number: 96-76947

Student Edition ISBN: 0-395-77992-8

Examination Copy ISBN: 0-395-84394-4

3 4 5 6 7 8 9 FFG - 03 02 01 00 99

Contents

Contents

Effective Sentences

Contents

Contents

Contents

Mechanics 379

Contents

Contents

Preface

The primary goal of *The Beacon Handbook* is to offer students clear, succinct, accessible explanations of the basic issues of grammar, usage, punctuation, and mechanics within the larger context of writing to communicate meaning.

Recognizing that a handbook must be complete, accurate, and accessible to be useful, *The Beacon Handbook* includes many features designed to enhance both accessibility and content.

Accessibility

"Quick Reference."   A "Quick Reference," placed near the beginning of each chapter, abstracts and presents succinctly the most important information in that chapter. "Quick References" can be used to preview or review chapters, or they can be drawn on for quick answers to students' pressing questions.

Clear Explanations.   Students are introduced to grammatical terms and principles through definitions and explanations couched in everyday language. Sample sentences, many accompanied by specific parenthetical explanations, illustrate discussions.

Tables and Other Graphic Displays.   Numerous tables, charts, lists, and checklists present information clearly and concisely. Checklists are especially useful for students working independently.

Thematic Exercises.   Each exercise, whether in sentence or paragraph format, treats a single topic, allowing students to apply newly learned information and skills within a realistic, coherent context of written expression.

Word Processing.   Because computers have introduced new possibilities for exploration and control of writing by writers at every level of experience, *The Beacon Handbook* offers specific, practical information and advice for using a word processor to improve writing fluency. Word-processing advice, clearly marked with the symbol ▦ , is incorporated into the text where it is most directly helpful, either within text discussions or in separate sections. Some advice, particular to a specific problem, will benefit only a few students; other advice will be of use to all students with access to a word processor; but even students without word processors may find it useful to adapt to paper some of the techniques described for the screen. Exercises marked with ▦ are available in ASCII files.

Content

The Writing Process.   *The Beacon Handbook* emphasizes the writing process—the discovery of meaning, expression, and form through planning, drafting, and revising—providing thorough grounding in writing the essay and the research paper, two formats typical in college writing.

Critical Thinking and Writing.   Chapter 5, "Critical Thinking and Writing," leads students through some of the basic concepts underlying critical thinking and writing skills, emphasizing the importance to communication—whether spoken, read, or written—of logical sequences of ideas, clearly and correctly articulated assertions, and apt and adequate supporting evidence.

Professional Samples.   Paragraph-length samples from respected writers such as Henry David Thoreau, E. B. White, Martin Luther King, Jr., and Joan Didion provide students with interesting reading as well as effective, varied models. In addition, samples from a wide variety of sources illustrate techniques of writing in different contexts.

Samples of Full-length Papers. *The Beacon Handbook* includes a full-length model of each of the three types of paper discussed in detail: the essay, the argument, and the research paper. "The Composing Process" follows Erica, a student writing about magazine advertisements, through her planning, drafting, and revising to her final paper. "Critical Thinking and Writing" contains Michael Brennan's "A Case for Discretion,"[1] annotated to show use of logical strategies. The research process and final paper of Shingo Endo, a student writer, illustrate "Research"; the paper, on music therapy, is annotated to show Shingo's rhetorical, stylistic, and technical choices.

The Research Paper. *The Beacon Handbook* describes and illustrates the entire research process, beginning with the selection and evaluation of potential topics and sources and ending with preparation of the final copy. Through the model of one student's research and paper, students see the relation among all stages and the bearing of each on the final paper. Coverage of proper documentation forms includes both the Modern Language Association of America[2] style and, in an appendix, the American Psychological Association[3] style.

Instructional Supplements

The Beacon Workbook, by Cynthia Frazer, Old Dominion University. A collection of 180 supplemental exercises accompanied by an instructor's manual with answers to all exercises.

Diagnostic Tests. Three forms of a fifteen-page test provided on photocopying masters, free to adopters.

---

1. Michael Brennan, "A Case for Discretion," *Newsweek* 13 Nov. 1995: *18.*
2. Joseph Gibaldi, *MLA Handbook for Writers of Research Papers,* 4th ed. (New York: MLA, 1995).
3. *Publication Manual of the American Psychological Association,* 4th ed. (Washington: APA, 1994).

Beacon Exercises and Review. A grammar and review program of nearly three hundred exercises available in computerized form for IBM® and Macintosh® computers, free to adopters.

Beacon Editing Exercises. Sixty-four thematic exercises available in computerized form as ASCII files, also free to adopters.

ACKNOWLEDGMENTS

My work on the fourth edition of *The Beacon Handbook* has been made infinitely easier and more productive because of the excellent staff at Houghton Mifflin. I am also grateful for the advice from a number of teachers who reviewed the previous editions in preparation for the fourth edition:

Jean Anaporte-Easton, West Virginia State College
Curtis W. Bobbitt, College of Great Falls, Montana
Steven L. Culbertson, Owens Community College, Ohio
Janet B. Hubbs, Ocean County College, New Jersey
Theresa M. Jackson, Western Iowa Technical Community College
Rose Mask Monroe, Baltimore City Community College
Allen Powell, Dallas Baptist University
Brenda Serotte, Lehman College, CUNY

In addition, I would like to thank Scott Davis, Librarian and Head of Information Services, Cunningham Memorial Library, Indiana State University, for his technical advice and insights; the students in my research-focused writing classes for their comments about the effectiveness of the explanations, samples, and exercises; and the teaching assistants in the Department of English, Indiana State University, for their suggestions and recommendations. In particular, I would like to thank Shingo Endo for allowing me to use his preliminary research work and his research paper as the basis for much of the discussion in the research unit.

As always, I wish to thank Judy, Chris, and Jenny for their patience, encouragement, and support.

R.P.

To the Student

The Beacon Handbook combines a brief introduction to writing with a complete yet compact reference to the conventions of standard English, the expected means for communication in college and the workplace. The first and seventh parts cover the process of writing essays and research papers, respectively; the other five parts describe and illustrate the conventions of English grammar, usage, punctuation, and mechanics.

Designed to be used efficiently, *The Beacon Handbook* organizes information in a consistent format. After reviewing *The Beacon Handbook*'s organization and learning to use its features, you will see that you can easily find the information you need, even when you are not sure what information you are looking for. And after you have found what you are looking for, *The Beacon Handbook*'s features also help you to understand clearly and apply effectively the principles of good writing.

Finding Information

Organization. The seven parts of *The Beacon Handbook* are divided into thirty-five chapters, each treating a specific aspect of composition or English grammar and usage. Each chapter is divided into precepts (rules to guide your work), coded with the chapter number and a letter of the alphabet; up to three levels of headings may subdivide precept sections. Look, for example, at Chapter 15, "Fragments": the first precept, coded 15a, reads "Revise fragments that are phrases." Two headings, "Fragments Lacking Subjects" and "Fragments Lacking Verbs," subdivide the discussion. For an example of subdivisions at more than one level, see precept 22d.

Note that precept numbers appear in the top outside corner of each page. These work like the guide words at the tops of dictionary pages; the precept number at the top of the left page indicates the first precept on that page, and the precept number at the top of the right page indicates the last precept on that page.

Guides to the Organization. The endpapers, the heavy pages used to join the book cover to the text pages, contain a brief outline of the book and a list of correction symbols similar to those your instructor will use to comment on your papers, with cross-references to relevant text sections.

The table of contents provides a complete outline of the text. See pages vii–xviii.

Two indexes, one to word-processing information (see pages 693–95) and a general index (see pages 696–730), provide detailed, alphabetical listings of the text's contents.

"Quick Reference." A "Quick Reference," located near the beginning of each chapter, lists in a clear, brief, accessible format the most crucial information in the chapter. See page 3.

Appendixes and Glossaries. The appendixes and glossaries provide useful information in accessible locations and formats. Five appendixes are included: Appendix A, on preparing computer and typed manuscripts (see pages 560–64); Appendix B, on the basic features of the American Psychological Association documentary style (see pages 565–91); Appendix C, on writing essay examinations (see pages 592–98); Appendix D, on the basic forms of business letters and résumés (see pages 599–610); and Appendix E, on writing about literature (see pages 611–53).

Two glossaries are included: the Glossary of Usage explains troublesome or often-confused words and provides examples of correct usage (see pages 654–71); and the Glossary of Grammatical Terms defines grammatical terms used in the book and provides an example of each (see pages 672–90).

Using Information

Examples, Tables, and Special Notes. Throughout the text, examples, tables, and special notes augment definitions and explanations. Use them to assure your understanding of and as convenient references to chapter concepts and information.

Examples, set off with extra space and distinguished by typeface and labels, illustrate the principle under discussion. Explanation of examples may follow in parentheses, when needed, to point out the pros and cons of specific choices. See page 277 for a sample.

Tables, charts, and lists present crucial information succinctly in an easily located, readable format. See pages 129, 315, and 512.

Computer Notes, Boxes, and Exercises. Advice for using a word processor to improve your writing appears in computer notes within discussions (see page 9) or separate computer boxes (see pages 55–56); both are marked with the symbol ■. Choose from among the strategies suggested according to your needs as a writer or the nature of a particular project. Try all of the strategies; by playing with the computer you will find your own best strategies and style of working.

You will notice that some of the exercises in *The Beacon Handbook* are also marked with ■. This means that those exercises may be available on disk from your instructor or in your writing lab. If so, you can complete the exercises using your word-processing program, which will enable you to correct, revise, and rewrite freely, without retyping. If the disk version is not available or you do not have access to a word processor, you can, of course, still complete the computer exercises as you would any of the others, by recopying them.

Whether you are using *The Beacon Handbook* as a text, with chapters assigned by your instructor, or as a reference, using it as necessary when you are writing for any of your courses or for your own reasons, a preliminary review of its features and information will give you increasing control of your writing.

THE BEACON HANDBOOK

THE
COMPOSING
PROCESS

1   Planning

Before sitting down at a desk or computer to write, you need to make plans. Whether these plans are formulated in your mind or on paper, you should begin to focus on particular subjects and make choices about ways to explore them. You will vary your planning strategies with each project as you respond to its individual requirements and challenges. This chapter explores some common and consistently helpful planning strategies.

Quick Reference

Planning strategies encourage exploration and discovery. Use the following approaches to think about your subject:

⟩ *Be open-minded about potential subjects.*

⟩ *Do not select a specific topic until you have explored the general subject from a variety of perspectives.*

⟩ *Develop topics that interest you. Your enthusiasm will come through in your writing and will engage your readers.*

⟩ *After determining your topic, clearly state the main idea in a working thesis statement that expresses the appropriate tone and includes any necessary qualifications.*

Note: The exercises in Chapters 1, 2, and 3 will take you from idea to final paper. Keep the work from each exercise to use in later exercises.

| 1a | > | **To begin, select a general subject.** |

Because the most effective writing develops from an interest in or commitment to a subject, select a general subject that appeals to you as you begin to plan your paper.

Do not limit your thinking. Instead, keep an open mind and consider various general subjects, such as the following, before selecting one.

Regular activities. Think of your routine activities: working, studying, listening to music, shopping, watching television, eating, exercising, reading. Any of these routines can yield interesting topics if thoughtfully explored.

General reading. Thoughts about, associations with, and responses to your general (non-course-related) reading in books, magazines, and newspapers can lead to interesting subjects.

Special interests. Do you see every foreign film that comes to local theaters or every television documentary on ecology? Can you write computer programs to track baseball statistics or compile a club newsletter? Such special interests make good subjects because the more you know about a subject, the more you will have to write about it.

People you know. The appearance, personality, behavior, and beliefs of the people you know can provide interesting subjects. Consider anyone you know—a newspaper vendor, your landlord, a professor—not just close friends and family.

Places you have visited. Have you been to Spain, Montreal, or the Grand Canyon? What about a relative's farm or business, your city's fire station, or the weight room at the local gym? Both familiar and unfamiliar places, explored in detail and without preconceptions, make interesting subjects.

Unusual experiences. If you have had experiences that most others have not had, you have the beginning of a good subject. Exploring these experiences on paper may lead you to insights both you and others will appreciate.

Problems people face. Personal, social, economic, and political problems demand attention. Serious problems to which you have given or would like to give serious thought can be provocative subjects.

Changes in your life. Think about significant changes in your life: going to college, getting a job, adjusting to the aging or death of a parent. Exploring your feelings and thoughts during and after these changes may provide a rewarding subject.

Likes and dislikes. Consider things you find appealing or unappealing: the network news, mystery novels, reunions, jazz. Consider especially the underlying attitudes and values that your preferences reveal, and be willing to discuss them openly.

Strong opinions. What strong opinions do you hold on important matters like censorship, U.S. immigration policy, or nuclear disarmament? Consider writing about the opinion that usually starts the liveliest discussions with your relatives or friends.

Social, political, and cultural events. Local, national, and international issues and events can be fascinating to write about, whether the topic is the politics of the Olympics, the collapse of a local bridge, or the latest Broadway musical hit. Consider especially events that you have followed closely.

Academic courses. The information, insights, and associations that you have absorbed in academic courses make productive subjects to explore in writing. Remember that not everyone learns the same things, even in the same courses.

EXERCISE 1.1 ❭ *General subjects*

For each of the twelve general subjects presented above, list at least two potential subjects for a paper, for a total of twenty-four.

| 1b | ❭ | **Develop ideas through planning.** |

Rather than move directly from selecting a general subject to writing a paper or an article, first take time to explore your general subject. Select and develop a manageably narrow topic by focusing on one aspect of the subject, consider your knowledge of and opinion about the topic, and explore alternative ways to develop ideas related to the topic.

Basics for composing on the word processor

Writers experienced in using word processors follow the steps below to avoid losing or misplacing their work.

Save your work frequently. Every fifteen to twenty minutes and whenever you leave your computer, however briefly, use the "save" command to ensure that your work will be stored in the computer's memory.

At the end of every writing session, print a paper copy, known as a *hard copy*, of your work. If the electronic version is lost, you will still have your work, and a hard copy will be useful when you reread and revise.

At the end of every writing session, make a backup disk copy of your work. Store your disks carefully to avoid damage from liquids, dust, heat, magnetism, and so on.

Provide distinctive, easily recognizable names for each file, clearly indicating the project and its stage of development. When you revise, copy and rename the file before working on it.

Arrange the stages of your projects into logical directories and subdirectories that can be easily located. Regularly print hard copies of your directories so that you can locate material at a glance even when you are not at your computer.

Identify your work by placing its directory and file name at the bottom of the last page. You will then easily be able to locate the electronic file corresponding to any hard copy.

Date drafts of your projects so that you can determine the most recent version.

Planning strategies provide opportunities to think about a subject and explore ideas. When you have the freedom to select your subject and narrowed topic, these strategies will help you to decide what to write about. When you work from an assigned general subject or narrow topic, these strategies will help you to discover ways to clarify and develop ideas about it. Sometimes completing one activity will be enough; sometimes you will need to try several.

Planning Strategies

Freewriting	Looping
Journal writing	Clustering
Journalists' questions	Brainstorming

Freewriting

Freewriting means writing spontaneously for brief, sustained periods of ten or fifteen minutes. Freewriting can be *unfocused* if you are searching for a subject, or it can be *focused* if you know the subject but are deciding how to approach it. Freewriting generally uses full, linked sentences, but because it does not impose any other formal constraints, it gives you an opportunity to relax and write down ideas that might not otherwise have occurred to you.

To begin, think briefly about your subject and then start writing about it. (If you do not have a subject, simply begin writing down whatever comes to mind.) Write quickly. Do not worry about grammar or mechanics, neatness or form. Avoid any urge to revise sentences or to worry about logical connections among ideas. Write down all your thoughts; write until you can think of nothing else to say.

Consider this freewriting sample, which helped Erica, a student writer, to identify a general subject for a paper assigned in her English class:

Over the weekend, Tarita and I stopped by Readmore Books so that she could find a book for her nephew's birthday. While she hunted in the children's section, I drifted over to the newsstand section to browse through the magazines, something that I've always liked to do. I moved slowly down the display—it was probably sixty feet long—simply looking at titles and cover designs. I saw old stand-bys like Time, Newsweek, Life, U.S. News and World Report, and TV Guide. But I also saw a lot magazines for people with special interests: Audio, Details, Parents, YM, Boating, Guns and Ammo, Ebony, Business Week, Esquire, Mademoiselle, Ladies Home Journal, American Health, House Beautiful, and many others. As I always seem to, I got to thinking about people I know and the magazines they regularly read. Dad reads Esquire; Mom reads Better Homes and Gardens; Jason reads Details; Danielle reads YM; I read Mademoiselle. And then, as I browsed, I began to watch people pick up magazines to leaf through them. A guy in a suit (was he on a lunch break?) picked up New Republic, and a woman who was obviously shopping (she had several bags from stores nearby) thumbed through Psychology Today. And I started to think about what their magazine choices said about them. Was I creating some harmless stereotypes? Yes, I was. But then Tarita found me, she bought her book, and we headed back to campus.

Notice that Erica's word choices are sometimes colloquial and vague, her sentences sometimes informal, and her ideas only loosely linked. But her ideas are flowing, and she is getting them down on paper.

To avoid mulling over the right word or revising a sentence until it is perfect—tendencies that interfere with the quickness and spontaneity that freewriting requires—turn off your computer screen or dim it so that you cannot read the words. Then simply type, free from the urge to pause or tinker. You will be surprised by how much writing you will do, and you can revise or correct the text later if you wish.

Journal Writing

Keeping a journal means recording your thoughts and observations regularly, for your own use, usually in a notebook reserved for that purpose. Like freewriting, journal writing gives you a chance to record ideas for later evaluation; journal writing, however, more often focuses on and systematically develops a specific topic or event. Reflective by definition, journal writing offers you the chance to explore privately and in detail thoughts and feelings about people, actions, events, ideas—in short, anyone or anything of interest or concern.

Keeping a journal will lead to ideas, insights, and further observations that you might not otherwise have had.

To make the best use of this strategy, try to write in your journal every day. Get into the habit of carrying your notebook with you, writing briefly or at length whenever a thought occurs to you or an event or comment interests you. Or try writing in your journal by appointment, choosing a convenient time such as first thing in the morning or just before dinner. Whenever and wherever you write in your journal, give it a long trial, perhaps a month, of making regular entries. Journal writing may seem awkward at first, but it will become easy and pleasurable as you find your own best method of working.

Erica wrote systematically in her journal about one aspect of her freewriting:

> *The magazines we read on a regular basis say something about us. After all, if we're willing to spend money, we must be getting something from what we read. But what is it? In part, of course, we find out information about subjects that interest us. Mom, I know, learns about flowers and food from reading Better Homes and Gardens; Jason finds out about music and general-interest topics from reading Details; Dad learns about many subjects from reading Esquire. In part, though, we learn about products through advertisements: I learn about new styles through the ads in Mademoiselle; Danielle discovers what's current by looking at the ads in YM. Because advertisers place their work in specific magazines (or change their ads to fit different groups), they must certainly have a sense of who is buying or subscribing to individual magazines. They, too, must be creating "portraits" of regular readers—and maybe those portraits reveal a great deal about us as readers.*

Erica's journal entry, though not fully focused or developed, draws connections more clearly than did her freewriting as she explores the facets of magazines that interest her most.

Journalists' Questions

For decades, journalists have used a reliable set of questions—
who, what, when, where, how, and *why*—to explore their subjects and to uncover the specific, detailed information that their
readers want to know. By using these questions as prompts
and refining them to suit your needs, you can pinpoint various
aspects of your subject, finding pertinent and interesting connections and information.

Erica specifically modified the journalists' questions to
extend her exploration of her subject, producing these notes:

Magazines and the People Who Read Them

Who reads magazines? Almost everyone: students, certainly, but
others, too; everyone in my family, most of my friends and casual
acquaintances, people who read for information, people who read
for entertainment.

What kinds of magazines do they read? News magazines (Time,
Newsweek); fashion magazines (Glamour, GQ); sports magazines
(Sports Illustrated, Boating); health magazines (American Health,
Muscle and Fitness); car magazines (Auto Week, Car and Driver);
computer magazines (PC World, Byte); home magazines (Home,
House Beautiful); and so on.

When do people read? Some start reading magazines as children;
some don't start till they're older. Some read at work; some read
during their spare time.

Where do people read their magazines? At libraries, at news-
stands, in grocery lines, at home (subscriptions), at work (professional materials), in waiting rooms.

How do people read magazines? Front to back, back to front; articles then ads, ads then articles; some people read them as they
come out each week or month; some people save them and then
read several at once.

> *Why do people read magazines? To gather information, to be entertained, to learn about trends and products, to reinforce perceptions, to challenge themselves, to learn about other people and topics.*

Some of Erica's questions yield more ideas than others. *What, how,* and *why* provided particularly specific and useful responses. The questions most useful for a given subject will vary, though any might provide useful details or lead to an interesting, focused topic.

Looping

Looping helps you to move from a general subject to a narrow topic through a series of progressively more specific freewritings. To loop, begin with a general subject and freewrite for five to ten minutes. Then circle one element or detail and freewrite again, focusing on it. Repeat the process as often as necessary until you decide on a specific, restricted topic within your original, general subject.

Erica's looping produced this series of brief paragraphs:

Freewriting

> *The magazines people read vary—as do the ways they read the magazines. But almost everyone I know comments at one time or another about (the ads in magazines). We look at ads to find out about new products, and sometimes we look at them to be entertained. Interestingly, though, the ads in any magazine create a composite view of the regular readership for the magazine.*

Loop 1

> *Ads in magazines can signal what regular readers are interested in, what they want to know about, and what they do. At least advertisers seem to create (target audiences) (ages, interests, preferences, etc.) and then pitch their ads to a stereotypical reader, not to the casual reader. Noticing the products advertised and the*

ways in which they are presented provides a useful glimpse at a magazine's readers.

Loop 2

In magazines geared to a specific age group—like YM, Details, New Woman, Esquire—there seem to be interestingly mixed signals. Though YM seems to be directed to teenage girls (that's the direction the articles take), the ads frequently create images that are more adult: they use older models, for example, and present images more appropriate for young women, rather than girls.

Notice the pattern in Erica's looping: she writes first on a general subject, then on a specific topic, and finally on a specific example. Looping frequently, though not always, follows this sequence, allowing you to explore a subject and perhaps to select a topic and method of development.

 The dimmed-screen approach described on page 9 works well with looping. Complete the first freewriting with the screen dimmed. Then turn the brightness up, read what you have typed, and select an aspect for further exploration. Turn the brightness down again and freewrite on your new topic. Repeat the process as often as is useful.

Clustering

Clustering, because it combines verbal and visual prompts, can lead to more flexible, nonlinear planning that emphasizes associations, rather than hierarchies, of ideas. Using this free-form approach may help you to pursue a looser, more creative exploration of your subject.

Begin a cluster with a circled key word or phrase in the center of a sheet of paper. Associating ideas freely, add lines radiating from the central idea leading to circled words or phrases that describe, define, or explain it. These ideas in turn will prompt further associations that branch out from them.

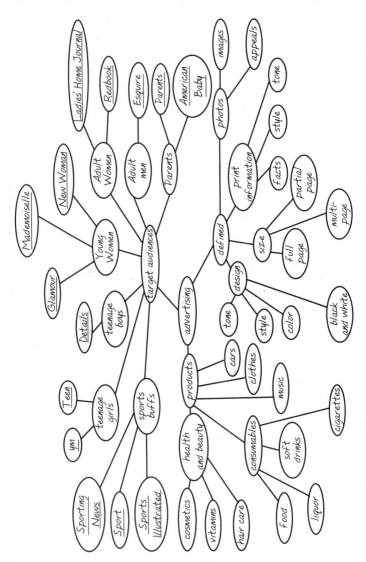

Continue adding ideas and connections as they occur to you. Evaluate your finished cluster. Use another color to trace the most interesting development and to cross out the ones that did not work. Look for self-contained satellite clusters that move beyond the original idea. Consider whether portions of your cluster correspond to portions of the paper you are planning, thus indicating an organization. Finally, consider clustering around a new idea suggested by your first cluster.

Erica, for example, began her clustering with the word *advertising*, which she had used repeatedly in her other planning exercises, and produced the cluster shown on page 14. Analyzing her cluster, Erica concluded that the branches "products" and "target audiences," by producing more specific and varied examples, illuminated *advertising* and each other intriguingly.

Clustering may not always produce ideas that you will be able to use in a paper, but because of its flexible, nonlinear form, it can lead you to surprising discoveries and provocative associations.

Brainstorming

Use **brainstorming** to produce a list of everything you can think of that is related to your subject. A brainstorming list generally comprises freely associated ideas expressed in words and phrases. It may be developed by an individual writer or by a group working together on one project.

Begin a brainstorming list by thinking briefly about your subject. Then write without pausing, using single words or short phrases, until you run out of ideas. Brainstorming should be done rapidly and spontaneously, so do not pause to evaluate, analyze, or arrange ideas.

Although lists are the most commonly used format for brainstorming, consider other, more graphic formats. Organize your ideas into trees, showing ideas branching out of one another, or into clusters, in which ideas radiate from and circle around the main idea. Use any format that is comfortable for you and that encourages the lively generation of ideas.

Erica's brainstorming produced this list:

Advertisements in Specialized Magazines

products advertised	*YM*
kinds of appeal	*New Woman*
match with audience	*Sport*
image created	*Esquire*
special products	*Ebony*
cars	*Parents*
clothes	*Details*
hair care	*Car and Driver*
consumables (food, drinks, etc.)	*Instructor*
Calvin Klein	*Time*
Hugo Boss	*stereotypes in ads*
Clearasil	*what ads say*
Coke	*what they look like*
Columbia House	*ads in multiple magazines*

Erica's long and varied list shows that she looked at her subject from many angles. The list reveals some connections among ideas but shows no formal arrangement.

To use a brainstorming list, arrange items in groups unified by a common idea or theme. Do not let your original list limit your thinking while grouping ideas. Drop items that do not fit into your groups, repeat items in several groups if appropriate, and add new items whenever you think of them.

Grouping Ideas

Classify by topics.

Identify examples.

Arrange chronologically.

Compare or contrast.

Classify by Topics

Items from your list will generally suggest logical classes or categories into which to subdivide your subject. Group items from your list into the appropriate categories. Sometimes an item from your list will be a comprehensive category that in turn suggests additional items. At this point in planning, categories need not be logically related.

Items from Erica's list suggested many categories, two of which are shown here:

Special-Interest Magazines	*Kinds of Products*
YM	special products
New Woman	cars
Sport	clothes
Esquire	hair care
Ebony	consumables (food, drinks, etc.)
Parents	
Details	
Car and Driver	
Instructor	
Time	

Identify Examples

Specific examples make writing livelier than do abstract discussions. Use examples drawn from your brainstorming list to focus your topic, adding details as you think of them.

Erica mentions several specific ads in her brainstorming list. Discussing one could unify her ideas or stimulate new ones. Here is a sample:

Calvin Klein

clothes ads

cologne ads

kinds of appeal

match with audience

image created

Arrange Chronologically

Many subjects suggest a chronological, historical, or narrative pattern in which a series of events or the stages in a single event are recounted in sequence.

Erica's subject, for example, could be further developed chronologically:

Seasonal Ads

clothes and other products

images by season

activities by season

indoor vs. outdoor

special seasonal events

Compare or Contrast

Often, similarities or differences among items on your brainstorming list will suggest logical groupings. Comparing similar items or contrasting dissimilar ones may lead to an interesting perspective on, or new items relevant to, your subject. Parallel lists, as in the following example, may be used to explore these relations. Revise your original entries as necessary to emphasize the points of comparison or contrast.

Younger Audience	*Older Audience*
school	work
friends or classmates	friends or coworkers
fun	fun or practical
relationships	relationships
soft drinks	liquor

EXERCISE 1.2 ❯ Planning strategies

Using several of the general subjects you listed in Exercise 1.1, try each of the planning strategies: freewriting, journal writing, journalists' questions, looping, clustering, and brainstorming-grouping.

1c ❯	**Select a specific topic for your paper.**

Having explored your general subject and discovered the aspects of it that interest you most, you should now work toward identifying a specific, narrowed topic.

To begin, review your planning materials. Then use these questions to decide on an effective topic:

Which topic seems most original? Look for interesting ideas, unusual connections, or unique observations.

Which topic interests you most? Notice recurrent ideas, repeated phrases, or often-used examples.

About which topic are you most informed? Notice your use of examples, specific details, facts, and names.

Which topic is the most useful? Look for problems to solve or contradictions to explore.

Which topic can you cover best in the space allowed for your paper? Consider a simple issue for a short paper but a complex issue for a long paper.

Finally, state your chosen topic in a sentence.

Reviewing her planning materials using the questions listed above, Erica discovered several distinct patterns. Specific examples, appearing in different planning contexts, suggested that Erica had extensive knowledge of and a keen interest in magazine advertisements suited for different audiences. Erica also saw that she had many ideas and opinions about perceptions that are created by these different ads. On the basis of these discoveries, Erica chose to classify ads that are targeted to readers of specific magazines. She would thus be able to use her experience, knowledge, and ideas to write a focused paper.

EXERCISE 1.3) *A specific topic*

Review your planning materials and select a specific topic. Then write a brief paragraph describing how you arrived at your selection. Describe your review of your planning materials, comment on how you selected some ideas and rejected others, and end the paragraph by stating your topic in a sentence.

| 1d | Identify your role, readers, and purpose. |

As you narrow your topic and develop and arrange the ideas of the paper, consider in detail the context for your writing: your role, readers, and purpose.

Your Role as a Writer

Consider your perspective on your topic. If you are writing about horse racing, are you writing from your experience as a spectator or as a jockey? Do you own a racehorse or oppose horse racing? What knowledge of and attitude toward the sport does each of these positions involve? Defining your individual perspective on the topic—whether you are writing as an authority, an unbiased observer, or a probing nonspecialist— will help you to make choices of content and presentation.

Erica has obviously looked at and thought about a wide variety of magazines and the ads they contain and can write without bias on their relative merits. Her familiarity with many magazines allows her to choose appropriate examples and discuss them in detail. She can write open-mindedly and with a broad perspective.

Your Readers

Consider carefully the expectations, concerns, and knowledge of your audience. To do this, first identify your readers by answering these questions:

What are the probable age, educational level, and experience of your audience?

What information, concerns, and interests do your readers probably share?

What choices of tone and language will help you to communicate best with your audience?

For example, twenty-year-olds and forty-year-olds have different experiences and concerns, so they are likely to be familiar with and interested in different examples. Erica might discuss the ads in *Details* for a younger audience and the ads in *Esquire* or *Time* for an older audience. Similarly, appropriate tone and language can vary with audience; one audience might understand and enjoy reading current slang, while another might be confused by it. Differences in education and information require differences in the amount of detail offered in explanations. An informed audience may realize at once that companies like Columbia House present different ads for different target audiences; an uninformed audience might not.

 Dim the screen on your computer and freewrite for five minutes about your audience. Using specific details, describe your audience as completely as possible—age, education, opinions, activities, favorite television shows—as if you were writing quickly to a friend. When you have finished, turn the brightness up, read what you have written, and introduce italic or boldface codes to highlight the most revealing details about your readers.

Erica decided that the audience for her paper—her teacher and college classmates—ranged in age from seventeen to forty-five, though most fell between seventeen and twenty-two. Looking at magazines was a common experience for the group, but to avoid lengthy descriptions, she decided to concentrate on a few well-known magazines. Erica realized, however, that her readers would not necessarily be familiar with all the magazines she wanted to discuss and that her paper would require fairly detailed descriptions. Finally, concluding that she had a useful point to make on a popular topic, she decided that her readers would expect informal language.

Your Purpose

Your purpose for writing is never simply to fulfill a course requirement. Any time you write with careful attention to your thoughts, information, and audience, an organizing purpose will emerge.

Most writing has one of four general purposes: expressive, referential, persuasive, or argumentative. Writing for college courses may serve any of these purposes. In **expressive writing,** writers express their individuality by sharing experiences, opinions, perceptions, and feelings. Expressive papers explore the writer's perspective. (**Literary writing,** not covered in this book, is a form of expressive writing in which writers share perceptions and insights using artistic forms such as the short story, poem, novel, or play.) In **referential writing,** writers share information and ideas, often gathered through systematic research. A writer's focus in a referential paper is on the topic and often on specialists' views, which must be carefully documented. (For a discussion of documentation, see Chapters 33–35.) In **persuasive writing,** writers present information and opinions intended to alter readers' views or perceptions. A persuasive paper relies on evidence to convince readers to rethink the topic; some research (properly documented) may be required. Finally, in **argumentative writing,** writers present their opinions on topics that have many possible viewpoints, supporting their positions using ideas, information, experience, and insights. A writer's focus in an argumentative paper is on the issues.

Begin thinking about your specific purpose by deciding which general purposes suit your needs. In most writing, the general purposes overlap. Most persuasive writing is also expressive, and referential writing is often persuasive. As you develop a paper and make choices about structure, content, and style, you will discover how purposes blend naturally.

Erica, for example, decided that her paper would be primarily referential because it would be based on a nonjudgmental assessment of magazine advertisements. The paper would have an expressive element as well, for it would reveal her perspective. Erica was unsure whether she would develop a persuasive element in her paper.

EXERCISE 1.4 ❭ *Role, readers, and purpose*

Make a list that characterizes your role, readers, and purpose for the paper you have been planning. Consider how the results of this analysis will influence further planning and drafting.

| 1e ❭ | **Write a working thesis statement.** |

After narrowing your topic and characterizing your role, readers, and purpose, you can begin to formulate a **working thesis statement**—a brief statement of your topic and your opinion on it—to guide your draft. Later in the writing process, you will refine the working thesis statement into a **final thesis statement**—generally a single sentence near the end of the introduction—that will guide your readers.

You may sometimes omit a thesis statement if you build meaning implicitly through examples, details, or description, leaving it to the reader to formulate the meaning. Such works are said to have an **implied thesis.** This method generally works best for very personal descriptive or narrative papers. For most writing, a thesis statement will help both you and your readers understand the organization and follow the development of ideas.

After a thoughtful review of your planning materials, moving from the topic to a working thesis statement should be a simple step. Review your planning materials, concentrating on recurrent or fully developed ideas. Analyze your role, readers, and purpose to discover the general approach you want to take. Ask yourself what you want readers to know or think about the topic and try to express the answer in a single sentence.

An effective thesis statement has three essential characteristics and may have three optional characteristics:

Essential

Identify a specific, narrow topic.

Present a clear opinion on, not merely facts about, the topic.

Establish a tone appropriate to the topic, purpose, and audience.

Optional

Qualify the topic as necessary, pointing out significant opposing opinions.

Clarify important points, indicating the organizational pattern.

Take account of readers' probable knowledge of the topic.

A carefully planned and written working thesis statement will help suggest the focus for your thinking and a structure for your writing. In the final paper, a well-expressed thesis statement will prevent confusion by clarifying for readers the paper's central idea. Ineffective thesis statements like these are not helpful:

Attics are places to store belongings.   (This topic lacks an opinion; it merely states a fact.)

Cats make weird pets.   (This narrowed topic contains an opinion, but it is imprecise, is stated too informally, and fails to qualify its criticism for readers who like cats.)

Liquor advertisements glamorize the drinking that leads to thousands of highway deaths each year. (The topic and opinion are clear, but this thesis statement ignores the variables in a controversial issue.)

First drafts of thesis statements are often as vague and incomplete as these. However, weak thesis statements can be revised to produce improved versions:

Attics are great places to store useless belongings. (The inclusion of *great* and *useless* defines the writer's opinion and establishes a humorous tone.)

Cats make unusually independent pets. (*Independent* is more precise and therefore clearer than *weird*. The change in wording creates a tone appropriate to a college paper.)

Although some advertisements now include warnings not to drink and drive, most continue to glamorize the drinking that leads to thousands of highway deaths each year. (This thesis statement still expresses a strongly held opinion, but the introductory qualification and the inclusion of *most* help make it more judicious than the original version.)

Here are Erica's attempts to write an effective thesis statement:

First attempt
Ads tell us a great deal about the regular readers of magazines.

(The topic is vague, and the sentence presents a fact, not an opinion.)

Second attempt
Magazine ads provide a useful way to understand the regular readers of magazines.

(The topic is clearer and an opinion is stated, but the thesis statement is still imprecise and ineffectively worded.)

Third attempt

> *Although people can be characterized by the magazines they read, examining magazine advertisements provides a useful way to understand who the regular readers of magazines are, not who they think they are.*

(The topic is more explicit, and placing the qualification first creates emphasis at the end.)

 When writing working thesis statements, take advantage of the computer's capability to copy easily. Type a first attempt at a thesis statement. Then copy it several spaces below (use the "copy" and "paste" commands). Leaving the original version in place, analyze and revise the copy. Copy the second version and revise it to produce the third, and so on. Keeping all versions allows you to reexamine choices of wording and tone without substantial retyping or a clutter of markings. You may want to return to earlier versions to reclaim discarded phrases or words.

EXERCISE 1.5 ❭ *Thesis statements*

Briefly evaluate each of the following thesis statements. Note the strengths and weaknesses of each. Revise any ineffective thesis statements by narrowing and focusing the topic, changing the tone, or adding an opinion or any necessary qualifications.

1. Some critics maintain that the *Iliad* and the *Odyssey* are the foundation works on which all subsequent literature in the Western tradition are based.

2. The 1996 Summer Olympics were held in Atlanta.

3. Contrary to commonly held opinion, anti-Communist hysteria in the United States predated the rabid speeches and accusations made by Senator Joseph R. McCarthy in the early 1950s.

4. Even though a lot of people will disagree, I think that prayer is okay in public schools.

5. By encouraging managers in some U.S. corporations to play with a matchbox, some string, and a candle, cognitive psychologists are passing on important lessons in creative problem solving.

6. The United States government should retaliate quickly against terrorism.

7. Achieving competency in a foreign language is among the highest rewards of education.

8. Women should not always be awarded custody of children in divorce settlements.

EXERCISE 1.6) *Thesis statements*

Write a thesis statement about your topic. Revise it as often as necessary to achieve a clear statement of the topic, your opinion on it, and any necessary qualifications. Consider carefully your role, readers, and purpose, and establish an appropriate tone.

 Planning on the word processor

After you have tried a number of the planning strategies in this chapter, start a file in which you record the guiding questions or categories of those that work best for you. For example, record the following:

the list of ways to think of topics (pages 4–5)

the questions used to narrow topics (page 20)

the categories for classifying information (pages 17–19)

the questions journalists use to anticipate their readers' questions (pages 11–12)

the key concepts and questions useful for analyzing
your role, readers, and purpose (pages 21–24)

the categories for evaluating your thesis (pages 24–27)

Include any additional comments, questions, or strategies
that you have developed on your own. Separate each strategy with a page break and mark it with a key word as a
heading so that you can use the "search" function to find
quickly the material you need.

When planning a piece of writing, call up your file of
planning strategies into a second window or screen and
use its contents as prompts for varying your approach to
your topic. Or "copy" and "paste" a specific set of planning
prompts to a separate file devoted to your topic and
expand them with relevant notes—examples, facts, questions, possible sources, and so on.

As you continue to write, you will develop new strategies
and modify old ones. Update your planning file from time to
time to take advantage of your increasing experience.

2 Drafting

Writing a rough draft is a rehearsal, an opportunity to explore possibilities for the arrangement and expression of ideas. In the drafting stage, you can organize ideas from your planning materials and experiment with ways to express them in sentences, paragraphs, and ultimately a complete, though not yet final, paper. Drafting a paper is rarely a neat and easy matter of fleshing out your notes, however. You must be flexible and open to new ideas that occur as you write, filling gaps and making new connections. Drafting begins the process of transferring ideas into sentences.

Quick Reference

Drafting is an opportunity for you to experiment with ways to express your ideas, knowing that you can revise the work later. As you draft your paper, keep these principles in mind:

❭ *Use the broad organizational pattern that emerges most naturally from your planning.*

❭ *Use outlining to help you achieve a logical structure for your ideas, but do not let the outline dictate your draft. Revise the outline when necessary.*

❭ *Use drafting to get ideas on paper in a reasonably coherent form without pausing too much over the exact expression or striving for technical correctness.*

❭ *Experiment with various techniques for introducing a paper that interests readers and concluding a paper that satisfies them.*

2a ⟩ **Organize your materials and continue to seek new ideas.**

Examine the materials you wrote during planning. Look for emerging patterns among ideas and for ideas that seem especially important or that illustrate your thesis especially well. Planning materials will generally suggest a natural pattern for organizing the paper. Some common organizational arrangements are chronological, spatial, and topical.

Chronological Arrangement

Chronological arrangement presents information in sequence, explaining what happened first, second, third, and so on. Personal narratives, such as a description of your first day at a new job, and narratives of events, such as a political debate, make good use of a chronological arrangement.

Spatial Arrangement

Spatial arrangement recreates the physical features of a subject. For instance, a writer might describe a town by "leading" readers from a residential area in the north to a commercial or industrial area in the south. Spatial arrangement has limited application, but when physical features are important, it can convey insights more effectively than any other method.

Topical Arrangement

Topical arrangement, a pattern often used in persuasive writing, organizes supporting ideas to present the thesis with the greatest possible emphasis. Topical arrangement can follow a number of patterns according to your purpose—from most important point to least important, for instance, or from simplest to most complex. Sometimes a mixed pattern works best.

For example, present the second-most important point first, interesting readers with strong material, and then sandwich in lesser points to fill out the discussion; use the most important point last, thus closing with especially convincing evidence.

Other Methods of Arrangement

The organizational patterns used to arrange ideas within paragraphs can also be used to organize full-length papers. Your planning materials, for example, may suggest one of these common patterns: analogy, cause and effect, process, classification, and definition. Erica's planning materials reveal an emerging classification pattern. The principles discussed in Chapter 4, "Paragraphs," can be expanded so that you use full paragraphs to develop each of your ideas within the overall organizational pattern.

EXERCISE 2.1 **)** *Organizing materials*

Review your thesis and planning materials from Chapter 1 and experiment with each of the organizational patterns described above. (For more information on alternative patterns, see section 4d.) Choose one pattern and then organize your planning materials according to the arrangement suggested by the pattern.

2b	>	Outline your paper.

Having selected a pattern of arrangement, prepare an **outline,** a structural plan using headings and subdivisions to clarify the main features of the paper and the interrelationships among them. Loosely structured, informal outlines provide simplicity and freedom, while highly systematic, formal outlines emphasize clarity and completeness. You can benefit from both kinds at different stages of writing. In the earliest stages of drafting—

when you are deciding what should come first, second, third, and so on—informal outlines work best. At later stages, use formal outlining to analyze your work for consistency, completeness, and logic. Experiment to discover what form of outlining works best for you, and when. Remember, informal and formal outlines are plans, not descriptions of what you must do. Sometimes plans do not work because they are flawed or incomplete. If your plan is not working, do not frustrate yourself by trying to make it work. Instead, decide why it does not work and make the appropriate changes.

Informal Outlines

Informal outlines, intended for your use only, may be simple lists marked with numbers, arrows, dots, dashes, or any other convenient symbol to indicate relative importance among ideas. Because they are not systematically composed, arranged, and labeled, informal outlines can be completed more easily and quickly than formal outlines.

Below is Erica's brief, informal outline.

Health

→ *focus of the articles*

→ *impressions from the ads*

Sport

→ *focus of the articles*

→ *impressions from the ads*

New Woman

→ *focus of the articles*

→ *impressions from the ads*

Because they make it possible to move items easily without retyping, word-processing programs are ideal tools for informal outlining. Prepare and then print a first version of your informal outline. Evaluate the outline, marking the printed copy with changes. Use the "cut" and "paste" functions on your computer to execute the changes, and then print a new version of the outline. A clean printed version of your informal outline is easier to work from than one with scribbled changes.

EXERCISE 2.2) Informal outlining

Compose an informal outline that arranges the large elements from your planning materials. Add missing details and examples as you continue to draft your paper.

Formal Outlines

When an outline is intended for readers, **formal outlines** are used because they adhere to a commonly accepted and under-stood system. After developing an informal outline, consider creating a formal outline as well.

Note the following conventions of formal outlines:

Indicate *major topics* with uppercase roman numerals (*I, II, III*). Each of these entries represents one or more whole paragraphs.

Indicate *subdivisions* of topics with uppercase letters (*A, B, C*). Each of these generally represents a cluster of sentences within a paragraph.

Indicate *clarifications* of subdivisions (examples, supporting facts, and so on) with arabic numbers (*1, 2, 3*). Each of these generally represents a sentence.

Indicate *details* in sentences with lowercase letters (*a, b, c*).

In addition, the following conventions are also observed:

Use parallel forms throughout. Use phrases and words in a **topic outline** and full sentences in a **sentence outline.** An outline may use topic sentences for major topics and phrases in subdivisions of topics (a **mixed outline**) but should do so consistently.

Include only one idea in each entry. Subdivide entries that contain more than one idea.

Include at least two entries at each sublevel.

Indicate the inclusion of introductions and conclusions, but do not outline their content.

Align headings of the same level at the same margin.

Many word-processing programs offer easy-to-use outlining features. These automatically position the roman numerals, capital letters, and other division indicators and correctly align the text that you supply for each level. If your word processor has these features, learn to use them. They will save you time and effort.

The formal outline below organizes Erica's materials. It is a mixed outline, using sentences at the roman numeral (paragraph) level and phrases for the topics within paragraphs.

INTRODUCTION

Thesis statement: Although people can be characterized by the magazines they read, examining magazine advertisements provides a useful way to understand who the regular readers of magazines are, not who they think they are.

I. Readers of Health magazine are, in fact, as health-oriented as the title suggests.

A. *Focus of articles: food, fitness, medical care, travel*

   1. *Emphasis on healthy living*

   2. *Emphasis on personal choices and activities*

B. *Ads: running shoes, fat-free or low-fat foods, self-help books, vitamins and supplements*

   1. *Emphasis on activity*

   2. *Geared to people of all ages*

II. *Readers of* Sport *are spectators of, not participants in, sports.*

A. *Focus of articles: basketball, hockey, baseball, golf*

   1. *Emphasis on statistics, teams, players, trends*

   2. *Emphasis on analysis*

B. *Ads: cigarettes, cars, liquor, chewing tobacco, memorabilia*

   1. *Emphasis on relaxation*

   2. *Geared to male fans, not players*

III. *Readers of* New Woman *have not escaped "old" stereotypes.*

A. *Focus of articles: relationships, self-discovery, health and fitness, work*

   1. *Emphasis on taking control of life*

   2. *Emphasis on self-help*

B. *Ads: makeup, cologne, book clubs (best-sellers), contraceptives*

   1. *Emphasis on externals*

   2. *Geared to women whose interests aren't really "new"*

CONCLUSION

Use the computer to revise your informal outline into a formal outline. Insert roman numerals and uppercase letters to
mark major divisions and then move elements to align them
correctly. Insert arabic numerals and lowercase letters, plus
additional clarifying materials, to show the degree of detail
that your paper will include. Use the word processor's
abilities to insert and reformat without retyping existing
materials.

EXERCISE 2.3 ❭ *Formal outlining*

*Using your informal outline from Exercise 2.2 as a starting point,
complete a formal outline, providing necessary elaboration. Create
either a mixed outline or a sentence outline, labeling it appropriately. Double-check your work against the guidelines for outlining
given on pages 34–35.*

| 2c | ❭ | **Write a rough draft of your paper.** |

The **rough draft** is the first full-length, written form of a paper.
It is usually messy and unfocused. Some parts develop clearly
and smoothly from planning materials, but others develop only
after three or four tries. That pattern is typical because writing
a rough draft is a shifting process that requires thinking, planning, writing, rethinking, replanning, and rewriting again.

Every rough draft has different requirements, varying from
paper to paper. Begin your rough drafts by working on the
body paragraphs, postponing work on the opening and closing
paragraphs. However, write with your thesis statement clearly
in mind. These additional general strategies are helpful:

Gather all your materials together. Your work can proceed
with relatively few interruptions if your planning materials
and writing supplies are nearby.

Work from your outline. Write one paragraph at a time, in any order, postponing work on troublesome sections until you have gained momentum.

Remember the purpose of your paper. As you write, concentrate on arranging and developing only the ideas presented in your outline or closely related ideas that occur to you.

Use only ideas and details that support your thesis statement. Resist any tendency to drift from your point or to provide interesting but extraneous details.

Remember your readers' needs. Include all information and explanations that readers will need to understand the discussion.

Do not worry about technical matters. Concentrate on getting ideas down on paper. You can attend to punctuation, mechanics, spelling, and neatness later.

Rethink and modify troublesome sections. If the organization of the paper is not working, if an example seems weak, or if the order of the paragraphs no longer seems logical, change it.

Reread sections as you write. Rereading earlier sections as you write will help you to maintain a reasonably consistent tone.

Write alternative versions of troublesome sections. When you come to a problematic section, write multiple versions of it and then choose the one that works best.

Periodically give yourself a break from writing. Interrupting writing too often creates problems with consistency of style or tone, but occasionally getting away from it will help you to maintain a fresh perspective and attain objectivity.

Drafting on the word processor

Composing at the computer can be fluid and productive. With the help of the "add," "delete," "move," and "reformat" features in your word-processing program, you will be able to generate a rough draft with relative ease, knowing that you can make both small and large changes without substantial retyping. Using a word processor now will enable you to do the following easily later:

Move words, phrases, sentences, and paragraphs.

Check spelling.

Check format and spacing.

Count the number of words.

Conduct "search" and "replace" procedures to change words and phrases.

Begin by copying your outline to a new file, renaming it, and proceeding to compose and type sentences that explain and expand its divisions. Set the line spacing at double-space for good readability; later, when you are ready to print your draft, set the line spacing at triple-space to provide extra room for making changes during revision.

Draft freely, without worrying about missing details, exact wording, or technical correctness. Devise your own system of symbols or key words to mark places in the draft to which you would like to return. Keep your system simple and use it consistently so that it becomes part of your drafting technique and does not interfere with it. The following are helpful strategies:

Use symbols unlikely to appear in your writing (such as *, #, >, +, or ~) or double end punctuation marks. You might use + to mark places needing development or additional details, !! to mark places needing examples, or ?? to mark places at which you are unsure of your information or opinions.

Use brackets or boldface to include alternate word choices or versions of sentences or longer passages.

Use abbreviations or distinctive symbols in place of frequently used long phrases or difficult-to-spell words and names.

Symbols, abbreviations, and key words can be located using the "search" function. Make your changes and then delete the symbol and unwanted material, or use the "replace" feature to substitute the full word or phrase for any abbreviated form.

Until you have completed your final draft, use the "move" function to save material you are tempted to delete. Alternate versions, digressions, examples, and so on, can be moved to the end of the draft, where they will be available for review and possible retrieval. Insert a page break and a heading, such as "Scrap" or "Discard," and hold this material separate from your draft but convenient to it.

For many writers, the process of drafting creates a flood of ideas, not all of them relevant to the project at hand. If that is the case for you, use the capabilities of your word processor to capture these ideas before they escape you. Open a second window screen or use your program's "notepad" feature to record ideas, images, questions, reminders, and so on for future use.

Remember to give your draft a clear, logical, recognizable file name; note the date at the beginning of the draft and the name at the end.

EXERCISE 2.4 ❭ *Rough draft*

Write a rough draft of your paper, using the guidelines given above. Work from your outline to ensure that each idea is supported by adequate detail.

| 2d | Plan your title and introductory and concluding paragraphs. |

Spend some extra time on the title and the beginning and ending paragraphs of your paper because first and final impressions are important. The best time to plan and write these special parts of a paper varies from one paper to the next. They can be developed, written, and rewritten at any time during planning, drafting, or revising.

Titles

A good **title** is at once descriptive, letting readers know what the paper is about, and imaginative, sparking readers' interest. To achieve these ends, try one or more of these strategies:

Use words or phrases that explicitly identify the topic. Search your draft for expressions that are clear and brief.

Play with language. Consider variations of well-known expressions. Use **alliteration** (repetition of the initial sounds of words) or **assonance** (repetition of internal vowel sounds of words).

Consider two-part titles, the first part imaginative, the second part descriptive. Separate the two parts with a colon.

Match the tone of the title to the tone of the paper. Use serious titles for serious papers, ironic titles for ironic papers, factual titles for factual papers, and so on.

Keep an open mind as you write titles; write as many as you can and select the one that best clarifies the topic for readers and piques their interest.

Erica began her search for an effective title by describing her topic in a phrase: "What magazine ads say about readers." Although the phrase labeled her paper clearly, it would not create any special interest among readers. She tried playing with language and considered "You Are What You Read—and Buy" (a variation of a well-known proverb) and "Print Ads and Preconceptions" (an experiment with alliteration). Erica then tried combining her descriptive title with her title using alliteration to create a two-part title: "Print Ads and Preconceptions: What Magazine Ads Say About Readers." She eventually combined her descriptive title with a brief phrase presented as a question to pique her readers' interest: "Mixed Signals? What Magazine Ads Say About Readers."

Introductions

The **introduction** to a paper creates interest and clarifies the subject and opinion for readers. Depending on the length of the paper, an introduction may be one or several paragraphs long.

As you prepare drafts of alternate introductions, keep these general goals in mind:

Adjust the length of the introduction to the length of the writing. A brief paper needs a proportionately brief introduction; a long paper requires a long introduction.

Match the tone of the introduction to the tone of the paper. A casual, personal paper needs an informal introduction, whereas a serious, academic paper requires a formal introduction.

Use the introduction to draw readers into the discussion. It must create interest, suggest the direction the paper will take, and indicate the paper's development.

Most openings begin with one or more of the following general strategies and end by presenting a specific thesis statement.

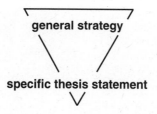

general strategy

specific thesis statement

Below are descriptions of ten of the most commonly used strategies for introductions, with examples.

Allusion

Refer to a work of art, music, literature, film, and so on, or to a mythical, religious, or historical person or event.

> Pity-and-terror, the classically prescribed emotional response to tragic representation, was narrowly restricted to drama by the ancient authorities. In my view, tragedy has a wider reference by far, and pity-and-terror is aroused in me by works of art immeasurably less grand than those which unfold the cosmic undoings of Oedipus and Agamemnon, Antigone, Medea, and the women of Troy. The standard Civil War memorial, for example, is artistically banal by almost any criterion, and yet I am subject to pity-and-terror whenever I reflect upon the dense ironies it embodies. —Arthur C. Danto, "Gettysburg"

Analogy

Make a comparison that is interesting, helpful, and relevant to the topic.

> Visiting Catalina Island is like stepping into a postcard of southern California in the 1930s: there are palm trees, sparkling seas, and Spanish-style buildings that gleam as white as a movie idol's smile.
> Couples once sailed here on white steamships to dance in a vast ballroom overlooking the harbor lights of Avalon, the island's only

town. Yachtsmen, families, beach buffs, and sports fishermen still flock to Avalon, which parties all summer but is pleasantly sleepy in the off-season. Many of Catalina's 2,900 residents came for the weekend—and simply never left. —Merry Vaughn Dunn, "The Island of Romance"

Anecdote

Begin with a short description of a relevant incident.

One summer day in 1923 I was taken with two small cousins by trolley westward over the Queensborough Bridge. We were making an excursion to a matinee at Roxy's. To our left as we clanged across the great web of the bridge I had my first full view of Manhattan, the buildings in their dreamy altitudes piling up down the island around the tallest of all, the Woolworth tower. A heat haze enriched light and shadow on the distant masses. Here and there small plumes of vapor appeared. As the vista slowly shifted, I felt the wonder expected of me as a visiting twelve-year-old from the Midwest. The city already belonged to myth, standing like Asgard beyond the East River water, more of the sky than of the earth. I felt, even so, some formless question stirring at the edge of my mind as to what sense of life that skyline honored or expressed. There was as yet nothing like it in the world. —Robert Fitzgerald, "When the Cockroach Stood by the Mickle Wood"

Definition

Define a term central to your topic. Avoid defining terms already understood, unless such a definition serves a special purpose.

One of the most interesting and characteristic features of democracy is, of course, the difficulty of defining it. And this difficulty has been compounded in the United States, where we have been giving new meanings to almost everything. It is, therefore, especially easy for anyone to say that democracy in America has failed.

"Democracy," according to political scientists, usually describes a form of government by the people, either directly or through their

elected representatives. But I prefer to describe a democratic society as one which is governed by a spirit of equality and dominated
by the desire to equalize, to give everything to everybody. In the
United States the characteristic wealth and skills and know-how and
optimism of our country have dominated this quest. —Daniel J.
Boorstin, "Technology and Democracy"

Description

Use a description of a scene, person, or event to establish context or mood for your topic.

A single knoll rises out of the plain in Oklahoma, north and west of
the Wichita Range. For my people, the Kiowas, it is an old landmark; and they gave it the name Rainy Mountain. The hardest
weather in the world is there. Winter brings blizzards, hot tornadic
winds arise in the spring, and in summer the prairie is an anvil's
edge. The grass turns brittle and brown, and it cracks beneath your
feet. There are green belts along the rivers and creeks, linear groves
of hickory and pecan, willow and witch hazel. At a distance in July
or August the steaming foliage seems almost to writhe in fire. Great
green and yellow grasshoppers are everywhere in the tall grass,
popping up like corn to sting the flesh, and tortoises crawl about
on the red earth, going nowhere in the plenty of time. Loneliness is
an aspect of the land. All things in the plain are isolate; there is no
confusion of objects in the eye, but *one* hill or *one* tree or *one* man.
To look upon that landscape in the early morning, with the sun at
your back, is to lose the sense of proportion. Your imagination
comes to life, and this, you think, is where Creation was begun.
—N. Scott Momaday, "The Way to Rainy Mountain"

Facts and Figures

Begin with specific, interesting, useful information or statistics.

The Crystal Palace, designed in 1850 by the English architect Joseph
Paxton to house showpieces of Victorian technology, was 1,848 feet
long and 408 feet wide. It supported 293,655 panes of glass, and
over the 140 days of its original use, it sheltered 6,063,986 people,

or roughly one-third the total population of the United Kingdom at the time. In his diary, the historian and statesman Thomas Babington Macaulay called the Crystal Palace "a most gorgeous site; vast; graceful; beyond the dreams of the Arabian romances." A detail that Macaulay failed to remark upon was that the great dome, or transept, of the Crystal Palace was framed in wood painted to look like steel merely to allay public fear that so vast and important an edifice could be held aloft by so "flimsy" a material as wood. Yet in relation to its density, wood is stiffer and stronger, both in bending and twisting, than concrete, cast iron, aluminum alloy, or steel.
—Karl J. Niklas, "How to Build a Tree"

New Discussion of an Old Subject

Explain why a topic that may be "old hat" is worth examining again.

As recently as 1960 infertility in couples was, to put the matter delicately, not a top priority for the medical establishment: it was a women's problem. Demographers routinely attributed the reproductive success of a couple to the woman if the fertility of the individuals was unknown. In other words, if a couple tried and failed to have children, the presumption was that the woman was barren, not that the man was sterile. In general, an infertile couple was regarded as exceptional.

These days infertility is not so casually dismissed. For one thing, the man falls under suspicion as well. The evidence of the past twenty years shows what, with hindsight, may always have been the case: that the male is a contributing factor in a couple's infertility 50 percent of the time—sexual equality with a vengeance.
—Diana Lutz, "No Conception"

Question

Use a question or a series of questions to provoke readers to think about your subject.

When did terra firma firm up? And what happened to it once it did?

These are among the great unanswered questions in earth science. Prevailing wisdom holds that the bulk of Earth's continental crust didn't form until at least 2.5 billion years after Earth's birth. And like scum floating on the surface of a bubbling broth, this early crust was too buoyant to founder into Earth's interior, melt and be recycled into the raw material for new crust. According to this view, most, if not all, of the continental crust ever formed is still present on the surface in one form or another, as it has never been recycled in the mantle. —Roslyn M. Dupré, "Earth's Early Evolution"

Quotation

Use what someone else has said or written in a poem, short story, book, article, or interview.

The AIDS epidemic is "one of those cataclysms of nature that have no meaning, no precedent, and, in spite of many claims to the contrary, no useful metaphor." So wrote Sherwin Nuland, who teaches medicine at Yale, in his book *How We Die: Reflections on Life's Final Chapter*. No metaphor, perhaps, but the epidemic's evolution underscores a grim truth: life is regressive. That is, people with problems have a high probability of acquiring more problems. —George F. Will, "An Epidemic's Evolution"

Startling Statement

Use an arresting statement to get readers' attention and arouse their interest.

The prevalence of malnutrition in children is staggering. Globally, nearly 195 million children younger than five years are undernourished. Malnutrition is most obvious in the developing countries, where the condition often takes severe forms; images of emaciated bodies in famine-struck or war-torn regions are tragically familiar. Yet milder forms are more common, especially in developed nations. Indeed, in 1992 an estimated 12 million American children consumed diets that were significantly below the recommended allowances of nutrients established by the National Academy of Sciences.

Undernutrition triggers an array of health problems in children, many of which can become chronic. It can lead to extreme weight loss, stunted growth, weakened resistance to infection and, in the worst cases, early death. The effects can be particularly devastating in the first few years of life, when the body is growing rapidly and the need for calories and nutrients is greatest. —Larry J. Brown and Ernesto Pollitt, "Malnutrition, Poverty and Intellectual Development"

Write sample introductions at the computer, where you can easily copy and revise them. Decide on a number of strategies and quickly type out a draft of each, incorporating your thesis statement by using the "copy" and "paste" commands to save typing time. Then print copies. Rereading the draft introductions in printed form is easy and gives you a clear sense of each one's length. Decide which introduction seems most effective, and move it to the beginning of the draft of your paper. You can always move it again and try another. Save all versions until you have completed your final draft; they may provide you with good ideas later.

Erica considered a number of introductions for her paper, trying to find one that would interest her readers as well as clarify her topic:

Anecdote

Tell about Tarita and me at the bookstore or tell about someone leafing through magazines in a doctor's or dentist's waiting room.

Description

Use an extended description of someone selecting a magazine from a newsstand or describe someone sitting down to read a magazine that has just arrived.

Allusion

Using one of the magazine promotions posted on campus bulletin boards, refer to the surprising variety of magazines available today; name magazine titles.

Erica considered the anecdote but decided that its personal, informal tone did not match the purpose for the paper, which was to be informative. The description of someone reading would be lengthy and, though potentially interesting, would require too long a transition to connect it with her topic. Alluding to specific magazines through a list of titles might seem superficial. Erica decided to combine the allusion with a brief anecdote to create interest, connect with readers' experiences, and suggest the wide range of her topic.

EXERCISE 2.5) *Title and introductory paragraphs*

Write several titles for your paper and select the most effective one. Then write two draft versions of the introduction, using the guidelines given above. Make sure that the strategies both create interest and clearly and appropriately introduce your topic.

Conclusions

A **conclusion** reemphasizes the point of the paper and provides an opportunity to create a desired final impression. Most conclusions begin with a brief but specific summary and then use a concluding strategy to present a general observation.

Some introductory strategies—such as allusion, analogy, anecdote, description, and quotation—can also be useful concluding strategies. The following strategies are particularly appropriate for conclusions.

Challenge

Ask readers to reconsider and change their behavior or ideas or to consider new behavior and ideas.

I wouldn't dream of arguing that we Americans have found the Holy Grail of cultural diversity when in fact we're still searching for it. We have to think hard about our growing pluralism. It's useful, I believe, to dissect in the open our thinking about it, to see whether the lessons we are trying to learn might stimulate some useful thinking elsewhere. We do not yet quite know how to create "wholeness incorporating diversity," but we owe it to the world, as well as to ourselves, to keep trying. —Harlan Cleveland, "The Limits of Cultural Diversity"

Framing Pattern

Frame your essay by modifying some central words, phrases, or images used in the introduction to reflect the progress in thought made in the paper. When appropriate, the introductory strategy may be repeated as the concluding strategy, intensifying the framing effect, as in the following example using description. (The corresponding introduction appears on page 45.)

The next morning I awoke at dawn and went out on the dirt road to Rainy Mountain. It was already hot, and the grasshoppers began to fill the air. Still, it was early in the morning, and the birds sang out of the shadows. The long yellow grass on the mountain shone in the bright light, and a scissortail hied above the land. There, where it ought to be, at the end of a long and legendary way, was my grandmother's grave. Here and there on the dark stones were ancestral names. Looking back once, I saw the mountain and came away. —N. Scott Momaday, "The Way to Rainy Mountain"

Summary

Summarize, restate, or evaluate the major points you presented in your paper. This strategy must be used carefully and thoughtfully to avoid becoming mere repetition.

The triumph of Abstract Expressionism is to be understood not as a minor instance of Cold War politics but as a major moment in the creative and intellectual life of New York City at its zenith as an art capital. We today might look at this moment with wonderment and nostalgia. But understanding what happened involves more than a heady whiff of the risk and the thrill of new possibilities refreshing the arts. It also means confronting some decisive changes in the very nature and purpose of art. As the twentieth century began, art was charged with a function it had never had before: It was to be a substitute for religion. By mid-century, art was being asked to serve as a replacement for politics as well. This was perhaps a burden that no art could ultimately bear, and the relative poverty of the visual arts today admonishes us to be a little skeptical of the claims made forty and fifty years ago, though it is easy enough to get intoxicated in the atmosphere of that era, so recent yet so far away.
—David Lehman, "The Artistic Triumph of New York"

Visualization of the Future

Predict what the nature or condition of your topic will be like in the near or distant future. Be realistic.

Will politicians respond? The science is solid but not 100 percent certain, and it will be a lot more expensive to contain carbon dioxide than it has been to limit CFCs. So the politicians probably won't respond, at least for now. Maybe the Nobel committee will someday give a prize to the scientists who conducted pioneering studies of global warming. Maybe the Republicans, if they're still in power, will take action. Or maybe it will be too late. —Michael D. Lemonick, "When Politics Twists Science"

Work at the keyboard to produce a draft of your conclusion. Work quickly, emphasizing important connections among ideas in the body paragraphs. Remember that you will be able to revise your work later.

Erica, though aware that her plans might change as she wrote her paper, considered several conclusion strategies:

Use a quotation from H. G. Wells: "Advertising is legalized lying."

Challenge readers to think about the magazines they and others read—and what the ads, as well as the articles, say about them.

As in the introduction, allude to specific magazines, varying the list, and suggest that readers reconsider their choices of magazines.

Erica ultimately decided to combine the strategies of challenge and allusion, to encourage thought and to frame the paper.

EXERCISE 2.6 ⟩ Concluding paragraphs

Write two draft versions of your conclusion. Make sure that the strategies are closely connected to the tone and topic of your paper.

3 Revising

Revision, which means "to see again," provides an opportunity for you to rethink, reorganize, rephrase, refine, and redirect your work. It allows you to polish your work, preparing it for readers by putting it into the best possible form.

Quick Reference

Revising is much more than proofreading and correcting technical errors. It is a rich opportunity to refine, clarify, and, if necessary, reconceive the paper, from its large to its small features.

> *Evaluate your content critically and delete or replace anything that does not effectively support your main idea.*

> *Improve the style of your paper by reworking sentences to make them varied, emphatic, and clear.*

> *Eliminate technical errors. These interfere with easy reading and draw attention away from your ideas.*

> *Use peer review for an unbiased response to your specific questions and an assessment of the strengths and weaknesses of the paper as a whole.*

> *Prepare the final copy of your paper, making any additional changes necessary and following accepted guidelines for manuscript preparation.*

You can revise by rereading your writing and making changes in content, sentence structure, word choice, punctuation, and mechanics all at once; such single-stage reworking is often called **global revision.** When you have sufficient experience with writing, you will be able to make global revisions. For now, it will be easier to revise in the three stages described in this chapter: **content revision, style revision,** and **technical revision.**

A Revision Sequence

Set aside the rough draft.

Reread the draft.

Revise content.

Revise style.

Correct technical errors.

Consult a peer editor.

Make final changes.

Prepare a final copy to submit.

| 3a | Set aside your rough draft for as long as possible. |

Fatigue and frustration can keep you from seeing your own work clearly, so it is important to take a break from writing after finishing your draft. By interrupting your work to relax briefly, you will be able to gain (or regain) objectivity about the draft before you begin revision.

Set aside your rough draft for as long as possible. Several days would be best, but if that is not possible, then stop working on the paper for at least several hours. Telephone a friend, listen to music, take a walk, or study for another course. Do *anything* that will rest and refresh your mind for writing and allow you to look at your work critically and with detachment.

3b ⟩ **Revise the content of your paper.**

Return to your paper to examine its content for clarity, coherence, and completeness. To guide your revision, consider the following questions:

Are the title and the introductory strategy interesting, clear, and appropriate in tone?

Does the thesis statement clearly present the topic and your opinion about it?

Do the topics of the paragraphs support the thesis statement? Are they clearly stated?

Are the topics presented in a clear, emphatic order?

Are the paragraphs adequately developed? Is there enough detail? Are there enough examples? Does the information in each paragraph relate to the thesis statement?

Are the summary and concluding strategy effective?

When you have many content revisions, do more than one revised draft.

Word processing and content revision

Revising papers written on a word processor can be relatively easy. Two basic approaches to computer revision are possible; the choice between them depends on how comfortable you feel working at the keyboard. Each is presented below.

"Hard-Copy" Revision

Working from a printed copy of the rough draft is best for writers who have limited experience with word processors or who are uncomfortable with computers.

Triple-space the draft; leave extra wide margins.

Hard-copy revision allows you to analyze several pages simultaneously, making it a good method for evaluating and correcting organizational and other large-scale problems.

Once you produce revision notes and rewritten portions of the draft, transfer them to the computer file, first making a backup copy of the original and giving it a different file name. This transfer stage makes hard-copy revision somewhat slower than "on-screen" revision.

Hard-copy revision works best for complex or extensive revisions, such as remedying problems with logical coherence and transitions.

Advice: Avoid the urge to "respect" a printed version just because it looks finished; it may still require major reworking.

"On-Screen" Revision

On-screen revision works best for writers familiar and comfortable with computers and word-processing programs.

Keep a backup copy of the original draft, giving it a different file name.

Work on only one screen at a time, evaluating each phrase, sentence, and paragraph and typing changes as you think of them.

Working on screen can be quicker than working on a hard copy.

On-screen revision works best for simple revisions: additions, deletions, and limited rearranging of material.

Use whichever approach best matches your needs and experience with computers. Remember that each approach will help you to incorporate content revisions without completely retyping or rewriting the paper.

Figure 1 shows the content revisions that Erica made in the rough draft of her first body paragraph: (1) she clarified several sentences, (2) she added important information about magazine ads that she had inadvertently omitted, (3) she deleted an example that she had decided was not effective, and (4) she added a sentence explicitly connecting the example to her thesis statement.

Figure 1

People think that Health magazine makes an appeal to people

who are concerned about general health, and the articles certainly
                    The Mar/Apr   in women
suggest that. A recent issue includes weight lifting, heart disease,
            iron
the use of suppliments, and healthy cooking—these all treat health

related topics. The ads in Health target reader that want to be

healthy. Several ads sell sport shoes, and 5 skin and hair care

advertisements point out vitamin and protien enrichment. Over 20
                that are low fat or fat free
ads promote foods. 11 ads promote vitamins, mineral suppli-

ments, and medicines. 1 ad tries to sell a mattress. And even the
            (a Chevy Lumina ad)   (Subaru Outback ad)
car ads emphasize safety or activity. Some of the ads show peo-
  Their is a clear connection among what the readers of Health read and
ple of all ages, making them nicely balanced. Clearly, their activites
  what they buy, proving that
match their topics of concern.

EXERCISE 3.1 ❭ *Content revision*

*Reread your draft and respond to the questions on page 55.
Unless you can answer each question with an unequivocal yes,
revise the draft until the content is clear, coherent, and complete.*

| 3c | Revise the style of your paper. |

Achieving clear, adequately developed content is the first step
in revision. The second step is achieving a clear and compelling presentation of that content.

When you have developed strong content in the paper,
refine its style, using these questions as a guide:

Do the lengths and types of sentences vary?

Do sentences clearly and concisely express their meaning?

Are word choices vivid, accurate, and appropriate?

Do most sentences use the active voice?

Do transitions adequately relate ideas?

Word processing and style revision

Style revision can be effectively done on the computer
because you can add to, delete from, and combine or separate your sentences without completely retyping the text.
Some specific guidelines follow:

Check sentence length. Have your word-processing program locate periods (most will end sentences) using the "search" command. As the program executes the search, notice the approximate number of lines the cursor skips. If it is pausing frequently within lines or on every line, some sentences are probably too short. If the cursor often skips three or more lines, some sentences may be too long.

Check for repeated expressions. Use the "search" command to locate words that you suspect you use too often. Especially look for slang, jargon, and technical terms, intensifiers like *very*, and proper names, all of which can be distracting if overused. Then change some of them.

Check for passive constructions. Search for forms of the verb *to be*, the auxiliary forms used to create passive sentences. When the search finds one of these verbs, reread the sentence, check for passive voice, and rephrase the sentence if necessary.

To get a sense of how the paper flows, read it aloud, with or without an audience, noting where word choices are awkward or where phrases are difficult to follow. Your hesitations while reading orally will help you to pinpoint areas that require reworking.

After revising the content of her paper, Erica considered the effectiveness of its style. She decided to make a number of major and minor changes: (1) she altered her word choices throughout the paragraph, making them more vivid, (2) she added transitions, and (3) she combined some short, choppy sentences to improve the flow of the paragraph. Erica's style revisions are shown in Figure 2.

Figure 2

People think that Health *magazine makes an appeal to people*

— with edits: People ~~think~~ *assume, for example,* that Health magazine ~~makes an appeal to people~~ *attracts readers*

who are concerned about general health, and the articles certainly

suggest that. The Mar/Apr 1996 issue includes weight lifting, heart

disease in women, the use of iron suppliments, and healthy cook-

ing—these all treat health related topics. The ads in Health *target*
                                                    Providing a useful corallary,

reader that want to be healthy. Several ads sell sport shoes, and 5
who live   lives   promote walking

skin and hair care advertisements point out vitamin and protien
                                   emphasize

enrichment. Over 20 ads promote foods that are low fat or fat
          , as well as good looks

free. 11 ads promote vitamins, mineral suppliments, and medi-

cines. And even the car ads emphasize safety (a Chevy Lumina ad)

or activity (Subaru Outback ad). Their is a clear connection among
                              In this case,

what the readers of Health read and what they buy, proving that
                                              suggesting

their activites match their topics of concern.
        correspond to   interests

EXERCISE 3.2) *Style revision*

*Revise the style of your paper by answering the questions on
page 58.*

| 3d | > | Eliminate technical errors and inconsistencies. |

Technical revision focuses on grammar, punctuation, mechanics, spelling, and manuscript form. After eliminating major
problems with content and style, consider the technical revisions that will make the paper correct and precise.

Ask yourself the following general questions and also watch for technical errors that you make frequently.

Are all words spelled correctly? (When in doubt, always look up the correct spelling in a dictionary or use your spellchecker.)

Are any necessary words omitted? Are any words unnecessarily repeated?

Is punctuation accurate? (See "Punctuation," starting on page 320.)

Are elements of mechanics properly used? (See "Mechanics," starting on page 379.)

Are all sentences complete?

Do nouns and pronouns and subjects and verbs agree in number and gender as appropriate?

Are all pronoun antecedents clear?

Are all modifiers logically positioned?

Make technical revisions slowly and carefully, paying particular attention to the kinds of errors that you have made in the past. If you are uncertain whether you have made an error, look up the applicable rule in this handbook.

Word processing and technical revision

Use word-processing capabilities to help you check for potential problems and make some technical revisions.

Check spelling. A spelling program (a standard feature of most word-processing programs) will search your manuscript for words not found in its dictionary. When the spelling program highlights a word that is suspect, consider the word carefully. It may be spelled incorrectly, or it may be a technical term or a proper name not found in the program's dictionary. Look up suspect words in a standard college dictionary. Spelling programs will also highlight words typed twice in succession. Remember that spelling checkers will not highlight a misspelled word that happens to be another word correctly spelled (for example, *hale* instead of *half*) nor a correctly spelled word used in the wrong context (for example, *their* instead of *there*). Always carefully proofread the spelling of your papers.

Check for specialized punctuation. Because some marks of punctuation—semicolons, colons, dashes, and parentheses—must be used with special care, use the "search" command to locate them in your manuscript; then double-check their use. For example, search for colons and then check to see that they are preceded by full sentences.

Check pronoun usage. Use the "search" command to find uses of pronouns (*he, she, they,* and others). Note whether each pronoun has a clear and correct antecedent (the word it refers to), and correct any unclear or inaccurate references.

After making her content and style revisions, Erica made her technical revisions: (1) she corrected spelling errors, (2) she inserted necessary italics, (3) she corrected her use of numbers, (4) she eliminated words inadvertently repeated, and (5) she corrected her punctuation. Erica's technical revisions are shown in Figure 3.

Figure 3

People assume, for example, that <u>Health</u> magazine attracts read-

ers concerned about general health. The articles certainly suggest

that. The ~~Mar/Apr~~ *March/April* 1996 issue includes articles on weight lifting,

heart disease in women, the use of iron suppl*e*iments, and healthy

cooking*;* these all treat health~~-~~related topics. Providing a useful

cor*o*a*l*lary, the ads in <u>Health</u> target reader*s* who live healthy lives.

Several ads promote walking shoes; *five* ~~5~~ skin and hair~~-~~care ~~adver-~~

~~tisements~~ *ads* emphasize vitamin and prot*ei*i*e*n enrichment, as well as

good looks; over *twenty* ~~20~~ ads promote foods that are low~~-~~fat or fat~~-~~free;

eleven 1~~1~~ ads promote vitamins, mineral suppl*e*iments, and medicines;

even the car ads emphasize safety (a *Chevrolet* ~~Chevy~~ Lumina ad) or activity

(*a* Subaru Outback ad). In this case, ~~the their~~ *there* is a clear connection

~~among~~ *between* what the readers of <u>Health</u> read and what they buy, sug-

gesting that their activit*i*es correspond to their interests.

EXERCISE 3.3 ❱ *Technical revision*

Return to your paper and examine it for technical errors, revising
to eliminate them as you work. Work slowly and carefully, using
Chapters 15–31 of this handbook to review rules of grammar,
punctuation, and mechanics.

| 3e | Use peer editing to help you revise. |

A peer editor, often another student in the course for which you are writing, will read your paper and evaluate its content, style, and technical correctness. In many composition classes, sessions are set aside for peer reviews; when they are not (or for other courses), ask another writer to read and respond to your paper—not to rework it for you but to point out anything incomplete, unclear, inconsistent, or incorrect.

If your instructor does not provide specific guidance for peer editing, consider these basic approaches:

Find a peer editor with writing experience and standards that are similar to yours. Ideally, your peer editor should be from your class because then you are likely to share similar expectations about audience, purpose, and requirements for the paper.

Ask a peer editor specific questions, focusing on issues of particular importance to you. If, for instance, you are concerned about the organization of your paper, ask for an assessment of the order of the information or paragraphs. If you have difficulties with subject-verb agreement, ask the peer editor to check agreement. Do not ask simply for an editor to read and praise the paper, for such an undirected review will not help you to revise. Rather, ask for specific comments matched to your needs—and expect criticism as well as praise.

Ask the peer editor to point out problems but to refrain from altering your paper. A good peer editor would note, for instance, that your introductory strategy does not reflect the tone or purpose of your paper but would leave it to you to reconsider and revise the strategy—if you agreed with this assessment. Do not expect the editor to rewrite your paper for you.

Consider carefully the comments and queries of a peer editor, but also trust your own judgment. Notes about confusing, incomplete, or incorrect passages will always require attention. But on matters of judgment or personal taste—specific word choices, titles, and so on—consider the editor's notations carefully but remember that the paper is *yours.* Make no subjective changes that do not seem right and necessary to you.

Peer editing does not substitute for your own careful evaluation and revision of your paper, and it will not eliminate all problems. It will, however, elicit useful responses to your work before you prepare the final copy.

EXERCISE 3.4 ⟩ *Peer editing*

Prepare for peer editing by listing four to six features that you would like an editor to check. They may relate to any aspect of the content, style, or technical correctness of the paper. Using your list of specific concerns and the following list of editing questions, ask a peer editor to evaluate your revised paper.

Introduction

Do the title and introductory strategy create interest? Are they appropriate?

Is the thesis statement appropriately positioned? Does it express a clear topic and opinion? Does it include any necessary qualifications and clarifications?

Body paragraphs

Is the order of the paragraphs appropriate? Would another arrangement work better?

Does the topic of each paragraph clearly relate to the thesis statement? Are topics developed sufficiently?

Are transitions smoothly made between sentences within paragraphs and between paragraphs?

65

Conclusion

Does the conclusion effectively summarize the key points of the paper?

Is the concluding strategy appropriate?

Style

Are the sentences varied, coherent, forceful, and smooth?

Are the word choices vivid, accurate, and appropriate?

Technical matters

Are the sentences grammatical?

Is the usage standard?

Are punctuation and mechanics correct?

Word processing and personal revision guidelines

Use the guidelines for revising content, style, and technical matters on pages 55, 58 and 60–61 as the basis for a personal file of revision guidelines. Type the questions listed, or as many of them as you regularly find useful in your writing, into a separate file. Add to the file reminders about frequent or recurring problems in your drafts and useful suggestions for improving your writing made by peer editors and teachers. Add a list of words you frequently misspell. Print a copy of the file to use when reviewing drafts, or use it on-screen, in a second window, as a personal revision checklist.

| 3f | > | **Prepare a final copy of your paper.** |

Most papers should be neatly and cleanly printed or typewrit-
ten, following the general manuscript guidelines that appear in
Appendix A, "Manuscript Form." Your instructor will explain
any specific requirements for preparing a final manuscript.

EXERCISE 3.5 ⟩ *A final copy*

*Prepare the final copy of your paper. Work carefully, proofreading
each page. As a safeguard, print a second copy of the final manuscript or make a photocopy. Submit the original copy of your
paper—on time.*

 ### *Word processing and preparing a final manuscript*

If you have been working on the computer, preparing the
final copy will be easy.

Make final changes. Having made most of your substantive changes during content, style, and technical revision, in all probability you will need to make only small
changes—for example, final adjustments in word
choice.

Insert paging codes. For your final copy, include your
name and the page number in the upper right corner of
each page. Using the program's "menu," usually with
the designation *headers* or *running heads*, insert the
codes to print name and page number. One code will
then run throughout the paper, and paging will be done
automatically.

Print a draft-quality copy for yourself. Using the draft mode, prepare a copy of the final paper to keep for yourself. Double-check to make sure that the manuscript format is accurate; if it is not, make necessary changes.

Print a high-quality copy to submit. Use a laser printer, if possible, to produce a manuscript that looks typed. If one is not available, use the best quality mode of the available printer.

| 3g | A sample paper. |

Erica Karschner   Karschner 1

Ms. Evans

English 104

January 17, 1997

Mixed Signals? What Magazine Ads Say About Readers

On the bulletin boards of most classroom buildings, students find--among the notices for apartments for rent, concerts, fund-raisers, and organizational meetings--flyers for magazine-subscription services. With phrases like "Education Discount" and "Save up to 80%," these flyers attract collegiate readers and often prompt them to order subscriptions to magazines that interest them. But what do the magazines they order say about them? Plenty. Even more interesting is what the ads in the magazines suggest

about regular readers. Although people can be characterized by the magazines they read, examining magazine
advertisements provides a useful way to understand who
the regular readers of magazines are, as well as who they
think they are.

People assume, for example, that Health magazine
attracts readers concerned about general health. The
articles certainly suggest that. The March/April 1996
issue includes articles on weight lifting, heart disease
in women, the use of iron supplements, and healthy cooking; these all treat health-related topics. Providing a
useful corollary, the ads in Health target readers who
live healthy lives. Several ads promote walking shoes;
five skin and hair-care ads emphasize vitamin and protein
enrichment, as well as good looks; over twenty ads promote foods that are low-fat or fat-free; eleven ads promote vitamins, mineral supplements, and medicines; even
the car ads emphasize safety (a Chevrolet Lumina ad) or
activity (a Subaru Outback ad). In this case, there is a
clear connection between what the readers of Health read
and what they buy, suggesting that their activities correspond to their interests.

People might also assume that <u>Sport</u> magazine attracts readers who find sports and sports activities appealing. The April 1996 issue, for example, includes articles on Grant Hill, the NCAA final four, the up-coming baseball season, NBA recruitment, hockey, and golf. Clearly readers of <u>Sport</u> have a broad interest in many sports. Yet the ads suggest other, not necessarily related, interests as well. The two ads for sports shoes are outweighed by five ads for cigarettes and three ads for chewing tobacco; the single ad for Gatorade has three corresponding ads for liquor. The six car and truck ads emphasize performance (Camaro's 200-hp 3800 V6) and power (Ram's "Magnum Power"). The only personal-care product advertised is shaving cream. A review of the articles and ads, as a result, suggests that <u>Sport</u> read-ers' interests and activities are not the same: they seem to be fans, not players.

People could also fairly assume that readers of <u>New Woman</u> are examining women's issues from a current per-spective. The articles certainly suggest that. In the March 1996 issue, for example, the articles focus on relationships with workaholics, sibling relationships, dealing with anger, job loss, alternative careers, nutrition, exercise, and fashion. However, a review of the ads gives a somewhat different view of readers. Twelve ads for personal products (deodorant, tampons, contraceptives) receive the greatest emphasis, followed by eight makeup ads (lipstick, foundation, mascara). With three or four ads apiece, the following products also suggest readers' interests: cologne, sports gear, clothes, shoes, medicines, food, cigarettes, and exercise equipment. It's a strangely mixed collection, suggesting that even "new" women can't escape the pull of "old" stereotypes.

Ads appear in magazines because companies have discovered through research what products will sell to which target audiences. As a result, the ads in magazines like Health, Sport, and New Woman can give us insights into the interests and buying patterns of their regular readers, showing us who they really are. So the next time you're sitting in a waiting room thumbing through copies of Details, Ladies' Home Journal, YM, Parents, Field and Stream, Business Week, or Psychology Today just to pass the time, direct your attention to the print ads: they can tell you more about regular readers of the magazines than you--or the regular readers--might think.

4   Paragraphs

Paragraphs focus on single facets of a subject. A single paragraph describes or explains one idea; as part of a series of paragraphs in a paper, a single paragraph develops one aspect of the paper's thesis. Paragraph length varies with the purpose of the paragraph, the nature of the material in the paragraph, and the function of the paragraph. To present ideas effectively, however, all paragraphs—short or long—must be unified, coherent, complete, and developed.

> ## Quick Reference
>
> Paragraphs, the building blocks of papers, must be focused, structured, and developed.
>
> ❭ Write paragraphs that develop single ideas, using topic sentences, when appropriate, to clarify your focus for readers.
>
> ❭ Use the stylistic techniques of transition and repetition to link ideas within and between paragraphs.
>
> ❭ Use varied methods of paragraph development, selecting patterns appropriate to the ideas that you generated during planning.

4a ❭ Develop unified paragraphs.

A **unified paragraph** includes information pertinent to the main idea and excludes information that is unrelated. Often a

Note: Many of the exercises in this chapter will take you through the steps of writing paragraphs. Keep the work from each exercise to use in later exercises.

topic sentence states the main idea explicitly and indicates by its phrasing the pattern of development that the paragraph follows.

Lack of unity is a common problem in early drafts. You can avoid blurring the focus of a paragraph by keeping the following points in mind.

Focus on One Topic

A unified paragraph develops one main idea only; it does not include information that is loosely related to the main idea or that constitutes an additional main idea. The following paragraph is not unified because it describes two museums (two topics) without establishing a connection between them.

> The Metropolitan Museum of Art in New York City is an impressive example of nineteenth-century architecture. Made of stone with massive columns and elaborately carved scrollwork, it is institutional architecture of the sort we expect in public buildings. Farther up Fifth Avenue, the Guggenheim Museum of Modern Art is built of reinforced concrete. This museum forms a spatial helix, a continuous spiral that expands as it rises; each level is marked by a narrow band of windows. Its design is severe and unusual.

Without any suggestion that the museums are being contrasted, the paragraph includes an unnecessary shift in topic as the discussion moves from one museum to the other. A topic sentence explaining the relationship between the Guggenheim and the Metropolitan Museum of Art would create focus, or each museum could be discussed in a separate, focused paragraph.

> The Metropolitan Museum of Art in New York City is a typical example of nineteenth-century public architecture. Made of stone, with massive columns, tall casement windows, and an elaborately carved entablature, it is institutional architecture that conveys the dignity we expect in great public museum buildings. It is reminiscent of the Louvre in Paris, the British Museum in London, and the National Gallery in Washington. Familiar yet impressive, it suggests a grand purpose.

Farther up Fifth Avenue, the Guggenheim Museum of Modern Art offers a contrasting, twentieth-century view of museum architecture. Built of reinforced concrete in the form of a spatial helix, a continuous spiral that expands as it rises, it is adorned only by a band of simple windows. In 1937, when it was designed by Frank Lloyd Wright, the building's severity made it seem very modern, very alien, and austere rather than august. Yet it changed the way Americans perceived institutional architecture, and we now find similar designs in a range of public buildings from libraries to high schools.

Include Relevant Details Only

Including a number of interesting details that are marginally related or irrelevant to the topic takes a paragraph in too many directions and destroys unity, as in this paragraph:

(1) Hurricanes are cyclones that develop in the tropical waters of the Atlantic Ocean. (2) Forming large circles or ovals, they have winds of 75 miles per hour or more and can measure 500 miles across. (3) Years ago, hurricanes were named after women—Irene, Sarah, and Becky, for example—but now they are also named after men. (4) They usually form hundreds of miles from land and then move slowly to the northwest at about 10 miles per hour. (5) For reasons unknown, they pick up speed rapidly when they reach the twenty-fifth parallel. (6) That means, in very practical terms, that they reach peak speed and destructive power by the time they hit North American coastlines. (7) Hurricanes that form in the Pacific Ocean are commonly called typhoons.

Here, all the material relates to hurricanes, but some of it only loosely. Sentences 1, 2, 4, 5, and 6 are factual descriptions of how the storms form and move. Sentences 3 and 7 include interesting but only marginally relevant information. The unity of the paragraph would be improved by omitting the unrelated material, which might fit into another paragraph.

Use Topic Sentences

A **topic sentence** presents a paragraph's main idea and indicates the writer's opinion about it. As succinct statements of an idea and intended development, topic sentences unify the paragraphs in which they appear. In long papers, the topic sentences of all body paragraphs, taken together, constitute the ideas and major illustrations that support the paper's thesis.

A topic sentence at the beginning of a paragraph works like a map, providing an overview that guides readers through the writing. A topic sentence at the end of a paragraph summarizes its ideas. Sometimes, especially in descriptive paragraphs, a topic sentence is unnecessary; readers will be able to infer the point from the paragraph as a whole. If you decide to omit a topic sentence from one of your paragraphs, remember that its absence may be confusing to your readers, who may not fully understand or may misinterpret your point.

Topic sentence at the beginning

Euphemisms thus serve as verbal placebos; they are particularly frequent when the ill-timed provocation could expose one to instant retaliation. Sports figures are always careful to speak with respect, even admiration, of their upcoming opponents, however inept. Precautionary and placatory euphemisms include variations on the theme, "They're a much better team than their record shows," and that minimal, thread-bare uncompliment, "They never give up." Everywhere except in politics (where it's accepted practice to toot one's own horn as loudly as possible), false modesty is useful protection against overconfidence on one's own part and provocation of the opponent. —Robert M. Adams, "Soft Soap and the Nitty-Gritty"

Topic sentence at the end

Slip out of shape and the system that delivers oxygen and nourishment to brain cells can quickly bog down. The heart gets sluggish. Arteries clog up with cholesterol-laden plaque. Blood flow to the tiny capillaries that feed brain cells may slow to a trickle. The result:

Neurons get less of the nourishment they demand and can't move electrical signals as fast. The mind slows. **A recent study even found that high blood pressure, a common fallout of aging, can lead to memory problems.** —Peter Jaret, "Think Fast"

No topic sentence

Whenever I had nothing better to do in San Salvador I would walk up in the leafy stillness of the San Benito and Escalón districts, where the hush at midday is broken only by the occasional crackle of a walkie-talkie, the click of metal moving on a weapon. I recall a day in San Benito when I opened my bag to check an address, and heard the clicking of metal on metal all up and down the street. On the whole no one walks up here, and pools of blossoms lie undisturbed on the sidewalks. Most of the houses in San Benito are more recent than those in Escalón, less idiosyncratic and probably smarter, but the most striking architectural features in both districts are not the houses but their walls, walls built upon walls, walls stripped of the copa de oro and bougainvillea, walls that reflect successive generations of violence: the original stone, the additional five or six or ten feet of brick, and finally the barbed wire, sometimes concertina, sometimes electrified; walls with watch towers, gun ports, closed-circuit television cameras, walls now reaching twenty and thirty feet. —Joan Didion, "Salvador"

Use the computer's capabilities to cut, copy, and paste materials to reposition your topic sentences, experimenting with different ways to create emphasis. Print copies of different versions and read and evaluate them, noting their relative effectiveness. Choose the version that best suits your purpose and tone to use in your draft.

EXERCISE 4.1) *Topic sentences*

The following paragraph lacks unity because it has a poor topic sentence. Revise the topic sentence to give the paragraph a clearer focus and then strike out any irrelevant material.

In the early days of television, children in major roles were good-natured, middle-class role models. Timmy, the boy on *Lassie*, had well-cut blond hair, sparkling eyes, a straight-toothed smile. He even had dimples. He was naive in a way children were only portrayed in early television. He ignored warnings, got into trouble, was rescued by his dog, and learned a new lesson each week—and the lesson always had to do with following adults' rules. Timmy, in an idealized way, always learned to like adult rules. Of course, Theodore (Beaver) Cleaver wasn't like that at all. He always got himself into trouble and certainly didn't have a dog to rescue him; in fact, he always got caught but he never really got punished. Children in today's programs have little in common with these two boys.

EXERCISE 4.2 ❯ *Topic sentences*

Using four of the subjects listed below, write topic sentences. Make sure that your topic sentences clearly identify the subject and indicate how you will discuss it.

Example

Subject: lawyers

Topic sentence: Lawyers sometimes act more as legal interpreters than as advocates.

1. Censorship on the Internet

2. Sibling rivalry

3. Nationalized health insurance

4. The Olympic Games

5. Religious prejudice

6. Standardized achievement tests

7. National parks

8. Political debates

9. Holiday celebrations

10. Water conservation

| 4b | Create coherent paragraphs. |

Effective paragraphs are clear and thorough and explain ideas and the connections among ideas. When sentences fit together well, a paragraph is coherent and readers are able to concentrate on what the paragraph says. The strategies used to achieve coherence are transition and repetition.

Transitional Words and Phrases

Transition is movement from one facet of a subject to another. Transitional words and phrases facilitate these shifts in focus. The English language is rich in such words and phrases. Coordinating conjunctions (*and, but,* and others), subordinating conjunctions (*although, since,* and others), and correlative conjunctions (*either . . . or, not only . . . but also,* and others) are the most commonly used transitional words and phrases. Use transitional words and phrases to establish relationships within sentences, between paragraphs, or among the parts of a paper. The following lists show some of the relationships you can establish by using transitional words and phrases and give examples of words and phrases that suggest each relationship.

Addition

also	furthermore
and	in addition
besides	moreover
equally	next
further	too

Similarity

also   moreover

likewise   similarly

Difference

but   on the contrary

however   on the other hand

in contrast   yet

nevertheless

Examples

for example   specifically

for instance   to illustrate

in fact

Restatements or summaries

finally   in summary

in brief   on the whole

in conclusion   that is

in other words   therefore

in short   to sum up

Result

accordingly   so

as a result   therefore

consequently   thereupon

for this reason   thus

Chronology

after	meanwhile
afterward	next
before	second
during	simultaneously
earlier	soon
finally	still
first	then
immediately	third
in the meantime	when
later	while

Location

above	opposite
below	there
beyond	to the left
farther	to the right
here	under
nearby	

The following paragraph makes use of a number of transitional words and phrases, each marked with italics, to emphasize the relationships among ideas.

In recent years, some doctors have begun diagnosing allergies by combining blood droplets with different allergens to determine a sensitivity. [Allergy specialist] Lieberman warns, *however*, that this method is less accurate, is more expensive, and takes longer to get answers than skin testing. *Generally*, doctors recommend the blood test when it might be dangerous to use the allergen directly on the skin—as might be the case in someone hypersensitive to bee venom, *for example*—or if a skin disease *such as* eczema makes it difficult to see the results of a skin test.—Cynthia Green, "Sneezy and Grumpy? See Doc"

Repeat Words and Phrases

Selective **repetition of words and phrases** can make writing unified and effective. To avoid monotony, use variations of key words or phrases, synonyms (words with the same meaning), and pronouns to create variety as you create unity. The following paragraph uses all three.

> *Laughter* is surely one of humanity's greatest gifts, for the ability to *laugh*—to appreciate the pleasure or *absurdity* in daily activities—allows people, young and old alike, to keep problems in perspective. Children are natural *laughers*. In situations, both appropriate and inappropriate, the *chuckles, giggles,* and outright *peals of laughter* of children can emphasize their innocence, their joyful ignorance of the problems of the world. *Levity* among adults is, unfortunately, far less common, but *it* is equally welcome. How fortunate are the adults who can react to potentially frustrating situations—a collapsed tent, a split seam in a pair of pants, a surprise guest—and see the sheer *laughability* of their attempts to maintain absolute control. *Laughter* expresses pleasure, eases tension, and lifts the spirit. *It* is a gift we should all share more often.

Repeat Sentence Structures

The **repetition of sentence structures** creates unity within a paragraph by presenting similar ideas in similar ways. If you strive for variety in most sentences, then selectively repeated patterns will stand out. The following excerpt from a lengthy paragraph uses repeated sentence structures (all italicized) to focus attention on similar activities.

But though I was initially disappointed at being categorized as an extremist, as I continued to think about the matter I gradually gained a measure of satisfaction from the label. *Was not Jesus an extremist for love:* "Love your enemies, bless them that curse you, do good to them that hate you, and pray for them which despitefully use you, and persecute you." *Was not Amos an extremist for justice:* "Let justice roll down like waters and righteousness like an ever-flowing stream." *Was not Paul an extremist for the Christian gospel:* "I bear in my body the marks of the Lord Jesus." *Was not Martin Luther an extremist:* "Here I stand; I cannot do otherwise, so help me God." *And John Bunyan:* "I will stay in jail to the end of my days before I make a butchery of my conscience." *And Abraham Lincoln:* "This nation cannot survive half slave and half free." *And Thomas Jefferson:* "We hold these truths' to be self-evident, that all men are created equal. . . ." So the question is not whether we will be extremists, but what kind of extremists we will be. —Martin Luther King, Jr., "Letter from Birmingham Jail"

Use the word processor to add transitions to your paragraphs. The program will automatically reformat your paragraphs without retyping. Copy your paragraphs and experiment freely with repeating words, phrases, and sentence structures. You can always return to your original version or try another. Print out your paragraphs and mark the transitional words and phrases, as in the example on page 81, to check for consistency of pronouns and other references and for excessive repetition.

EXERCISE 4.3 ❭ *Transitions and repeated sentence elements*

Notice the use of transitional words and phrases and repetition in the following paragraphs, and comment on the purpose and effectiveness of each use.

One great difficulty in getting straightforward answers is that so many of the diseases in question have unpredictable courses, and some of them have a substantial tendency toward spontaneous remission. In rheumatoid arthritis, for instance, when such widely disparate therapeutic measures as copper bracelets, a move to Arizona, diets low in sugar or salt or meat or whatever, and even an inspirational book have been accepted by patients as useful, the trouble in evaluation is that approximately 35 percent of patients with this diagnosis are bound to recover no matter what they do. But if you actually have rheumatoid arthritis or, for that matter, schizophrenia, and then get over it, or if you are a doctor and observe this happen, it is hard to be persuaded that it wasn't *something* you did that was responsible. Hence, you need very large numbers of patients and lots of time, and a cool head.

Magic is back again, and in full force. Laetrile cures cancer, acupuncture is useful for deafness and low-back pain, vitamins are good for anything, and meditation, yoga, dancing, biofeedback, and shouting one another down in crowded rooms over weekends are specifics for the human condition. Running, a good thing to be doing for its own sake, has acquired the medicinal value formerly attributed to rare herbs from Indonesia. —Lewis Thomas, "On Magic in Medicine"

EXERCISE 4.4 ❱ *Transitions and repeated sentence elements*

Revise one of your paragraphs to make effective use of transitional words and phrases and repeated words, phrases, and sentence structures.

| 4c | ❭ | **Write complete paragraphs.** |

Paragraphs vary in length. Short paragraphs can be emphatic and useful for presenting simple ideas, but too many in succession may seem choppy and leave ideas undeveloped. Long paragraphs are necessary for presenting complex ideas, but too many in a row may become tiring and make the ideas too concentrated. The best general rule about paragraph length is to make paragraphs long enough to explain ideas fully and to serve their purpose in a paper—and no longer. Look at the following paragraphs, which vary considerably in length.

Brief paragraph

The drama begins to unfold with the arrival of the corpse at the mortuary. —Jessica Mitford, "Behind the Formaldehyde Curtain" (This one-sentence paragraph creates an emphatic transition to a lengthy technical discussion of embalming procedures used by morticians.)

Moderate paragraph

Mathew Brady, the brilliant archivist of American Civil War photography, is known as much for his innovation as for his imagery: By bringing his horse-drawn darkroom to the battlefield, Brady and his corps of photographers created a new way of looking at human conflict. How fitting, then, that the countless photos he amassed are once again on the cutting edge of technology—this time as a searchable digital archive administered by the Library of Congress. —"Glory, Duty, and Death" (This moderate-length paragraph uses two long sentences to identify Brady's innovations in photography and link him to recent computer trends.)

Long paragraph

Poor Columbus! He is a minor character now, a walk-on in the middle of American history. Even those books that have not replaced his picture with a Mayan temple or an Iroquois mask do not credit him with discovering America—even for the Europeans. The Vikings, they say, preceded him to the New World, and after that the Europeans, having lost or forgotten their maps, simply neglected to cross the ocean again for five hundred years. Columbus is far from being the only personage to have suffered from time and revision. Captain John Smith, Daniel Boone, and Wild Bill Hickok—the great self-promoters of American history—have all but disappeared, taking with them a good deal of the romance of the American fron-

tier. General Custer has given way to Chief Crazy Horse; General Eisenhower no longer liberates Europe single-handed; and indeed, most generals, even to Washington and Lee, have faded away, as old soldiers do, giving place to social reformers such as William Lloyd Garrison and Jacob Riis. A number of black Americans have risen to prominence: not only George Washington Carver but Frederick Douglass and Martin Luther King, Jr. W. E. B. Du Bois now invariably accompanies Booker T. Washington. In addition, there is a mystery man called Crispus Attucks, a fugitive slave about whom nothing seems to be known for certain except that he was a victim of the Boston Massacre and thus became one of the first casualties of the American Revolution. Thaddeus Stevens has been reconstructed—his character changed, as it were, from black to white, from cruel and vindictive to persistent and sincere. As for Teddy Roosevelt, he now champions the issue of conservation instead of charging up San Juan Hill. No single President really stands out as a hero, but all Presidents—except certain unmentionables in the second half of the nineteenth century—seem to have done as well as could be expected, given difficult circumstances.
—Frances FitzGerald, "Rewriting American History" (In this lengthy paragraph near the beginning of her essay, FitzGerald uses a series of examples to establish the scope of the essay.)

A complete paragraph presents ideas clearly, along with enough supporting detail to satisfy readers. Although supporting detail will vary from paragraph to paragraph, depending on purpose and length, complete paragraphs are usually developed through the use of specific examples, facts, and description, as described in section 4d.

EXERCISE 4.5 〉 Complete paragraphs

Use one topic sentence from Exercise 4.2 to construct a paragraph that elaborates on your central idea.

EXERCISE 4.6 ⟩ *Complete paragraphs*

Use the topic sentence that follows and the accompanying examples (or others of your choosing) to construct a paragraph that is complete enough to satisfy a reader's expectations.

Topic sentence

In recent years, presidents' wives have provided a useful focus on national issues.

Examples

Eleanor Roosevelt: minority and women's rights and international cooperation

Jacqueline Kennedy: historical preservation and the fine arts

Lady Bird Johnson: environmental protection, forestation, and parks preservation

Betty Ford: substance-abuse programs and the arts

Nancy Reagan: substance-abuse programs and foster-child programs

Barbara Bush: substance-abuse programs and literacy programs

Hillary Rodham Clinton: health care reform and education.

| 4d | ⟩ | **Vary the organization and development of paragraphs.** |

Organize Paragraphs in Alternative Ways

Deductive Structure

A **deductive paragraph** begins with a topic sentence and continues with supporting descriptions, examples, and facts. This paragraph has a deductive structure:

A third party with an even national appeal but lacking plurality support within any state will be stymied by the electoral college. Millard Fillmore and the Know-Nothings won 21 percent of the popular vote in 1856, but received only 2 percent of the electoral vote. Republican William Howard Taft was the choice of 23 percent of the voters in 1912, but of less than 2 percent of the electoral college. That same year, Theodore Roosevelt mounted the biggest third-party challenge of the twentieth century, taking 28 percent of the popular vote, yet he ended up with just 17 percent of the electoral vote. Most recently, we had Ross Perot's 1992 campaign, when he won nearly 20 percent of the popular vote but didn't earn a single electoral vote. —Walter Berns, "Third Parties and the Presidential Race"

Inductive Structure

The inverse of the deductive paragraph, an **inductive paragraph** begins with descriptions, examples, and facts and ends with the topic sentence. This structure builds suspense, heightens interest, and emphasizes details over generalization. Despite these advantages, the inductive structure should be used selectively to avoid dulling its effect or frustrating readers by asking them too often to wait for the main idea. This paragraph has an inductive structure:

On that particular day [4 September 1893] Beatrix Potter decided to write a letter, which was to become famous. It was to five-year-old Noel Moore, the youngest son of her ex-governess Annie Moore, a delicate boy who was often ill and who found great comfort in the generously illustrated letters that arrived regularly from "Yours affectionately, Beatrix Potter." This particular letter began: "My dear Noel, I don't know what to write to you, so I shall tell you a story about four little rabbits whose names were Flopsy, Mopsy, Cottontail and Peter. They lived with their mother in a sand bank under the root of a big fir tree. . . ." The letter continued with the whole of the now famous story of Peter Rabbit. —Judy Taylor, "The Tale of Beatrix Potter"

EXERCISE 4.7) Deductive and inductive structure

> *Using two of the topic sentences you wrote for Exercise 4.2, write one deductive and one inductive paragraph. Underline the topic sentence in each and number the details in the margin of the paper. Be ready to explain why you chose the paragraph structure you did for developing each topic sentence.*

Develop Your Paragraphs

Purpose

Let purpose determine the development of your paragraphs. Although it is possible first to select an appropriate pattern of development and then to fit information to the pattern, the result is often awkward or mechanical. A better strategy is to complete some planning activities, decide on a general purpose and thesis for the whole paper, outline the information, and then write the first draft, letting the patterns of the paragraphs develop naturally. In this way, each paragraph extends and strengthens the paper's purpose.

For example, in her brief essay "In Bed," Joan Didion narrates her history of ignoring, fighting, and finally learning to live with migraine headaches. In the course of eight paragraphs, Didion vividly describes and provides facts on the effects, course, and treatment of this illness; she narrates her own experience from childhood; and, ultimately, she persuades readers that such afflictions can be beneficial when they remind us of the beauty and serenity of life.

Descriptions

All writing benefits from apt and vivid details that evoke the five senses. In your writing, search for words that describe your subject's sights (*burgundy* sweater, *glistening* chrome), sounds (*faint* tapping, *shrill* laughter), textures, (*corrugated* tin, *leath-*

ery skin), tastes (*salty* crackers, *tart* berries), and smells (*fishy* odor, *lilac* scent). Be specific, and try for both originality and accuracy.

> To new arrivals in London, it seemed pitch black out of doors, too, but not, by 1943, to Londoners. People had become conscious again of the phases of the moon, the light from the stars. They had regained their country eyes. The darkness was full of noises, the echo of footsteps, of people talking, the cries for taxis. Sound itself seemed amplified and dependable in the half-blindness of the street. The smell was of dust, of damp plaster in the air, and of the formaldehyde scent of the smoke from the dirty coal that lodged in the yellow fog. The stained sandbags, the rust, the dull, peeling paint, damp that made great dark lines down the walls, made London seem like a long-neglected, leaky attic. —Mary Lee Settle, "London—1944"

Examples

One of the most effective methods for developing a paragraph is through the use of specific, appropriate examples. Be precise; name names. Instead of "a dramatic program," write "*ER.*" Instead of "a school in the Midwest," write "University of Chicago." To be convincing, examples need to be precise but also representative. Do not use extremely positive or negative examples that will seem to readers exceptional rather than typical. Often, presenting a single extended example will best show readers how you reached your conclusion. One useful way to present examples fully is to answer the journalists' questions: *who, what, when, where, how,* and *why.*

> Consider the Commerce Department, that wellspring of corporate welfare, that Oscar Mayer of Washington Pork, home to more than 100 separate trade programs. Initially, Republicans wanted to abolish the department—a move they estimated would save $7.8 billion over five years. Given that the department's budget was $5.3 billion in 1994 alone, why such skimpy savings? Because Republicans intended to shift most of the department's functions to new entities.

Among them, the *New York Times* observed, "would be a United States Science and Technology Administration, a National Marine Resources Administration, and an Economic Development Regional Administration." —Don Feder, "The 104th Congress: Verdict Pending"

Facts

Using facts and technical and statistical information effectively demonstrates how and why you reached your conclusion. Be as specific as possible. Rather than write that a car costs "a lot," write "$64,000." Rather than write that tuition has "increased dramatically" in the last decade, write "26 percent." If you use facts that you have gathered yourself, simply incorporate them in your writing. If your facts come from research, be sure to include full documentation (see pages 509–24 for guidelines).

Avalanches are triggered most frequently in the periods during and immediately following heavy snowstorms. The slopes most likely to avalanche will be the lee slopes, where wind-deposited snow compacts into slabs that precariously balance on the unstable snow underneath. Other variables in the avalanche equation include temperature changes, as well as the steepness and shape of the slope. Convex slopes tend to be more dangerous than concave slopes; those that fall from a 30- to 50-degree angle pose the greatest risk. Steep drops of 60 degrees or more avalanche almost constantly, so the snow seldom builds up to dangerous depths. Cornices, which are windswept waves of hard-packed snow that form on the lee side of exposed ridgelines, should be strictly avoided. —Keith McCafferty, "Avalanche!"

Comparison and Contrast

Comparison and contrast bring together two subjects in order to analyze their respective similarities and differences. Use this technique to explain the unfamiliar in terms of the familiar or to explore the features or qualities of your subjects.

A topic sentence should offer a clear synthesis of the compared or contrasted elements.

Comparison and contrast paragraphs can be structured in two ways: whole-to-whole and part-to-part. **Whole-to-whole, development** (or **divided development**) fully discusses first one subject and then the other. The topic sentence of a paragraph with this pattern generally emphasizes the two subjects, subordinating features or qualities.

In the waning years of the nineteenth century, two remarkable women, exact contemporaries living at opposite ends of the immense American diversity, dissented from the cultural shibboleths and popular taste of their time in the way they wrote about the life they knew best. Kate Chopin (1851–1904) was consciously defiant of the decencies and sexual prudery of the late 1890s, and sought to uncover the sensuality and discontent of women which the stultifying conventions of the age refused to acknowledge. Sarah Orne Jewett (1849–1909) preferred to look back rather than forward to the emancipated future envisioned by Mrs. Chopin; her sensibility and values were deeply anchored in the past of a rural New England that was rapidly disappearing in her lifetime, but she, too, shunned the idealized versions of actuality which a culture dedicated to gentility demanded of its literature. —Pearl K. Bell, "Kate Chopin and Sarah Orne Jewett"

The second pattern for comparison and contrast, **part-to-part development** (or **alternating development**) provides a point-by-point, alternating comparison between two subjects. The topic sentences generally emphasize qualities, features, or consequences following from the topic.

In 1973 I stayed in the four-story Erawan Hotel, then one of the tallest buildings around. Small lizards skittered over the moist walls like leaf shadows. Today the new Erawan stands 22 floors high and has a disco and a gym. In a huge glass lobby filled with trees, Thais, Americans, Japanese, and Germans make deals to the clink of spoons on china cups. The sidewalks outside are filled with young workers striding to their offices. Thailand's economic success is most obvious in the cities, but it filters into the countryside as well. Where families once tended small paddies just outside Bangkok, large tractors now groom the sweeping fields of commercial farms. Many farms have given way to golf courses in the past decade. On quiet side roads where I once slowed for water buffalo, I now dodge motorcycles piloted by young Thai men in love with speed. —Noel Grove, "The Many Faces of Thailand"

Analogy

An **analogy** illuminates a subject by pointing to an unexpected connection between dissimilar things. This quality of the unexpected can make writing vivid, but be sure to select or construct analogies in which the connections are reasonable and clear. The following example contains one extended analogy.

The garment industry is like a pyramid, with retailers—department stores like Bloomingdale's, Macy's, Sears, and others—at the top. They buy their fashions from companies like Liz Claiborne and Guess?, who are known as manufacturers although they rarely make their own clothes. The majority farm out their work to thousands of factory owners—the contractors whose factories are often sweatshops. Contractors are the small fry in the pyramid; they are often undercapitalized entrepreneurs who may be former garment workers themselves, taking in a small profit per garment. At the bottom of the pyramid is the worker, generally a woman—and sometimes her child—who is paid $0.50 or $1 for a dress that costs $120 at retail. As a general rule, prices within the pyramid follow a doubling effect at each tier. The contractors double their labor costs and overhead when quoting a price to the garment companies, which, in turn, calculate their overhead and double that to arrive at a price to charge the retailer. The retailer then doubles this price, and sometimes adds still more, to assure a profit even after two or three markdowns. —Helen Zia, "Made in the U.S.A"

Cause and Effect

Analyzing an event or condition often involves asking why it happened or how it came to be—that is, inquiring into its known or likely causes. Remember that a single cause may have multiple effects, and a single effect multiple causes. Remember, too, that a cause and effect relationship is not established by mere association. It is not necessary to document the relation in your paragraph, but if you are speculating, make that clear to your readers.

As populations are restricted in size, they lose some of the genetic varieties composing the internal variability of the species. When individual organisms become more uniform within the populations, the species as a whole loses its ability to adapt to changes in the environment. The organisms also become in effect more closely related to one another (because their genes are overall more similar). The rate of inbreeding consequently increases, which in a few extreme cases reduces vigor and fertility of individuals and renders the species as a whole still more vulnerable. —E. O. Wilson, "Endangered Species"

Process Analysis

To describe how something is done or made or how something happens, you need to describe accurately and completely the series of steps involved. A paragraph describing a process is generally presented chronologically, as in this example.

The process Perkins has evolved is a fairly complicated one, open to variation at each stage. With the gather of glass on the blowpipe, a large amount is lowered into a wooden mold with the help of assistants. Once the mold is removed, the glass is further manipulated on the marvering table. After careful placement into the annealing oven (where it cools for 50 hours), upper edges or sides may be cracked or broken slightly to give each piece its individual character before painting. Then the entire sculpture is sandblasted. The broken shards are reassembled onto the piece after oil painting is completed. The layering on of colors is crucial and, to that end, Perkins uses Winsor & Newton Liquin, a drying medium he adds to the paints, which were chosen to insure conservation properties in consultation with a paint chemist at the local art supplier, Daniel

Smith, Inc. Finally, a coat of clear picture varnish coats the work.
—Matthew Kangas, "Danny Perkins: Grunge Glass"

Classification

A large subject can be examined by dividing it into its parts or
subgroups. Establish meaningful, consistent criteria for division,
supplying readers with the information they need to distinguish
among the classes. Subgroups should not overlap.

> For present purposes, it will be useful to distinguish four degrees of
> poverty: *destitution*, which is lack of income sufficient to assure
> physical survival and to prevent suffering from hunger, exposure, or
> remediable or preventable illness; *want*, which is a lack of enough
> income to support "essential welfare" (as distinguished from com-
> fort and convenience); *hardship*, which is lack of enough to pre-
> vent acute, persistent discomfort or inconvenience; and *relative
> deprivation*, which is lack of enough to prevent one from feeling
> poor by comparison with others. —Edward C. Banfield, "Several
> Kinds of Poverty"

Definition

Definitions clarify thinking and writing, explaining terms and
concepts to readers. A **formal definition,** such as those in dictionaries, places the subject in a class and then distinguishes it
from other items in the same class.

> The goal of the measurement is easy to understand. According to
> Isaac Newton, any two material objects in the universe attract each
> other with a force that is proportional to the mass of the objects
> and that diminishes with their distance from each other. To quantify
> this phenomenon, physicists define as G the magnitude of the
> attraction that two one-kilogram masses, exactly one meter apart,
> exert on each other. Strictly speaking, G is an odd quantity with no
> intuitive meaning, so for this reason physicists take the liberty of
> referring to it in more familiar terms as a force. —Hans Christian
> Von Baeyer, "Big G"

An **informal** (or extended) **definition** may describe the subject, provide examples of it, or compare or contrast it with some other thing. The following paragraph contains examples of both types of definition.

Gardeners have long squabbled over what wildflowers are. Purists insist that they are native plants that grew before the arrival of the Europeans. Others include naturalized plants in the classification—those introduced from other parts of the world that reproduce freely in their nonnative habitat. Opinion these days favors the definition that includes both native and naturalized plants. Weeds, incidentally, are just wildflowers that grow when they are not wanted. Noxious weeds are plants that the authorities have determined threaten human health or agricultural practices. Some common attractive weeds are Queen Anne's lace (*Daucus carota*), chicory (*Cichorium intybus*) and even oxeye daisy (*Chrysanthemum leucanthemum*). —Eva Hoepfner, "Wildflower Meadows"

EXERCISE 4.8 ❭ *Paragraph development*

Write a paragraph using one of the following methods of development. Use one of the topics provided, or select one of your own.

Descriptions: an incident of prejudice, a scene showing family support, a situation in which trust was crucial, a depiction of a smoothly run business

Examples: the need for urban planning, the importance of energy conservation, the practical value of hobbies, the increasing dependence on computers

Facts: high costs of education, everyday uses of mathematics, basic equipment necessary for cooking, questionable recruitment procedures in college athletics

Comparison and contrast: seeing a horror film on television and at a theater, celebrations in different cultures, two specialized magazines, your language patterns with close friends and with parents

Analogy: preparing for a date and for a religious ritual, political ads and soft-drink ads, a college campus and a city, marriage and a corporate merger

Cause and effect: a death in the family, the farming crisis in the United States, a major industry closing in your city, personal financial difficulties

Process analysis: preparing a speech, analyzing a work of literature, buying a stereo, applying for college admission

Classification: types of museums, kinds of cartoon strips, types of radio stations, kinds of football fans

Definition: interactive videos, patriotism, a good parent-child relationship, luck

5   Critical Thinking and Writing

All purposeful verbal communication—whether speaking, listening, reading, or writing—requires critical thinking, that is, an active, focused engagement with the topic. When people speak or write, they first synthesize ideas and experiences and then communicate their insights or observations to others. Conversely, when people listen or read, they actively seek to comprehend the insights and observations of others, thus responding to the speaker's or writer's intended communication.

The systematic study and practice of critical thinking and writing improves all forms of communication by fostering substantive, precise, and thorough analysis, expression, and response. This chapter explores the techniques of critical thinking as they apply to both reading and writing.

Quick Reference

By thinking critically when you read and write, you will improve your understanding of others' writing and their understanding of yours.

》 *Think critically, actively focusing on the topic and its development.*

》 *Support different kinds of assertions with the appropriate kinds of evidence.*

》 *Evaluate discussions to determine whether supporting evidence is adequate.*

》 *Recognize patterns of fallacious reasoning. Challenge them in what you read and avoid them when you write.*

5a > **Think critically, focusing actively on the topic and its development.**

Critical thinking involves systematic and rigorous scrutiny and evaluation of ideas—in both what you read and what you write. When you read a paper, article, report, or book that argues a position, think about it critically, actively examining and evaluating its purpose, assumptions, evidence, and development. Ultimately, you must decide whether it has succeeded in establishing the validity of its position.

To work as a writer, you must use your critical thinking skills to clarify and support your own purposes, assumptions, evidence, and development. Your general goal in thinking critically when you write is to make certain that you demonstrate the validity of your position.

Critical thinking, then, can be used as you read, to deconstruct someone's thought processes, and as you write, to construct a presentation that will effectively convey your ideas.

Three basic patterns of reasoning—induction, deduction, and warrant-based reasoning—organize ideas and evidence in different ways, reflecting differences in thinking patterns. Be aware of these patterns as you read and write.

Inductive Reasoning

Induction builds from specific evidence (observations, experiences, examples, facts, statistics, testimony) and then, through interpretation, derives a **claim** (described as a conclusion or a generalization). The soundness of inductive reasoning depends on careful evaluation and description of evidence, reasonable interpretation, and clear expression of the claim.

Consider this evidence regarding Maxwell Elementary School:

- Children at MES have an absence rate higher than the school district average.

- Children at MES have the second-lowest standardized test scores in the school district.

- More children at MES receive suspensions because of fighting than do children at other elementary schools in the district.

- Fewer children at MES go on to graduate from high school than the district average.

You could make several different claims based on a review of this evidence: (1) Maxwell Elementary School students face greater obstacles to success than do children at other elementary schools in the district, (2) Maxwell Elementary School students experience a disproportionately high amount of educational interference, and (3) Maxwell Elementary School students are less likely to succeed than are students at other schools.

While reading and writing, analyze the cumulative evidence that leads to a claim or claims. As this example shows, slightly different interpretations of the same evidence can result in different, though related, claims.

Deductive Reasoning

Deduction begins with a general claim (or premise) and then clarifies or illustrates the original claim with supporting information. The effectiveness of deductive reasoning depends on a reasonable claim, thorough description of related evidence, and sound use of logic in reaching a conclusion.

For example, consider this general claim, which many people believe: Children learn from the example set by the adults around them. Interestingly, the support for a general claim like this varies as much as the writers who support it. The supporting evidence could be presented positively, through examples related to work, education, human relations, good health, fiscal responsibility, and so on. Conversely, the same generalization

5a comp   The Composing Process

could be supported negatively, through examples related to drug and alcohol abuse, physical violence, crime, compulsive behavior, and so on.

While reading and writing, analyze the original claim and the evidence used to support it. As the example above shows, different kinds of evidence can illustrate the same claim.

Warrant-Based Reasoning

Warrant-based reasoning begins with an idea expressed as a claim (or conclusion); it is presented in conjunction with related evidence. The **warrant** is the underlying assumption, often unstated, that establishes a relationship between the claim and the evidence, in the same way a warranty (from the same root word) makes a claim ("this product will work for at least one year") based on evidence ("this product has been tested and has worked for at least one year").

Claim
Hospice care is the most beneficial medical care for the elderly.

Evidence
Hospice care provides homelike settings with familiar living arrangements.

Warrant
Homelike settings, with more familiar living arrangements, are beneficial.

Carefully evaluate warrants, especially unstated ones. An invalid warrant, even an implicit one, leads to unreasonable claims.

Because college admissions tests are administered nationwide, they are an effective measure of student potential. (The implicit warrant is that widely used tests are effective. Because this notion is questionable, the conclusion is questionable as well.)

EXERCISE 5.1 **)** *Patterns of critical thinking*

To practice applying the principles of critical thinking, complete the following arguments. Compare your responses with those of your classmates to see the variations that occur when people interpret the same evidence.

Inductive Argument

Evidence

Tuition costs have increased, on the average, 5–15 percent yearly.

Books often cost $50–$100 per course.

Student fees average $200 per year.

School supplies can cost well over $200 a year.

Room and board now averages between $4,000 and $6,000.

Claim

_____

_____

Deductive Argument

Claim

We have become a society of complainers.

Evidence

_____

_____

_____

_____

Warrant-Based Argument

Claim

Computers have improved people's lives.

Evidence

People keep records efficiently, conduct business quickly, and communicate easily.

Warrant

_____

_____

_____

_____

EXERCISE 5.2 ❭ *Claims, evidence, and warrants*

Identify the claims, evidence, and warrants (both implicit and explicit) in the following paragraph.

Low wages and lack of job security create frustration. . . . This leads to a 40 percent turnover rate among congressional staffers. There is something to be said for new blood, but not when a complete transfusion is taking place about every two years. The result is not only a less efficient staff but in the long run a less effective Congress. Without experienced staff, there is no institutional memory—those who will recall what happened on an issue four years before. Without them, in fact, Congress becomes more vulnerable to criticism even from the people it most benefits. —Jonathan Yates, "'Reality' on Capitol Hill"

5b	Analyze purpose, audience, and content.

To read and write effectively, you must analyze the roles of purpose, audience, and content in ensuring communication. See section 1d for more information on audience and purpose.

Evaluate Purpose

To think critically about a piece of writing—one that you are reading or one that you are writing—you must evaluate its general purpose. Although writing can serve a variety of purposes simultaneously, four types apply to both spoken and written communication.

Purposes of Writing

Expressive writing shares perceptions and experiences, generally those gathered from personal observations. Personal essays and letters, poetry, and fiction are examples of expressive writing.

Referential writing shares information and ideas, generally those gathered through systematic research. Reports, research papers, memoranda, and informational articles in newspapers and magazines are examples of referential writing.

Persuasive writing presents information and observations with the specific intent of convincing readers to alter their perceptions or to take action. Letters to newspaper editors, requests, petitions, arguments in law courts, and advertisements are examples of persuasive writing.

Argumentative writing presents ideas, information, experiences, and insights to articulate an opinion about an arguable topic. Argumentative writing articulates an opinion and illuminates the topic. Debates, political speeches and articles, newspaper editorials, and essays of criticism and analysis are examples of argumentative writing.

Recognizing the different purposes that expressive, referential, persuasive, and argumentative writing serve—and recognizing when these goals overlap—will help you to test the validity of a paper's assumptions and presentation. For instance, a single apt, well-written example may effectively illustrate a point in an expressive paper but be inadequate support to convince readers in a persuasive paper on the same topic. The different reasons for writing establish different expectations for development.

Understanding an Audience

To improve your work as a critical reader and writer, examine and evaluate the needs, demands, and challenges of your reading audience and assess how to meet their needs.

Questions About Readers

- How much will they already know about the topic?

- How skeptical might they be about your claims?

- What preconceptions or misconceptions might they have?

- What kinds of evidence will they require?

- What kinds of objections will they raise?

- What needs will they bring to the reading?

To write a balanced, informed paper that clearly acknowledges the needs of varied readers, consider how the opposition might refute your claims. Similarly, how might you refute theirs? How might you reconcile these opposing views?

Freewrite about objections to your views or use two columns, listing your most important evidence on the left and an opponent's response on the right. Keep these opposing views in mind when writing, conceding points when necessary and countering objections when appropriate. You cannot accommodate all readers, but you can attempt to anticipate the needs, expectations, and objections of critical readers.

Use the word processor to generate and organize thoughts about your audience.

- *Use freewriting to describe your audience.* Turn off or dim your computer monitor and freewrite about your audience, using the questions listed above as guidelines. Assess your audience fairly, respecting opposing views. Record your thoughts quickly.
- *Organize your thoughts about your audience.* Using the audience description you have generated, group ideas and assess your audience's general needs.
- *Brainstorm for objections to your position.* If your topic is controversial, some members of your audience will disagree with your claims. Use the computer to construct a brainstorming list of objections; then supply the counterarguments.

Summarize General Content

Reading is an active process of interpreting written symbols (words) to reveal a writer's meaning or content. As a reader, you must first decide what is being said before you can evaluate its effectiveness or validity. The simplest technique for articulating a writer's content is to summarize it, in your mind or on paper.

A **summary** is a brief restatement in your own words of the central idea presented in a short written work or in a portion of a longer work. For brief texts of only a few paragraphs, a summary may be a single sentence; for longer texts, a complete summary may require several sentences or a whole paragraph.

Strategies for Writing Summaries

- Look for the writer's thesis statement or topic sentence. It will present the most direct, comprehensive statement of the central idea.

- Read the text carefully and then put it aside; do not look at the text while writing your summary.

- Select and restate the central idea(s) only.

- Omit details, explanations, examples, and clarifications.

- Express the text's main idea(s) in your own words, not in the writer's.

- Name the author or source explicitly in the summary, and provide a page citation.

Learning to write a summary takes practice, but the skill is valuable for your reading and your writing. Expect to revise a summary several times to make it brief, accurate, and complete.

To demonstrate how summaries work, first read the following passage from an article in the *State Department Bulletin* on international trade competition and trade deficits:

> What are the sources of competitive pressure on U.S. industry? Some competitive pressures result, in the normal course of events in a dynamic world economy, from shifting patterns of comparative advantage. As countries develop and mature they move into new lines of production and exports. The accumulation of capital, new technologies, and product innovations abroad may make nations internationally competitive in a new product line, and their exports can put pressure on existing producers elsewhere. While we may wish to protect ourselves from disruptive import surges, it is in our long-run interest to adjust to these changing conditions by either increasing our own competitiveness in these product lines or moving resources into other areas where our comparative advantage resides. While such adjustment is painful for the affected industries

in the short run, the process is the mechanism through which the benefits of economic advance in one country are shared internationally. Certain U.S. industries are finding this adjustment very difficult and painful, but we should not confuse their plight with the problem of the overall trade deficit. —Elinor G. Constable, "International Competition, Trade Deficits, and National Policy"

A clear, concise, and complete summary of Constable's paragraph requires several drafts:

First attempt

Trade competition arises for a number of reasons.   (Though concise, this summary is too simplistic.)

Second attempt

Trade competition arises as foreign countries develop their technologies and enter world markets. (Although this summary is clearer than the first, it presents only part of Constable's point. It needs further elaboration.)

Third attempt

When trade competition arises because foreign countries develop their technologies and enter world markets, U.S. companies must improve their own technologies or shift to other areas of trade. (This summary presents the major points of Constable's paragraph.)

Fourth attempt

Elinor G. Constable, in "International Competition, Trade Deficits, and National Policy," notes that when trade competition arises because foreign countries develop their technologies and enter world markets, U.S. companies must either improve their own technologies or shift to other areas of trade (60).   (Citing the author, title, and page number completes the summary.)

Use a word processor to help you create and revise a clear and concise summary.
■ *Draft the summary.* Working at the keyboard, type out the first version of your summary.

- *Refine the summary.* Use the "add" and "delete" capabilities of a word processor to incorporate overlooked central ideas and to eliminate extraneous details.
- *Add clarifying information.* Incorporate the author, title, and page number of the original work.

EXERCISE 5.3) Summaries

Write a summary of each of the following paragraphs.

1. The tropical rain forest north of Manaus, like that in many other parts of the Amazon basin, is being clear-cut from the edge inward. It is being lifted up from the ground entire like a carpet rolled off a bare floor, leaving behind vast stretches of cattle range and cropland that need artificial fertilization to sustain even marginal productivity for more than two or three years. A rain forest in Brazil differs fundamentally from a deciduous woodland in Pennsylvania or Germany in the way its key resources are distributed. A much greater fraction of organic matter is bound up in the tissues of the standing trees, so that the leaf litter and humus are only a few inches deep. When the forest is felled and burned, the hard equatorial downpours quickly wash away the thin blanket of top soil.
—Edward O. Wilson, "The Superorganism"

2. In social organizations which embody a strong class system, such as military units and large business concerns, there are many territorial rules, often unspoken, which interfere with the official hierarchy. High-status individuals, such as officers or managers, could in theory enter any of the regions occupied by the lower levels in the peck order, but they limit this power in a striking way. An officer seldom enters a sergeant's mess or a barrack room unless it's for a formal inspection. He respects those regions as alien territories even though he has the power to go there by virtue of his dominant role. And in businesses, part of the appeal of unions, over and above their obvious functions, is that with their officials, headquarters, and meetings they add a sense of territorial power for the staff workers. It is almost as if each military organization and business concern consists of two warring tribes: the officers versus the other ranks, and management versus the workers. Each has its special home base within the system, and the territorial defense pattern thrusts itself into what, on the surface, is a pure social hierarchy. Negotiations between managements and unions are tribal battles fought out over the neutral ground of a boardroom table, and are as much concerned with territorial display as they are with resolving problems of wages and conditions. Indeed, if one side gives in too quickly and accepts the other's demands, the victors feel strangely cheated and deeply suspicious that it may be a trick. What they are missing is the protracted sequence of ritual and counter-ritual that keeps alive their group territorial identity. —Desmond Morris, "Territorial Behavior"

| 5c | Evaluate evidence. |

Evidence is the illustrative material used to support a claim. As a researcher, analyze what kinds of evidence sources offer and how well they use it. As a writer, select and present evidence with care, because critical readers will examine the evidence to decide whether it substantiates your claims. Evidence can be classified as facts and statistics, examples, and expert testimony.

Facts and Statistics

Facts are verifiable pieces of information (58,135 American soldiers died in the Vietnam War); **statistics** are mathematical data (approximately 65 percent of soldiers killed in Vietnam were in the U.S. Army). Well-chosen facts and statistics clarify and, consequently, support many of the claims made in writing. However, be skeptical about the use of factual and statistical information; authors with special interests may manipulate information to support their claims.

Examples

Examples are individual cases that illustrate claims (the Watergate cover-up as an example of the abuse of executive power). Examples from personal experience are considered primary evidence; examples from other people's experiences are considered secondary evidence. To be effective, examples must be relevant, representative, and complete.

Relevant Examples

Relevant examples illustrate a claim in a timely way and present single cases that correspond effectively to the larger issue presented in the claim. In supporting a paper about film censorship today, D. W. Griffith's *Intolerance* (1918) would not be a relevant example. The film's depiction of adultery (its most controversial element) is not controversial today. The use of a more recent example, such as Oliver Stone's *Natural Born Killers* (1994), would address current censorship issues. In another way, relevance is also determined by how well the example correlates with the claim. To illustrate the claim that Jimmy Carter was an ineffectual president, a relevant example might be the mishandling of the hostage crisis in Iran; such an example corresponds to the seriousness of the claim and illustrates it in an important way. An example about the embarrassments caused by President Carter's brother Billy ignores the important values presented in the claim and does not address President Carter's effectiveness as a leader.

Representative Examples

Representative examples are neither extremely positive nor extremely negative. Extreme examples are exceptions, and thoughtful readers find them unconvincing. In a paper on the negative effects of state lotteries on family finances, for instance, a $6-million winner would not be representative, nor would a person who spent the family food money on lottery tickets—neither example convincingly supports the assertion.

Complete Examples

Complete examples provide sufficient information to allow readers to see how the examples work as evidence. Incorporating responses to the journalists' questions (*who, what, when, where, how,* and *why*) is one useful way to guarantee completeness. Adding a summary can further clarify important connections.

Expert Testimony

Expert testimony in written work, like expert testimony in court trials, is a statement of opinion or a judgment made by an expert or authority in a field. For example, a specialist in labor practices, or a statistician working with government hiring data, could speak authoritatively to support a claim about sexual discrimination in government hiring. A feminist critic of literature would not necessarily have any expertise with regard to hiring practices, even though he or she might have an informed opinion on discriminatory hiring practices.

Appeals

Appeals to readers stress the logic of claims, emphasize the ethical nature of positions, and focus on the emotional nature of discussions. Most writing blends these appeals so as to emphasize multiple perspectives. Analyzing the techniques writers use will improve your understanding of their work; as a writer, you can recognize the techniques at your disposal.

Appealing to Logic

Appeals to logic emphasize evidence, offering facts and statistics to support a claim. The following paragraph emphasizes technical information—thereby appealing to logic—to support the position that chemical poisoning is gradually decreasing.

> It took the social activism of the 1960s and early 1970s to bring about controls. The Lead-based Paint Poisoning Prevention Act banned the manufacture and sale of leaded paint and directed the Department of Housing and Urban Development (HUD) to develop a strategy for removing old paint from old housing. In the mid-1970s the Food and Drug Administration (FDA) pressured the food industry to remove lead solder from the seams of baby-food and baby-formula cans. According to the EPA, more than 161,000 metric tons of lead tainted the air in 1975. In an effort to lower this atmospheric pollution the agency ordered oil companies to start phasing out lead additives in gasoline beginning in 1977. By 1984 the count had fallen by 75 percent, to 39,000 metric tons. Each year since, the levels have continued to fall. —Michael Weisskopf, "Lead Astray: The Poisoning of America"

Appealing to Ethics

Appeals to ethics stress the writer's trustworthiness, honesty, fairness, clarity, and directness. The following paragraph establishes the writer's knowledge of and fairness to opposing views; by carefully qualifying his statements, he establishes an ethical perspective.

> In the great debate over legalizing recreational drugs, the least convincing assertion of the pro-legalizers is that drug use might not even increase as a result. I can state for certain that drug use would increase. I don't use drugs now. If they were legal, I would use them. Or, rather, if marijuana were legal, I would use it occasionally instead of the legal drug I now use regularly, alcohol. To be sure, increased respect for the law is not the only reason so many middle-class, middle-age people have abandoned marijuana: you're also no longer so carefree about where your mind might take you on automatic pilot, especially in public. But society's official disapproval is a substantial deterrent. Without it, many of us would sneak the odd toke or two. —Michael Kinsley, "Glass Houses and Getting Stoned"

112

Appealing to Emotion

Appeals to emotion emphasize the needs, desires, hopes, and expectations of readers, particularly sympathy and self-interest. The following paragraph, emphasizing the personal and emotional dimensions of health care, appeals to readers' sympathy.

Obviously the decisions that must be made when an elderly patient faces a medical crisis are difficult ones for everyone—patient, loved ones, doctors, hospitals and health-care personnel alike. When a satisfying, although perhaps restricted, life is possible if treatment is successful, the decisions are easy: You do everything you can. But when someone has had a medical crisis and is in failing health with little hope of recovery; when all the painful, costly, possibly degrading though heroic measures may gain no more than a few extra days or weeks or, maybe, months for a patient who is probably miserable and often unconscious, the decisions are more difficult and individuals may vary widely in their preferences—if, indeed, they are given a choice. —Roy Hoopes, "Turning Out the Light"

EXERCISE 5.4) *Evidence*

Identify the kinds of evidence used in the following paragraphs. Discuss with class members why this evidence is effective and consider alternative ways to support the claims in the paragraphs.

Spurred by a scientific consensus that significant greenhouse-effect warming will occur in the early decades of the next century, delegates from 46 countries at a Conference on the Changing Atmosphere held in Toronto have called for an urgent action plan. The conferees, who included scientists and policymakers (but no senior U.S. Government official), recommended that governments initially reduce emissions of carbon dioxide—thought to play a major role in greenhouse warming—by 20 percent before the year 2005.

Some workers maintain that greenhouse warming, which results when trace gases prevent infrared radiation from the earth's surface from escaping to space, has already set in; indeed, a scientist at the National Aeronautics and Space Administration (NASA) is searching for a greenhouse "fingerprint" in existing data. The four warmest years in a century of instrumental records have fallen within the 1980s, and the first five months of 1988 were the hottest five-month period ever recorded.

One climate analyst, James E. Hansen of NASA's Goddard Institute for Space Studies, told a Senate subcommittee in Washington just before the Toronto conference that the recent warming could be ascribed "with a high degree of confidence" to the greenhouse effect. At Toronto the delegates kept an open mind about whether the greenhouse effect has contributed to the warmth of the 1980s. They agreed, however, that past emissions of greenhouse gases make significant warming inevitable. Indeed the most recent computer models predict that accumulating trace gases will harm the lower atmosphere sooner than expected.

Carbon dioxide, which is increasing by 0.4 percent each year because of combustion of fossil fuels and the destruction of tropical forests, accounts for half of the predicted warming. Other greenhouse gases include methane, which is increasing at an even faster rate, and the synthetic refrigerants and solvents called chlorofluorocarbons (CFCs).

The consensus view was that a global warming of between three and nine degrees Fahrenheit is likely to occur by the middle of the next century if emissions are not curtailed. It is impossible to say what the climatic consequence for particular regions would be—the current U.S. drought, for example, cannot necessarily be blamed on the greenhouse effect. Nevertheless, some studies suggest that continental interiors will become dryer as greenhouse warming occurs. The sea level is expected to rise by at least 30 centimeters over the next 50 to 100 years. —Tim Beardsley, "Winds of Change"[1]

| 5d | Avoid logical fallacies. |

Logical fallacies are errors in thinking and writing that result from faulty logic. Try to identify logical fallacies to evaluate the accuracy of what you read; strive to avoid logical fallacies in what you write.

Hasty Generalization

A **hasty generalization** is a conclusion based on too little evidence, suggesting a superficial investigation of an issue.

> The Bedderman Street Housing Project cost hundreds of thousands of dollars and is now a shambles. Federally subsidized housing is a waste of taxpayers' money. (One failed housing project is not enough evidence to support the claim that the whole system of subsidized housing has failed. A larger sampling is necessary to justify such a sweeping claim.)

Oversimplification

Oversimplification ignores the complexities, variations, and exceptions relevant to an issue.

> The influx of foreign cars almost destroyed the American automobile industry. (Imported cars caused some problems for the industry, but so did high prices, overly large cars with poor designs, dated technology, poor gas mileage, and other factors.)

Either/Or

The **either/or fallacy** suggests that only two choices exist when, in fact, there are more. This type of thinking is not only illogical (because multiple alternatives are almost always available) but also unfair (because ignoring complexities and choices distorts a discussion).

For the sake of learning, we must maintain the firmest kind of discipline, including corporal punishment, in our public schools, or we can expect chaos, disorder, and the disintegration of education as we know it. (The two alternatives presented are extremes: firm discipline resulting in order versus relaxed discipline resulting in chaos. The statement both ignores moderate methods of maintaining discipline and asserts that without firm discipline the worst will happen. It is highly manipulative.)

Begging the Question

Begging the question distorts a claim by including a secondary idea that requires proof, though none is given.

Since Senator Hillard is a pawn of major corporations, we can expect him to support their interests instead of ours. (The writer provides no evidence that Hillard is controlled by corporations. The statement attempts to mislead readers by asserting that an affiliation exists, rather than proving that it does.)

Sometimes begging the question is done very subtly, through word choice.

The antiwar demonstrators of the 1970s should be remembered as the cowards that they were. (The writer uses the word *cowards* to define the group without making any attempt to prove the implicit warrant that protesting is cowardly.)

Association

Fallacies of association suggest that ideas or actions are acceptable or unacceptable because of the people who are associated with them. Such a fallacy ignores that ideas or actions should be evaluated on their own merits.

The bombers were Irish, so obviously the Irish people support terrorism. (This assertion links all people in Ireland with a small group of terrorists. Such reasoning ignores the fact that terrorists often act on their own or in groups and do not necessarily represent a country's people.)

Non Sequitur

Non sequitur, a Latin phrase meaning "it does not follow," presents a conclusion that is not the logical result of a claim or of evidence that precedes it.

Japanese children spend forty percent more time in the classroom than, and perform better than, American children. American parents should take more interest in their children's schooling. (Both statements may be true, but the writer does not establish any logical connection between them.)

Bandwagon

The **bandwagon fallacy** suggests that if a majority of people express a belief or take an action, everyone else should think or do the same. Such arguments give the weight of truth or inevitability to the judgments of the majority, which may not be justified.

Over 70 percent of Americans favor tariffs on imports from China, and you should, too. (The argument falsely implies that the force of public opinion alone should sway undecided opinion. Such arguments are often bolstered by statistics from studies or surveys, but the use of numbers alone does not sufficiently support the writer's position. The advisability of tariffs should be decided on the basis of their effect on national and international interests, not on possibly uninformed or self-interested and emotional opinions.)

Red Herring

A **red herring** is an irrelevant issue introduced into an discussion to draw attention from the central issue.

State boards of education should not vote to spend money for art and music programs when so many of our children fail to read at their grade levels. (Deplorable as the children's poor preparation in reading may be, it has no bearing on the quality, or benefit to students, of arts education programs.)

117

ost Hoc, Ergo Propter Hoc

Post hoc, ergo propter hoc—a Latin phrase meaning "after this, therefore because of this"—suggests a cause-and-effect relationship between two actions, even though one action simply preceded the other.

> Since Bill Clinton became president, stock market values have risen. Clearly, Clinton's administration has been good for investors. (Although stock values rose after Clinton became president, there is not necessarily a connection between the events.)

Ad Hominem

Ad hominem, a Latin phrase meaning "to the man," is an attack on the people involved with an issue, rather than the issue itself. By shifting focus from ideas to people, writers fail to address the real issues.

> Universities should not grant honorary degrees. After all, Walter Hale, who received a degree from Lawrence University, is supposedly linked to organized crime. (The main issue should not be Hale but rather honorary degrees. The mention of Hale inappropriately sidetracks the discussion and fails to make any case against the degrees themselves.)

False Analogy

A **false analogy** is a comparison that is not based on relevant points of similarity. For an analogy to be logical, the subjects must be similar in several important, not superficial, ways.

> If eighteen-year-olds are old enough to get married, vote, and serve in the military, they are old enough to drink alcohol. (This analogy falsely suggests that activities performed when under complete control have a bearing on an activity that often results in lack of control. The comparison is based on strained similarities.)

EXERCISE 5.5 ⟩ *Logical fallacies*

Identify and explain the logical fallacies in the following sentences.

1. Jean Genet's plays should not be regarded so highly. After all, he was a thief and served time in prison.

2. Many Nobel Prize winners in science used animals in their experiments, so using animals in research must be acceptable.

3. I saw a man on a road crew sitting in the back of a truck reading a magazine and drinking a Coke. Obviously, road-crew jobs are extremely easy.

4. If the federal government stopped paying child support, fewer unmarried women would have children.

5. If business people can deduct the cost of their lunches, then factory workers should have the same right.

6. To reduce the deficit, all we have to do is increase taxes.

7. Unless we outlaw all corporate donations to candidates, all our politicians will become pawns of business.

8. New York has exceptional museums, beautiful parks, varied entertainment, and fabulous restaurants. It is a great place to raise a family.

9. Any student who tries hard enough is sure to make an *A* in the introductory speech class.

10. Since smoking marijuana is immoral, we should punish anyone caught using it.

5e	⟩	**A sample argument.**

The following article appeared in the "My Turn" section of *Newsweek* magazine, 13 November 1995. Numbered annotations listed on pages 122–24 identify important features and strategies.

A Case for Discretion

By Michael Brennan

1. I stood before federal district court judge Kimberly Frankel. The date was May 28, 1995; the place, Portland, Ore. I had just pleaded guilty to five shoplifting charges and one felony count of cocaine possession.

2. In a similar case in San Diego, Steven White, 32, faced a mandatory sentence of 25 years to life for shoplifting a $130 VCR. He decided instead that a bullet through the brain was the less painful way to go. The suicide note he left offered apologies to his parents for the heartbreak he caused them, but suggested that spending that much time in prison was too high a price to pay for a misdemeanor. The sentence White faced was a result of one of the many federal and state "mandatory minimum" sentencing acts that have been enacted by Congress and various state legislatures since 1986. White's case fell under California's so-called "three strikes you're out" law.

3. Like me, White had a sporadic history of heroin addiction and nonviolent criminal offenses. His first two strikes—burglary convictions—dated to 1983. His "third strike"—the shoplifting charge, which occurred in 1994—was elevated to a felony by being classed as "petty theft with a prior conviction of theft." Two judges pleaded with prosecutors not to seek the 25-to-life sentence that the recently enacted law called for. They refused.

4. Many groups oppose mandatory minimum sentences, including the National Association of Veteran Police Officers, the U.S. Sentencing Committee, the American Bar Association and Families Against Mandatory Minimums. Supreme Court Chief Justice William Rehnquist calls mandatory minimums "a good example of the law of unintended consequences."

5. There are currently 1.2 million people incarcerated in federal and state prisons in this country. The majority of them are up on drug-related crimes, and many are there as a result of mandatory minimum sentences. The average cost of housing a federal prisoner is $20,804 annually. It is ultimately the taxpayer

6. who foots this enormous bill. Furthermore, the hodgepodge of state and federal mandatory drug sentences sometimes leads to violent offenders—Florida's rapists, robbers and murderers, for example—being released early to make room for nonviolent, first-time drug offenders serving lengthy, mandatory-minimum sentences.

7. Ironically, I came close to being classed as a violent offender. On one of my shoplifting sprees I struggled with a Fred Meyer's department-store security guard as I tried to escape her grasp. If she had described my desperate struggle as resistance and my shoplifting partner's presence as a threat, I could have been charged with robbery 2, which now carries a mandatory five-year sentence under Oregon's Measure 11. But the issue is only partially whether the punishment fits the crime. There are a number of federal prisoners doing life without parole for marijuana sales, for example, while rapists are routinely paroled after only four years.

8. The more central question, however, is this: is it the American way to remove all discretion from judges and invest prosecutors with an extraordinary degree of power? Are there no circumstances—youth, a previously clean record or varying levels of culpability among codefendants—that might mitigate the degree of punishment that must be meted out? Not under any of the mandatory minimum sentences.

9. In my case, by the time I appeared before Judge Frankel I had behind me a 15-year on-again, off-again history of heroin addiction that resulted in numerous petty-theft convictions, three felony heroin-possession convictions and four stints in county jails.

Judge Frankel was free to weigh this unsavory history against what I had accomplished in the four drug-free years prior to my recent relapse. After my release from jail in 1989 I went

10. from a homeless ex-offender to a working writer. I also initiated and managed a self-help work project in Boston that successfully employed 19 individuals who were dealing with homelessness, AIDS, addiction and mental illness.

The judge, using the discretionary powers that have been an integral part of the American judicial system for 200 years, sentenced me to 30 days in jail, 90 days of work-release, $700 in restitution fees, and two years' probation. The work-release program allowed me to pay society back through community-work programs, maintain family connections, and earn money at outside work to pay a substantial portion of my incarceration costs and to save funds for post-release living expenses.

11.   Contrast my experience with that of Stephanie Lomax, a former Portland, Ore., resident whose family shared her story with me. Lomax and two codefendants were convicted in Nebraska on conspiracy charges involving crack cocaine. White House drug czar Lee Brown recently stated that crack-cocaine mandatory sentences primarily affect African-Americans, thus adding a racial bias to federal drug laws. He calls crack-cocaine mandatory sentences "bad law" based on "bad information."

12.   Lomax, a 25-year-old pregnant black mother and first-time offender with no previous criminal history, continues to maintain her innocence. She was sentenced to life without parole. This means, literally, that she will die in the same prison system where she gave birth to the child she can no longer hold.

13.   Americans are understandably frightened and frustrated by the impact of drugs and crime on society. One can only hope that our fears have not also destroyed our sense of compassion and justice, and that we can still respond to Stephanie Lomax (and untold thousands like her).

14.   "Does anyone care about what is going on in the system today?" she writes from her cell at the Pleasanton federal prison in California. "I am poor. I have no assets and I'm very much in need of help. Can you help me and my family?"

Annotations

1. Brennan begins his inductive argument with an anecdote, incorporating selected details from his personal experience. To create interest, he does not relate his sentence; instead he withholds information, knowing that readers will be curious enough to continue with the essay.

2. Brennan adds a related example, this time providing information about White's sentence and his suicide. The facts of the case—particularly the fact that the VCR was valued at only $130—increase the emotional appeal of this example.

3. A transitional paragraph, linking the two cases, allows Brennan to define key terms and move forward with his discussion.

4. Although Brennan has yet to articulate the central idea of his argument (that mandatory sentencing is unacceptable), he incorporates expert testimony to influence readers' thinking. Citing national law-enforcement and legal associations that oppose mandatory sentences is especially effective, since they deal most directly with criminals; citing Supreme Court Chief Justice Rehnquist's opposition has even more impact.

5. Brennan next incorporates useful and important facts—including the number of people incarcerated and the average yearly cost for housing each prisoner. The sentence "It is ultimately the taxpayer who foots this enormous bill" appeals to readers' self-interests, since most readers are taxpayers who want their money well spent.

6. Brennan closes the paragraph with a statement that includes two implied warrants: (1) violent offenders deserve long sentences and (2) drug offenders do not necessarily deserve long sentences.

7. To establish the inconsistency of sentencing patterns, Brennan provides a related example, showing how his case might have been handled more stringently.

8. This paragraph offers Brennan's implied thesis, presented as questions that he hopes readers will answer in the way

he proposes. Implicit in his questions are several warrants: (1) judges should have discretion in sentencing offenders, (2) prosecutors should not have undue power, and (3) individual circumstances should influence individual sentences.

9. Brennan establishes his ethical position by acknowledging his personal history in a straightforward fashion; such candor often appeals to readers.

10. By relating information about the self-help work project, Brennan further appeals to readers by showing that his concerns are not wholly selfish: he has, in fact, contributed to society in positive ways, in spite of his illegal activities.

11. By introducing an extended example (which he uses to draw his argument to a close), Brennan provides further balance for his argument. He is able to use additional expert testimony—this time from a White House appointee—to introduce the issue of racial bias as it affects mandatory sentencing.

12. The details from Lomax's case are introduced simply, without description. The starkness of the information matches the starkness of Lomax's situation.

13. Brennan appeals to his readers by acknowledging their general frustration with drug-related crimes.

14. An emotional appeal developed from the extended example used in the essay gives Brennan a chance to personalize the effects of mandatory sentencing. If readers sympathizes with Lomax and understand her plight, then one can assume that such sympathy and understanding will transfer to the larger issue. That, at least, is Brennan's design.

EFFECTIVE SENTENCES

6 Understanding Parts of Speech

Sentences consist of words used in specific ways according to their parts of speech. Words combined into phrases, clauses, and sentences create meaning.

This chapter explores the parts of speech so that you will be able to use each of them flexibly and precisely to compose effective sentences.

Quick Reference

Learning about the parts of speech is a means to an end: Technical knowledge of sentence elements allows you to analyze and improve your sentences.

⟩ *Use the most specific nouns that suit the meaning of your sentence.*

⟩ *Use only pronouns that have clear antecedents.*

⟩ *Use verbs whose tenses create the time distinctions you intend.*

⟩ *Use coordinating conjunctions to join equivalent elements; use subordinating conjunctions to join subordinate and independent clauses; use correlative conjunctions in pairs.*

English has eight parts of speech: nouns, pronouns, verbs, adjectives, adverbs, conjunctions, prepositions, and interjections. Learning to identify parts of speech in sentences is not an end in itself but a means to understanding how words work together in sentences. Knowing this, you can analyze your writing, identifying and eliminating grammatical inconsistencies and building sentences that convey your exact meaning.

When analyzing the parts of speech in a sentence, note carefully how the words function. Remember that the same word can be used in different ways in different sentences. In the following sentences, the word *stone* appears as a noun, a verb, and an adjective.

Noun

Stone—limestone, marble, and granite—is a common material for statuary.

Verb

In ancient times, it was common to *stone* criminals.

Adjective

Many campus buildings constructed in the 1930s and 1940s have *stone* façades.

| 6a | > | Nouns |

A **noun** names a person, place, thing, idea, quality, or condition and can be proper, common, collective, abstract, or concrete.

Proper Nouns

Proper nouns name specific people, places, and things: *Emily Dickinson, Berlin, Corvette*. They are always capitalized.

Nakia lost her *Minolta X700* while vacationing in *Kenya*.

Common Nouns

Common nouns name people, places, and things by general type: *poet, city, sports car.* They are not capitalized.

My *friend* lost her thirty-five-millimeter *camera* while vacationing in a foreign *country.*

Collective Nouns

Collective nouns name groups of people or things; although each group includes two or more members, it is usually considered *one* group: *team, class, group, audience.*

The *congregation* at St. Stephen's has raised $3000 for the *homeless.*

Abstract Nouns

Abstract nouns name ideas, qualities, and conditions: *freedom, honesty, shyness.*

Concrete Nouns

Concrete nouns name things or qualities perceptible by the senses: *table, pepper, warmth, noise.*

| 6b | > | Pronouns |

Pronouns substitute for nouns. Generally, a pronoun refers to a previously stated noun, called an **antecedent.**

The movers dropped the desk while carrying *it* up the stairs. *They* immediately filled out a damage report, *which* required John's signature. (*It, they,* and *which* are the pronouns; *desk, movers,* and *report* are the antecedents.)

Pronouns are classified as personal, possessive, reflexive, interrogative, demonstrative, indefinite, and relative, depending on their function in a sentence.

Personal Pronouns

Personal pronouns substitute for nouns that name people or things. The form of the pronoun depends on the gender and number of the antecedent and whether the pronoun is a subject or an object (see pages 280–84 and 288–95).

Subject		Object	
Singular	*Plural*	*Singular*	*Plural*
I	we	me	us
you	you	you	you
he		him	
she	they	her	them
it		it	

The archer was distracted by noisy people in the crowd, so *she* delayed the shot until the referee had quieted *them*. (*She* and *them* are the pronouns; *archer* and *people* are the antecedents.)

Possessive Pronouns

Possessive pronouns show ownership.

Singular	*Plural*
my, mine	our, ours
your, yours	your, yours
his, his	
her, hers	their, theirs
its, its	

For each pair, use the first form, often called a **pronoun-adjective,** with a noun; use the second form if the pronoun stands alone in place of a noun.

> Thomas, *your* solution is more practical than *mine.* (*Your,* a pronoun-adjective, modifies the noun *solution; mine* stands alone but also implies reference to the same antecedent, *solution.*)

Reflexive Pronouns

Reflexive pronouns show that someone or something in the sentence is acting for or on itself; if used to show emphasis, they are sometimes called **intensive pronouns.**

Singular	*Plural*
myself	ourselves
yourself	yourselves
himself	
herself	themselves
itself	

Self-related action

The state senators voted *themselves* a raise for the third time in a decade. (*Themselves* shows that the senators raised their own wages.)

Emphasis

Although his friends offered to help paint the apartment, Russell preferred to do it *himself*. (*Himself* emphasizes that Russell wanted no help.)

Reflexive pronouns require antecedents within the same sentence and, as a result, should not be used as subjects.

Faulty

Joan and *myself* renovated the house. (*Myself* cannot function as the subject of the sentence.)

Correct

Joan and *I* renovated the house *ourselves*. (*I* is the suitable subject pronoun; *ourselves*, with *Joan and I* as the antecedent, is correctly used to show emphasis.)

Interrogative Pronouns

Interrogative pronouns are used to ask questions.

Subject	Object
who	whom
whoever	whomever
Other interrogative pronouns	
what	whose
which	

Who won the Nobel Peace Prize this year?

To *whom* should I send the application?

Which musical had the longer Broadway run, *Les Misérables* or *Phantom of the Opera?*

Demonstrative Pronouns

Demonstrative pronouns are used alone to substitute for specific nouns.

Singular	*Plural*
this	these
that	those

Used with nouns, these four words function as **demonstrative adjectives.** If the antecedent of the demonstrative pronoun is unclear, use the demonstrative adjective with the noun.

Confusing
   Godfrey hesitated before speaking. That helped him to control his emotions.   (Does *that* refer to hesitating or speaking or both?)

Clear
   Godfrey hesitated before speaking. That pause helped him to control his emotions.

Indefinite Pronouns

Indefinite pronouns, pronouns without specific antecedents, serve as general subjects or objects in sentences. When using an indefinite pronoun as a subject, remember that some are singular and some are plural and choose the verb that agrees with the indefinite pronoun you are using.

Common Indefinite Pronouns

Singular

another	either	no one
any	everybody	nothing
anybody	everyone	one
anyone	everything	somebody
anything	neither	someone
each	nobody	something

Plural

all	few	several
both	many	some

When used alone, these words are pronouns. Some of these words can also modify nouns and thus serve as pronoun-adjectives: *any* passport, *another* guess, *several* women.

> *Someone* is sure to discover that the dates on the schedule are inaccurate.   (Singular pronoun is the subject of the sentence.)

> *Several* are available on the table at the back of the lecture hall. (Plural pronoun is the subject of the sentence.)

> *Both* archaeologists agree that their earlier finds were misleading. (Pronoun-adjective modifies *archaeologists*.)

Relative Pronouns

Relative pronouns substitute for nouns already mentioned in the sentence and are used to introduce adjective or noun clauses.

To refer to people	
who	whoever
whom	whomever

To refer to things	
that	which
what	whichever
whatever	

To refer to people or things
that (generally for things)
whose (generally for people)

Novelists *who* achieve notoriety quickly often fade from view just as quickly.

Anger *that* is not expressed is often the most damaging.

People *whose* children attend private schools pay for education twice, through taxes and through tuition.

Sometimes the relative pronoun *that* can be left out (understood) in a sentence where the noun-clause relationship is clear without it. As a general rule, use *that* to introduce essential information, but use *which* to introduce information that can be omitted.

An object *that is more than one hundred years old* is considered an antique.   (The clause is essential to the meaning of the sentence.)

The steamer trunk, *which we found in Aunt Pauline's attic,* belonged to my great grandfather.   (The clause can be omitted without altering the meaning of the sentence.)

 Although relative pronouns embed information in sentences, too much embedded material can make sentences difficult to read. Use your word processing program's "search" function to locate uses of relative pronouns. Decide whether sentences with several pronouns might be more effective if separated.

EXERCISE 6.1 ﹚ *Nouns and pronouns*

Underline the nouns and pronouns in each of the following sentences and label each according to type.

1. Acupuncture, a medical treatment, developed centuries ago in China.

2. The acupuncturist uses extremely thin gold needles to pierce a patient's skin.

3. Patients frequently receive sedation before the treatment begins and the needles are implanted.

4. The areas where the needles are inserted do not necessarily correspond to the areas of discomfort or pain.

5. Those who have been helped by acupuncture strongly advocate the treatment.

6. Why should those of us who have not tried acupuncture question their satisfaction?

7. Teams of Western scientists have studied acupuncture and found no physiological explanations for its success.

8. Yet success rates for patients who have faith in the procedure suggest that we can learn more than we already know about the psychological effects of medical treatments.

9. Ironically, while acupuncture has been attracting attention in Europe and the United States in recent years, its use in China has declined.

10. Some say acupuncture is merely a medical hoax, but others continue to search for scientific explanations for its apparent success.

EXERCISE 6.2 ⟩ Nouns and pronouns

 Revise the following paragraph, replacing some nouns with pronouns to achieve a smoother style.

Theodore Roosevelt, the twenty-sixth president of the United States, was an individualist. Nonetheless, Roosevelt served the public well. Roosevelt's individualistic tendencies were illustrated first by Roosevelt's attempts at boxing, an uncommon activity for an upper-class gentleman at Harvard. After Roosevelt's graduation, Roosevelt made a trip west, where Roosevelt experimented briefly with ranching and cowboy life. Roosevelt returned to the East to serve in the government, but in 1898 Roosevelt resigned Roosevelt's post as secretary of the navy to organize the Rough Riders, a regiment formed to fight in the Spanish-American War. The Rough Riders found Roosevelt to be an able leader, and though the Rough Riders did not follow Roosevelt up San Juan Hill as legend has it, the Rough Riders did fight with Roosevelt in Cuba. Roosevelt returned to the United States a hero; Roosevelt's notoriety helped Roosevelt to win the mayoral race of New York. Two years later, Roosevelt was elected vice president in spite of opposition from political bosses and industrial leaders. Political bosses and industrial leaders must have found Roosevelt's freewheeling individualism unsettling and certainly unpredictable. The political bosses and industrial leaders fought Roosevelt in Roosevelt's antitrust actions when Roosevelt became president after McKinley's assassination. Throughout Roosevelt's presidency and the rest of Roosevelt's life, Roosevelt continued to act as an individual but with the public good in mind.

6c ⟩ **Verbs**

A **verb** expresses an action (*organize, sing*) or a state of being (*seem, was*). Grammatically complete sentences contain at least one verb, and effectively chosen verbs make writing clear, exact, and interesting.

Types of Verbs

The three types of verbs are action, linking, and auxiliary.

Action Verbs

Action verbs express both physical and mental activities.

> *action verb*
> |
> Gayle *parked* her car on a designated snow route.

> *action verb*
> |
> She *thought* the snow would stop.

Action verbs are either intransitive or transitive. **Intransitive verbs** do not need direct objects (a person or thing that receives the action of the verb, like *car* in the first example above) to complete their meaning.

> *subj.*   *intrans. verb*
> | |
> The negative ad *campaign backfired*.   (Without a direct object, the sentence is still clear.)

Transitive verbs require direct objects to complete their meaning.

```
           subj.    trans. verb          d.o.
            |          |                   |
```
At last, *Gerald completed* the *experiment*.   (Without the direct object *experiment*, the sentence's meaning would be unclear.)

Some verbs can be either intransitive or transitive, depending on the meaning of the sentence.

```
         subj.  intrans. verb
          |         |
```
Some *artists paint* for several months without completing a single work.

```
         subj.       trans. verb          d.o.
          |              |                  |
```
Leonardo da Vinci painted very few *works*.

Linking Verbs

Linking verbs express either a state of being or a condition.

Common Linking Verbs			
Forms of to be			
am	be	being	was
are	been	is	were
Other linking verbs			
appear	feel	look	seem	sound
become	grow	make	smell	taste

Forms of *to be* join the subject of a sentence or clause with a complement (either a predicate noun or a predicate adjective), creating a parallel relationship.

With predicate nouns

linking verb

Brad *is* the best player on the soccer team.   (*Brad* [subject] = *player* [predicate noun]. The predicate noun further identifies Brad.)

With predicate adjectives

linking verb

Woodrow Wilson *was* enthusiastic about the League of Nations. (*Woodrow Wilson* [subject] = *enthusiastic* [predicate adjective]. The predicate adjective describes Wilson.)

Auxiliary Verbs

Auxiliary verbs (or **helping, verbs**) work with other verbs to create verb tenses or to form questions.

Common Auxiliary Verbs			
***Forms of* to be**			
am	been	is	were
are	being	was	
Other auxiliary verbs			
can	do	has	might	should
could	does	have	must	will
did	had	may	ought to	would

aux. verb   verb
   | |
Ophelia *will enter* from stage right.

aux. verb   verb
    | |
Greenpeace *must oppose* chemical dumping in our waterways.

When modifiers are used, they often separate the auxiliary from the main verb. In forming questions, the auxiliary usually precedes the subject. Auxiliary verbs always precede main verbs.

aux. verb   mod.   verb
   | | |
Ophelia *will probably enter* from stage right.

aux. verb   verb
  | |
Must Greenpeace *oppose* chemical dumping in our waterways?

EXERCISE 6.3 ❭ Verbs

Underline and label the verbs in the following sentences.

1. Stoics are people who accept their fate without question.

2. They have learned not to concern themselves with what they will be unable to change or to waste time worrying about what is past.

3. Modern stoics have as their model, though they may not know it, a fourth-century Greek philosopher.

4. Zeno and his followers believed that the Fates (goddesses in Greek mythology) determine people's destinies.

5. Modern-day stoics, however, must grapple with Judeo-Christian beliefs that teach us that we have free will.

Forms of Verbs

In English, verbs have three principal parts or forms: the infinitive, the past tense, and the past participle. The **infinitive** is a verb's primary form (*work, cope*); it is often used with *to*. For regular verbs, the **past tense** and **past participle** are formed by adding *-ed* or *-d* to the infinitive (*worked, coped*).

Principal Parts of Regular Verbs

Infinitive	Past tense	Past participle
select	selected	selected
inform	informed	informed
open	opened	opened

Many common English verbs are irregular and form the past tense and past participles in a variety of ways. Because there is no predictable pattern for these verbs, it is helpful to become familiar with the principal parts of common irregular verbs.

Principal Parts of Common Irregular Verbs

Infinitive	Past tense	Past participle
arise	arose	arisen
awake	awoke, awakened	awakened
be	was/were	been
beat	beat	beaten, beat
begin	began	begun

Infinitive	*Past tense*	*Past participle*
bend	bent	bent
bite	bit	bitten
blow	blew	blown
break	broke	broken
bring	brought	brought
build	built	built
burst	burst	burst
catch	caught	caught
choose	chose	chosen
come	came	come
cost	cost	cost
creep	crept	crept
deal	dealt	dealt
dig	dug	dug
dive	dived, dove	dived
do	did	done
drag	dragged	dragged
draw	drew	drawn
dream	dreamed, dreamt	dreamed, dreamt
drink	drank	drunk
drive	drove	driven
eat	ate	eaten
fall	fell	fallen
fight	fought	fought

Infinitive	*Past tense*	*Past participle*
find	found	found
fly	flew	flown
forbid	forbade, forbad	forbidden
forget	forgot	forgotten, forgot
freeze	froze	frozen
get	got	got, gotten
give	gave	given
go	went	gone
grow	grew	grown
hang (to suspend)	hung	hung
hang (to execute)	hanged	hanged
have	had	had
hear	heard	heard
hurt	hurt	hurt
keep	kept	kept
know	knew	known
lay (to put)	laid	laid
lead	led	led
lend	lent	lent
let	let	let
lie (to recline)	lay	lain
lie (to tell an untruth)	lied	lied
lose	lost	lost
make	made	made

Infinitive	*Past tense*	*Past participle*
read	read	read
ride	rode	ridden
ring	rang	rung
rise	rose	risen
run	ran	run
say	said	said
see	saw	seen
send	sent	sent
set (to put)	set	set
shake	shook	shaken
shine	shone, shined	shone, shined
shoot	shot	shot
shrink	shrank, shrunk	shrunk, shrunken
sing	sang	sung
sink	sank	sunk
sit (to take a seat)	sat	sat
slay	slew	slain
sleep	slept	slept
speak	spoke	spoken
spin	spun	spun
spring	sprang	sprung
stand	stood	stood
steal	stole	stolen
sting	stung	stung

Infinitive	Past tense	Past participle
strike	struck	struck, stricken
strive	strove, strived	striven
swear	swore	sworn
swim	swam	swum
swing	swung	swung
take	took	taken
teach	taught	taught
tear	tore	torn
throw	threw	thrown
wake (to wake up)	woke, waked	woken, waked
waken (to rouse)	wakened	wakened
wear	wore	worn
wring	wrung	wrung
write	wrote	written

Verb Tenses

English has three simple tenses (present, past, and future); three perfect tenses (present perfect, past perfect, and future perfect); and six progressive tenses, one corresponding to each simple and each perfect tense.

Distinguishing among verb tenses will enable you to understand in reading and use in writing the clear, precise time distinctions they express.

Present Tense

The **present tense** indicates an existing condition or state, something occurring at the present time, or a habitual action.

The plums *are* ripe.   (existing condition)

I *hear* a baby crying.   (occurring at the present time)

Marla *plays* the cello.   (habitual action)

Past Tense

The **past tense** indicates that something has already occurred and is in the past.

The architectural plans *arrived* last week.

Future Tense

The **future tense** indicates that something will happen in the future. Form the future tense by adding the auxiliary *will* to the infinitive.   (*Shall*, an alternative auxiliary, is rarely used in current American writing.)

Sasha's poem *will appear* in next month's issue of the magazine.

Present Perfect Tense

The **present perfect tense** indicates that something began in the past and continues into the present or that it occurred at an unspecified time in the past. Form the present perfect tense by using the auxiliary *has* or *have* plus the past participle of the verb.

Marcus *has joined* the Navy.   (beginning in the past, continuing to the present)

Inclement weather *has* always *created* problems for farmers. (unspecified time)

Past Perfect Tense

The **past perfect tense** indicates that an action was completed before some time in the past. Form the past perfect tense by adding the auxiliary *had* to the past participle.

> Great cities *had flourished* in the Western Hemisphere long before Spanish explorers reached North and South America.

Future Perfect Tense

The **future perfect tense** indicates that an action will be completed before a certain time in the future. Form the future perfect tense by adding the auxiliaries *will have* to the past participle.

> In fifty years, we *will have depleted* many of the earth's natural resources.

Progressive Tenses

For every basic tense, an equivalent **progressive tense** exists that indicates continuing action. Form the progressive tenses by using a form of the verb *to be* (*am, are, is, was, were, will be, has been, have been, had been,* or *will have been*) and the present participle (*-ing*) form of the verb.

Progressive tenses	
Present progressive	*is playing*
Past progressive	*was playing*
Future progressive	*will be playing*
Present perfect progressive	*has been playing*
Past perfect progressive	*had been playing*
Future perfect progressive	*will have been playing*

EXERCISE 6.4 ❭ *Verb tenses*

Underline the verbs in the following sentences and label each verb with its tense.

1. In 1947, Kenneth Arnold, a pilot, described saucer-shaped objects that traveled at great speeds.

2. Since then, thousands of people around the world have reported similar "unidentified flying objects" (UFOs).

3. During the 1950s and 1960s, Project Bluebook, a division of the U.S. Air Force, attempted to explain these sightings and found that most were misinterpretations of natural phenomena.

4. By the late 1960s, Project Bluebook had served its purpose—it reassured military and civilian populations that the earth was not being watched or attacked—and was consequently disbanded.

5. Today, some people still claim to see bright, formless objects in our skies—and no doubt such claims will continue.

EXERCISE 6.5 ❭ *Verbs*

The following passage from Benjamin Franklin's letter describing how to reproduce his electrical experiments is written primarily in the present tense. Reconstruct the passage as though Franklin had written a narrative of his procedure. Make appropriate changes in the verbs. (Hint: Many verbs will be in the past tense.)

Make a small cross of two light strips of cedar, the arms so long as to reach to the four corners of a large thin silk handkerchief when extended; tie the corners of the handkerchief to the extremities of the cross, so you have the body of a kite; which being properly accommodated with a tail, loop, and string, will rise into the air, like those made of paper; but this being silk, is fitter to bear the wet and wind of a thunder-gust. To the top of the upright stick of the cross is to be fixed a very sharp-pointed wire, rising a foot or more above the wood. To the end of the twine, next the hand, is to be tied a silk ribbon, and where the silk and the tie join, a key may be fastened. This kite is to be raised when a thunder-gust appears to be coming on, and the person who holds the string must stand within a door or window, or under some cover, so that the silk ribbon may not be wet; and care must be taken that the twine does not touch the frame of the door or window. . . . And when the rain has wet the kite and twine, so that it can conduct the electrical fire freely, you will find it stream out plentifully from the key on the approach of your knuckle. —Benjamin Franklin, "Letter to Peter Collinson"

| 6d | Adjectives |

An **adjective** modifies or limits a noun or pronoun.

Questions adjectives answer

What kind?	*auburn* hair
Which one?	the *fourth* presentation
How many?	*sixteen* guests
Whose?	*Jeffrey's* assessment

Forms of Adjectives

Adjectives come in three forms: positive, comparative, and superlative.

Positive Adjectives

A **positive adjective** modifies a noun or pronoun without suggesting any comparisons.

These are *clear* instructions.

Comparative Adjectives

A **comparative adjective** compares two people, places, things, ideas, qualities, conditions, or actions.

These are *clearer* instructions than those we had last time.

Superlative Adjectives

A **superlative adjective** compares three or more items.

These are the *clearest* instructions I've received so far.

Kinds of Adjectives

Regular Adjectives

A **regular adjective** precedes the word it modifies. Several adjectives can modify the same word.

adj.   adj.   noun   adj.   adj.   noun

There is a *red wool jacket* hanging in *Aby's hall closet.* (*Red* jacket, *wool* jacket; *Aby's* closet, *hall* closet.)

When adjectives in a series function together as one modifier—that is, when each word alone cannot modify the noun or pronoun—hyphenate the series of words.

In 1982, American car manufacturers reintroduced *two-tone cars.* (not *two* cars or *tone* cars but *two-tone* cars; but *Detroit* manufacturers or *car* manufacturers, so *Detroit car manufacturers*, not *Detroit-car manufacturers*)

Predicate Adjectives

A **predicate adjective** follows a linking verb but modifies the subject of the sentence or clause.

pred. adj.
|

The sleeping child was obviously *content.*

When adjectives in a series work as a unit but are in the predicate-adjective position, do not hyphenate them.

Toni's comments were *off the cuff,* but they were sensible.

Articles and Demonstrative Adjectives

The **articles**—*a, an,* and *the*—and the **demonstrative adjectives**—*this, that, these,* and *those*—also function as adjectives.

The shortest distance between two points is *a* straight line.

Those forms go in *this* folder.

| 6e | Adverbs |

Adverbs modify verbs, adjectives, other adverbs, phrases, clauses, or entire sentences. Although many adverbs end in *-ly,* many do not, and many words ending in *-ly* are not adverbs. Use an *-ly* ending as a guide, but identify adverbs by their function in sentences.

The lonely widower was treated well by his neighbors. (*Lonely* is an adjective; *well* is an adverb.)

Questions adverbs answer

How?	*slowly* approached
When?	laughed *first*
Where?	searched *everywhere*
How often?	praised *repeatedly*
To what extent?	*thoroughly* disliked

Forms of Adverbs

Adverbs come in three forms: positive, comparative, and superlative.

Positive Adverbs

A **positive adverb** modifies a verb, an adjective, another adverb, a phrase, a clause, or an entire sentence but does not suggest a comparison.

Michael types *quickly*.   (modifies the verb *types*)

Michael types *very* quickly.   (modifies the adverb *quickly*)

Comparative Adverbs

A **comparative adverb** compares two actions or conditions.

Michael types *more quickly* than I do.   (modifies *types,* comparing the two typing speeds)

Superlative Adverbs

A **superlative adverb** compares three or more actions or conditions.

Of all the people on the newspaper staff, Michael types the *most quickly*. (modifies *types*, comparing the typing speeds of Michael and the group)

EXERCISE 6.6 〉 *Adjectives and adverbs*

Underline the adjectives and adverbs in the following sentences and draw arrows to show the word or group of words that each modifies.

1. American folklore has created a number of important national heroes, among them Abraham Lincoln.

2. Lincoln, the sixteenth president of the United States, was a man destined to become a legend.

3. His solemn, idiosyncratic appearance made him an easily recognizable figure, and his pivotal role during the Civil War clearly made him an important historical character.

4. Yet the reverential anecdotes and the blatant fabrications about him must surely seem questionable.

5. Lincoln's early life, though austere, was not backward, yet the rail-splitting Abe of the rustic log cabin in New Salem far overshadows the sophisticated lawyer that Lincoln clearly was in Springfield.

6. Lincoln belonged to no Christian church, yet he was often depicted in Christ-like terms as an always suffering, always kind, and always patient man.

7. Folklore has undoubtedly skewed the biographical facts of Lincoln's life, but it has created a fascinating—albeit false—vision of a man.

EXERCISE 6.7 ❭ *Adjectives and adverbs*

*Underline the adjectives and adverbs in the following paragraph
and indicate with an arrow the word or group of words that each
modifies.*

My favorite spot at Aunt Ruth and Uncle Dan's house is the small,
secluded patio just outside their bedroom. Every time I quietly open
the sliding doors and step outside, I know I will feel more peaceful.
The 10-by-10-foot patio is brick, meticulously set in a herringbone
design. A comfortable, well-padded lounge chair provides a place
to sit, and a small redwood table is a convenient spot to place my
usual drink, a tall glass of Aunt Ruth's lightly spiced tea. Once comfortably seated, I always enjoy the various flowers, my favorite feature. Close to the front edge of the patio are pink, plum, red, and
yellow moss roses, gently trailing their waxy green stems onto the
dull red bricks. Slightly back, radiating away from the patio, are
miniature yellow and orange marigolds, with their dense, round
flowers set against dark green, sharp-edged leaves. Close behind
those are Aunt Ruth and Uncle Dan's prize roses—white, pink, red,
and yellow tea roses that are carefully pruned. The small buds, usually a darker color, contrast noticeably with the large open blossoms that always remind me of fine damask. I always love to
escape from the cheerful but noisy family activities to this secluded
spot where the flowers are so beautiful. Inevitably, a visit to this flo-
ral oasis makes me feel more tranquil than before.

| 6f | ❭ | **Conjunctions** |

Conjunctions link words, phrases, or clauses. They show relationships of equivalence, contrast, alternatives, chronology, and
cause and effect. Conjunctions may be coordinating, subordinating, or correlative.

Coordinating Conjunctions

Coordinating conjunctions link equivalent sentence parts.
They are the most commonly used conjunctions.

	Coordinating conjunctions		
and	for	or	yet
but	nor	so	

In a desk drawer in his office, Todd always keeps a needle *and* thread.   (joining nouns)

Struggling for modernity *but* ruling in the old style, Peter the Great imposed a tax on beards.   (joining phrases)

Subordinating Conjunctions

Subordinating conjunctions introduce subordinate clauses (those that cannot stand alone as sentences) and link them to independent clauses (those that can stand alone as sentences).

	Common subordinating conjunctions		
after	because	so that	whenever
although	before	that	where
as	even if	though	whereas
as if	even though	unless	wherever
as long as	if	until	whether
as though	since	when	while

subordinate clause

While Gilbert was stationed in the Philippines, he returned home only once.

subordinate clause

Interest rates will rise *as long as* the national debt grows.

Correlative Conjunctions

Correlative conjunctions always work in pairs and give additional emphasis to parts of sentences. The words, phrases, or clauses joined by these correlative constructions must be in parallel form.

Correlative conjunctions	
both . . . and	neither . . . nor
either . . . or	not only . . . but also

Both Mobil *and* Atlantic Richfield underwrite programs for the Public Broadcasting Service.

A successful gardener *not only* selects plants carefully *but also* attends to them painstakingly.

Conjunctive Adverbs

Conjunctive adverbs connect ideas in independent clauses or sentences. Like other adverbs, conjunctive adverbs can appear in any position in a sentence. (See sections 22c and 22d for information on punctuating conjunctive adverbs.)

Common conjunctive adverbs

accordingly	however	next
also	incidentally	nonetheless
besides	indeed	otherwise
consequently	instead	similarly
finally	likewise	still
further	meanwhile	then
furthermore	moreover	therefore
hence	nevertheless	thus

Conjunctive adverbs show relationships similar to but with a slight shift in focus or emphasis from those shown by conjunctions. For example, the coordinating conjunctions *but* and *yet* signal a simple contrast between balanced clauses; the subordinating conjunctions *although, even though,* and *though* signal contrast but emphasize one clause over the other; the conjunctive adverb *however* signals contrast but keeps the clauses separate.

Coordinating conjunction
Children learn to use computers with ease, *but* most adults learn with some difficulty.

Subordinating conjunction
Although children learn to use computers with ease, most adults learn with some difficulty.

Conjunctive adverb
Children learn to use computers with ease. Most adults, *however*, learn with some difficulty.

Since they are punctuated differently (see section 22c), it is important to distinguish between short conjunctive adverbs and other short conjunctions. A simple method is to count the letters in the word: all conjunctive adverbs contain at least four letters, while coordinating conjunctions contain either two or three letters.

EXERCISE 6.8) *Conjunctions*

Use conjunctions to combine the following sets of sentences. Some rewording will be necessary.

1. Geography is the study of land masses. It includes the study of territorial divisions. It includes the study of bodies of water.

2. Geography was once studied as a separate course in public schools. It has now been subsumed by the social studies curriculum in most schools.

3. American students today are not receiving sufficient instruction in geography. They are not making the effort to learn the material.

4. College students in 1950 took a geography test sponsored by the *New York Times*. College students in 1984 took the same test. The comparative scores were startling.

5. Scores in some areas dropped 50 percent. That is not surprising. Seventy-two percent of the 1984 sample group said they had received little instruction in geography.

6g 〉 Prepositions

Prepositions link words in sentences. **Prepositional phrases** consist of a preposition, a noun or pronoun (the object of the preposition), and, frequently, modifiers.

$$\overset{\textit{prep.}}{\underset{|}{\;}} \quad \overset{\textit{obj.}}{\underset{|}{\;}}$$

We seem to be losing the fight *against crime*.

$$\overset{\textit{prep.}}{\underset{|}{\;}} \quad \overset{\overset{\textit{pron.}}{\textit{adj.}}}{\underset{|}{\;}} \quad \overset{\textit{adj.}}{\underset{|}{\;}} \quad \overset{\textit{obj.}}{\underset{|}{\;}}$$

Because of his heretical views, Galileo was excommunicated.

Common Prepositions

Single-word prepositions

about	by	outside
above	concerning	over
across	despite	past
after	down	since
against	during	through
along	except	throughout
among	for	till
around	from	to
at	in	toward
before	inside	under
behind	into	underneath
below	like	until
beneath	near	up
beside	of	upon
besides	off	with
between	on	within
beyond	onto	without
but	out	

Multiple-word prepositions

according to	in addition to	in spite of
ahead of	in case of	inside of
as well as	in front of	instead of
because of	in place of	rather than

Prepositional phrases modify specific words or phrases, functioning sometimes as adverbs (answering questions like *when, where,* or *how often)* and sometimes as adjectives (answering questions like *what kind* or *whose).*

    prep. *obj.*   *prep.*   *obj.*

Our flight landed *in Montreal ahead of schedule.*   (Adverbial functions: Where did it land? When did it land?)

   prep. *obj.*   *prep.*   *obj.*

Novels about families often describe conflicts between parents and

    obj.

their children.   (Adjective functions: What kinds of novels? What kinds of conflict?)

EXERCISE 6.9 ⟩ *Prepositions*

Underline the prepositional phrases in the following paragraph and label the preposition and object in each phrase.

The dog has got more fun out of Man than Man has got out of the dog, for the clearly demonstrable reason that Man is the more laughable of the two animals. The dog has long been bemused by the singular activities and the curious practices of men, cocking his head inquiringly to one side, intently watching and listening to the strangest goings-on in the world. He has seen men sing together and fight one another in the same evening. He has watched them go to bed when it is time to get up, and get up when it is time to go to bed. He has observed them destroying the soil in vast areas, and nurturing it in small patches. He has stood by while men built strong and solid houses for rest and quiet, and then filled them with lights and bells and machinery. His sensitive nose, which can detect what's cooking in the next township, has caught at one and the same time the bewildering smells of the hospital and the munitions factory. He has seen men raise up great cities to heaven and then blow them to hell.—James Thurber, "A Dog's Eye View of Man"

| 6h | > | **Interjections** |

Interjections express surprise or other emotion or provide transitions in sentences.

> *Okay,* I'll try the steamed oysters if you insist.

> *Oh no!* You used aluminum foil in the microwave oven?

Strong interjections may be punctuated like a sentence, with a period or an exclamation point; milder interjections are joined to a sentence with a comma. Because most interjections are conversational and generally do not clarify a sentence's meaning, use them sparingly in formal writing.

EXERCISE 6.10 **)** *Parts of speech*

Indicate the part of speech of the numbered words and phrases in the following paragraphs. For verbs, name the specific tense.

In the (1) *old* days, when I (2) *was writing* a great deal of (3) *fiction,* there would come, once in a while, moments when I was (4) *stymied.* (5) *Suddenly,* I would find I (6) *had written* (7) *myself*

(8) *into* a hole and could see no way out. To take care of that, (9) *I* developed a (10) *technique* which (11) *invariably* worked.

It was simply this—I (12) *went* (13) *to* the movies. Not just any movie. I had to pick a movie which was loaded with action (14) *but* (15) *which* made no demands on the (16) *intellect.* (17) *As* I watched, I did my best to avoid any (18) *conscious* thinking concerning my (19) *problem,* and (20) *when* I came out of the movie I knew exactly what I would have to do to put the story back on track.

It never failed.—Isaac Asimov, "The Eureka Phenomenon"

Revising parts of speech with a word processor

Use your word processor to improve the wording of your sentences. Make a backup copy of your draft and then experiment with parts of speech.

Substitute pronouns. Examine your draft for sentences where pronouns, rather than nouns, would create coherence and transition and eliminate repetition. Delete selected nouns and replace them with appropriate pronouns.

Change verb tense. To change the method of development of a paper—for example, from explaining a process to narrating an event, or vice versa—use the "delete" feature to change verb tenses to suit your new purpose.

Add clarifying words and phrases. After finishing a draft, make sentences more specific by inserting concrete, vivid adjectives and adverbs; the word-processing program will automatically reformat your sentences to accommodate these changes.

Understanding Sentences

Sentences contain at least a subject and a verb, and express a complete thought. Although sentences do not depend on groups of words outside themselves to make their meanings clear, they may contain words, phrases, and clauses, in addition to the essential subject and verb, that enhance their internal clarity. This chapter will help you to recognize the parts that make up sentences and to use these parts to form expressive, coherent sentences.

> ## *Quick Reference*
>
> *Learning about parts and kinds of sentences will give you the technical knowledge you need to analyze and revise your writing.*
>
> ❯ *Sentences must include a subject and a predicate.*
>
> ❯ *Phrases cannot stand alone but must be parts of sentences.*
>
> ❯ *Subordinate clauses cannot stand alone but must be joined to independent clauses.*
>
> ❯ *Use subjects, predicates, phrases, and clauses to create simple, compound, complex, and compound-complex sentences.*

| 7a | > | **Distinguish among parts of sentences.** |

A **sentence** consists of at least a subject and verb. As the simplest complete expression of meaning, it is therefore the basic unit of written communication. Understanding the parts of sentences will help you to understand how to express your meaning coherently and effectively.

Subjects

The **subject** of a sentence is the person, place, thing, idea, quality, or condition that acts or is acted upon or that is described or identified in the sentence.

> *subj.*
> |
> *Gauguin* fled to the South Pacific in search of unspoiled beauty and primitive innocence.

The subject can consist of one or more nouns or pronouns, together with any related modifiers. The subject generally appears near the beginning of a sentence, but it can appear in other positions as well.

Subjects of sentences can never be part of prepositional phrases, because the nouns and pronouns in prepositional phrases serve as objects of the preposition and therefore cannot also be subjects.

Subjects can be simple, compound, and complete.

Simple Subjects

A **simple subject** consists of a single word.

> *simple subj.*
> |
> *Machiavelli* changed the way rulers thought about governing. (*Machiavelli* performed the action, *change.*)

Sometimes the subject *you* is unstated but understood in an imperative sentence (a request or command).

[*You*] Open the door this minute!

Compound Subjects

A **compound subject** consists of two or more simple subjects joined by a conjunction.

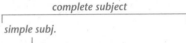

Locke and *Descartes* had different views on knowledge.

Complete Subjects

A **complete subject** contains the simple subject plus any words modifying it: adjectives, adverbs modifying adjectives, and prepositional phrases.

```
                    complete subject
┌──────────────────────────────────────────────┐
  simple subj.
     |
```
The *supplies* for a basic design course need not be expensive.

EXERCISE 7.1 ❯ *Subjects*

Underline the complete subjects in the sentences below. Bracket and label simple subjects; bracket compound subjects and draw an arrow joining the simple subjects within them.

1. The musical, a combination of drama and music, developed as a distinctly American art form.

2. Emerging from vaudeville traditions, productions like George M. Cohan's *Little Johnny Jones* offered engaging tunes like "Yankee Doodle Boy" and "Give My Regards to Broadway" in very predictable plots.

3. However, in 1927, Jerome Kern and Oscar Hammerstein presented *Show Boat*, the first major musical based on a respected novel, and changed musicals forever.

4. *Oklahoma!, South Pacific, My Fair Lady,* and *West Side Story* remain the most lasting contributions of the 1940s and 1950s, the golden years of the American musical.

5. In recent decades, British musicals have enjoyed both critical and popular success on Broadway, while American productions have often seemed uninspired by comparison.

Predicates

The **predicate** of a sentence expresses the action or state of being of the subject. It states what the subject of the sentence does, what it is, or what has been done to it.

                             predicate

As a child prodigy, Mozart *was paraded* through the aristocratic

   predicate

houses of Europe.

A predicate consists of one or more verbs, together with any modifiers or complements. (Complements are discussed on pages 168–71.) Like subjects, predicates can be simple, compound, or complete. In questions, the parts of the predicate are usually separated by the subject.

Simple Predicates

A **simple predicate** consists of the verb and any auxiliaries.

     simple predicate

Machiavelli *changed* the way rulers thought about governing.

Compound Predicates

A **compound predicate** consists of two or more verbs joined by a conjunction.

compound predicate

simple pred.

Compact discs *have revolutionized* the recording industry and, for

simple pred.

the most part, *have replaced* albums as the most popular recording form.

Complete Predicates

A **complete predicate** consists of the simple or compound predicate plus all related modifiers: adjectives, adverbs, prepositional phrases, and any complements.

complete predicate

simple pred.

The supplies for a basic design course *need* not *be* very expensive.

EXERCISE 7.2 ❭ *Predicates*

Underline the complete predicates in the sentences below. Bracket and label simple predicates; bracket compound predicates and draw an arrow joining the simple predicates within them.

1. Professional ice hockey associations were first formed in Canada near the beginning of the twentieth century.

2. The first major league, the National Hockey Association, was founded in 1910 and included teams only from eastern Canada.

3. The following year, the Pacific Coast League organized teams from western Canadian cities, cities from the American northwest, and later other American cities.

4. In 1917, the National Hockey Association was reorganized to form the National Hockey League.

5. Since then, teams from both Canada and the United States have competed throughout the regular season and have vied for the Stanley Cup, the symbol of the League championship.

EXERCISE 7.3) Subjects and Predicates

Underline and label the simple and compound subjects and predicates in each of the following sentences.

Most tarantulas live in the tropics, but several species occur in the temperate zone and a few are common in the southern U.S. Some varieties are large and have powerful fangs with which they can inflict a deep wound. These formidable looking spiders do not, however, attack man; you can hold one in your hand, if you are gentle, without being bitten. Their bite is dangerous only to insects and small mammals such as mice; for man it is no worse than a hornet's sting.

Tarantulas customarily live in deep cylindrical burrows, from which they emerge at dusk and into which they retire at dawn. Mature males wander about after dark in search of females and occasionally stray into houses. After mating, the male dies in a few weeks, but a female lives much longer and can mate several years in succession. In a Paris museum is a tropical specimen which is said to have been living in captivity for 25 years. —Alexander Petrunkevitch, "The Spider and the Wasp"

Complements

A **complement** completes the meaning of a transitive verb. Complements follow the verb and are part of the complete predicate. They can be simple or compound.

Direct Objects

Direct objects complete the action of a transitive verb by answering the questions *what* or *whom*.

Senator Packhard supported *the doomed Equal Rights Amendment.* (*What* did Senator Packhard support?)

Indirect Objects

Indirect objects indicate to whom or for whom the action of the transitive verb is intended. Indirect objects follow transitive verbs but always precede direct objects.

The librarian handed *Michael* the videotape. (*To whom* did the librarian hand the videotape?)

Predicate Nouns

Predicate nouns follow linking verbs and restate or identify the subject of a sentence.

Agnes De Mille was a skillful and innovative *choreographer.* (*Choreographer* restates the subject, *De Mille.*)

Predicate Adjectives

Predicate adjectives follow linking verbs and modify the subject of a sentence.

De Mille's choreography was sometimes *playful,* frequently *surprising,* and often *austere.* (*Playful, surprising,* and *austere* describe the subject, *choreography.*)

EXERCISE 7.4 ⟩ *Complements*

Underline the complements in the sentences below and label them as direct objects, indirect objects, predicate nouns, or predicate adjectives. Draw an arrow between the parts of compound complements.

1. The year 1896 was not only a tribute to humanity's best but also a reflection of humanity's worst characteristics.

2. At the Democratic Convention, William Jennings Bryan gave his "Cross of Gold" speech and sparked interest in an uneventful campaign.

3. The British Patent Office granted Guglielmo Marconi a patent for the wireless telegraph.

4. When the United States Supreme Court handed down its *Plessy* v. *Ferguson* decision, it established a "separate but equal" standard that institutionalized racism.

5. Athens, Greece, was the site of the first modern Olympiad.

6. Alfred Nobel was the benefactor of an endowment that began by awarding yearly prizes in peace, science, and literature.

EXERCISE 7.5 ⟩ *Complements*

Underline and label the complements in the following paragraph.

Henry Reed was class valedictorian. He was a small, very black boy with hooded eyes, a long, broad nose and an oddly shaped head. I had admired him for years because each term he and I vied for the best grades in our class. Most often he bested me, but instead of being disappointed I was pleased that we shared top places between us. Like many Southern Black children, he lived with his grandmother, who was as strict as Momma and as kind as she knew how to be. He was courteous, respectful and soft-spoken to elders, but on the playground he chose to play the roughest games. I admired him. Anyone, I reckoned, sufficiently afraid or sufficiently dull could be polite. But to be able to operate at a top level with both adults and children was admirable. —Maya Angelou, "Graduation"

Phrases

Phrases are groups of related words that cannot function as independent sentences because they lack subjects or predicates or both; phrases must be part of a sentence. The three most commonly used kinds of phrases are prepositional phrases, verbal phrases, and appositive phrases; they function as nouns, adjectives, or adverbs. A fourth kind, absolute phrases, modifies whole sentences.

Prepositional Phrases

A **prepositional phrase** consists of a preposition, its object or objects (a noun or pronoun), and any modifiers; it functions most often as an adjective or adverb and less often as a noun.

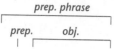

The dog limped *across the yard to the lighted doorway.*   (Both phrases work as adverbs, answering the question "*Where* did the dog limp?")

My anxiety *about the dental work* was intense.   (The phrase works as an adjective, answering the question "*Which* anxiety?")

EXERCISE 7.6 ❯ *Prepositional phrases*

Insert parentheses around the prepositional phrases in the follow-ing sentences and then underline the word or words that each phrase modifies.

1. The once inexact study of weather has become a highly complex science in the last few decades.

2. The National Weather Service currently uses computers to syn-thesize data it receives from satellites, balloons, ground stations, and airplanes.

3. Once computers at the National Meteorological Center compile this information, it is relayed by a variety of electronic means to regional weather stations where teams evaluate the results.

4. The findings of the National Severe Storms Forecast Center (NSSFC) in Kansas City, Missouri, are particularly useful because its team channels information about potentially dangerous storms to affected areas.

5. Using data from the NSSFC, local meteorologists issue a wide range of watches and warnings, notably for tornadoes, severe thunderstorms, blizzards, and hurricanes.

6. By providing systematically gathered and carefully organized information, weather forecasters can warn people of danger— protecting millions of dollars' worth of property and saving thou-sands of lives.

Verbal Phrases

Verbal phrases combine **verbals** (verb forms used as nouns, adjectives, and adverbs) with complements or modifiers. There are three types of verbals: gerunds, participles, and infinitives. Like verbals, verbal phrases function in sentences as nouns, adjectives, or adverbs.

Gerund Phrases   **Gerunds** are *-ing* forms of verbs that function as nouns.

Reading is my favorite winter sport.

Gerund phrases combine a gerund and its complements and modifiers; the entire phrase works as a noun.

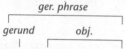

Climbing Mount Everest was their lifelong ambition.   (The gerund phrase is the subject of the sentence.)

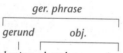

I enjoy *playing* chamber music.   (The gerund phrase is the direct object of *enjoy*.)

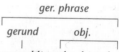

Harrison reread the instructions for *assembling* the bicycle.   (The gerund phrase is the object of the preposition *for*.)

EXERCISE 7.7 **》** *Gerund phrases*

Underline the gerund phrases in the following sentences. Bracket the objects and modifiers.

1. Learning a second language is a complicated task, but it is a rewarding one.

2. The benefits can be as simple as reading a menu in a foreign restaurant, a book in a used-book store, an untranslated quotation in a scholarly work, or a magazine in a library.

3. Working for international corporations is one career option open to people trained in a second language.

4. Traveling outside the United States is especially enjoyable when reading and speaking a country's language is possible.

5. Through studying other languages, people become sensitive to language itself, and that sensitivity can increase their effectiveness as thinkers, readers, writers, speakers, and listeners.

Participial Phrases   **Participles** appear in two forms: the **present participle** (*climbing, going*) and the **past participle** (*climbed, gone*). See the discussion of participles and the list of irregular verbs on pages 141–45.

Scowling, the tax assessor repeated the question. (*Scowling* is a present participle modifying *tax assessor.*)

Exhausted, the basketball player collapsed onto the bench (*Exhausted* is a past participle modifying *player.*)

Participial phrases combine a participle and its modifiers; the phrases work as adjectives. Like other adjectives, participial phrases must be placed near the nouns and pronouns they modify.

> *part. phrase*

> *part.*

Standing on the wooden bridge, Nathan watched small leaves float

> *part. phrase*

> *part.*

by, *swirling* along in the current.   (The first participial phrase modifies *Nathan*; the second modifies *leaves.*)

```
                    part. phrase
  ┌─────────────────────────────────────┐
  │  part.                              │
  │   │
```

Seated in a chair far from the door, Carlos had not noticed his friends' arrival.   (The participial phrase modifies *Carlos*.)

EXERCISE 7.8 ❯ *Participial phrases*

Insert parentheses around the participial phrases in the following sentences and label the participles as present or past. Then underline the word that each phrase modifies.

1. Challenged by books like E. D. Hirsch's *Cultural Literacy* and Allan Bloom's *The Closing of the American Mind,* Americans have reassessed their educational system.

2. Articles have appeared in the popular media, questioning the assumptions of these books and, at the same time, criticizing our educational system.

3. Enticed as they are by eye-catching but often misleading headlines and titles, writers have provided misleading clues about the goals of these books.

4. Limited by time and length constraints, television and print journalists have offered elliptical, abbreviated summaries of Hirsch's and Bloom's positions, oversimplifying their statements.

5. Talk-show hosts, by sensationalizing discussions of Hirsch's and Bloom's books, have failed to help viewers address important educational concerns.

6. Such problems in evaluating educational problems, made worse by American tendencies to oversimplify, will persist until Americans consent to read Hirsch's and Bloom's books for themselves.

Infintive Phrases   **Infinitives** combine the word *to* with a verb's primary form; they are used as nouns, adjectives, or adverbs.

To win was her only goal.   (*To win* works as a noun—the subject of the sentence.)

The office manager is an important person *to know*.   (*To know* works as an adjective, modifying *person*.)

Travis was too excited *to sleep*.   (*To sleep* works as an adverb, modifying *excited*.)

Infinitive phrases combine an infinitive and its complements and modifiers; these phrases function as nouns, adjectives, or adverbs. When infinitive phrases are used as adjectives, they should be placed near the nouns they modify. When they work as adverbs, however, they can appear in a variety of positions, as can other adverbs.

Rachel must learn *to control* her temper if she wants *to get* along in this office.   (Both infinitive phrases work as nouns. Both are direct objects, describing *what* Rachel must learn and *what* she might want.)

```
     inf. phrase
  ┌──────────────┐
   inf.
 ┌──────┐
```
To be responsible, we must act without prejudice.   (The infinitive phrase, working as an adjective, modifies *we*.)

```
                    inf. phrase
              ┌──────────────────┐
                    inf.
                 ┌──────────┐
```
The experiment was too dangerous *to contemplate* seriously.   (The infinitive phrase, working as an adverb, modifies the predicate adjective *dangerous*.)

EXERCISE 7.9) Infinitive phrases

Underline the complete infinitive phrases in the following sentences and label each phrase as a noun, adjective, or adverb.

1. It is hard to believe how much wood and how many wood products Americans use without being aware of them.

2. To start off our mornings, many of us eat cereals packaged in cardboard boxes while reading newspapers made from wood pulp.

3. To go about our daily routines, we move between rooms built with two-by-fours, walk on hardwood floors, and open wooden doors, often oblivious to the structural uses to which wood is put.

4. We talk on the telephone—to convey messages or simply to converse—without thinking that wood resins are used in the plastic casing for the phone, let alone that millions of wooden telephone poles help to make such communication possible.

5. Many of us use pencils to write with, paper to write on, and desks or tables to write at—all products of forest-related industries.

6. To conceive of how many trees are necessary to support the activities of even one person is virtually impossible.

Appositive Phrases

Appositives explain, describe, define, identify, or restate a noun. They provide either necessary explanation or nonessential information. In the latter case, the appositive must be separated from the rest of the sentence by commas.

The painting *American Gothic* has been amusingly used in many advertisements.   (Because *American Gothic*, the appositive, is necessary to the meaning of the sentence, no commas are needed.)

Mitchell, *a hopelessly disorganized person,* was audited by the IRS and fined $1,000. (Because the appositive provides nonessential information, it is set off with commas.)

EXERCISE 7.10) *Appositives*

Combine the following pairs of sentences to form single sentences containing appositives. Be sure to use commas where needed.

Example

The American Kennel Club recognizes more than one hundred breeds of purebred dogs. The American Kennel Club is the primary organization of dog breeders.

The American Kennel Club, the primary organization of dog breeders, recognizes more than one hundred breeds of purebred dogs.

1. Sporting dogs hunt by smelling the air to locate game. Pointers, setters, retrievers, and spaniels are typical sporting dogs.

2. Working dogs serve or once served as herders, sled dogs, and guards. The group called working dogs comprises twenty-eight separate breeds.

3. Terriers hunt by digging. Their digging is an activity for which their strong front legs are natural.

4. Nonsporting dogs include nine breeds most usually kept as pets. Many nonsporting dogs are descended from breeds in other classifications.

5. Most toy dogs have been bred down from larger breeds of dogs. Toy dogs are almost always kept only as pets.

Absolute Phrases

Absolute phrases consist of nouns and participles, usually with modifiers, and modify whole sentences rather than individual words. They can be positioned anywhere in a sentence but must be separated from the rest of the sentence by commas.

> *Her feet aching from the six-mile hike,* Lisa stretched out under a tree to rest.

> Lisa stretched out under a tree to rest, *her feet aching from the six-mile hike.*

> Lisa, *her feet aching from the six-mile hike,* stretched out under a tree to rest.

EXERCISE 7.11 ❯ Phrases

Underline and label the prepositional, gerund, participial, infinitive, appositive, and absolute phrases in the following sentences.

1. Intrigued by the history of Great Britain, many Anglophiles are Americans obsessed by England and English things.

2. To learn about their "adopted" country, Anglophiles often subscribe to magazines like *British Heritage.*

3. They also read materials in books and newspapers that offer insight into the English way of life.

4. Many Anglophiles, their daily schedules rearranged, watched the satellite broadcasts of the royal weddings of Charles and Diana and of Andrew and Sarah.

5. Anglophiles, often people who feel displaced in the rush of American activities, find pleasure in learning about "that sceptered isle."

6. Visiting England is the lifelong dream of most Anglophiles, but spending time there often spoils illusions that have developed through years of active fantasizing.

EXERCISE 7.12) Phrases

Place in parentheses and label the prepositional, appositive, and absolute phrases in the following paragraph. Then underline the gerund, participial, and infinitive phrases and label each one.

When in the winter of 1845–6, a comet called *Biela* became oddly pear-shaped and then divided into two distinct comets, one of the astronomers who observed them, James Challis of Cambridge, averted his gaze. A week later he took another peep and *Biela* was still flaunting its rude duality. He had never heard of such a thing and for several more days the cautious Challis hesitated before he announced it to his astronomical colleagues. Meanwhile American astronomers in Washington D.C. and New Haven, equally surprised but possibly more confident in their own sobriety, had already staked their claim to the discovery. Challis excused his slowness in reporting the event by saying that he was busy looking for the new planet beyond Uranus. When later in the same year he was need-lessly beaten to the discovery of that planet (Neptune) by German astronomers, Challis explained that he had been preoccupied with his work on comets. —Nigel Calder, "Heads and Tails"

Clauses

A **clause** contains both a subject and a predicate and can be either independent or subordinate.

Independent Clauses

An **independent clause** (sometimes called a **main clause**) is grammatically complete and can be used alone as a simple sentence or combined with other clauses to form other sentence types (see pages 184–86).

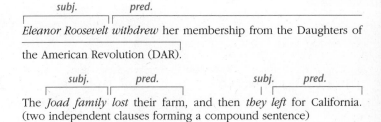

Eleanor Roosevelt withdrew her membership from the Daughters of the American Revolution (DAR).

The *Joad family lost* their farm, and then *they left* for California. (two independent clauses forming a compound sentence)

Subordinate Clauses

A **subordinate clause** (sometimes called a **dependent clause**) contains a subject and predicate but is grammatically incomplete and must be joined to an independent clause to express a complete idea. Subordinating conjunctions and relative pronouns establish this dependent relationship.

because she objected to the DAR's discriminatory practices

To make a subordinate clause grammatically complete, join it to an independent clause or revise it into a simple sentence by eliminating the subordinating conjunction or relative pronoun.

Eleanor Roosevelt withdrew her membership from the Daughters of the American Revolution (DAR) *because she objected* to the DAR's discriminatory practices.   (complex sentence)

Eleanor Roosevelt withdrew her membership from the Daughters of the American Revolution (DAR). *She objected* to the DAR's discriminatory practices.   (two simple sentences)

Subordinate clauses function in sentences as nouns, adjectives, or adverbs, depending on what information they provide.

Noun clause

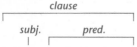

Whoever wrote this paper should pursue graduate study. (used as the subject of the sentence)

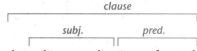

Even the White House knows *that military spending is out of control.* (used as the direct object of *knows*)

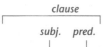

Sell the land to *whoever agrees not to develop it.* (used as the object of the preposition *to*)

Adjective clause

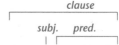

The armor *that Mordred wore* was rusty and dented. (modifies *armor*)

Adverb clause

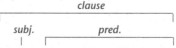

Jessica paints more carefully *than I usually do.* (modifies *carefully*)

EXERCISE 7.13   ) Clauses

Underline the subordinate clauses in the following sentences and indicate whether they are used as nouns, adjectives, or adverbs.

1. Wherever I hang my hat is home.

2. Don't count your chickens before they hatch.

3. Absence makes the heart grow fonder.

4. All that glitters is not gold.

5. Fools rush in where angels fear to tread.

EXERCISE 7.14   ) Clauses

The following paragraph contains a number of subordinate clauses. Underline them and indicate whether they are used as nouns, adjectives, or adverbs.

When the credits run at the end of a film, audience members who stay to read them discover the names of people whose contributions are sometimes as important to the film as the actors' are. For instance, producers control and organize the entire film production, finding people who will finance the project and finding creative people who will actually make the film. That directors are in charge of the filming is well known, but many people do not realize that directors also choose and coach actors and find locations and select technicians. When the filming is finally completed, editors begin their work. They take thousands of feet of film, select the best shots, and piece together the version of the film that audiences eventually see. Besides the producers, directors, and editors, hundreds of other people are involved in the making of a film. Learning who they are and what they do makes audience members more appreciative of the combined efforts involved in film making.

| 7b | > | **Distinguish among kinds of sentences.** |

The four basic sentence types are simple, compound, complex, and compound-complex. Learning to recognize their different structures and purposes will help you to use them to improve the effectiveness of your writing.

Classifying Sentences by Structure

Simple Sentences

A **simple sentence** is an independent clause that contains at least one subject and one predicate. However, simple sentences may have compound subjects, compound predicates, and compound complements, as well as multiple modifiers and phrases.

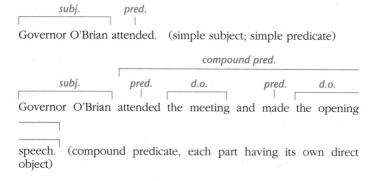

Governor O'Brian attended.   (simple subject; simple predicate)

Governor O'Brian attended the meeting and made the opening

speech.   (compound predicate, each part having its own direct object)

Compound Sentences

Compound sentences contain at least two independent clauses, each with its own subject and predicate. The clauses are usually joined by a comma and a coordinating conjunction, but they can be joined by a semicolon, with no coordinating conjunction.

subj.	pred.	conj.	subj.	pred.

Bluebirds are getting scarcer, but ornithologists do not know why.

subj.	pred.		subj.

Dickens assailed the workhouses in *Oliver Twist*; in *Bleak House* he

pred.

took on the Courts of Chancery.

Complex Sentences

Complex sentences contain one independent clause and one or more subordinate clauses. The clauses are joined by either subordinating conjunctions or relative pronouns.

Subordinate clauses may be positioned at the beginning, middle, or end of the sentence. Each position conveys a different emphasis. Note the placement of commas in the examples.

	sub. clause		ind. clause
conj.	subj.	pred.	subj.

Because shortages exist in government-run shops, Soviet citizens

pred.

often purchase goods through the black market.

ind. clause

subj.	pred.

Soviet citizens often purchase goods through the black market

sub. clause

conj.	subj.	pred.

because shortages exist in government-run shops.

sub. clause

conj.	subj.	pred.

Soviet citizens, because shortages exist in government-run shops, often purchase goods through the black market. (In this case, the subordinate clause interrupts the independent clause.)

Compound-Complex Sentences

Compound-complex sentences contain at least two independent clauses and one subordinate clause.

sub. clause   *ind. clause*

conj.	subj.	pred.	subj.	pred.

Because the zoo was closed on Monday, we visited the United

ind. clause

conj.	subj.	pred.

Nations instead, and we visited the zoo on Tuesday.

EXERCISE 7.15   **❭**   *Sentence structures*

Combine the following groups of simple sentences to form compound, complex, or compound-complex sentences. Create at least one sentence of each type. Label your revised sentences.

Example

Hoover Dam supplies water and electricity to Los Angeles and surrounding areas. The dam was originally built to control the flow of the Colorado River.

Although Hoover Dam currently supplies water and electricity to Los Angeles and surrounding areas, it was originally built to control the flow of the Colorado River.   (complex)

1. In the early 1900s, the Palo Verde and Imperial valleys seemed ideal for development. At times floods washed away crops. At other times crops withered.

2. In 1918, the Bureau of Reclamation submitted a report. The report suggested building a dam. The dam would improve water control.

3. Water control was the primary goal for the project. Generating electricity was a secondary goal.

4. The Bureau of Reclamation designed the dam. Six companies worked on the project. It was a joint venture that involved an average of 3,500 workers a day.

5. The finished dam is 726 feet high. It is 1,244 feet long. It contains 4,400,000 cubic yards of concrete. That is enough to pave a one-lane road from New York to San Francisco.

EXERCISE 7.16 **)** *Sentence structures*

Label each sentence in the following paragraph as simple, compound, complex, or compound-complex.

Rodeo, like baseball, is an American sport and has been around almost as long. While Henry Chadwick was writing his first book of rules for the fledgling ball clubs in 1858, ranch hands were paying $25 a dare to a kid who would ride five outlaw horses from the rough string in a makeshift arena of wagons and cars. The first commercial rodeo in Wyoming was held in Lander in 1895, just nineteen years after the National League was formed. Baseball was just as popular as bucking and roping contests in the West, but no one in Cooperstown, New York, was riding broncs. And that's been part of the problem. After 124 years, rodeo is still misunderstood. Unlike baseball, it's a regional sport (although they do have rodeos in New Jersey, Florida, and other eastern states); it's derived from and stands for the western way of life and the western spirit. It doesn't have the universal appeal of a sport contrived solely for the competition and winning; there is no ball bandied about between opposing players. —Gretel Ehrlich, "Rules of the Game: Rodeo"

Classifying Sentences by Purpose

In addition to classifying sentences by grammatical structure, writers classify sentences by their purpose.

Declarative Sentences

A **declarative sentence** expresses a statement.

"God does not play dice." —Albert Einstein

Exclamatory Sentences

An **exclamatory sentence** expresses an emphatic statement.

"Give me liberty or give me death!" —Patrick Henry

Imperative Sentences

An **imperative sentence** expresses a command.

"Ask not what your country can do for you—ask what you can do for your country." —John F. Kennedy

Interrogative Sentences

An **interrogative sentence** asks a question.

"What *is* the answer? . . . In that case, what is the question?" —Gertrude Stein

EXERCISE 7.17 ❭ *Sentence purposes*

Label each of the following sentences as declarative, exclamatory, imperative, or interrogative. Then experiment, rewriting each sentence in each of the three remaining forms.

1. "Tell me what you eat, and I will tell you what you are." —Anthelme Brillat-Savarin.

2. "Education is what survives when what has been learnt has been forgotten." —B. F. Skinner

3. "One only dies once, and it's for such a long time!" —Molière

4. "How can we know the dancer from the dance?" —W. B. Yeats

Revising sentences with a word processor

Writing with a word processor gives you considerable freedom to make sentence-level revisions. Make a backup
copy of your draft and then experiment with your writing.
Consider, for instance, these specific ways that you can
use the computer to try different forms and effects:

Combine sentences. Word processors allow you to
combine sets of sentences to create varied sentence
types with retyping.

Break down sentences. If, on rereading your draft, you
decide that some sentences seem too long or complex,
use the computer to deconstruct them easily into
briefer, more readable sentences.

Revise sentence patterns. Using the "cut" and "paste"
commands, transform simple sentences into other, more
varied sentence types containing appositives, absolute
phrases, subordinate clauses, and other patterns. Try
recasting some declarative sentences as exclamatory,
imperative, or interrogative sentences.

The freedom to rearrange sentences will be a great help to
you during revision. You can always return to your original
version by using the "cut" and "paste" functions to retrieve
sections of your backup copy.

8 Sentence Variety

8a ⟩ Vary sentence length.

Varying sentence lengths helps create effective paragraph rhythm. A paragraph of short sentences can seem undeveloped and choppy; a paragraph of long sentences can seem dense and difficult.

Short Sentences

Although short sentences present one idea clearly, too many of them in succession can make writing seem awkward and simplistic. A few well-placed short sentences, however, can enhance variety and add emphasis.

Our senator maintains two elaborate houses, one in our state and one in Washington, D.C. Although I understand the reasons for having two homes, owning two $300,000 residences seems needlessly extravagant. In short, I disapprove.

Medium Sentences

Medium-length sentences allow space to connect ideas and add details, while remaining clear and easy to read. Medium-length sentences are the most versatile and should form the core of your writing.

Although I enjoy televised boxing, I am often dissatisfied with network commentaries. All too often, sportscasters' comments are superficial, pointing out the obvious—like who is winning—rather than helping me to understand the sport.

Long Sentences

Long sentences establish complex interrelationships and include substantial amounts of amplification and clarification. Use long sentences sparingly to emphasize relationships and to incorporate significant details.

For more than a century, the *Statue of Liberty*, in all its majesty, has stood at the entrance to New York Harbor, welcoming immigrants, travelers, and returning Americans and symbolizing the freedoms we value.

EXERCISE 8.1 ⟩ *Sentence length*

Expand, combine, or divide the sentences in the following paragraph to achieve variety and effective expression.

Medieval castles, strongly built of native stone, served as homes for the nobility, but in times of brigandage and war they also served as fortresses and as shelters for the peasants who lived nearby.

Sometimes castles also served as prisons, treasure houses, or seats of local governments because they were secure and centrally located, although access to castles was sometimes limited because some castles, notably those in central Europe, were built on irregular terrain. Some castles were attractive. Some used drawbridges. Battlements, also called parapets, were the tall, structural walls from which soldiers observed the countryside, and during battles these same soldiers positioned themselves in these lofty places to shoot arrows or hurl rocks at the invaders below. Most people know of castles from films.

| 8b | Vary sentence types. |

Although the four basic sentence structures are simple, compound, complex, and compound-complex, the effect of these structures varies depending on the types of sentences: loose, periodic, or balanced.

Loose Sentences

Loose sentences, the most common type, first present major ideas (the subject and verb) and then provide other information. This pattern is satisfying and easy for readers.

Dr. Zhivago is a typical David Lean film, with panoramic scenes, larger-than-life characters, and universal implications.

Periodic Sentences

Periodic sentences, less common than loose sentences, create suspense and emphasis by placing the main idea or some part of it at the end of the sentence.

After having spent thousands of dollars and hundreds of hours renovating the townhouse, the Petersons sold it.

Balanced Sentences

Balanced sentences use parallel elements—words, phrases, and sometimes whole clauses—to create interest and emphasis.

I practiced; I ran; I lost.

One brother was refined, intelligent, and persuasive, but the other was crude, shrewd, and domineering.

EXERCISE 8.2 ⟩ *Types of sentences*

Label each of the following sentences as loose, periodic, or balanced; then revise each sentence into one of the other types.

1. Almanacs, published yearly in book or pamphlet form, include calendars, citations for important dates, information about geography and weather, and a myriad of other facts.

2. Almanacs are informative and practical, yet they are also idiosyncratic and entertaining.

3. Though generally associated with colonial American farmers and navigators, almanacs have as their precedents the works of an unsuspected group: Persian astrologers.

4. Over the years, sailors have relied on the *Nautical Almanac*, farmers have used the *Old Farmer's Almanac*, and amateur weather forecasters have depended on the *Ford Almanac*.

5. With its proverbs, its lists of counties and roads, its advice on planting, its selections of verse, and its astrological information, *Poor Richard's Almanack* is probably the best-known early almanac.

6. Contemporary almanacs are best represented by works such as the *Information Please Almanac*, compendiums of widely divergent statistics on thousands of topics.

| 8c | Vary sentence beginnings. |

Although subjects and verbs in subordinate or independent clauses begin most sentences, writers can create variety by positioning other sentence elements first.

Beginning with Adverbs

Adverbs can appear in many positions in sentences. Using them at the beginning creates variety.

The ornithologist cautiously approached the eagle's nest.

Cautiously, the ornithologist approached the eagle's nest.

Beginning with Adjectives

When an adjective phrase modifies the subject of the sentence, move it to the beginning of the sentence to create variety.

Jason, exhausted and dirty, collapsed in the armchair.

Exhausted and dirty, Jason collapsed in the armchair.

Beginning with Prepositional Phrases

Move adverbial prepositional phrases to the beginning of the sentence.

The pope did not restrict his travel after the attempt on his life.

After the attempt on his life, the pope did not restrict his travel.

Beginning with Verbal Phrases

Verbal phrases (gerund, participial, and infinitive phrases) make effective beginnings. Make certain, however, that the phrase modifies the subject of the first clause; otherwise, you will create a *dangling modifier*.

Incorrect

Worried that it might be stolen, the manuscript was placed in a secret vault. (The beginning phrase cannot modify *manuscript;* therefore, it is a dangling modifier.)

Correct

The monks, worried that the manuscript might be stolen, placed it in a secret vault.

Worried that the manuscript might be stolen, the monks placed it in a secret vault.

Beginning with Conjunctive Adverbs and Transitional Expressions

Create variety by occasionally placing conjunctive adverbs and transitional expressions at the beginning of sentences.

The subscription price for *Architectural Record,* for instance, is almost half of the newsstand price.

For instance, the subscription price for *Architectural Record* is almost half of the newsstand price.

Beginning with Coordinating Conjunctions

Coordinating conjunctions usually join independent clauses in compound sentences, but they can also be used to introduce a sentence closely related to the one preceding it.

International terrorism has made many world travelers more cautious than they used to be, but some travelers seem naively indifferent to potential threats from terrorists.

International terrorism has made many world travelers more cautious than they used to be. But some travelers seem naively indifferent to potential threats from terrorists.

*EXERCISE 8.3) Varying sentence structure
                and beginnings*

> *Most of the sentences in the following paragraph are loose.
> To make the writing more varied and interesting, combine
> some sentences, restructure others into periodic or bal-
> anced form, and experiment with different sentence
> beginnings.*

Landscaping serves more than an aesthetic function, even if few
people realize it. Small shrubs and bushes protect a building's foundation, sheltering it from summer heat and winter cold. Large
shrubs and small trees provide windbreaks for buildings, providing
protection, especially in the winter, from strong winds that can
affect interior temperatures and subsequently heating costs. Large
trees shade a building during the summer, keeping the sun's warming rays off the building's roof and consequently keeping the building cool. Landscaping does improve the looks of a building, often
enhancing architectural details and softening harsh lines, but the
surprise for many people is that landscaping can pay for itself in
energy savings, which means it has practical as well as aesthetic
benefits.

8d	Vary sentence relationships by using
	coordination and subordination.

Coordination

Coordination joins two or more independent clauses with a
comma and one of the coordinating conjunctions: *and, but, for,
nor, or, so,* and *yet.* The resulting compound sentences bring
balance and emphasis to writing.

Linking or Contrasting

To avoid a monotonous series of simple sentences while still
giving equal stress to the main ideas, join closely related main

clauses with a coordinating conjunction. The resulting compound sentence will give writing an even, balanced rhythm.

> Tamiko does not like watching television, *but* she does like shooting videotapes.

> Vail had a foot of fresh snow, *but* Katrina postponed her skiing trip.

Varying Conjunctions

Each of the seven coordinating conjunctions links ideas in a slightly different way. For example, although *but* and *yet* both indicate contrast and are roughly interchangeable, they create slightly different impressions for the reader. For instance, *yet* expresses contrast more strongly and is more formal than *but*.

> Estella was a heartless girl, *but* Pip loved her anyway.

> Estella was a heartless girl, *yet* Pip loved her anyway.

In another example, *for* and *so* indicate a cause-and-effect relationship but require that clauses appear in a different order. Hence, they achieve different effects.

> There is no room for delay, *so* there is no room for doubt. (With *so,* the cause precedes the effect, and the effect is slightly emphasized.)

> There is no room for doubt, *for* there is no room for delay. (With *for*, the effect precedes the cause, and the emphasis shifts slightly to the cause.)

Avoiding Excessive Coordination in a Series of Sentences

The balance of clauses in compound sentences can create a monotonous rhythm if it is overused. Look, for instance, at this series of coordinated sentences:

Several weeks before the last snowfall, the ground thaws, and the wintered-over spinach turns green. Some of the leaves begin to grow, but most remain dormant for a few weeks more. The plants grow rapidly in the middle of March, and by April we are eating fresh spinach salad.

By the third sentence, an annoying and potentially distracting rhythm has developed. Remember not to rely too much on any one sentence pattern.

Several weeks before the last snowfall, when the ground thaws, the wintered-over spinach turns green. Although some of the leaves begin to grow, most remain dormant for a few weeks more until the middle of March, when the plants grow rapidly. By April we are eating fresh spinach salad.

Avoiding Excessive Coordination Within Sentences

Three or more identically structured clauses in a single sentence can effectively link ideas and create interest and an emphatic rhythm. When clauses are dissimilar in structure or meaning, however, try other methods to join the ideas.

Awkward coordination

Americans have become concerned about stimulants in foods, and they have started using products without caffeine, and to accommodate them restaurants now regularly serve decaffeinated coffees and teas. (These clauses lack balance. The first two explain trends among Americans, but the third describes an effect of these trends.)

Effective subordination

Because Americans have become concerned about stimulants in foods and have started using products without caffeine, restaurants now regularly serve decaffeinated coffees and teas to accommodate them. (The first two clauses are joined and then related to the effect.)

Effective subordination

Americans, concerned about stimulants in foods, have started using products without caffeine, and to accommodate them restaurants now regularly serve decaffeinated coffees and teas. (With some necessary rewording, one clause has been reshaped as a verbal phrase.)

Because excessive coordination is distracting and inter-feres with sentence variety, use your word processor's "search" function to locate coordinating conjunctions. Determine whether their use is excessive, and experiment with the alternative methods in this chapter for linking ideas and creating variety and emphasis.

EXERCISE 8.4 〉 *Coordination*

Revise the following sentences to achieve effective coordi-nation and to eliminate excessive coordination.

1. Many American cities are now concerned with maintaining their architectural characters. Building codes control the development of new buildings.

2. Codes often restrict the kinds and sizes of buildings that can be constructed. Architects must design structures that match the scale of existing buildings.

3. Many cities, such as Boston and San Francisco, need the vast commercial space provided by tall office buildings. These sky-scrapers often cannot be built in some areas because of protec-tive codes.

4. City dwellers do not want the severe shadows cast by tall build-ings. They do not want small, historical, and architecturally inter-esting buildings dwarfed by monolithic towers.

5. Citizens are now aware that poorly planned cities become unliv-able, and, as a result, they have been supportive of new building

codes, but city development is now more challenging than it once was, for cities must now grow by controlled, aesthetically consistent patterns.

Subordination

Subordination joins at least one independent clause with at least one subordinate clause, forming a complex sentence that indicates the relative importance of ideas. Different subordinating conjunctions (*after, because, when, until,* and others) create differences in meaning and emphasis.

Establishing Levels of Importance

To avoid a monotonous series of simple sentences or the awkward rhythm of too many compound sentences, join related clauses with a subordinating conjunction. The resulting complex or compound-complex sentence will stress the relative importance of ideas while producing a varied rhythm.

Jessica stripped two coats of shellac and three coats of paint from the table *before* she discovered that the walnut was in excellent condition.   (The sentence emphasizes the multiple stages of stripping over the discovery of the wood beneath.)

Because viewers expect quick overviews with many visual aids, television newswriters must plan brief, attention-getting news stories.   (The sentence emphasizes the effect of viewers' expectations on newswriting.)

Using Relative Pronouns

Relative pronouns (*that, which, who,* and others) embed clauses within sentences, adding clarity and producing variety. The information in the embedded relative clause is clearly less important than the information in the independent clause.

One of T. S. Eliot's best poems is "The Love Song of J. Alfred Prufrock," *which* is also one of his earliest. (The relative clause embeds secondary but useful information.)

Avoiding Excessive Subordination

When too much secondary information is included in a sentence, ideas can become muddled. Consider the following sentence:

> Although many films about adolescence concentrate on the awkward and often unsatisfying relationships that exist between teenagers and their parents, most of these films take a satiric approach, presenting parents as fools or tyrants and, as a result, defusing through laughter much of the tension in the real relationships because the depicted relationships are so extreme, so absurd.

Although grammatically correct, this sentence is poorly planned. Revision into three sentences improves its rhythm and clarity.

> Many films about adolescence concentrate on the awkward and often unsatisfying relationships that exist between teenagers and their parents. Most of these films, however, take a satiric approach, presenting parents as fools or tyrants. Because the relationships depicted in these films are so extreme, so absurd, much of the tension of real relationships is defused through laughter.

EXERCISE 8.5) *Subordination*

Use subordinating conjunctions and relative pronouns to combine the following sets of sentences into a coherent paragraph.

1. Some people never visit art museums or exhibitions. Their only contact with art is through "public art." Public art is sculpture and other works displayed in public places.

2. Monuments are one kind of public sculpture. Statues and plac-
   ards are the most common kinds of monuments. These monuments commemorate historical events or honor individuals or
   groups of people, such as veterans.

3. People often walk through plazas and courtyards near government buildings. Sculpture is often displayed in these areas. This
   sculpture is frequently commissioned by the government.

4. Most people are comfortable with traditional, realistic statuary of
   people. Many people are less at ease with abstract sculpture.

5. Many people say nonrepresentational sculpture doesn't "look
   like anything." In time, some grow more accepting. They learn
   to enjoy modern sculpture's use of form, texture, and material.

6. Sculpture enriches public space. It provides visual and tactile
   stimulation. It also sometimes provides pleasure. It even supplies
   topics for conversation.

EXERCISE 8.6 ❭ *Coordination and subordination*

*Revise the following paragraph by using coordination and
subordination to indicate the relative importance of ideas
and to improve the variety of the sentences.*

Dermatologists continually warn people about the danger of ultraviolet rays. Many people seem intent on getting dark suntans.
During the summer, beaches and pools are crowded with people.
These people want to "catch some rays." They smear on creams,
lotions, and oils. They can accelerate the sun's natural modification
of skin pigments. They want to get deep tans. They lie on towels or
stretch out on lounge chairs for hours, defiant of doctors' stern
advice. In most cities, tanning salons are quite popular. "California"
tans are not always possible everywhere. For a fee, usually between
three and ten dollars, people can lie down and subject themselves
to artificial sunlight. This artificial sunlight is produced by ultraviolet
bulbs. Many people think a tan looks healthy. Overly dark tans, in
fact, cause serious skin damage. This damage can last a lifetime.

Revising for sentence variety with a word processor

Take advantage of the word processor to create needed variety and emphasis in your sentences.

Move sentence elements. Using the "cut" and "paste" features, shift elements to the beginnings of sentences to create variety. Such moves will require you to change capitalization and punctuation—alterations that are much easier and faster on a word processor than on a typewriter.

Vary sentence structures and lengths. Look for a series of short sentences to combine through coordination or subordination. Look for excessively long sentences to break up. Look for repeated sentence types, and restructure some for greater variety and more effective expression.

9 Emphasis

Emphasis underscores the significance of main ideas and makes supporting ideas and details clear and vivid. To control emphasis, therefore, is to control meaning. In addition to using other methods—such as choosing words carefully (see Chapters 13 and 14), constructing cohesive paragraphs (Chapter 4), and using subordination and coordination (Chapter 8)—emphasize people and actions by writing active sentences and by writing concisely.

Quick Reference

Emphatic sentences stress the most important ideas, allowing readers to concentrate their attention according to the writer's purpose. Control emphasis in the following ways:

❭ *Write active sentences to stress the doer of an action.*

❭ *Write passive sentences to stress the receiver of an action or to stress that the doer of the action is unknown.*

❭ *Strip sentences of all unnecessary words, phrases, and clauses to highlight words crucial to meaning.*

9a ❭ **Use active and passive sentences to create different kinds and degrees of emphasis.**

Active Sentences

Verbs in the active voice create **active sentences:** the subjects of the sentences act.

Lin Su invested two thousand dollars in the commodities market.

Passive Sentences

Verbs in the passive voice create **passive sentences:** the subject of the sentence is acted upon. A passive verb requires auxiliaries. Note that a passive sentence does not always specify the person completing the action. When the sentence identifies the person who initiates an action, the person is named in a prepositional phrase beginning with *by*.

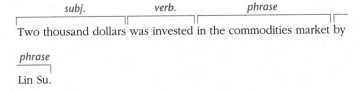

Two thousand dollars was invested in the commodities market by

phrase

Lin Su.

Emphasis

Stressing Who or What Acts

An active sentence emphasizes the doer of an action. It establishes a clear, strong relationship between the subject and verb.

> The *restorer damaged* a portion of the fresco when he cleaned it. (The damage is clearly due to the restorer's error.)

When the results of an action are more important than the doer, or when the doer is unknown, passive sentences effectively express the meaning.

> The fresco *was* irreparably *damaged* during its restoration.

In most cases, however, clarity, precision, and force make the active voice the better choice. Notice the ambiguity in the following passive sentence:

> A portion of the fresco was damaged when the restorer cleaned it. (It is not clear that the damage was the restorer's fault.)

The choice of an active or a passive verb allows subtle but significant shifts in meaning and emphasis.

Active
> The 1980 eruption of Mount St. Helens destroyed more than sixty million dollars' worth of property.   (The use of *eruption* with the active verb *destroyed* emphasizes the violence of nature.)

Passive
> More than sixty million dollars' worth of property was destroyed by the 1980 eruption of Mount St. Helens.   (This sentence shifts the emphasis to the loss of property.)

Stressing Action

The passive emphasizes action over the doer of the action; thus, it is especially useful for describing universal or widespread conditions or events.

Passive
> Open-heart surgery to repair faulty valves is now commonly performed across the United States.   (The surgical procedure is most important here, not the individual doctors who perform it.)

Active
> Doctors across the United States now commonly perform open-heart surgery to repair faulty valves.   (This construction emphasizes the doctors who perform the procedures.)

As a general guide to usage, write active sentences when "who is doing what" is most important. When "what is being done" is most important, passive sentences may better serve your purpose.

EXERCISE 9.1) *Active and passive sentences*

Determine which of the following sentences should be left in the passive voice and briefly state your reasons. Revise the remaining sentences into the active voice.

1. Biographies are often written by people who know their subjects well, either from personal contact or through study.

2. The *Life of Samuel Johnson,* a famous early biography, was written by James Boswell, a personal friend of Johnson.

3. In typical fashion, facts, anecdotes, and quotations were recorded in Boswell's diary and then translated into the biography.

4. When people like Benjamin Franklin choose to write their autobiographies, experiences are often presented to create a positive impression.

5. The lives of famous people like Lincoln were once described reverently by biographers.

6. Balanced treatments of positive and negative qualities are frequently presented by contemporary biographers.

7. A multifaceted view of the Roosevelts' relationship is presented in *Eleanor and Franklin*, a biography of the couple by Joseph P. Lash.

8. An essentially negative portrait of Pablo Picasso emerges in the Stassinopoulos-Huffington biography of the twentieth-century artist.

9. Contemporary autobiographies are usually written by well-known people with the help of professional writers.

10. *My American Journey,* a recent autobiography, was written by Colin Powell and a cowriter to chronicle Powell's rise in the military establishment.

9b	Make your writing as concise as possible.

Concise writing expresses meaning in as few words as possible. Such writing is precise, clear, and emphatic. To write concisely, choose concrete, exact words and avoid needless repetition by eliminating words, phrases, and clauses that do not add meaning. Your sentences need not be short—some long sentences are concise and some short sentences are not—but to highlight important ideas, they should contain no extraneous words.

In a first draft, concision will probably not be your goal. Rather, concentrate on developing ideas and connecting them effectively. When revising, however, search for the words and expressions that most clearly and concisely express your meaning.

Unnecessary Repetition of Words and Ideas

Deliberate, controlled **repetition,** as in the following example, emphasizes important ideas:

We forget all too soon the things we thought we could never forget.
—Joan Didion

But such effects, if overused, can irritate readers and so should be used rarely.

Avoid unintentional, excessive, or monotonous repetition. In revising your writing, delete unnecessary words and rearrange the sentence to read smoothly.

During the 1930s and 1940s, the studio renowned for film musicals was MGM studio.

In the 1930s and 1940s, MGM studio was renowned for film musicals.

Rely on specific word choices to make your ideas clear. Do not elaborate needlessly. **Redundancy,** or repeating ideas, adds useless words and irritates readers.

The smile on Corrine's face showed that she was pleasantly elated by the reception of her new poem.   (Where else could a smile be but on her face? Could elation be anything but pleasant?)

Corrine's smile showed that she was elated by the reception of her new poem.

Eliminating Wordiness

Eliminating Expletive Constructions

Sentences beginning with expletive constructions (*it is, here is, here are, there is,* and *there are*) weaken the impact of ideas by obscuring the subject and verb. Other, stronger words in the sentence can often better express your meaning. Revise your writing to eliminate expletives. Strike them out and use the remaining, substantive words to present the same idea.

There are three kinds of qualifying exams routinely used by the admissions committee.

The admissions committee routinely uses three kinds of qualifying exams.

Eliminating Wordy Expressions

Wordy expressions bog down writing. Phrases like *at this point in time* and *because of the fact that* add unnecessary words without enhancing either sense or sound. Many such expressions can be shortened or have clear, concise substitutes.

Due to the fact that an accident blocked the road, I was late.

Because an accident blocked the road, I was late.

Concise Alternatives to Wordy Expressions

Wordy	*Concise*
at this point in time	now
by means of	by
in order to	to
in the event that	if
of the opinion that	think
until such time as	until

Eliminating Empty Phrases

Phrases such as *in my opinion, I believe, it seems,* and *I suppose* add little meaning to a sentence but blur its focus and slow its pace. Readers may take these phrases to mean that you are unsure of your ideas or information. Unless your purpose is to compare your opinion with someone else's, such phrases serve no purpose and should be dropped from your writing.

It seems that athletes in triathlons are masochistic.

Athletes in triathlons seem masochistic.

Eliminating *to be* Verbs

To be verbs weaken sentences by depriving them of strong verbs and adding words. Many words in English have multiple forms, usually including a verb form that can replace weak *to be* verbs. Examine your sentences containing *to be* verbs for words that might yield verbs.

Research assistants *are responsible for completing* most day-to-day experiments *and recording* the results.

Research assistants *complete* most day-to-day experiments *and record* the results.

Eliminating Nonrestrictive Clauses and Modifying Phrases

Nonrestrictive clauses (clauses not essential to the meaning of the sentence) that contain *to be* verbs can be reduced to appositives (phrases restating a noun or pronoun). Because appositives contain no subject or verb, they are more concise than clauses.

Chemicals found in aerosols have damaged the Earth's ozone layer, *which is our main protection from solar radiation.*

Chemicals found in aerosols have damaged the Earth's ozone layer, *our main protection from solar radiation.*

When it will not affect the rhythm or clarity of a sentence, change prepositional and verbal phrases to one-word or multiword modifiers. When multiword modifiers precede a noun, they are often hyphenated.

The colors *of the tapestry* were distorted *by a nearby window made of stained glass*.

A nearby stained-glass window distorted the *tapestry's* colors.

EXERCISE 9.2 ⟩ *Concision*

Through revision, make these wordy sentences concise; note the number of words saved.

1. It is known to scientists who study such matters that an average of four trillion gallons of precipitation falls on the United States each and every day.

2. Falling from the overcast sky, heavy rains and snows fill our lakes, rivers, streams, and waterways, as well as replenish water supplies in our reservoirs.

3. There are some areas of the continental United States that are known to receive annually fewer than five inches of rain each year.

4. Other parts of the United States experience the benefit of more than twenty inches of precipitation or rain in a calendar year.

5. Precipitation—which includes rain, snow, sleet, and drizzle—is crucial to the national well-being of the United States.

6. Most of the people who think about it are aware that water is used to satisfy the needs of people, plant life, and animal life; however, they often fail to consider the fact that water is also in use in important industries.

7. I am of the opinion that water distribution should be under the management of a separate and independent national agency.

8. Until such time as we have a national policy for the management of water supplies, we can expect to have imbalances in the supplies of water in this country.

EXERCISE 9.3 〉 *Concision*

Make the following paragraph, bloated with useless words, more concise.

To be capable of understanding the development and use of paper and how that use came about, we must make our way back hundreds of years to China. By most estimates, paper was invented by the Chinese, who created it in 105 B.C. As a matter of fact, it was kept as a secret by the state for hundreds of years. As far as we know, most transcriptions were done on bamboo sheets. The Moors discovered the Chinese invention in A.D. 750. They became aware of it when they were at war with the Chinese. The Moors established and forged the link to Europe. In 1100, there was a paper mill for making paper established in Toledo, Spain. Gradually, the use of paper began to spread across Europe in a slow manner. Paper was able to reach Rome in approximately 1200, and it was a cause for the Catholic Church to feel threatened by the "new" invention. The church opposed the introduction of something that was so unfamiliar. According to the church, documents written on paper were not legally binding due to the fact that the church did not consider paper permanent. Still, paper began to be used by people instead of parchment, which was treated animal skin. People were greatly intrigued and fascinated as well by the new medium, which was cheaper and more convenient than parchment had ever been or could ever be. The use of paper reached English soil by 1400, and then it reached America by 1690. Soon, there was no other universally accepted writing surface that was used everywhere by virtually everyone. At this point in time, we take paper for granted and use it daily. We do not even acknowledge the fact that it was once a revolutionary new invention.

Creating emphasis with a word processor

To create more emphasis in your writing, try these two methods on your word processor.

Find and replace to be *verbs.* Use the "search" command to check for a variety of *to be* verbs: *am, are, is, was, were,* and others. Not every *to be* verb will need to be replaced, but replacing some with more forceful verbs will make your sentences more emphatic.

Search for and replace expletive constructions. Many word-processing programs allow for multiword searches. If yours does, look for *there is, there are, it is,* and other expletive constructions. Strike them out and revise the sentence by using more forceful subjects and predicates.

Parallelism

Parallelism brings symmetry to coordinate sentences and sentence elements; symmetry, in turn, enhances clarity. Parallelism requires that ideas of equal importance be expressed in similar ways or that words or phrases used together in similar ways appear in identical grammatical form: nouns with other nouns, verbs with other verbs of the same tense, predicate adjectives with other predicate adjectives, and so on.

> *Quick Reference*
>
> *Parallelism creates clarity by stressing the balance between similar words, parts of sentences, or entire sentences.*
>
> ❯ *Independent clauses joined by coordinating conjunctions must be parallel to be grammatical.*
>
> ❯ *Clauses and phrases joined by correlative conjunctions must be parallel to be grammatical.*
>
> ❯ *Prepositions, conjunctions, pronouns, and sentence structures arranged in parallel constructions convey meaning clearly and effectively.*

| 10a ❯ | **Maintain parallelism in constructions by using coordinating conjunctions: *and, but, for, nor, or, so,* and *yet.***

When a coordinating conjunction is used in a sentence, the joined elements should appear in identical grammatical form.

Nonparallel

All her employers found Jan to be intelligent, able, and a hard worker.   (*Intelligent* and *able* are predicate adjectives; *hard worker,* a predicate noun, is not parallel.)

Parallel

All her employers found Jan to be *intelligent, able,* and *hard working.*

Nonparallel

To have dreams is important, but living them is even more important.   (*To have dreams,* an infinitive phrase, and *living them,* a gerund phrase, are not parallel.)

Parallel

To have dreams is important, but *to live them* is even more important.

| 10b | Maintain parallelism in sentences by using correlative conjunctions: *both . . . and, either . . . or, neither . . . nor,* and *not only . . . but also.* |

Correlative constructions present balanced alternatives that require parallel treatment.

Nonparallel

The aim of a teacher should be both to inspire and educate.   (In correlative constructions, infinitive forms must be repeated, not mixed with present-tense verbs.)

Parallel

The aim of a teacher should be both *to inspire* and *to educate.*

> **10c** ⟩ Repeat sentence elements—prepositions,
> conjunctions, relative pronouns, clauses—for
> correctness, clarity, emphasis, or effect.

In brief sentences, prepositions and subordinating conjunctions can sometimes be omitted from the second part of a parallel structure. In longer sentences, repeat prepositions and subordinating conjunctions.

Repetition for Correctness and Clarity

Nonparallel

Bela Karolyi coached Mary Lou Retton, an exceptional vaulter and who was also an outstanding performer in the floor exercise. (Use of the coordinating conjunction *and* requires parallel structures in the phrases it links.)

Parallel

Bela Karolyi coached Mary Lou Retton, *an exceptional vaulter* and *an outstanding performer in the floor exercise.*

Parallel

Bela Karolyi coached Mary Lou Retton, *who was an exceptional vaulter* and *who was also an outstanding performer in the floor exercise.*

Unclear parallel

When the summer days grow increasingly longer and noticeably hotter and work becomes especially frustrating, I head to the cabin at Bishop's Point for a cool and relaxing break. (The length of the opening subordinate clause makes the parallel construction difficult to follow without repeating the subordinating conjunction, *when.*)

Clear parallel
> *When* the summer days grow increasingly longer and noticeably hotter and *when* work becomes especially frustrating, I head to the cabin at Bishop's Point for a cool and relaxing break.

Repetition for Emphasis and Effect

Throughout a paper or paragraph, varied sentence structures help maintain readers' interest. In some cases, however, closely linked ideas expressed in a series of parallel sentences can create clarity and heighten interest.

> His voice quavered audibly; his face blushed hotly; his hand trembled violently.

Consider in detail the parallel structures of these elements:

Possessive pronouns	Subjects	Verbs	Adverbs
His	voice	quavered	audibly;
his	face	blushed	hotly;
his	hand	trembled	violently.

EXERCISE 10.1 〉 *Parallelism*

Revise the following sentences to improve parallelism.

1. "As Ye Plant, So Shall Ye Reap" is a moving essay about the plight of migrant workers and which is somewhat controversial.

2. Over the years, César Chávez used his political power to draw attention to the harsh treatment of these workers, to garner

support from politicians, and orchestrate boycotts of selected
produce.

3. Not only are migrant workers exploited in the Southwest but
   also in other parts of the Sunbelt.

4. The work of these laborers, extremely tedious and which needs
   to be controlled by labor laws, is traditionally undervalued.

5. To supply better wages and providing better working conditions
   should be our goal.

EXERCISE 10.2 ❭ *Parallelism*

   *Locate and correct faulty parallelism in the following
        paragraph.*

Americans like to play it safe, so it is not surprising that they want
the places where they play to be safe. Not so very long ago, however, amusement parks were poorly supervised, dirty, and they
were rather tasteless. On hot summer Saturdays, American families
would head to places with names like Chain-of-Rocks Park to have
a good time. Once there, they found that the parking facilities were
not only randomly planned but also no guards patrolled the area.
The parks themselves were poorly maintained, with litter on the
sidewalks, with oil running on the sidewalks, and food having been
left to spoil on the tables. The attendants appeared to be people
with nothing better to do and who wash or shave only infrequently.
They seemed to be alternately indifferent, callous, or they sometimes appeared to be threatening. Probably because of these unappealing qualities and other safety concerns, the amusement parks of
an earlier time have been replaced by well-maintained, clean, and
the attractiveness of today's Six Flags, King's Island, and Disney
parks. Yesterday's grimy and chaotic amusement parks have been
replaced by today's safe, sanitized theme parks.

Achieving parallelism with a word processor

Use your word processor to identify and revise problems with parallelism.

Locate conjunctions. Because parallelism is most often required in constructions using coordinating and correlative conjunctions, use the "search" function to find them. Search for *and* or *either . . . or,* for instance, and double-check parallelism in sentences containing these words.

Make necessary changes. When you discover elements that are not parallel, use the "delete" command to remove the nonparallel element and then replace it with a parallel one.

11   Pronoun Reference

To create variety and unity in your writing, substitute pronouns for overused nouns. To make your meaning clear, however, you must follow certain patterns of pronoun usage.

> ## Quick Reference
>
> *A pronoun must refer clearly to a specific noun, its antecedent; otherwise, the meaning of a sentence can become confused.*
>
>) *Make sure that a pronoun has one antecedent, not several.*
>
>) *Be certain that a pronoun's reference is clear, not vague or general.*
>
>) *Make sure that reflexive pronouns have antecedents in the same sentence.*

11a ⟩ Avoid unclear pronoun references.

Unclear pronoun references result when antecedents are ambiguously placed, broad or vague, or implied rather than stated. Readers associate pronouns with the nearest antecedents. To avoid confusion, be sure that the antecedents of the pronouns you use are specific, clear, and appropriately positioned.

Ambiguous References

Ambiguous references result when more than one noun could be a pronoun's antecedent.

Ambiguous

The scuba instructor gave Patrick a detailed account of the history of the sport. He thought the lecture was a waste of time. (Did the instructor feel dissatisfied, or did Patrick?)

Clear

Even though he thought the lecture was a waste of time, the scuba instructor gave Patrick a detailed account of the history of the sport. (The rule of nearness suggests that *he* refers to the scuba instructor.)

Vague References

General or broad antecedents result in **vague references** and confused readers.

Vague

The members of Israel's Knesset requested more military aid from the United States. This was approved by Congress. (Did Congress approve of the request, or did Congress approve the aid?)

Clear

Upon the request of members of Israel's Knesset, Congress approved more military aid.

Implied References

An **implied antecedent** suggests a reference but does so confusingly, leaving to the reader the writer's work of creating clear, precise thought and expression.

Unclear

The Theater-in-the-Round is not very innovative, but they usually do technically polished productions. (*They* has no direct antecedent.)

Clear

Although the directors at the Theater-in-the-Round are not very innovative, they usually do technically polished productions.

| 11b | Use reflexive pronouns (those ending in *-self* or *-selves*) to refer only to the subjects of sentences. |

Reflexive pronouns serve only as indirect or direct objects.

```
                  reflex.  indirect
      subj.        verb.    obj.    d.o.
```
Carlotta Monterey gave herself credit for Eugene O'Neill's stability in his last years.

Use a personal pronoun in place of a reflexive pronoun if the subject of the sentence is not the antecedent. A reflexive pronoun should never be the subject of a sentence.

Incorrect

Wilbur and myself disagree about the effectiveness of amplified sound on stage.

Correct

Wilbur and I disagree about the effectiveness of amplified sound on stage.

| 11c | Use pronouns to refer to antecedents in the same sentence or in the immediately preceding sentence. |

When pronouns and antecedents are separated by too many words, references become vague or unclear. Too-frequent use of a pronoun becomes monotonous. Alternate between using a noun and using a pronoun.

Charlie Chaplin began his work in American films with the Keystone Cops. Although ~~Chaplin's~~ *his* early roles were limited, they gave him a chance to demonstrate his considerable talents. Chaplin later showcased his talents in a one-reeler titled *The Tramp*. In that film, ~~Chaplin~~ *he* introduced the character that was to win him wide acclaim. ~~He~~ *Chaplin* later produced, wrote, directed, and starred in such films as *The Kid, City Lights,* and *Modern Times*.

(Although the entire paragraph is about Chaplin and consequently is not confusing, it is improved by alternating Chaplin's name with pronouns.)

For clarity, observe the convention of restricting pronoun references to sentences within the same paragraph, even when the reference seems clear.

. . . Chaplin later produced, wrote, and starred in such films as *The Kid, City Lights,* and *Modern Times*. ~~His~~ *Chaplin's* importance in Hollywood soon became clear. In fact, he, Mary Pickford, and Douglas Fairbanks split from their studios to form the studio United Artists. . . .

EXERCISE 11.1   〉   *Pronoun reference*

Clarify the pronoun references in the following sentences.

Example

Although *Macbeth* is based on Scottish history, he modified historical evidence to create a compelling tragedy.

Although *Macbeth* is based on Scottish history, Shakespeare modified historical evidence to create a compelling tragedy.

1. In the opening act, the witches tempt Macbeth and Banquo with promises of greatness. They certainly are strange.

2. Teachers have long felt that *Macbeth* is a Shakespearean tragedy that appeals to students. They find *Macbeth* a valuable introduction to Shakespeare's other, more complicated works.

3. Although *Macbeth* has violence at its core, Nedah, Louis, and myself found the Polanski film version bloodier and more perverse than necessary.

4. The elements of Japanese kabuki theater merge well with the symbolic dimensions of *Macbeth*. They make kabuki productions of *Macbeth* very appealing.

5. In the last act of *Macbeth*, it implies that conditions in Scotland will return to normal.

Checking pronoun references with a word processor

Use the "search" function to locate pronouns; then check for clear antecedents.

Locate personal pronouns. Your subject will determine what pronouns you use most often. Search for these pronouns and examine their use for ambiguous, vague, or implied antecedents.

Locate reflexive pronouns. Search for these pronouns and make certain that their antecedents appear in the same sentences.

Positioning Modifiers

Modifiers explain, describe, define, or limit a word or group of words. Position modifiers so that the relationship between them and the words they modify is clear.

| 12a ⟩ | **Position modifiers to create clarity and smoothness in sentences.** |

To be effective, modifiers must be placed where they create clear meaning.

Positioning Long Modifiers

If a long modifier separates the subject from the verb or the verb from the object, reposition the modifier.

Ineffective

Poe's "The Telltale Heart" is, however disturbing its main premise may be, a spellbinding story.

Effective

However disturbing its main premise may be, Poe's "The Telltale Heart" is a spellbinding story.

Positioning Prepositional Phrases and Subordinate Clauses

Because readers instinctively use nearness as a guide to understanding modification, place prepositional modifiers near the words they modify.

Unclear

Huck and Jim were impressed by the view of the mansion, on the raft.   (The mansion was on the raft?)

Clear

On the raft, Huck and Jim were impressed by the view of the mansion.

Unclear

In spite of his successful command of forces in the Pacific, President Truman relieved Douglas MacArthur of his military duties. (Truman commanded forces in the Pacific?)

Clear

President Truman relieved Douglas MacArthur of his military duties, in spite of his successful command of forces in the Pacific.

Positioning Limiting Modifiers

Limiting modifiers such as *hardly, nearly,* and *only* substantially change the meaning of a sentence. Place them carefully and double-check to see that your intended meaning is clear.

229

He simply stated the problem.   (Stating the problem is all he did.)

He stated the problem simply.   (He made the problem easy to understand.)

We had time only to meet him.   (We had time for nothing else.)

We had time to meet only him.   (We met no one else.)

Positioning Modifiers near Infinitives

Try not to place a modifier between *to* and an infinitive. Although this usage is common in conversation and is acceptable to some linguists, it is best to avoid split infinitives.

Split infinitive
> After rereading "Ode on a Grecian Urn," Ralph began *to quickly prepare* his report.

Always acceptable
> After rereading "Ode on a Grecian Urn," Ralph quickly began *to prepare* his report.

| 12b | ⟩ | Avoid dangling modifiers. |

A phrase that appears at the beginning of a sentence but that does not modify the subject of the sentence is a **dangling modifier.** Sentences with dangling modifiers are unclear and illogical. Eliminate dangling modifiers by repositioning the misplaced phrases.

Dangling
> *Leaping high above the waves,* Michael watched the dolphins. (Michael was not leaping; the dolphins were.)

Clear
> Michael watched the dolphins leaping high above the waves.

Dangling

When still in high school, my father expected me to be home by midnight. (You were not out that late when your father was in high school. You probably were not even born!)

Clear

When I was still in high school, my father expected me to be home by midnight.

| 12c | Avoid squinting modifiers. |

Squinting modifiers are words or phrases that could modify either the words before them or the words after them.

Squinting

Armand said *before ten o'clock* he would reach the summit. (He spoke before ten o'clock? Or he would arrive before ten?)

Clear

Armand said he would reach the summit before ten o'clock.

When a modifier is in an ambiguous position, you may be able to clarify the meaning of the sentence by inserting the relative pronoun *that* in the appropriate position.

Ambiguous

Walter said *during the meeting* Monica misrepresented her case. (Did Walter comment during the meeting? Or is that when Monica distorted her case?)

Clear

Walter said *that* during the meeting Monica misrepresented her case. (Here, *that* clarifies when Monica spoke.)

Walter said during the meeting *that* Monica misrepresented her case. (Here, *that* clarifies when Walter spoke.)

EXERCISE 12.1 ⟩ *Positioning modifiers*

The following sentences contain misplaced modifiers. Revise the sentences to make the modification clear and effective.

1. The problems of alcoholism, no matter whether they affect adults, adolescents, or even children, need to be honestly addressed.

2. Drinking is, though acceptable within most groups in American culture, socially, physically, and economically costly.

3. Families and coworkers often fail to honestly assess the drinking habits of alcoholics and, as a result, fail to immediately encourage alcoholics to seek professional help.

4. People who drink often have liver trouble, among other medical and social problems.

5. When inebriated, family members endure the emotional and physical abuse of alcoholics.

6. Alcoholics must admit often that their drinking problems are severe before they can get help.

EXERCISE 12.2 ⟩ *Positioning modifiers*

The following paragraph contains a variety of misplaced modifiers. Revise the sentences to make the modification clear and effective.

Helping my uncle with his one-acre garden taught me that victories in the garden are won the hard way. My uncle and I, each morning before it got too hot, would do maintenance work. We would pull small infestations of weeds by hand and then spray, with a post-emergent herbicide, larger growths of weeds. Then we would mulch the plants whose foliage did not protect the soil from the sun's drying rays. Using straw and sometimes black plastic sheets, we would, trying not to damage low leaves, encircle the stalks of the plants. Covered with parasitical bugs, we would sometimes have to spray plants with a pyrethrin mixture. Once we got started, we worked often without talking. A few comments seemed to be enough on the growth of the asparagus or the tomatoes. Once, however, Uncle Charles told me during our work sessions I was a conscientious worker when he felt talkative. As the days passed, I began to, because of my own hard work, realize how much effort goes into gardening. I must say that grown with so much care, I now appreciate my fruits and vegetables more than I used to.

Positioning modifiers with a word processor

Use your word processor to improve the effectiveness of modifiers.

Reposition modifiers. When modifiers must be moved, use the "cut" and "paste" commands to make the changes. You will also need to alter punctuation and mechanics using the "delete" command.

Insert the relative pronoun that *when necessary to prevent misreading.* Your word-processing program will automatically reformat the sentence.

DICTION

13 Using Meaning and Tone

Through **diction,** the choice and use of words for effective communication, you make your meaning clear to readers. Specific word choices affect the tone of writing, implying your perception of yourself, your readers, your subject, and your purpose in writing.

Quick Reference

Selecting appropriate words requires a strong sense of your purpose and your audience.

⟩ *Use formal or informal diction, depending on the tone that you want to achieve in your paper.*

⟩ *Choose words that your readers will understand.*

⟩ *Select words whose denotations suit your meaning and whose connotations suit your purpose.*

⟩ *Use specific words that convey your meaning clearly and efficiently.*

⟩ *Use idioms correctly; note especially the correct preposition in phrasal idioms.*

| 13a ⟩ | Consider your word choices. |

American English consists of many regional and social dialects that can be broadly classified as standard or nonstandard. **Standard English** is just that: standard, established usage for speaking and writing. Employ its grammatical principles and accepted word choices for most formal writing, including academic and professional; educated readers expect its use in most of what they read. **Nonstandard English**—often used in conversation, fiction, and informal writing—occasionally uses ungrammatical constructions and colloquial, regional, or personal words and expressions.

In the early stages of writing—planning, organizing, and writing a rough draft—do not pause to consider your diction, standard or otherwise. However, when revising a rough draft, consider word choices carefully. Use the following guidelines, the Glossary of Usage starting on page 654, and your dictionary to choose the words that best convey the meaning and tone you want.

Formal Diction

Used in most academic and professional writing, **formal diction** differs somewhat from the word choices of everyday conversation. When addressing important subjects (death, religion, politics, or culture, for example), select formal diction.

Formal diction generally excludes slang and contractions and uses the third person (*he, she, it, they*). Choose the most exact words to express meaning and organize words carefully to achieve the desired tone. The following paragraph, informal in the first draft, is revised in the second draft to achieve the formal tone suited to the subject.

Informal diction and tone

The effects of divorce on children change with the kids' ages. Little kids, one to four, often don't get it when their parents yell at each other, but they usually know something's wrong. They tend to get down, stopping eating and talking, or to act up, getting loud and wild. Bigger kids, from four to eight, have a better idea of what's going on. Because they don't know any better, they're always asking embarrassing questions like "Why are you and Mommy yelling at each other?" These kids often get edgy, flunk in school, and carry a heavy load of guilt.

Formal diction and tone

The effects of divorce on children vary with the children's ages. Very young children, from one to four, often do not fully comprehend the problems between their parents, but they usually sense the tension. They may become depressed, stop eating or talking, or demand attention through loud misbehavior. Older children, from four to eight, more clearly recognize relationships in turmoil. Lacking social adeptness, they often ask embarrassing and candid questions such as "Why are you and Mommy yelling at each other?" These children may become nervous, do poorly in school, and feel responsible for their parents' problems.

Informal Diction

Informal diction is the language of conversation. Use informal diction most of the time, especially for subjects like travel, sports, and popular culture.

Informal diction often includes contractions and uses first-person pronouns (*I, me, my,* and so on) and sometimes includes slang and regionalisms. It can serve your purposes well in a nonacademic composition, such as a personal-experience paper. The following paragraph, with its personal point of view, effectively employs informal diction.

When I was about eleven, my parents got a divorce. I wasn't surprised. For months before, I had known something was wrong, although I wasn't sure what. Mom and Dad would alternately argue about trivial matters and then turn silent, not speaking to each other for days. Then one day, Dad just quietly moved out. It was a relief for everyone, and now, ten years later, Mom and Dad are good friends.

Diction and Audience

A good idea supported with pertinent examples and facts may confuse readers if the words you choose do not accurately convey your intended meaning. To assess the appropriateness of your diction for your audience, consider these questions:

How well developed are your readers' vocabularies? If your readers are well educated or well read, their vocabularies are probably extensive, and you have a wide choice of words to use to present ideas. On the other hand, if you suspect that your readers' vocabularies are not well developed, adjust your diction to present your ideas clearly yet simply.

Do your readers understand the technical vocabulary of the subject? Readers who are familiar with your subject will understand its technical terminology, and you can use it freely. If readers are not familiar with your subject, however, do not assume that they will understand its specialized vocabulary. Instead, define key words or use everyday equivalents for technical terms.

What level of diction will your readers expect? Most readers expect standard diction in most writing; some prefer formal diction for some topics; others prefer informal diction for all topics. If formal diction suits your purpose, you should comply with readers' expectations by omitting slang, contractions, and regionalisms from your writing. If your purpose justifies informal diction, comply with readers' expectations by choosing words freely. Remember, too, that for some subjects, readers expect a well-chosen blend of formal and informal language, a combination often termed **moderate diction.** To answer questions about the level of particular words or phrases, refer to the Glossary of Usage starting on page 654, a general dictionary, or a dictionary of usage.

You cannot completely match word choices with readers' knowledge, needs, and expectations, but you should make an effort to analyze your audience and write in language that they will understand and appreciate.

EXERCISE 13.1 ❯ *Formal and informal diction*

The diction of the following sentences about the novel Native Son *is too informal. Revise the sentences to increase their formality.*

1. Many readers are grossed out when Bigger Thomas bashes the rat in the opening scene of the novel.

2. The Daltons, a filthy rich family, had made a bunch of money by ripping off poor tenants in slum housing.

3. Their daughter Mary and her left-wing friends were into hanging out in restaurants in black neighborhoods.

4. Bigger took off after he accidentally did Mary in.

5. Once the cops nabbed Bigger, he was put on trial and then sent up the river.

| 13b | Select words whose denotations and connotations match your meaning. |

Words are defined in two ways, by their denotations and by their connotations.

Denotations

Denotations are dictionary meanings—short, specific definitions. They present the explicit meanings of words and exclude the subtle shades of meaning that words acquire from use in specific contexts.

Connotations

Connotations are the secondary and sometimes emotional meanings of words. They suggest meaning beyond the explicit denotation. Connotations can create difficulties for beginning writers who do not consider the implied meanings of the words they choose. Make sure that the connotations of the words you use match your purpose.

Consider Connotations

Two words often share the same denotation (and hence are synonyms) but have distinct connotations. Connotations can be classified as positive, negative, or neutral.

Positive connotation

The *delegation* of students protested outside the administration building. (*Delegation* implies an orderly, duly constituted, and representative gathering.)

Negative connotation

The *mob* of students protested outside the administration building. (*Mob* suggests lack of control and implies a threat.)

Neutral connotation

The *group* of students protested outside the administration building. (*Group* simply denotes "a number of people.")

EXERCISE 13.2) Connotations

 Revise the following sentences to replace words whose connotations seem inappropriate.

1. Airport security has become restrictive in the last few years, as folks who travel a lot have discovered.

2. At every concourse in major airports, people dawdle in lines, waiting to have their carry-on luggage inspected.

3. At these security checkpoints, people sometimes get peeved about passing their stuff through scanning devices, but every once in a while, someone is flabbergasted when his or her luggage sets off the alarm.

4. The security guards interrogate people whose luggage sets off the alarm to see if they have a reasonable excuse, and then the checking continues.

5. Although these security checks are an annoyance, they help to keep air travel inviolate.

13c	**Select abstract or concrete words to suit your meaning.**

Abstract words name intangibles, such as concepts, qualities, or conditions: *truth, loyalty, laziness, freedom, poverty.* **Concrete words** name tangibles: *fire hydrant, bagel, razor, rabbit, silo.* For some purposes, abstract words effectively present general ideas. The vividness of concrete words, however, adds interest and specificity appropriate to all writing.

Abstract
Poverty demoralizes people.

Concrete
Being unable to pay bills, buy suitable clothing, feed one's children well, and own some small conveniences demoralizes parents who want comfortable homes for their families.

The following diagram illustrates the continuum of specificity.

Most General			**Most Specific**
←			→
Games	Card games	Wagering card games	Poker
Trees	Fruit trees	Apple trees	Granny Smith apple trees
Animals	Mammals	Marine mammals	Whales

Whales can be made more exact by specifying *blue whales, sperm whales,* or *killer whales.* Although you may not always have this many alternatives, choose the most specific word possible to clarify your meaning.

1. *Women* in *fiction* are sometimes shrewder than *men.*

2. *Heroines* in *novels* are sometimes shrewder than *heroes.*

3. *Romantic heroines* in *nineteenth-century novels* are sometimes shrewder than *their lovers.*

4. *Catherine* in <u>*Wuthering Heights*</u> is shrewder than *Heathcliff.*

Sometimes a generalization best suits your purpose, in which case the third sentence may be the best. However, do not forget the importance of specificity. Readers of the first sentence could easily and justifiably supply their own details, thinking wrongly, for instance, that the writer means that women in contemporary short stories are sometimes shrewder than their fathers. To avoid such misinterpretation, make your meaning clear by using specific diction.

EXERCISE 13.3) Specific words

The following sentences present general ideas. Clarify their meanings by replacing general words with specific ones.

1. Politics is expensive.

2. The crowd at the convention was big.

3. Family members of politicians often have personal problems.

4. The candidate won the election.

5. Television influences politics.

| 13d | Use the established forms of idioms. |

Idioms, groups of words that together establish an idiosyncratic meaning, are often illogical if examined word for word. For example, *break it up,* commonly understood to mean "stop fighting," does not make sense when examined one word at a time. *Break,* to split into two or more pieces, creates a visual image of fighters separating. *It,* though indefinite, clearly refers to the implied subject, *fight. Up* defies explanation unless it is considered part of the idiom *break up.* Other unanalyzable idioms include *pick up (the house), take a shower, fall in love,* and *catch a cold.* Such idioms have developed along with our language, and although they may not make literal sense, they are understood.

Not all idioms are equally acceptable in formal writing. If you use an idiom, use it carefully and use its established form. The correct use of many phrasal idioms, such as those in the following list, depends on using the correct preposition. If you are in doubt about which preposition to use, check the list or a dictionary.

243

Phrasal idioms

---

agree with (someone)

agree to (a proposal)

angry with (*not* angry at)

charge for (a purchase)

charge with (a crime)

die of/die from

differ with (meaning "to disagree")

differ from (meaning "to be unlike")

in search of (*not* in search for)

intend to (*not* intend on)

off (*not* off of)

plan to (*not* plan on)

similar to (*not* similar with)

sure to (*not* sure and)

to search for

try to (*not* try and)

type of (*not* type of a)

wait for (someone or something)

wait on (meaning "to serve")

Whenever you are confused about the meaning of an idiom, consult a dictionary.

EXERCISE 13.4) *Idioms*

Select the appropriate idioms for the following sentences.

1. The National Geographic Society (NGS), founded in 1888, is a (type of a/type of) organization with diverse interests and goals.

2. On the one hand, the NGS often goes (in search of/in search for) exotic flora and fauna to describe in articles and broadcasts.

3. On the other hand, NGS also (tries and/tries to) make Americans aware of simple but subtle differences between peoples of different cultures.

4. Although the format for NGS television programs does not (differ with/differ from) that of other nature documentaries, they are nonetheless uniformly more fascinating.

5. With more than 10.5 million members, NGS will be (sure to/sure and) flourish into the twenty-first century.

| 13e | Use slang and regionalisms selectively. |

Both **slang** and **regionalisms** are exclusive, informal vocabularies, intelligible to a restricted group. In the case of slang, the restriction is generally to a social, professional, or cultural group; in the case of regionalisms, the restriction is to a specific geographic area.

Slang tends to change rapidly and to be in use for only brief periods. In speech, slang can be refreshingly direct and shows that speakers are aware of current language trends. If the use of a slang expression becomes broad enough, the expression may be absorbed into acceptable written English. Until that happens, however, slang has little place in formal writing. Slang is so quickly dated and so informal, and its meaning is so

often inexact to those outside the originating group, that it
does not communicate very clearly.

> That class was *the pits*.   ("A waste," as in peach pits? "A cavity in
> the ground," as in the La Brea Tar Pits?)

> When I saw how far ahead I was, I felt *wicked*.   ("Evil"? Wicked
> good? Wicked bad?)

Regionalisms are understood within the bounds of a restricted geographic area, but beyond that area their meaning
becomes lost. Like slang, regionalisms should be avoided
because they can muddle communication.

> Early in November, we ordered the *tags* for our car.   (Although *tags*
> will be clear to readers from some areas of the East, use the more
> common expression *license plates* to ensure the understanding of
> readers from other areas.)

EXERCISE 13.5   ❭   Slang and regionalisms

*Make a list of five slang terms or phrases and five regionalisms in
current use. Then write two sentences for each one. In the first
sentence, use the slang or regionalism; in the second, translate
the slang or regionalism into standard English.*

Example:

The insurance plan to supplement Medicare was a *rip-off*.

The insurance plan to supplement Medicare was a *fraud*.

| 13f | ❭ | **Use euphemisms selectively.** |

Euphemisms are "nice" words substituted for specific words
whose connotations are negative, unpleasant, or unappealing.
Instead of saying that soldiers were *killed*, a press release might

say that they *gave their lives*. Instead of saying that people are being *fired*, a notice might say they are being *let go*. Instead of saying that a customer is *overweight*, a salesclerk might say that she is *full-figured*. Seldom fooled by euphemisms, readers instinctively supply the appropriate translation.

Euphemism	*Translation*
financial enticements	bribes
the oldest profession	prostitution
corporal punishment	spanking
placed in custody	arrested
hair-color enhancer	dye

Some euphemisms establish a buffer around painful feelings—as when *passed away* replaces *died*—but even this use should be infrequent.

EXERCISE 13.6 ⟩ *Euphemisms*

Revise the following sentences to eliminate euphemistic words and phrases.

1. Weddings are often not inexpensive displays by people and for people who fail to consider their less-than-genuine behavior.

2. Elaborate and expensive, many weddings must be financed through deferred-payment plans.

3. Even brides who are in the family way often wear traditional white bridal gowns.

4. Many less-than-honest people who do not attend worship services regularly insist on being married in houses of God.

5. Ironically, many of these marriages—begun with such elaborate
   display—end in marriage dissolutions.

Revising meaning and tone with a word processor

When you are working on a paper, use the word processor's "delete" and "insert" capabilities to adjust the diction.

Make changes as you type the draft. As you reread on
the screen, delete words that do not fit naturally in the
sentences.

Insert codes for later changes. If the right word does not
occur to you as you work, use a symbol such as ^ or ~
to mark the place. At a pause in your work, use the
"search" function to find the symbols and return to the
sentence to consider the appropriate word choice.

Make "hard-copy" changes. Print a copy of the paper,
examine your word choices, and then return to your
computer to delete ineffective words and substitute better ones.

14   Choosing Effective Words

Ineffective word choices—such as clichés, pretentious or sexist language, and jargon—weaken writing by distracting or irritating readers and by obscuring ideas. You need to be aware of and avoid such problems. This chapter addresses the most common difficulties.

Quick Reference

Avoid hackneyed or imprecise word choices that muddy writing and distract readers from central ideas.

❭ *Eliminate clichés and other trite expressions.*

❭ *Use words to clarify your meaning, not to impress readers; avoid pretentious language and jargon.*

❭ *Use figurative language to enliven and illuminate your writing; avoid overused, illogical, or mixed figures of speech.*

❭ *Avoid sexist language; it is often inaccurate and may be offensive.*

14a ❭   Avoid clichés and triteness.

A **cliché** is an overused expression that has lost its original inventiveness, surprise, and, often, meaning. **Triteness** describes words and phrases that have been overused: they are stale, uninteresting, and frequently vague.

Clichés

Readers finding clichés in your writing will assume that you did
not take the time to think through your ideas or consider original ways to express them.

Complete the following phrases.

last but not _____

beat around the _____

fit as a _____

in the final _____

red as a _____

Most people can supply the missing words easily. If you use
such phrases in your writing, readers will find them equally
predictable—and boring. Rather than relying on clichés in your
own writing, devise phrases that express your meaning exactly,
in your own words.

Triteness

Trite words and phrases have been used so often, and so
thoughtlessly, that they have lost all appeal and interest. If you
discover trite expressions in your writing, strike them out and
replace them with less predictable word choices that create
interest and clarify your ideas.

Trite

The report of the Educational Task Force was *very thorough*.
(*Thorough* is so common and used in so many contexts that it hardly clarifies the meaning of the sentence.)

Improved
The report of the Educational Task Force included a general pref-ace, a fifteen-chapter text, and twenty-seven appendixes presenting research data. (The use of details to explain the features of the report improves the clarity of the sentence.)

Eliminating triteness is especially easy to do on a word processor. Simply delete the trite word or phrase and insert a carefully chosen replacement. If you are aware that you overuse certain trite expressions, use the "search" function to find and replace them.

EXERCISE 14.1 ❱ *Clichés and trite expressions*

Revise the following sentences to eliminate clichés and trite expressions.

1. Some monuments have struck a chord with the American people and can remind each and every one of us of the value of public memorials.

2. The Statue of Liberty is an awe-inspiring national monu-ment, symbolizing how America opened its arms to European emigrants.

3. The simplicity of the Tomb of the Unknown Soldier and the low-key military display puts a lump in the throats of many visitors.

4. One out-of-the-ordinary monument, St. Louis' Gateway Arch, reaches to the sky in a sweeping curve of shiny stainless steel.

5. With its marble as smooth as glass, the Vietnam Memorial is a plain and simple monument honoring the tens of thousands of soldiers who gave their lives for their country.

| 14b | Avoid pretentious language. |

A rich and varied vocabulary is an asset, but the words used in any given piece of writing must be geared to its specific audience and purpose. Using **pretentious language** to impress rather than to communicate with readers is generally ineffective. Avoid stilted language, even in formal writing. Not only is pretentious diction dishonest, but it often makes simple ideas difficult to grasp and complicated ideas impossible to understand. If you do not translate pretentious diction into natural words, your readers have to do so.

Pretentious

> *Prior to* the purchase of the *abode,* the Enricos carefully *ruminated* about how *residential payments* would affect their *cash flow.* (The stilted word choices here, some poorly chosen synonyms and some jargon, require a translation.)

Natural

> *Before* the Enricos purchased the *house,* they carefully *thought* about how *mortgage payments* would affect their *finances.* (This sentence uses natural diction and is therefore easily understood on the first reading.)

Although a thesaurus, or a book of synonyms, may help you to find alternative ways of stating a point, it should be used carefully. Use only words that are a natural part of your vocabulary, avoid clichés, and never choose words whose connotations you do not understand. Using a thesaurus to find impressive or unusual words results in pretentious writing.

EXERCISE 14.2) Pretentious language

Revise the following paragraph to eliminate pretentious language and use language that is more natural. (Suggestion: Make this a personal narrative.)

When one participates in commencement ceremonies, one is often fraught with a mixture of emotions. One senses relief because one's time in high school is terminating. Conversely, one feels uncertain about what lies ahead. Some students will seek employment immediately, other students will approach matrimony, and yet other students will pursue additional academic studies. For this diversity of students, commencement exercises symbolize an uncertain transmutation in their lives.

| 14c | Avoid jargon.

Jargon is the technical vocabulary of a specialized group. Doctors, mechanics, weather forecasters, teachers, carpenters, and publishers all have special words that they use in certain contexts. When writing is directed to a specific group, the use of the group's jargon may be acceptable (perhaps even necessary). When you write for a wide audience, however, translate jargon into common terms.

Jargon	*Translation*
urban open space *(city planning)*	a city park
precipitation *(weather forecasting)*	rain, snow, sleet
telephone surveillance *(law enforcement)*	wiretapping
discourse community *(communication)*	audience
merchantable dwelling *(real estate)*	a house that will sell

Jargon

The city council recommends a systematic program of greening for our arterials as a means to revitalize our declining streetscape.

Translation

The city council recommends that we plant trees along our main streets to make them appear less neglected.

EXERCISE 14.3 ❭ Pretentious diction and jargon

Translate these pretentious, jargon-laden sentences into natural, clear writing.

1. An excessive proportion of American citizenry improvidently pass their days ignoring quotidian dangers to health.

2. The abundance of vehicular collisions attests to the fact that the people of the United States of America are oblivious to safety-inducing guidelines for automobile management.

3. The numbers of persons who imbibe an excess of distilled spirits is also a depression-inducing statistic.

4. The inhalation of toxic fumes from smoking materials, although prohibited in most business establishments, continues to have a negative impact on the health aspect of the male and female population sectors.

5. The personal and private ownership and use of firearms and related paraphernalia account for the accidental demise of scores of people in each twelve-month period.

| 14d | ❭ | **Use figures of speech cautiously.** |

Figures of speech may be single words, phrases, or longer expressions. They add vitality to writing, most often by making unexpected or suggestive connections between dissimilar things. Metaphors and similes are the most common and useful figures of speech.

Metaphors compare two things, one familiar and one less familiar, to provide a useful or interesting association or insight.

> Dr. Mantera's criticism of the proposal was all thunder and no lightning. (The implication is that the criticism was mere noise with no illumination or insight.)

Similes are direct comparisons using the connectives *like, as,* or *as if.*

> Rob accelerated his car, shifting lanes quickly and rounding corners at high speed, as if he were making the final lap at the Indianapolis 500.

Original and apt figures of speech can enliven your writing, but they should be used to illuminate and clarify your ideas, not to decorate them. Be careful to avoid clichés.

Effective metaphor

> Ron, a *modern Tom Sawyer,* enjoys harmless trickery and mild adventure.

Ineffective metaphor

> After the laughter stopped, Bernice gave Rinaldo an *icy* stare. (The modifier is a cliché.)

Effective simile

> Cleo is *like a Duracell battery:* she's always starting something, and it lasts longer than we ever expect.

Ineffective simile

> Darryl's grades are solid *as a rock.* ("Solid as a rock" is a cliché.)

Extended or multiple related figures of speech must present a uniform impression, drawing on logically consistent images, locales, experiences, or circumstances. Without this consistency, the image is confused—often laughably so.

Confusingly mixed

Like an agile deer, the politician leaped into the fray. (Agile deer do leap, but they are shy animals unlikely to seek conflict. Moreover, "leaped into the fray" is a cliché.)

Logically linked

Like an agile deer, the politician leaped over obstacles to the proposal. (The agile deer leaping over obstacles is a logical, consistent image.)

EXERCISE 14.4   ❭   *Figures of speech*

 Revise the ineffective figures of speech in the following sentences.

1. Like good soldiers, athletes get down to the work that training sessions require and rise to the occasion.

2. Swimmers fly through lap after lap during practices, building the tireless endurance necessary in races.

3. Like kangaroos, basketball players jump for balls and then fire them down the court, hoping to hone skills to use in games.

4. With catlike speed, sprinters shoot from starting blocks over and over again, trying to perfect an opening move that will put them miles above the rest.

5. Like trains speeding down the tracks, football linesmen practice rushing and tackling, leaving other players in their wake.

| 14e | Avoid sexist language. |

Sexist language implies, generally through choices of key nouns and pronouns, that the subject applies only to males or only to females. Because it fails to reflect the diversity of contemporary society, sexist language is narrow-minded and inaccurate.

Avoid using sex-specific pronouns when the antecedent is not sex-specific and avoid nouns that arbitrarily or from empty tradition restrict meaning to one sex or the other. When choosing nouns, learn to notice the subtle—and sometimes not so subtle—implications of your choices.

Sexist

A psychiatrist is bound by professional oath to keep his patients' records confidential. (Many psychiatrists are women, so this statement is not accurate.)

Nonsexist

A psychiatrist is bound by professional oath to keep his or her patients' records confidential. (The use of *his or her* eliminates the sexist bias in the sentence.)

Nonsexist

Psychiatrists are bound by professional oath to keep their patients' records confidential. (The use of plural forms is often an easy way to avoid sexist language.)

Sexist

According to family records, my forefathers came to the United States from France in 1806. (Fore*mothers* had to come too, or there would not have been any children.)

Nonsexist

According to family records, my ancestors came to the United States from France in 1806.

EXERCISE 14.5 ⟩ *Sexist language*

The following passage was written in 1872, when sensitivity to sexist language was not common. Rewrite the passage to eliminate sexist language—but do not change the meaning of the passage.

The blight which threatens theoretical culture has only begun to frighten modern man, and he is groping uneasily for remedies out of the storehouse of his experience, without having any real conviction that these remedies will avail against disaster. In the meantime, there have arisen certain men of genius who, with admirable circumspection and consequence, have used the arsenal of science to demonstrate the limitations of science and of the cognitive faculty itself. They have authoritatively rejected science's claim to universal validity and to the attainment of universal goals and exploded for the first time the belief that men may plumb the universe by means of the law of causation. —Friedrich Nietzsche, *The Birth of Tragedy*

| 14f ⟩ | Avoid neologisms and archaisms. |

Neologisms, recently coined words or word forms, appear in current speech (and in some journalistic and technical writing) and then very often fade away. In formal writing, avoid using new terms unless no other word can express your meaning.

Some neologisms are so expressive and apt that they become widely used and universally acceptable. *Stereo, fallout,* and *refrigerator* were once newly coined words that have long since become standard.

Questionable

Access from one Internet site to another is simplified through a *hot connect*. (*Internet,* once a neologism, is now standard. *Hot connect* is still jargon, vague to the uninformed, and colloquial.)

Better

Access from one Internet site to another is simplified through a *direct electronic connection.*

Archaisms, words once in common use but no longer standard, seem affected and disruptive in contemporary writing. Words no longer in use—like *yon* ("over there") or *betwixt* ("between")—or words no longer used in a given sense—like *save* in the sense of "except"—make writing artificial and pretentious.

Artificial

We adults sat and reminisced *whilst* the children played along the shore. (No one says *whilst* anymore, and no one should write it.)

Natural

We adults sat and reminisced *while* the children played along the shore.

EXERCISE 14.6 〉 *Neologisms and archaic words*

Revise the following sentences to eliminate words or phrases that are either too new or too old to be standard usage.

1. Methinks that romance novels deserve more attention from serious readers than they have often received.

2. Betwixt the covers of romance novels as varied as *Wuthering Heights* and *The Lady and the Highwayman,* readers will find quickly paced stories of intrigue and love.

3. The heroines and heroes of these novels are ofttimes innocent, sincere, and trusting people whose lives are threatened by erstwhile friends who are really enemies.

4. With their inherent reliance on historical context, these infotainment novels provide readers with knowledge of past societies, as well as reading pleasure.

5. Although the reading of romance novels does not require much intellectual input from readers, these books provide innocent pleasure and distraction.

Choosing effective words with a word processor

Beyond general uses of word-processing programs to delete and substitute words, consider these specific approaches:

Replace neologisms. As you check a paper by using a spell-checking program, the program will highlight words not found in its dictionary. Neologisms, because they are new and in limited use, will not appear. The spell checker will draw your attention to these words, and you can then decide whether they or standard substitutes best serve your purposes.

Check for sexist use of pronouns. Use the "search" command to look for masculine pronouns: *he, him, his,* and *himself.* When the antecedent is not exclusively male, change the pronoun to *he or she, him or her,* and so on, or change the antecedent, pronoun, and verb to plural forms.

GRAMMAR

15 Fragments

Fragments are capitalized and punctuated as if they were sentences, but they are not sentences. They may be phrases lacking subjects or verbs, or they may be subordinate clauses. Four strategies for correcting fragments appear in sections 15a and 15b.

Although fragments are common in speech, notes, rough drafts, and writing that imitates speech, formal writing generally requires complete and grammatical sentences that state ideas fully. The use of fragments for special effect is discussed in section 15c.

Quick Reference

Fragments distract readers and shift their attention away from your ideas to the mechanics of your writing. To avoid this, follow these suggestions:

❭ *Make sure that your sentences contain subjects and verbs, the basic sentence elements.*

❭ *Be sure to use subordinating conjunctions in complex and compound-complex sentences, not in subordinate-clause fragments.*

❭ *Use intentional fragments selectively for special effect, remembering that excessive use distracts and annoys readers.*

| 15a | Revise fragments that are phrases. |

Correct fragments that lack subjects or verbs by supplying the missing element or by combining the fragment with a complete sentence.

Fragments Lacking Subjects

Fragments without subjects may be verb phrases (free-standing predicates and complements); they may also be verbal phrases (phrases using gerunds, participles, and infinitives [see pages 172–76]). Eliminate these fragments by adding a subject or by joining the fragment to an appropriate sentence.

Fragment

    Brian is addicted to reading mystery novels. Reads one a week.

Complete

    Brian is addicted to reading mystery novels. *He* reads one a week. (A subject pronoun has been added.)

Complete

    Brian, who is addicted to mystery novels, reads one a week. (The fragment has been joined to a related sentence.)

Fragment

    Jay has one ambition. To travel around the world.

Complete

    Jay's one ambition *is* to travel around the world. (The infinitive phrase is joined to the sentence.)

Fragments Lacking Verbs

Fragments without verbs are usually subjects and related modifiers, appositives, or absolute phrases. Correct these fragments by adding a verb or joining the appositive or absolute phrase to a nearby sentence.

Fragment

Rachel, an avid collector of china figurines. She pays eighty-five dollars for extra insurance coverage.

Complete

Rachel *is* an avid collector of china figurines. She pays eighty-five dollars for extra insurance coverage.   (A verb has been added.)

Complete

Rachel, an avid collector of china figurines, *pays* eighty-five dollars for extra insurance coverage.   (The fragment has been joined to a related sentence.)

 Use your word processor to correct phrasal fragments quickly and easily by inserting subjects or verbs. Be sure to change capitalization and punctuation as required by the new sentence.

15b ⟩ **Revise fragments that are subordinate clauses.**

A subordinate clause must be joined to an independent clause to form a grammatical sentence. Correct subordinate-clause fragments by dropping the subordinating conjunction to form a simple sentence or by joining the subordinate clause to one or more independent clauses to form a complex or compound-complex sentence.

Fragment

Some students have to postpone starting college. Because the cost of attending has risen.

Complete

Some students have to postpone starting college. The cost of attending has risen. (The subordinating conjunction has been dropped.)

Complete

Some students have to postpone starting college because the cost of attending has risen. (Here the subordinate clause becomes part of a complex sentence.)

Complete

Because the cost of attending college has risen, some students have to postpone starting.

 Your word processor will help you to join phrases and subordinate clauses to related sentences quickly and easily. Use the "cut" and "paste" features and experiment with ways to reposition these groups of words to form new expressive, grammatical sentences.

| 15c | Use fragments sparingly for special effect. |

Fragments can be effective and acceptable, even in final drafts, when they are used to isolate and thus emphasize a key word or phrase. Use this strategy selectively to achieve emphasis or to supply an answer to a question.

G, PG, R, X. These symbols are used to classify films and to restrict the audiences that see them. Although the coding system represents an admirable effort to protect children, does it work? No. Many parents disregard the implied advice of the rating system, and few theater owners adhere to its guidelines when selling tickets.

EXERCISE 15.1 ❯ *Fragments*

Eliminate the fragments in the following paragraph by adding subjects or verbs or by combining the fragments with complete sentences.

The National Board of Teaching Standards was formed to address matters of teacher training and certification. Because of inconsistencies that exist among states. Some states require prospective teachers to take a preprofessional skills test. To establish the reading, writing, and mathematical skills of future teachers. But not others. All states require expertise in content areas. Approximates that of traditional majors in each subject area. States require additional work in educational theory and practice. Usually fifteen to twenty semester hours of work. These pedagogical courses, ones emphasizing general principles of teaching and general patterns of learning. No matter how theoretically sound these courses may be, inconsistencies exist. Since states establish their requirements individually. As a result, teachers moving from one state to the other may not be fully prepared to meet requirements. Future teachers need the coordinated efforts of state departments of education. To develop uniform educational programs. Especially with prospects of taking the National Teacher's Exam.

EXERCISE 15.2 ❯ *Fragments*

The following paragraph includes a number of fragments. Some are intended for special emphasis, but others are clearly grammatical errors. Correct the ineffective fragments and explain why the others should remain.

New York. St. Louis. Knoxville. New Orleans. Los Angeles. These cities have all hosted those pretentious, glorious, overly expensive, and enjoyable activities known as world's fairs. Filled with exhibits, amusements, and restaurants. World's fairs offer people a chance to learn about the world while enjoying themselves. At these large fairs, nations from around the world build pavilions to showcase their national achievements. Often sending examples of their best technology, art, and historical treasures. Dancers, singers, and musicians. Enjoy seeing native costumes and folk dances that illustrate the diversity of the world's cultures. Sometimes, even specialties of individual fairs have become common later on. St. Louis, the city where the ice-cream cone was invented. It has since become a favorite treat worldwide. World's fairs, originally planned to "bring the world closer together." But do they continue to serve this original purpose? Not really. Because people now travel by airplane and can see the countries of the world. They see much more than can be seen in national exhibits at world's fairs.

Comma Splices and Fused Sentences

Comma splices and fused sentences contain two or more independent clauses that are not properly punctuated. In a **comma splice** (also called a **comma fault**), the independent clauses are incorrectly joined with only a comma. In a **fused sentence** (also called a **run-on sentence**), independent clauses are placed one after the other, with no punctuation.

Correct comma splices and fused sentences by changing the punctuation or structure of the sentence.

Quick Reference

Comma splices and fused sentences are never acceptable in writing, because they incorrectly merge ideas.

❯ *Use a period to separate the independent clauses in comma splices or fused sentences.*

❯ *Use a semicolon, a comma and a coordinating conjunction, or a subordinating conjunction (and a comma if necessary) to join independent clauses.*

❯ *Remember that conjunctive adverbs may be used only within independent clauses or sentences, not to join them as coordinating or subordinating conjunctions do.*

16a ❯ **Separate the independent clauses in a comma splice or a fused sentence by using a period to form two sentences.**

Comma splice

Many artists and musicians are extremely fashion conscious, they view their clothes as a form of self-expression.

Separate sentences

Many artists and musicians are extremely fashion conscious. They view their clothes as a form of self-expression.

| 16b | Join the independent clauses in a comma splice or a fused sentence by using a semicolon to form a compound sentence. |

Fused sentence

In the 1950s, members of English departments felt their programs were too diverse they split into departments of literature, composition, linguistics, and speech communication.

Compound sentence

In the 1950s, members of English departments felt their programs were too diverse; they split into departments of literature, composition, linguistics, and speech communication.

| 16c | Correct a comma splice or a fused sentence by using a comma and a coordinating conjunction to form a compound sentence or by using a subordinating conjunction to form a complex sentence. |

Use the coordinating conjunctions (*and, but, for, nor, or, so,* and *yet*) with a comma to link independent clauses grammatically to form a compound sentence. Use subordinating conjunctions (*although, because, since, while,* and others) to join independent clauses to form complex or compound-complex sentences.

Comma splice

The sky diver hurtled toward the ground, she felt no fear.

Compound sentence
  The sky diver hurtled toward the ground, but she felt no fear.

Fused sentence
  NASA delayed the shuttle launch the ground crew wanted to check
  the on-board computers again.

Complex sentence
  NASA delayed the shuttle launch because the ground crew wanted
  to check the on-board computers again.   (When the subordinate
  clause ends the sentence, a comma is unnecessary if the meaning is
  clear.)

Fused sentence
  Many cabinet members work for only four to eight years with the
  president they continue to work in Washington as consultants to
  major firms.

Complex sentence
  Although many cabinet members work for only four to eight years
  with the president, they continue to work in Washington as consultants to major firms.   (When the subordinate clause begins the sentence, a comma is required.)

| 16d | **Do not mistake conjunctive adverbs for coordinating or subordinating conjunctions.** |

Conjunctive adverbs (*besides, furthermore, however, nevertheless, still, then, therefore,* and others) logically connect ideas,
but they do not link independent clauses grammatically as
coordinating conjunctions do. When a conjunctive adverb
appears in a comma splice or fused sentence, correct the sentence by using a period or semicolon to separate the independent clauses.

Comma splice
Corporate mergers are often like marriages, however, some unfriendly ones are like abductions.

Correct
Corporate mergers are often like marriages. However, some unfriendly ones are like abductions.

Correct
Corporate mergers are often like marriages; however, some unfriendly ones are like abductions.   (The use of the semicolon establishes a closer link between the ideas.)

EXERCISE 16.1 ⟩ *Comma splices and fused sentences*

Correct these faulty sentences by changing their punctuation or structure.

1. *Rock 'n'roll* is a generic term used to describe a wide variety of musical styles, nonetheless, each musical style remains distinct.

2. The term *pop music* was coined in the 1950s, it describes music that cuts across socio-ethnic lines and appeals to a wide audience.

3. *Acid rock* describes the amplified, electronic music of mid-1960s artists in this subgenre of rock music were often part of the counterculture of drugs.

4. *Disco's* emphasis on highly synthesized electronic music with an insistent rhythm made it popular dance music, nevertheless, its popularity faded in only a few years.

5. Black American music, sometimes called *soul music* and sometimes *rhythm and blues,* developed from gospel music its acceptance in conservative white culture attests to the power of music to break down barriers.

6. With its emphasis on shock value, *punk rock* created a brief sensation in the world of music people soon grew tired of being shocked by performers who often lacked musical skill.

EXERCISE 16.2 〉 Comma splices and fused sentences

Correct the comma splices and fused sentences in the following paragraph by adding periods, commas and coordinating conjunctions, semicolons, or subordinating conjunctions.

Book censorship in American high schools has become a standard practice these days, individuals and groups have applied pressure to school boards everywhere. The books that have been censored range widely in subject they range widely in literary quality as well. No book seems to be beyond the reach of book censors. Books treating sexual situations, like *A Farewell to Arms,* have been banned, books that contain questionable language, like *The Catcher in the Rye,* have been banned, too. *The Grapes of Wrath* has been censored in some communities because of its presentation of socialist ideology, *Lord of the Flies* has been removed from libraries because of its violence. Even a book like *The Adventures of Huckleberry Finn* is now being brought into question it has racially demeaning dialect. The American Library Association has come to the defense of these books, however that has not kept them on bookshelves and reading lists in many American high schools.

Revising comma splices and fused sentences with a word processor.

Use a word processor to revise comma splices and fused sentences, taking advantage of its ability to make small changes that do not require the retyping of whole sentences.

Separate faulty sentences. Divide comma splices and fused sentences into separate simple sentences. Be sure to change capitalization and punctuation.

Insert coordinating conjunctions to join independent clauses correctly.

Join clauses with subordinating conjunctions. Use the "cut" and "paste" functions to experiment and find the best placement for clauses and coordinating conjunctions. You may also need to add commas.

17 Agreement

Subjects and verbs must agree in number; pronouns and antecedents must agree in number and gender.

Quick Reference

Errors in subject-verb or pronoun-antecedent agreement are easy to correct if you remember these basic principles.

❭ *Verbs must agree in number with the subject of the clause or sentence. Do not be misled by intervening words.*

❭ *Let the meaning of the subject (singular or plural) guide your choice of verbs; watch especially compound subjects with* and *or* or, *indefinite pronouns, collective nouns, and plural words with a singular meaning.*

❭ *Make sure that pronouns have clear antecedents with which they agree in both number and gender.*

❭ *Let the intended number of the antecedent guide your choice of pronouns; watch especially compound subjects with* and *or* or, *indefinite pronouns, collective nouns, and plural words with a singular meaning.*

17a ❭ Subjects and verbs must agree in number.

Verbs agree with the subject of the sentence, not with intervening words. Words that separate subjects and verbs, especially nouns that serve as objects of prepositions, should not influence your choice of verbs.

The *swallows* of Capistrano *are* becoming noticeably less predictable. (*Capistrano,* a singular noun in a prepositional phrase,
does not affect verb choice.)

Compound Subjects Joined by *And*

Compound subjects joined by *and* require plural verbs.

```
        compound subj.     plural verb
```
The defendant and *her counsel were* both angered by the verdict.

However, compound subjects that are seen as one unit are
singular and require a singular verb.

"Tragedy and triumph" describes Britain's lonely resistance to Hitler
during the grim days of 1940.

Subjects Joined by *Or, Nor, Either . . . Or,* or *Neither . . . Nor*

Or, nor, and so on do not indicate multiple subjects; they indicate alternative subjects. The verb, therefore, should agree with
the number of the subjects considered individually.

Singular subjects
  Either walking or running strengthens the heart. (Walking
  strengthens; running *strengthens.*)

Plural subjects
  Recordings or books as gifts *please* most people. (Recordings
  please; books *please.*)

When a compound subject contains both plural and singular
elements, the verb agrees with the nearer element.

Singular and plural elements
  Neither the designer nor the *engineers like* the prototype.

Plural and singular elements

Neither the engineers nor the *designer likes* the prototype.

When a singular noun follows a plural noun in a compound subject, the required singular verb, though grammatically correct, may seem awkward. If a sentence seems awkward, revise it.

The prototype satisfies neither the engineers nor the designer.

Indefinite Pronouns

Indefinite pronouns (*anyone, each, either, everybody, none, someone,* and others) have no specific antecedents. Some, such as *both* and *all,* are always plural and require plural verbs, but most are singular and require singular verbs. Be especially careful using pronouns like *everyone* or *everybody,* which require singular verbs even though *every-* sounds plural; *-one* or *-body* should guide you.

Somebody attends to the correspondence while she is gone.

Both assign papers during the first week of class.

Everyone brings her or his book to class on Friday.

Every and *each* used as adjectives require singular verbs, even when the subject is compound.

Every man, woman, and child *was* evacuated before nightfall. (*Every* emphasizes the people individually, so a singular verb is appropriate.)

Each actor and musician *was* asked to stand to be acknowledged. (*Each* emphasizes individuals and requires a singular verb.)

Collective Nouns

Collective nouns stressing group unity require singular verbs; collective nouns stressing the individuality of group members require plural verbs.

Group unity
The *committee votes* by a show of hands. (The committee as a whole follows this procedure.)

Individuality of group members
The Supreme Court act according to their individual consciences. (Each member acts separately, so the plural form is correct.)

If collective nouns stressing individuality sound awkward with plural verbs, revise the sentence by including "members of" or a similar word or phrase that clearly requires a plural verb.

The Supreme Court justices act according to their individual consciences.

Expletive Constructions

Expletive constructions (*here is, here are, there is, there are, there was,* and *there were*) depend for meaning on the noun complement (the noun that follows the construction); the verb in the expletive phrase must agree in number with the noun. A singular noun requires *is;* a plural noun requires *are.*

Here *is* the first *chapter* of my forthcoming novel.

There *are* many unimaginative *programs* on television.

 Your word processor can help you locate and check your uses of expletive constructions. Use the "search" function to find *here is, here are, there is, there are, there was,* and *there were.* Make sure that the verb in each expletive agrees with its noun complement.

Relative Clauses

The relative pronouns (*who, which,* and *that*), when used as the subject of a clause, agree in number with their antecedents.

> Flooding in the spring is a *threat* that *requires* our attention. (*That* refers to *threat,* a singular predicate noun. Consequently, the relative clause requires a singular verb.)

> People once believed in the *pseudo-sciences* of physiognomy and astrology, which *have* now lost their credibility. (*Which* refers to *pseudo-sciences,* a plural object of a preposition. The verb in the relative clause must, therefore, be plural.)

Linking Verbs

Linking verbs agree with the number of the subject, not the number of the predicate noun.

> A major *expense* of operating a school *is* salaries for administrators, teachers, and custodians. (Although *salaries* is plural, the subject of the sentence is *expense,* a singular noun. Therefore, the verb must also be singular.)

Plural Nouns with Singular Meanings

Plural nouns such as *news, politics, electronics,* and *mumps* often have singular meanings. When used in a singular sense, they require singular verbs.

Fractions, measurements, money, time, weight, and volume considered as single units also require singular verbs.

Plural noun
> *Geriatrics* successfully *discredits* the prejudice that senility is inevitable in the elderly. (*Geriatrics* is a single discipline and requires a singular verb.)

Plural unit

> *Six hundred dollars seems* a reasonable price.   (The dollar amount, considered *one* price, requires a singular verb.)

Common exceptions to this principle are *scissors* and *trousers*. Though units, they are considered plural. When used with the phrase *a pair of,* however, *pair* dominates and requires a singular verb.

> The *scissors need* sharpening.   (The logic is that scissors have two functional parts, making the plural verb appropriate.)

> This *pair* of scissors *needs* sharpening.   (The word *pair* emphasizes that the parts act as a single unit, making the singular verb necessary.)

Titles

Even when the words in a title are plural, the title of a single work requires a singular verb.

> *Leaves of Grass illustrates* the best and worst characteristics of nineteenth-century American verse.   (*Leaves of Grass* is the title of one long poem, so a singular verb is required.)

Words Used as Words

Words used as words require singular verbs. This rule applies even when the word discussed is plural.

> *Media* is often inaccurately *substituted* for *medium*.   (*Media,* a plural noun, requires a singular verb when discussed as a word.)

> In news broadcasts, *persons has become* a standard but annoying substitute for the word *people*.   (*Persons,* a plural noun, requires a singular verb when discussed as a word.)

EXERCISE 17.1   ⟩   *Subject-verb agreement*

Select the verb that maintains subject-verb agreement.

1. Archaeologists (studies/study) the buildings, tools, and other artifacts of ancient cultures.

2. Every archaeologist, especially field researchers, (know/knows)
of a historic site ruthlessly desecrated by treasure-seekers.

3. Despite international agreements, unscrupulous museums or a
wealthy private collector (compete/competes) for every major
artistic discovery, stolen or not.

4. But laws and international policing (reduce/reduces) yearly the
number of destroyed sites and stolen artifacts.

5. Excavations—better controlled than ever by teams of university
archaeologists, students, local workers, and national representatives—(proceed/proceeds) slowly these days, avoiding the damage inflicted by yesterday's "grave robbers."

6. *Digs* (is/are) the current jargon used to describe excavation sites.

7. Recent decades (has seen/have seen) few finds of the historical
significance of the discovery of Tutankhamen's tomb in 1922, but
research in various locales (continue/continues).

8. For archaeologists, five or ten years (seem/seems) a reasonable
time to work at a single site, so new finds will be made—but
more slowly than in the past.

EXERCISE 17.2   ⟩   *Subject-verb agreement*

*The following paragraph contains many errors in subject-
verb agreement. Correct the misused verbs and then draw
arrows to the subjects with which each verb agrees.*

There is more and more adults attending college at a later age. Their motives, either to change careers or to get the education they missed, varies. Anyone walking on a college campus see students in their thirties, forties, fifties, and even sixties carrying books and talking with friends. Almost every class and laboratory now include at least one of these "nontraditional" students. Because their home and job situations and their preparedness differs from those of eighteen- to twenty-two-year-olds, these students face problems that surprises a younger student. Some of these adults organizes their schooling around full-time jobs. Others care for families, as well as attends class. Nobody going to college and getting a degree find it easy, but an adult student with adult responsibilities have extra problems to cope with. As this situation becomes more common, everyone adjust, however, a process that already have begun. Even the media recognize this trend in American education. With humor and sympathy, the television show *Mad about You* provide insights into the problems adults face when attending college. Who knows? Given a chance today, maybe even Lucy Ricardo or John Walton might enroll in a class or two.

| 17b | **Pronouns and their antecedents must agree in number and gender.** |

Singular antecedents (the words to which pronouns refer) require singular pronouns; plural antecedents require plural pronouns.

sing.
antecedent
sing.
pronoun

Genghis Khan ruled *his* vast empire with great cruelty.

plural
antecedent
plural
pronoun

Children need encouragement and guidance from *their* parents.

Pronouns must also agree with the gender of their antecedents.

fem.   *fem.*
antecedent   *pronoun*

Queen Elizabeth II rules *her* empire as a constitutional monarch.

Plural pronouns do not specify gender, but singular pronouns specify masculine, feminine, or neuter gender.

Pronoun Forms

	Subjective	*Objective*	*Possessive*	*Reflexive*
Masculine	he	him	his	himself
Feminine	she	her	hers	herself
Neuter	it	it	its	itself

Pronoun-Antecedent Agreement and Sexist Language

The masculine pronouns (*he* and its variations) were once acceptable substitutes for antecedents whose gender was undetermined and thus might be either male or female. This usage is unacceptable today, even in formal writing, because it excludes women without justification and consequently reinforces stereotypes.

To avoid this problem, use plural antecedents and pronouns when possible or rephrase the sentence. Do not use a plural pronoun like *their* with a singular antecedent; this creates a problem in pronoun-antecedent agreement. Another possible solution, using pronouns in pairs (*he or she, his or hers, he/she,* and so on) should be used sparingly, since it can lead to distracting repetition and awkward rhythm in sentences.

Sexist

A good *surgeon* carefully explains procedures to *his* patients.

Nonsexist but incorrect

A good *surgeon* carefully explains procedures to *their* patients. (The plural *their* does not agree with the singular *surgeon*.)

Nonsexist and correct

Good *surgeons* carefully explain procedures to *their* patients. (Here a plural noun is used with a plural pronoun.)

Nonsexist and correct

Good *surgeons* carefully explain procedures to patients.   (Here the possessive pronoun is omitted without substantial loss of meaning.)

Nonsexist and correct

A good *surgeon* carefully explains procedures to *his or her* patients.

To express generalizations based on individual experiences, use a specific antecedent instead of a general noun. That, in turn, will dictate a specific pronoun choice and help you to avoid sexist language.

Dr. Knepper, like all good surgeons, carefully explains procedures to his patients.

Compound Antecedents Joined by *And*

Compound antecedents joined by *and* require plural pronouns.

compound antecedent	*plural pronoun*

Female *whales* and *dolphins* fiercely protect *their* young.

Antecedents Joined by *Or, Nor, Either . . . Or,* or *Neither . . . Nor*

Compound subjects joined by these words present alternative, not multiple, subjects, so pronouns refer to each subject individually.

Singular antecedents
> *Neither Gladstone nor Disraeli* graciously accepted criticism of *his* plans for the British government.   (Gladstone/*his*; Disraeli/*his*)

Plural antecedents
> Did *the Greeks or the Romans* consider Zeus *their* principal god? (Greeks/*their*; Romans/*their*)

When part of a compound antecedent is singular and part is plural, the pronoun agrees with the nearer antecedent.

Singular and plural antecedents
> The dean or the *students* must modify *their* terms.   (students/*their*)

If the construction sounds awkward, place the singular noun first or consider rewriting the sentence.

Correct but awkward
> The students or the *dean* must modify *her* terms.   (dean/*her*)

Better
> If the *dean* will not change *her* terms, the *students* will have to change *theirs*.   (dean/*her*; students/*theirs*)

Indefinite Pronouns as Antecedents

Indefinite pronouns (*anyone, each, either, everybody, none,* and others) are usually singular in meaning and take singular pronouns. However, some indefinite pronouns (*all, most, some,* and others) are plural in meaning and take plural pronouns. Let the number of the indefinite pronoun guide you.

> *Anyone* who works as a war correspondent risks *his or her* life frequently.   (*Anyone* refers to people one at a time, as does the pronoun cluster *his or her.*)

> *All* signed the petition, and then *their* regional representative sent it to national headquarters.   (*All* refers to the signers in the aggregate, so the plural *their* is correct.)

Collective Nouns

When collective nouns stress group unity, they take singular pronouns; when collective nouns stress the group as a collection of individuals, they take plural pronouns.

Group unity
> The *audience* showed *its* approval by applauding loudly.   (The audience is perceived as a single unit, creating a unified response.)

Individuality within the group
> The *audience* raised *their* voices in song.   (This sentence stresses the many voices of the audience members.)

EXERCISE 17.3 **❭** *Pronoun-antecedent agreement*

Insert appropriate pronouns in the following sentences.

1. Greeks, Romans, Egyptians, Indians, and virtually every other civilized group had one or more methods of keeping _____ dwellings cool in summer months.

2. For example, all of these peoples hung water-soaked mats in _____ doorways to develop cooling moisture.

3. Leonardo da Vinci, with _____ usual inventiveness, created the first mechanical fan in about 1500, _____ power provided by running water.

4. The 1838 British House of Commons was the first to enjoy systematic control of ventilation and humidity during _____ sessions.

5. Neither Alfred Wolff (in 1902) nor Willis Carrier (in 1911) realized the impact _____ work would have on later generations.

6. After 1931, a passenger riding on the Baltimore & Ohio railroad could travel to _____ destination in air-conditioned comfort.

7. When Stuart Cramer first used the phrase _air conditioning_ in 1906, _____ almost certainly didn't know that _____ newly coined term would be in universal use today.

8. Few people who live in temperate climates or who work in high-rise buildings would want to give up _____ air conditioning in the summer.

EXERCISE 17.4 ⟩ Pronoun-antecedent agreement

Most pronouns in the following paragraph have been omitted. Insert appropriate pronouns, maintaining correct pronoun-antecedent agreement.

Everyone who works in the United States must pay _____ income taxes on or before April 15. An employee of a traditional business has _____ taxes withdrawn in each pay period and at the end of the year receives _____ yearly statement, the W2 form. Neither employees nor the employer can decide how _____ tax accounts will be handled, but employees determine what percentage of taxes will be taken from _____ wages. For a self-employed taxpayer, the procedure for determining _____ taxes is not so clear. Artists, writers, freelance contractors, and other people whose incomes fluctuate must estimate _____ incomes for the year and pay _____ taxes in installments. Anyone who has ever tried to estimate how productive _____ will be in the next year can appreciate the difficulty a self-employed person has in estimating how much _____ will owe at the end of the year. In the past, the self-employed were granted some leniency in paying _____ taxes. However, in 1987, in spite of objections from some of _____ constituents, Congress voted to penalize people whose estimated tax payments were less than 90 percent of _____ taxes due.

Maintaining agreement with a word processor

Use the computer's capabilities to discover and correct errors in subject-verb and pronoun-antecedent agreement.

Locate conjunctions. Use the "search" function to locate *and, or,* and related conjunctions. Check for agreement problems.

Check pronouns and antecedents. Use the "search" function to locate specific pronouns. Once you have located them, check the sentence to make sure that the antecedent and pronoun are correctly matched in number and gender. If they are not, change either the pronoun or the antecedent. Check masculine pronouns carefully to avoid sexist use.

Revise agreement errors. Use the "delete" and "insert" capabilities to change verbs and pronouns that do not agree with their subjects or antecedents.

Experiment with solutions to agreement errors. Convert all nouns to plurals, for example, to avoid problems with sexist use of pronouns.

18 Pronoun Case

The **case** of a pronoun indicates the pronoun's grammatical relationship to the other words in the sentence. Pronoun case is indicated by changes in form (*I, me,* or *mine,* for example) or by changes in position in the sentence, as in the following example.

```
subj.      obj.  poss.
case       case  case
 |          |     |
 I gave them his address.
```

> ### Quick Reference
>
> *Follow these rules and suggestions to avoid problems with pronoun case.*
>
> ❯ *Personal pronouns used as subjects in clauses and sentences require the subjective case (*I, he, we, *and* they, *for example); pronouns used as objects require the objective case (*me, him, us, *and* them, *for example).*
>
> ❯ *Use a personal pronoun in the possessive case (*my, his, our, *and* their, *for example) to modify a noun or a gerund.*
>
> ❯ *Distinguish among* who *and* whoever *(the subjective-case forms),* whom *and* whomever *(the objective-case forms), and* whose *(the possessive-case form).*
>
> ❯ *Do not confuse possessive-case pronouns (for example,* its*) with contractions (for example,* it's, *meaning "it is").*

Nouns and pronouns used as subjects or predicate nouns are in the **subjective case.** Nouns or pronouns used as direct objects, indirect objects, or objects of prepositions are in the **objective case.** Nouns or pronouns used to show ownership are in the **possessive case.**

Case Forms of Personal Pronouns

	Subjective	*Objective*	*Possessive*
Singular			
1st person	I	me	my, mine
2nd person	you	you	your, yours
3rd person	he, she, it	him, her, it	his, her, hers, its
Plural			
1st person	we	us	our, ours
2nd person	you	you	your, yours
3rd person	they	them	their, theirs

Case Forms of *Who* and Related Pronouns

Subjective	*Objective*	*Possessive*
who	whom	whose
whoever	whomever	

Most pronouns and all nouns in the subjective case (*some-one, Alicia*) form the possessive case by adding *'s* (*someone's, Alicia's*) or only an apostrophe if the word ends with *s* (*teach-ers', Chris'*). The objective case is most frequently indicated by change of position.

Personal pronouns and relative pronouns produced with variations of *who* change forms in all three cases.

Do not confuse possessive-case pronouns, which do not use an apostrophe, with contractions that sound the same: *its* and *it's* ("it is"), *theirs* and *there's* ("there is"), and *whose* and *who's* ("who is").

| 18a > | **Pronouns used as subjects or as predicate nouns require the subjective-case form.** |

Subjective case

Although *he* got a *D* in freshman composition, Faulkner went on to become one of America's most honored writers.

When a sentence has a compound subject, isolate the parts of the subject to help you choose the appropriate pronoun.

Compound subject

Just after sunrise, Kendal and *she* waded into the stream to fish. (Kendal waded; *she* waded; consequently, *Kendal and she* waded.)

A predicate noun restates the subject and so requires the subjective case. Sometimes, however, this construction sounds excessively formal. Observe this pronoun-case rule in formal writing, but consider revising your sentence for less formal writing contexts. For example, invert the subject and predicate noun.

We discovered that "the mad scribbler" was *he*. (The predicate noun, signaled by the linking verb *was,* must be in the subjective case.)

We discovered that *he* was "the mad scribbler." (This sentence sounds less formal but is still correct.)

| 18b | Pronouns used as direct objects, indirect objects, or objects of prepositions require the objective-case form. |

A direct object answers the question *whom* or *what*. An indirect object answers the question *to whom* or *for whom*. Pronouns that answer these questions should be in the objective case.

Direct object
Susan B. Anthony challenged sexist and racist assumptions; we should respect *her* for that.

Indirect object
Although Rasputin was feared by the Russian nobility, Czar Nicholas and Czarina Alexandra gave *him* their absolute trust.

Object of preposition
The Medici family supported the arts in Renaissance Florence; many of the greatest works of Michelangelo, Leonardo, and Botticelli were created for *them*.

When a preposition has a compound object, isolate the parts of the object to help you choose the appropriate pronoun.

The contract had to be signed by both *him* and Eileen. (by *him*; by Eileen)

18c   Pronouns showing ownership or modifying a gerund require the possessive-case form.

Possessive Pronouns Used with Nouns

The possessive pronouns *my, your, his, her, its, our, your,* and *their* modify nouns. They act as adjectives in sentences and are sometimes called pronoun-adjectives.

> Although *my* exam scores were higher than Sarah's scores, *her* speeches were clearly better than mine.   (The pronouns in the possessive case serve as pronoun-adjectives.)

Possessive Pronouns Used Alone

The possessive pronouns *mine, yours, his, hers, its, ours, yours,* and *theirs* are sometimes used alone as subjects, predicate nouns, direct objects, indirect objects, or objects of prepositions.

> The blue car outside is *mine; his* is the red one.   (Both pronouns are in the possessive case, but *mine* works as a predicate noun and *his* as a subject.)

Possessive Pronouns Modifying a Gerund

When modifying a gerund (an *-ing* verb that functions as a noun), pronouns must be in the possessive case, serving as pronoun-adjectives.

> I was annoyed by *his* interrupting the speaker.   (The annoyance resulted from the person's *interrupting,* not from the person himself.)

> The director commented that *their* dancing was the best part of the musical number.   (The best part was their *dancing,* not them.)

18d	Sentence structure determines the case of pronouns in appositives, with nouns, and in elliptical constructions.

Pronouns in Appositives

When a pronoun in an appositive restates the subject of a clause, use the subjective case. When a pronoun in an appositive restates an object, use the objective case.

The two assistant managers, Gerald and *he,* were responsible for preparing the quarterly reports. (Because *Gerald and he* restates *two assistant managers,* the subject of the sentence, the pronoun must be in the subjective case.)

Certificates of merit were given to the runners-up, Abigail and *her.* (*Abigail and her* restates *runners-up,* the object of the preposition, so the pronoun must be in the objective case.)

We or *Us* with Nouns

When using *we* or *us* with a noun, choose the case that would be correct if the noun were omitted.

I think that *we* bicyclists should demand special cycling lanes on campus. (Without *bicyclists,* the clause reads *we should,* a correct use of the subjective case.)

Organizational policy prohibits *us* committee members from meeting informally. (Without *committee members,* the clause reads *policy prohibits us,* a correct use of the objective case.)

Pronouns in Elliptical Constructions

In **elliptical constructions** (constructions in which words are omitted or understood), use the case that would be appropriate if all the words were included. If the pronoun used alone sounds too formal, add the omitted words.

The Piersons arrived twenty minutes later than *we*. (The complete thought is that they arrived twenty minutes later than *we arrived*.)

EXERCISE 18.1 ⟩ *Pronoun case*

Supply the correct pronouns in the following sentences.

1. Hans Christian Andersen, the son of a shoemaker, began _____ adult life as an actor.

2. _____ failed on the stage, but because the king granted _____ a scholarship, Andersen was able to begin _____ writing career.

3. _____ writing of novels, plays, and long poems is almost completely forgotten, but almost everyone knows a few of _____ best fairy tales.

4. Ironically, Andersen did not set out to write fairy tales, but _____ wrote _____ first four to make money quickly.

5. Those stories succeeded beyond _____ expectations, and subsequently European nobility and royalty honored _____ for _____ work.

6. Although Andersen's tales may not be as well known as those of the brothers Grimm, _____ use of irony and humor, rather than violence, makes _____ work very appealing.

7. "The Emperor's New Clothes," one of _____ most ironic tales, alienated _____ from some of _____ noble patrons.

8. Today's readers, however, can enjoy the irony without insult and take delight in what was, for _____, a troublesome piece.

9. The best children's writers—and _____ is among them—delight us as children and intrigue us as adults, providing in simple tales some lessons on life.

10. If you think about Andersen as a failed actor who became a world-famous writer of fairy tales, you'll discover why "The Ugly Duckling" was one of _____ favorites; in a professional sense, at least, it was _____ story.

| 18e | Distinguish between the subjective-case forms *who* and *whoever* and the objective-case forms *whom* and *whomever.* |

Who and *Whoever*

Use the subjective-case forms *who* and *whoever* as subjects of sentences, clauses, and questions.

Who among us has not heard of the lost city of Atlantis? (*Who* is the subject of the question.)

Salvador Dali was an artist *who* took delight in shocking his contemporaries. (*Who* is the subject of the clause.)

The foundation will offer a scholarship to *whoever* writes the most creative essay. (*Whoever* is the subject of the clause; although the preposition *to* might suggest that the objective case is required, the whole clause, not the word *whoever,* is the object of the preposition.)

Whom and *Whomever*

Use the objective-case forms *whom* and *whomever* as direct objects, indirect objects, and objects of prepositions.

Whom should we invite to speak to the alumni? (*Whom* is the direct object of *invite*.)

The board will probably approve the appointment of *whomever* we select. (*Whomever* is the direct object of *select*.)

 Use the "search" feature to locate *who, whoever, whom,* and *whomever.* Then double-check the sentence to be sure that you have used them correctly. If you have not, use the "delete" and "add" functions of your word processor to make the necessary changes.

EXERCISE 18.2) Pronoun case

 Use who, whom, whoever, *and* whomever *correctly in the following sentences.*

1. The Better Business Bureau, a nonprofit organization, was founded to help people _____ are victims of questionable business methods and deceptive advertising.

2. Consumers should first address complaints to _____ has acted in an unbusinesslike manner.

3. The Better Business Bureau is a group to _____ consumers can turn if they still are not satisfied.

4. The Better Business Bureau will answer questions and suggest strategies to _____ calls, but it cannot take legal action against suspected businesses.

5. Since the Better Business Bureau refers cases to government agencies, however, it helps ensure that businesspeople _____ are unethical do not continue to exploit consumers.

EXERCISE 18.3) *Pronoun case*

Indicate whether the italicized pronouns in the following paragraph are in the subjective, objective, or possessive case. Be ready to explain your decisions.

When *I* came out of prison,—for some one interfered, and paid that tax,—*I* did not perceive that great changes had taken place on the common, such as *he* observed *who* went in a youth and emerged a tottering and grey-headed man; and yet a change had to *my* eyes come over the scene,—the town, and State, and country,—greater than any that mere time could effect. *I* saw yet more distinctly the State in which *I* lived. *I* saw to what extent the people among *whom I* lived could be trusted as good neighbors and friends; that *their* friendship was for summer weather only; that *they* did not greatly propose to do right; that *they* were a distinct race from *me* by *their* prejudices and superstitions, as the Chinamen and Malays are; that in *their* sacrifices to humanity *they* ran no risks, not even to *their* property; that after all *they* were not so noble but *they* treated the thief as *he* had treated *them,* and hoped, by a certain outward observance and a few prayers, and by walking in a particular straight though useless path from time to time, to save *their* souls. This may be to judge *my* neighbors harshly; for *I* believe that many of *them* are not aware that *they* have such an institution as the jail in *their* village. —Henry David Thoreau, "Civil Disobedience"

19   Verb Tenses

Tenses are the forms of verbs that indicate when things happened or existed in relation to when they are described. Tenses also indicate whether an action or state of being continued over time or whether it has been completed. Tenses are formed through the use of auxiliary verbs and changes in verb endings.

Quick Reference

Verbs, along with subjects, form the core of sentences. The use of effective verbs will strengthen your writing.

> Use the correct verb tense and form to express your meaning accurately.

> Use present tense to describe beliefs, scientific principles, works of art, and repeated or habitual actions.

> Use sequences of tenses correctly to clarify the time relations in your writing.

> Use verb mood correctly to indicate your opinion on the factuality or probability of your sentence.

Regular Verbs

Regular verbs form tenses according to consistent patterns. (For an example of a full conjugation of the verb *to learn,* see page 299.)

To Learn

Present tense	learn(s)
Past tense	learned
Future tense	*will* learn
Present perfect tense	*have* (or *has*) learned
Past perfect tense	*had* learned
Future perfect tense	*will have* learned
Progressive tenses	
Present progressive	*am (are)* learning
Past progressive	*was (were)* learning
Future progressive	*will be* learning
Present perfect progressive	*has (have) been* learning
Past perfect progressive	*had been* learning
Future perfect progressive	*will have been* learning

Irregular Verbs

Irregular verbs form tenses through changes in word form.

To Go

Present tense	go(es)
Past tense	went
Future tense	will go
Present perfect tense	have (or has) gone
Past perfect tense	had gone
Future perfect tense	will have gone

> **19a** ⟩ **Use the simple tenses to describe actions or conditions occurring or completed within the time specified.**

The simple tenses are the present, past, and future.

Present Tense

Use the **present tense** to describe events occurring or conditions existing in the present.

> He *concedes* your point.

In addition, there are some special uses of the present tense.

Repeated or Habitual Actions

Use the present tense to describe a habitual or frequently repeated action or series of actions or to explain standard procedures.

> Air traffic controllers *work* long, tension-filled shifts.

> *Deposit* a coin into the slot; *wait* for the tone; then *dial* the number.

General Beliefs and Scientific Principles

Use the present tense to assert accepted beliefs.

> Every child *deserves* adequate nutrition, clothing, housing, and a good education.

Express scientific and other principles in the present tense.

> The force of gravity *determines* the flow of water in rivers and streams.

> *Do* unto others as you would have them *do* unto you.

Descriptions of Works of Art

Use the present tense to describe and discuss works of art—literature, music, dance, painting—prehistoric through contemporary.

> In Coleridge's *Rime of the Ancient Mariner,* the narrator *learns* and compulsively *repeats* to others the lesson of the sacredness of all life.

> Picasso's *Guernica contains* images of chaos and terror.

Past Tense

Use the **past tense** to describe actions completed or conditions that existed in the past. In writing, you will use the past tense more often than any other tense, because much of what you write about has already occurred.

> Henry Ford *created* the Model T but, more importantly, *perfected* the industrial assembly line.

Future Tense

Use the **future tense** to describe actions or conditions that will or are expected to occur or exist in the future.

> The committee *will hold* its next meeting in Geneva, Switzerland.

| 19b | Use the perfect tenses to describe actions or conditions in relation to other actions or conditions. |

The perfect tenses are the present perfect, past perfect, and future perfect.

Present Perfect Tense

Use the **present perfect tense** to describe actions that occurred or conditions that existed at an unspecified time in the past or that began in the past and continue to the present.

> Since I *took* a music appreciation class, Beethoven's piano concertos *have been* favorites of mine.   (*Took* is in the past tense because the class is over; *have been* is in the present perfect tense because the preference began in the past and continues to the present.)

Past Perfect Tense

Use the **past perfect tense** to describe past actions or conditions that were completed before some other past action or condition.

> Until Lincoln *was elected* in 1860, the Republican party *had achieved* very little since its founding in 1854.   (*Had achieved* establishes the limited success of Republicans before the other past event, Lincoln's election.)

Future Perfect Tense

Use the **future perfect tense** to describe actions that will be completed or conditions that will exist in the future but before a specific time.

> Almost all businesses *will have converted* to computerized bookkeeping by the turn of the century.   (The "turn of the century" is in the future. Converting to computerized bookkeeping will also be in the future, but before A.D. 2000.)

> **19c** Use the progressive tenses to describe actions
> or conditions beginning, continuing, or ending
> within the present, past, or future.

Progressive tenses stress the continuing nature of actions or conditions.

The Japanese *are sharing* a large part of the costs for operating the United Nations. (The present progressive tense shows a continuous action.)

The American government *has been supporting* the United Nations since its founding. (The present perfect progressive tense describes a continuing process that began in the past.)

To avoid unnecessary wordiness, use the progressive tenses only when necessary to express continuing actions or states.

President Bush was trying to avert an increase in the minimum wage.

President Bush tried to avert an increase in the minimum wage.

> **19d** Use tenses in logical sequences to show
> precisely and accurately the relationships
> among actions and conditions.

Verb tense signals chronology, indicating when actions occurred or conditions existed in relation to when they are described. Logical sequences of tenses clarify the relationship among actions and conditions.

Sequences of present and past tenses cause few problems for writers, but more complicated verb-tense sequences may. Use the following rules for guidance.

Infinitives

Infinitives (*to swim, to subscribe, to record*) assume the tense indicated by the main verb.

Brainwashing *attempts to convince* people *to give up* their beliefs. (The infinitives coordinate with the present-tense verb *attempts*.)

Fidel Castro *led* the revolution *to overthrow* Cuba's dictator and subsequently *guided* the country's efforts *to institute* Communist reforms.   (The infinitives automatically coordinate with the past-tense verbs.)

Present Participles

The **present participle,** like the infinitive, assumes the tense of the main verb.

Having a fixed rate of interest, bonds *appeal* to wary investors more than stocks do.

Speaking to the American people in his first inaugural address, Franklin Roosevelt *reassured* them that "the only thing we have to fear is fear itself."

Past Participles and Perfect Participles

Past participles (*hurried, welcomed, driven*) and **perfect participles** (*having hurried, having welcomed, having driven*) indicate that the action or condition they describe occurred before that of the main verb.

Dressed as a man, Aurore Dupin (who used the pen name George Sand) *attended* the theater when women were not allowed to go.

Having won a record nine gold medals in Olympic swimming, Mark Spitz *retired* from competition.

Use of Tenses in a Subordinate Clause

Past Tense or Past Perfect Tense in a Subordinate Clause

When the verb in an independent clause is in the past or the past perfect tense, the verb in the subordinate clause must also be in the past or the past perfect tense.

Once scientists *discovered* that fluorocarbons damage the ozone layer that protects the Earth from ultraviolet radiation, environmentalists *protested* against their use in commercial products. (The use of the past tense *protested* in the independent clause establishes that this series of actions took place in the past.)

Before bacteria and viruses *were discovered*, diseases *had been explained* in superstitious ways. (The use of the past perfect *had been explained* establishes that nonscientific explanations existed before the scientific ones.)

Present, Future, Present Perfect, or Future Perfect Tense in a Subordinate Clause

When the verb in the independent clause is in the present, future, present perfect, or future perfect tense, any tense can be used in the subordinate clause. These tenses and combinations of tenses create numerous possibilities for expressing chronological relationships precisely and accurately. Be sure to arrange the tenses logically so that your meaning is clear.

Some scientists currently *think* that exercise *will prolong* life.

Although Molière's *Tartuffe was written* in 1665, its comments on religious hypocrisy and exploitation still *have* meaning today. (Literature of the past still speaks to contemporary audiences.)

EXERCISE 19.1 ⟩ *Tenses*

Revise the following sentences, written primarily in the present tense, by changing them into the past tense.

1. The design team for the theater production meets to review the script for the play.

2. They talk about specific concerns and mention any special needs they should consider.

3. The discussion turns to potential problems in lighting the production, as it always does, because the theater—a renovated movie house—is modified less than is needed.

4. The lighting designer says, once again, that the theater will need major electrical work before a computerized lighting system can be installed.

5. Completing the discussion of lighting, the team turns its attention to the set for the play.

6. The play chosen—*Who's Afraid of Virginia Woolf?*—requires a single set, one room in a history professor's house.

7. The designers describe productions they have seen.

8. The costumer describes a production that was done in Baltimore.

9. The lighting designer remembers a collegiate production she saw in Iowa.

10. The director says he wants this set to be more realistic in its details than others he has seen.

11. As is usually the case, the team leaves after the first meeting, having made only a few key decisions.

EXERCISE 19.2 ⟩ *Tenses*

Identify the tenses of the numbered verbs in the following paragraphs. Be prepared to explain why each tense is used.

Are owls truly wise? The Greeks (1) *thought* so, identifying them with Athena, goddess of wisdom. In medieval illustrations, owls (2) *accompany* Merlin and share in his sorcery. In fairytales they rival the fox for cunning. Children's picture books (3) *show* them wearing spectacles, mortarboard, and scholar's gown. Soups and other confections made from owls (4) *have been credited* with curing whooping cough, drunkenness, epilepsy, famine, and insomnia. The Cherokee Indians used to bathe their children's eyes with a broth of owl feathers to keep the kids awake at night. Recipes using owl eggs (5) *are reputed* to bestow keen eyesight and wisdom. Yet these birds are no smarter, ornithologists (6) *assure* us, than most others. A museum guide in Boston once (7) *displayed* a drowsy-looking barn owl on his gloved wrist, (8) *explaining* to those of us assembled there how small the bird's brain actually was. "You (9) *[will] notice* the head of this live specimen appears to be about the size of a grapefruit," he said, "but it's mostly feathers." Lifting his other hand, he (10) *added,* "The skull, you (11) *see*, is the size of a lemon. There's only room enough inside for a birdbrain, not enough for Einstein!" We all laughed politely. But I was not convinced. Sure, the skull (12) *was* small. The lower half was devoted to jaw and most of the upper half to beak and eye-holes. Yet enough neurons could be fitted into the remaining space to enable the barn owl to catch mice in total darkness. They can even snatch bats on the wing, these princes of nighttime stealth. We have to invent sonar for locating submarines, radar for locating airplanes; neither (13) *is* much use with mice or bats. Barn owls can also see dead—and therefore silent—prey in light one-hundredth as bright as we would need. Like the ability to saw a board square or judge the consistency of bread dough, that might not amount to scholarship, but it (14) *is* certainly a wisdom of the body. It (15) *has worked* for some sixty million years. —Scott Sanders, "Listening to Owls"

| 19e | Use the mood of a verb to indicate your opinion on the probability or factuality of your sentence. |

Verbs in English may have one of three **moods:** indicative, imperative, or subjunctive. Grammatical mood does not refer to or equal psychological mood; the word *mood* in the grammatical sense derives from "mode," meaning "manner," the way in which something appears, is done, or happens.

Definition and Use of Moods

Use the **indicative mood** to make statements or ask questions about conditions or actions that are considered facts.

Air travel is one of the safest modes of transportation.

Use the **imperative mood** to make statements (commands) about actions or conditions that should or must become facts.

Fasten your seat belt and prepare for take-off.   (The subject, *you,* is omitted or understood, as is generally the case in the imperative.)

Use the **subjunctive mood** to make statements or ask questions about actions or conditions that you doubt, wish for, or consider hypothetical or contrary to fact. The subjunctive is also used to present requests and demands.

If the terminal were redesigned, airport security would be easy to maintain.   (Note that both clauses express conditional, nonfactual states: The terminal has not been redesigned, and security is not easy to maintain.)

Her doctor recommended that she get a flu vaccine this year.   (The first clause describes a past action; the second clause uses the subjunctive to describe a requested action.)

However, clauses beginning with *if* use the indicative when they describe factual conditions, as in the following example:

If the terminal was redesigned, it was difficult to see any improvement.   (Both clauses are in the indicative past tense because they
describe actual events and perceptions.)

The subjunctive, which can sound extremely formal and even
stilted, is now rarely used in English, except for conditional
expressions, such as the examples above, and other idiomatic
expressions, such as the following:

Let it *be*.

God *save* the Queen!

I move that the committee secretary *forward* the report to the
mayor.

He asks that his privacy *be* respected.

If I *were* you, I'd enter the contest.

Forming the Moods

Most expressions in English are in the indicative mood, which
is formed using any and all of the verb tenses covered in 19a
through 19c above. The imperative mood is formed using the
present tense, as in the example on page 308.
Only the subjunctive has distinct forms. The verb *to be* in the
subjunctive differs from its indicative forms in both the present
and the past tense; the forms, identical in the singular and plural, are, respectively, *be* and *were*.

If the report *be* true, let us act quickly.   (present tense)

If she *were* in charge, she would have acted.   (past tense)

Subjunctive forms for verbs other than *to be* differ from the
indicative only in the third person singular of the present tense,
in which the -*s* ending is dropped.

May the weather *continue* clear.

This last example illustrates the sometimes formal tone of statements in the subjunctive. Often, a correct version in the indicative can be substituted.

If the report is true, we should act quickly.

I hope that the clear weather continues.

EXERCISE 19.3) *Mood*

Where appropriate, revise the verbs in the following sentences to correct their use of mood.

1. Increasingly, working parents in the United States are asking that every employer acknowledges the childcare problem.

2. A single parent especially often wishes a company-operated childcare facility was available at or near his or her place of work.

3. Lateness would probably decline if a parent was able to make one trip to a single location, instead of a separate trip to a childcare facility and then the usual trip to work.

4. If Congress was to partially subsidize childcare facilities, many companies might help their employees by providing on-site childcare.

5. But even if a company was to provide on-site childcare, problems in assuring sufficient daycare facilities would still exist.

20   Adjectives and Adverbs

In most instances, you naturally use adjectives and adverbs correctly. Occasionally, however, misusing adjectives and adverbs is likely if you do not think carefully about which word they are modifying. The following guidelines should help to solve most problems in adjective and adverb usage.

> ### Quick Reference
>
> Adjectives and adverbs refine the meaning of a sentence, but to do so effectively they must be used correctly.
>
> ⟩ Use adjectives to modify nouns and pronouns.
>
> ⟩ Use adverbs to modify verbs, adjectives, and other adverbs.
>
> ⟩ Use positive adjective and adverb forms when no comparison is made; use comparative forms to compare two items; use superlative forms to compare three or more items.
>
> ⟩ Distinguish between troublesome adjective and adverb pairs.

20a ⟩ Adjectives modify nouns and pronouns.

Make sure that the word modifying a noun or pronoun is an adjective. Isolate the word and its modifier, placing the modifier first, to see if the pair sounds correct. When you are uncertain, consult a dictionary to find the correct adjective form.

Treasure Island, an *exciting* novel by Robert Louis Stevenson, is a
classic of *adolescent* fiction.   (*Exciting* modifies *novel; adolescent*
modifies *fiction.*)

Jim Hawkins, the *young* hero, is *resourceful* and *brave.*   (*Young*
modifies *hero; resourceful* and *brave* modify *Jim Hawkins.*)

20b	Adverbs modify verbs, adjectives, and other adverbs.

Make sure that the word modifying a verb is an adverb. Isolate
the pair of words to see if the pair sounds correct. The adverb
should make sense before or after the verb. When you are
uncertain of a word's adverb form, consult a dictionary.

H. G. Wells, a political and social reformer in Victorian England, is
best known *today* for two brief works: *The War of the Worlds* and
The Time Machine.   (*Best* and *today* both modify *is known.*)

Adverbs that modify adjectives and other adverbs are intensifiers, stressing the specific modifications of the primary modifier. Because some intensifiers—*very, especially, really,* and
truly—are used so frequently, they may have the paradoxical
effect of weakening the impact of your statement. Use them
only when they are necessary to your meaning.

Unfortunately, Wells's ingenious science fiction has spawned some
very bad science fiction films.   (*Very* intensifies the adjective *bad.*)

This sentence would be improved if the writer substituted a
single, stronger adjective (for example, *appalling* or *dreadful*)
or a more specific, descriptive adjective (for example, *boring,
unbelievable,* or *exploitative*) for *very bad.*

20c › **Use positive, comparative, and superlative adjectives and adverbs correctly.**

Positive Adjectives and Adverbs

Positive adjectives and **adverbs** imply no comparisons: *recent, soon, clearly, fortunate.*

                adj.   *adj*

The set for *The Passion of Dracula* was *ornate* and *eerie*.

                     adj.

The scene changes were made *quickly.*

Comparative Adjectives and Adverbs

Comparative adjectives and **adverbs** establish differences between two similar people, places, things, ideas, qualities, conditions, or actions. Adjectives and adverbs form comparatives in two ways. One-syllable modifiers add the suffix *-er: sooner, paler.* (See also the table of irregular adjectives and adverbs on page 315.) Multisyllable modifiers use *more* or *less* to form the comparative: *less easily, more recent.*

A number of two- and three-syllable adjectives use the *-er* form (and *-est* for the superlative). Use the *-er* and *-est* forms with multisyllable words that have the following characteristics:

  L sound in the last syllable: *simple*

  Accent on the last syllable: *severe*

Some other multisyllable adjectives (pretty, narrow) form the comparative irregularly (prettier, narrower). Consult a dictionary if you are unsure of how to form a specific comparative or superlative.

comp. adj.   comp. adj.

The set for *The Passion of Dracula* was *more ornate* and *eerier* than anyone expected.

comp. adv.

The scene changes for this production were made *more quickly* than they were for *Hedda Gabler*.

Superlative Adjectives and Adverbs

Superlative adjectives and adverbs compare a person, place, thing, idea, quality, condition, or action with three or more similar items. Superlatives are the most emphatic adjective and adverb forms. One-syllable words form the superlative by adding the suffix -est: soonest, palest. Multisyllable adjectives and adverbs generally form the superlative by using most or least: least easily, most recent. (But see also the note on exceptions under the discussion of comparative forms on page 313.)

super. adj.

The set for *The Passion of Dracula* was the *most dramatic* and

super. adj.

eeriest one I have seen.

During this production season, the scene changes in *Dracula* were

super. adv.

made *most quickly*.

Positive	Comparative	Superlative
bad	worse	worst
good	better	best
little	less / littler	least / littlest
many / much / some	more	most
well	better	best
badly	worse	worst

Double Comparatives and Superlatives

Only one change is needed to form the comparative or superlative of an adjective or adverb. To use both a suffix and a helping word is unnecessary and incorrect.

Incorrect

Madonna rose to superstardom *more faster* than even she expected.

Correct

Madonna rose to superstardom *faster* than even she expected.

Incorrect

Kliban's cartoons of cats are the *most funniest* ones I have seen.

Correct

Kliban's cartoons of cats are the *funniest* ones I have seen.

Incomparable Adjectives

Because of their meanings, some adjectives cannot suggest comparisons of any kind. Examples of such words are *central, dead, empty, impossible, infinite, perfect, straight,* and *unique.* Use only the positive form of such modifiers.

Incorrect

James Joyce's *Ulysses* was the *most unique* novel I have read. (Unique means "one of a kind" and cannot suggest a comparison.)

Correct

James Joyce's *Ulysses* is a *unique* novel. (This sentence uses *unique* in its proper, positive form.)

Correct

James Joyce's *Ulysses* was the *most unusual* novel I have read. (*Unusual* is a quality that can be compared.)

20d	Distinguish carefully between troublesome adjective and adverb pairs.

Use *bad,* the adjective form, to modify nouns and pronouns, even with sensory or linking verbs (*appear, feel, look, smell, taste, sound,* and forms of *to be*). Use *badly* only to modify a verb.

That was a *bad* rendition of *Rhapsody in Blue.*

After sitting in the sun for two hours, Monica felt *bad.*

After dozens of art classes, Anita still painted *badly.*

Use *good,* the adjective form, only to modify a noun or pronoun. Use *well* as an adverb to mean *satisfactory;* use *well* as an adjective to mean *healthy.*

Louise was a very *good* pianist.

The rehearsal went *well* last night.

Although Anton had a slight fever, he said he felt *well* enough to play in Saturday's game.

Other troublesome adjective and adverb pairs appear in the Glossary of Grammatical Terms beginning on page 672.

EXERCISE 20.1 ❱ *Adjective and adverb forms*

Select the appropriate adjective or adverb forms in the following sentences.

1. Current methods of building construction will make homes (affordable/more affordable/most affordable) than they were in the past, without sacrificing quality.

2. Although prefabricated homes have always been (easily/more easily/most easily) constructed than conventionally built homes, they were not always built (good/well).

3. Now, however, factory construction of major structural elements is (increasing/increasingly) impressive.

4. Many home units—like kitchens and bathrooms—are being constructed with their plumbing and wiring embedded in wall units; then these "core construction blocks" are fitted together (quick/quickly/more quickly) in various ways.

5. Because installing plumbing and wiring is (costly/more costly/most costly) than other phases of construction, these "core blocks" keep on-site construction costs (low/lower/lowest).

6. With the money saved from structural costs, a homeowner can concentrate on architectural trim and interior design work that can make his or her home (unique/more unique/most unique).

EXERCISE 20.2 ⟩ *Adjectives and adverbs*

Correct the errors in adjective and adverb use in the follow-ing paragraph.

Tapestries, fabrics with pictures woven into them, were used in medieval churches and palaces more often as decorations but sometimes as insulation in the chilly buildings. The most unique tapestries were produced in Arras, France, where the art of weaving pictures reached its perfectest form in the 1400s. The tapestry mak-ers of Arras worked so good that the word *arras* was soon used as a synonym for *tapestry*. The tapestries that have survived from the 1400s and 1500s are in various states of repair. Some, like the set of tapestries called *The Hunt of the Unicorn,* are in real sound condi-tion. Their colors are still vibrant. The more famous panel of the set shows a unicorn sitting within a circular fence, surrounded by flow-ers and foliage of the brightest colors. Unfortunately, other tapes-tries have been treated bad over the centuries, and their colors are faded or their yarns damaged. Weaving tapestries is a most complex craft that has been sporadically and more simplistically revived in the last hundred years, but we will probably never approximate the more intricate and reverential nature of tapestries done in the late Middle Ages.

Using the word processor to evaluate adjective and adverb use

Beyond basic strategies for revision, a word processor can help you to solve special problems with adjectives and adverbs.

Search for intensifiers. Use the "search" function to find words like *very, really,* and *especially.* Eliminate all of the intensifiers that do not convey crucial meaning.

Search for comparatives and superlatives. Use the
"search" function to find *more, most, less,* and *least.*
Then make sure that the comparative or superlative form
is aptly chosen. With some word-processing programs,
you can search for specific sets of letters, not just separate words. If your program has that capability and if you
have special problems with comparatives and superlatives, consider searching for *-er* and *-est* combinations.

PUNCTUATION

21 End Punctuation

Three marks of punctuation can end sentences: the period (.), the question mark (?), and the exclamation point (!). These forms of punctuation also serve a few other purposes.

Quick Reference

End punctuation clearly and simply indicates the end of a sentence and its intended effect.

❭ *Use periods to end sentences that make statements, issue commands, or ask indirect questions.*

❭ *Use question marks to end sentences that ask direct questions.*

❭ *Use exclamation points to end sentences that express strong feeling.*

21a ❭ **Use periods after sentences making statements, issuing commands, or asking indirect questions.**

Statement

Cigarette smoking is hazardous to your health.

Command

Stop smoking today.

Indirect question

The Surgeon General asked whether the students understood the risks of smoking. (The sentence implies that the Surgeon General asked a question, but the sentence itself is not a question. The word order of the main subject and verb indicates that the sentence is a statement.)

| 21b | Use question marks after direct questions.

A question mark is one of two indicators of direct questions; the other is inverted word order of the subject and any part of the verb. (Indirect questions end with periods and use normal word order; see section 21a.) The verb in a question includes a helping verb not necessarily present in a statement.

Question

Did the president know of the illegal actions of his advisers?

Statement

The president knew of the illegal actions of his advisers.

Some writers use question marks in parentheses to indicate uncertainty. This usage should be avoided in formal writing.

Awkward

The Chinese invented paper in A.D. 105(?) but kept it a state secret for hundreds of years.

Better

The Chinese invented paper around A.D. 105 but kept it a state secret for hundreds of years.

21c ⟩ **Use exclamation points after sentences and interjections to express strong feeling or indicate special emphasis.**

An exclamation point may follow a sentence or an interjection.

Sentence

"I know not what course others may take; but as for me, give me liberty or give me death!" —Patrick Henry

Interjection

"Well! Some people talk of morality, and some of religion, but give me a little snug property." —Maria Edgeworth

Exclamation points should be used sparingly, especially in formal writing. Not many sentences or interjections require the emphasis that exclamation points provide.

EXERCISE 21.1 ⟩ *End punctuation*

Add the end punctuation required in the following paragraph, capitalizing where necessary to indicate new sentences.

Harry Truman, the thirty-third president, was a spirited leader with a penchant for candor he assumed the presidency in 1945, after Franklin Roosevelt's death, and until he left office in 1953 repeatedly challenged assumptions about how presidents ought to behave his presidency was marked by controversy Truman made the decision to drop nuclear bombs on Hiroshima and Nagasaki; he supported the Marshall Plan to help Europe recover from the devastation of World War II; he sent American troops to Korea a sign of his unquestioning acceptance of responsibility for key decisions, one of Truman's favorite slogans became nationally known: "the buck stops here" another of his favorites was "if you can't stand the heat, get out of the kitchen" supporters, using Truman's own flavorful

language often shouted this refrain: "give 'em hell, Harry" Truman
made many difficult decisions and never attempted to avoid the
controversy that resulted or to blame others for his decisions was
he a great president that is a judgment best left to history, but he
certainly was an honest and an interesting one

 *** Word processing and end punctuation***

A word processor will help you to avoid problems with
overuse or incorrect use of question marks and exclamation points.

Find and check your use of question marks. Use the
"search" command to locate question marks. Check
the sentence to make sure that the subject and verb
are inverted. If you discover a question mark following an indirect question, revise the sentence or the
punctuation.

Find and replace most exclamation points. Use the
"search" command to locate all exclamation points in
your papers. For all but the most necessary and emphatic uses, delete the exclamation points and replace them
with periods.

22 Commas

Commas separate and clarify the relationships among single words, phrases, and clauses. If commas do not appear where they are needed, thoughts can merge or overlap confusingly.

Confusing

As the speaker finished his audience stood to cheer. (Without a comma after *finished*, the sentence momentarily suggests that the speaker finished the audience.)

Clear

As the speaker finished, his audience stood to cheer.

Quick Reference

Use commas to clarify and separate sentence elements.

) *Use commas to separate items in a series.*

) *Use commas to separate clauses in compound sentences.*

) *Use commas to set off introductory subordinate clauses in complex and compound-complex sentences.*

) *Use commas to set off introductory words and phrases that serve as adverbs.*

) *Use commas to set off nonrestrictive information.*

) *Use commas to set off statements that signal direct quotations.*

22a ⟩ **Use commas to separate three or more items in a series.**

Separate a series of three or more parallel words, phrases, or clauses with commas. Although the comma immediately preceding the conjunction may be omitted, a comma there is always correct and may prevent confusion.

Nouns or Verbs in a Series

The faces of George Washington, Thomas Jefferson, Abraham Lincoln, and Theodore Roosevelt are carved into Mount Rushmore. (Commas separate each noun in the series.)

A good reporter asks questions directly, listens attentively, and takes notes accurately and quickly. (Commas separate all verbs in the series.)

Adjectives and Adverbs in a Series

When two or more adjectives independently modify a single noun, use commas to separate each one. Similarly, when several adverbs separately and equally modify a verb or an adjective, separate them with commas. No comma separates the last modifier in the series from the word modified.

The ancient, dilapidated depot is slated for demolition. (*Ancient* depot; *dilapidated* depot; each adjective functions independently.)

The ornithologist slowly, calmly, and carefully approached the injured goose. (*Slowly* approached; *calmly* approached; *carefully* approached; each adverb functions independently.)

To test the independence of modifiers, reverse the order of the modifiers or substitute *and* for each comma. If the sentence still makes sense, the adjectives or adverbs are *coordinate* and should be separated by commas. If the sentence does not make sense, the modifiers are *cumulative* and do not require commas (see section 23d).

> The *dilapidated and ancient* depot is slated for demolition. (The modification is clear, and the sentence makes sense.)

Phrases and Clauses in a Series

Phrases

Letters by Churchill, to Churchill, and about Churchill have become important and valued historical documents.

Clauses

At the turn of the century, the need for social reforms erupted into pitched battles as muckrakers exposed business corruption, industrial leaders challenged their accusations, and politicians sided with the powerful industrialists.

EXERCISE 22.1 ❭ *Commas*

 Insert commas where needed in the following sentences.

1. Computers are now commonplace equipment in homes schools and businesses.

2. It is amazing how quickly completely and smoothly most people have become acclimated to the new technology.

3. Computerized cash registers are now common in grocery stores at movie houses in discount stores and even at gas stations.

4. Computers in public and private libraries have made it possible for people to search for books print lists of available materials and complete research quickly.

5. Today our mail comes with computer labels our bank statements arrive with spread-sheet accounts of transactions and even our grocery store receipts have computer lists of products we've bought.

| 22b | Use a comma to separate clauses in compound and compound-complex sentences. |

Compound Sentences

Most independent clauses joined by a coordinating conjunction must be separated by a comma. When the clauses are brief and when no confusion is likely, the comma may be omitted. Using a comma, however, is always correct.

Price supports for dairy products greatly help farmers, and consumers benefit as well.   (Without a comma after *farmers,* the initial reading might inappropriately link *farmers* and *consumers* as direct objects.)

Making mistakes is common but admitting them is not.   (Because these clauses are brief and because confusion is unlikely, the comma may be omitted.)

Do not mistakenly place a comma before every coordinating conjunction. Place a comma only before coordinating conjunctions that link independent clauses. Conjunctions that connect only two words, two phrases, or two dependent clauses usually do not require commas.

Compound-Complex Sentences

One comma separates the independent clauses in a compound-complex sentence. When a compound-complex sentence begins with a subordinate clause, however, a comma must also be used to show where the subordinate clause ends and the independent clause begins.

> Once people learn to use computers and laser printers, personal publishing becomes possible, and many small organizations print their own materials.

EXERCISE 22.2 ⟩ *Commas*

Combine these simple sentences to form compound, complex, or compound-complex sentences. Insert any necessary commas.

1. *Buffalo* is the name usually used to refer to American bison. It is a common name used to describe several hundred kinds of large wild oxen worldwide.

2. Water buffalo in India have been domesticated for centuries. South African buffalo have resisted domestication and run wild. Small buffalo on Pacific islands remain wild as well.

3. In North America, especially on the Great Plains, huge herds of buffalo once roamed. By 1900, the bison population of approximately 20 million was reduced to fewer than six hundred.

4. William Hornaday, an American zoologist, worked to protect the remaining bison. He felt their extinction would be shameful. He encouraged the National Forest Service to build fenced areas for small herds.

5. Today, bison are kept in captivity. They cannot be trained or domesticated. They are of zoological rather than practical interest.

> **22c** Use a comma after most introductory words, phrases, and subordinate clauses.

Introductory Words

Because conjunctive adverbs (*however, subsequently,* and others) and some adverbs are nonrestrictive sentence elements, they must be set off by commas (see section 22d).

Conjunctive adverb

Subsequently, testimony proved that President Nixon was deeply involved in illegal activities.

A conjunctive adverb used to link compound sentences joined by a semicolon should also be followed by a comma.

Impeachment proceedings seemed imminent; therefore, Nixon resigned from office.

Adverb

First, children require good nutrition to grow and learn properly. (The comma prevents confusion; without it, readers might think that *first* is an adjective modifying *children.*)

Introductory Phrases

When a transitional expression (*for example, in other words, in fact,* and others) or an opening prepositional or verbal phrase is used as an adjective or adverb, separate the phrase from the rest of the sentence with a comma.

Transitional expression

For example, most organization newsletters are now generated by laser printers to achieve the look of typeset copy without the cost.

Prepositional phrase

After twenty years of promoting feminist causes, the National Organization for Women has achieved some of its goals but continues to address new ones.   (The comma signals the end of the introductory phrase and the beginning of the main idea of the sentence.)

If an introductory prepositional phrase is brief and if the meaning is clear without a comma, the comma may be omitted.

In April Americans pay income taxes.

Verbal phrase

Crouching in a makeshift hut of sticks and grasses, Jane Goodall observed the chimpanzees at play.   (The introductory participial phrase is adjectival, modifying *Goodall*.)

Introductory Subordinate Clauses

When a subordinate clause begins a sentence, use a comma to separate it from the independent clause that follows.

Because mosquitoes are such a problem in southern coastal cities like New Orleans, city workers spray with insecticides each evening.   (The comma marks the end of the subordinate clause.)

EXERCISE 22.3 ❭ *Commas*

 Insert commas where needed in the following sentences.

1. Built during the third and fourth centuries the catacombs of Rome are the most famous in the world.

2. Intended for use as burial sites the passages and rooms were used for other purposes too.

3. According to legend early Christians kept the bodies of Saint Peter and Saint Paul hidden for a time in the catacombs.

4. In addition Christians often took refuge in the catacombs because the catacombs were protected by Roman law.

5. Curiously use of the Roman catacombs ceased in A.D. 400.

 Use a comma to separate nonrestrictive information from the rest of the sentence.

Restrictive information, essential to the meaning of a sentence, supplies the distinctions that give ideas specificity. Such information is not set off by commas. Nonrestrictive information does not supply distinctions central to the meaning of a sentence. Because nonrestrictive information can be omitted, it is set off by commas from the rest of the sentence. Nonrestrictive elements may be single words, phrases, or clauses.

Nonrestrictive Words

Conjunctive Adverbs

Use commas to set off conjunctive adverbs. When they appear at the beginning or end of a sentence, use one comma to set them off. When they appear in the middle of a sentence, use two commas.

At end of sentence
Many people admired Nixon's command of international policy. They remained suspicious of his politics, however.

In midsentence
Newspaper reports suggested Nixon's involvement in Watergate. The president, however, claimed he had committed no crimes.

The words *yes* and *no,* mild interjections, and names in direct address

Use commas to separate the words *yes* and *no,* interjections, and names in direct address from the rest of a sentence.

Yes and direct address

"Yes, Virginia, there is a Santa Claus." —Francis Church (The comma after *yes* separates it from the rest of the sentence; the comma after *Virginia* separates this name used in direct address.)

Interjection

Okay, so it was Franklin who said, "In this world nothing is certain but death and taxes."

Nonrestrictive Phrases

Transitional Expressions

Transitional expressions *(for example, as a result,* and so on) are nonrestrictive and should therefore be separated from the rest of the sentence. Use a single comma if the expression appears at the beginning or end of a sentence; use two commas if it appears in the middle of a sentence.

Nixon, in fact, remained an astute commentator on foreign affairs.

Absolute Phrases

Absolute phrases modify entire sentences. Because these phrases are nonrestrictive, they must be set off by commas. Use a single comma if the phrase appears at the beginning or end of a sentence; use two commas if it appears in the middle of a sentence.

At end of sentence
> Franklin Roosevelt was the first president to fly in a commercial airplane, a fact unknown to most people.

In midsentence
> Gandhi, the goal of Indian independence achieved, retired from public life.

Prepositional and Verbal Phrases

When prepositional and verbal phrases supply information that is not essential to the meaning of a sentence, use commas to set them off from the rest of the sentence.

Prepositional phrase
> J. D. Salinger, above all else, values his privacy.   (The prepositional phrase *above all else* requires commas because it can be omitted without substantially altering the sentence's meaning.)

Verbal phrase
> *M*A*S*H**, challenging idealized assumptions about war, achieved surprising success.

Appositives

Appositives restate proper nouns. Nonrestrictive appositives add clarifying but not essential information and are set off by commas.

> Frank Lloyd Wright, an architect in the early twentieth century, felt that the design of a building should be suited to its surrounding.

Nonrestrictive Clauses

Nonrestrictive clauses that begin with a relative pronoun (*which, who, whose, whom, whoever,* and *whomever*) can be omitted without substantially changing the meaning of a sentence. Because they are not essential, nonrestrictive clauses must be set off by commas.

The Starry Night, which is prominently displayed in the Museum of Modern Art in New York, exemplifies Van Gogh's use of rich colors applied in bold strokes. (The information in the relative clause is set off by commas because it does not add to the essential meaning of the sentence.)

Picasso, who became one of the most successful and wealthiest artists in the world, started out ignored and impoverished during his early years in Paris.

22e	Use a comma to set off sentence elements that express contrast.

Because words and phrases that provide contrasting details do not function grammatically as parts of a sentence, they should be separated from the rest of a sentence by commas.

Shaw's first love was music, not theater.

The BBC, unlike American public television networks, is completely financed by the government.

EXERCISE 22.4 ❯ *Commas*

 Insert commas where needed in the following sentences.

1. *Beowulf* which is one of the earliest examples of Anglo-Saxon literature still appeals to those who like adventure stories not only to scholars.

2. The character Beowulf with a combination of heroic and religious qualities goes to the aid of Hrothgar the leader of a noble tribe.

3. The most famous episode of *Beowulf* the battle between Beowulf and the monster Grendel is a marvelous mix of supernatural and traditional Christian elements.

4. *Beowulf* is a historical-literary milestone; it is however a popular classic as well.

5. The plot elements of *Beowulf*—fights with supernatural beasts and tests of moral strength for example—remain standard elements in today's science fiction films perhaps explaining why *Beowulf* remains so popular.

| 22f | Use a comma to set off expressions that signal direct quotations. |

Commas separate expressions such as *he said* and *she commented* from the quotations they identify. These expressions can be used at the beginning, in the middle, or at the end of a quotation.

> In an ongoing battle of wits, Lady Astor once said to Winston Churchill, "Winston, if you were my husband, I should flavor your coffee with poison." (Note that the comma precedes the opening quotation mark.)

> "Madam," Churchill replied, "if I were your husband, I should drink it."

Or:

> "Madam, if I were your husband, I should drink it," Churchill replied.

> **22g** Use commas according to convention in numbers, dates, addresses, place names, and titles.

For easy reading and comprehension, most numbers of one thousand or more are divided by placing a comma between groups of three digits, moving from the right.

1,271   1,300,000

Dates written in month-day-year order require a comma between the day and the year, and in sentences a comma must also follow the year.

December 7, 1941, marked the beginning of America's involvement in World War II.

If dates are written in day-month-year order, or if only the month and year are given, no comma is needed.

Martin Luther King, Jr., was born on 15 January 1929; his birthday has been designated a national holiday.

The stock market crash of October 1929 precipitated the Great Depression.

Addresses written on one line or within a sentence require commas after the street name and between the city and state. Zip codes follow, with two spaces before and no comma after when written on a single line. When written within a sentence, zip codes appear with just one space before and with a comma after.   (See Business Writing, Appendix D.)

709 Sherwood Terrace, Champaign, Illinois 61820

Information on the water rights issue is available by writing the newspaper directly at *Courier-Journal,* 822 Courier Road, Wendel, Vermont 05753, to the attention of the editor.

Parts of place names are separated by commas even when they include only city and state or city and country. Within a sentence, a comma also follows the last item in the place name—essentially making the last item an appositive.

Marietta, Georgia   Ontario, Canada

Elsa, Illinois, is always 10 to 15 degrees cooler than nearby towns and cities because it is nestled in the bluffs along the Mississippi River.

Titles and academic and professional degrees that follow an individual's name should be set off with commas.

Adele Zimmerman, professor emerita, spoke at the alumni luncheon on Saturday.

Fernando Rivera, M.D., and Sean Mullican, Ph.D., coordinated the county's alcohol-abuse program.

When roman numerals follow the name of a private individual, monarch, ship, and so on, no commas are required.

Louis XIV of France was known as the "Sun King" because of the splendor of his court.

Commas are required with the abbreviations *Sr.* and *Jr.,* however.

Louis Gosset, Jr., won critical acclaim for his aggressive portrayal of a drill sergeant in *An Officer and a Gentleman.*

EXERCISE 22.5) *Commas*

 Insert commas where needed in the following paragraphs.

A. Although zoos provide opportunities to see many exotic animals up close the facilities for the animals do not always allow them to pursue or visitors to observe natural habits. Rhesus monkeys very small primates do not seem cramped in small places; they do not appear to suffer or experience any ill effects from their confinement. Chimpanzees however seem noticeably depressed in areas that do not allow them to move about freely. Orangutans highly intelligent primates also seem despondent. However the jungle cats tigers and leopards seem to suffer most. They pace in their cages or lie inactive and inattentive. These large primates and big cats which are usually among a zoo's main attractions require more space and some distance from the crowds of eager spectators. In recent years zoo keepers who have the animals' best interests in mind have begun building habitats for these larger animals. Most zoos have paid for these building projects which can be quite elaborate from general funds. Other zoos have launched major advertising campaigns hoping for individual donations. Still others stressing commitment to the community have appealed to major corporations. These large building projects should continue for they provide improved living conditions for large wild animals. As we maintain zoos that entertain and educate people we must also remember that the animals that live there should not suffer for our benefit.

B. Alaska the forty-ninth state joined the Union on January 3 1959. The largest state geographically covering 586412 square miles Alaska is also the least populated with only 479000 people. In fact the entire state has fewer people than many American cities of moderate size let alone Chicago Los Angeles or New York. Yes the contrast in physical size and population presents an anomaly but Alaska's history is full of such anomalies. Juneau its capital city has approximately twenty thousand people making it roughly the same size as Texarkana Arkansas; Augusta Maine; and Winchester Nevada. Alaska has fewer schools than many other states but has the highest teachers' salaries in the nation. Contradictions such as these have always been present. In 1867 when William H. Seward secretary of state arranged the purchase of Alaska for $7200000 most people thought the purchase was foolish. But "Seward's Folly" as the acquisition was called turned out to be not at all foolish. Rich deposits of minerals oil and natural gas have made Alaska one of America's greatest assets. (For more information on Alaska write to the Alaskan Chamber of Commerce 310 Second Street Juneau Alaska 99801.)

Word processing and commas

If you have problems with comma use, a word processor will provide a convenient means for eliminating them.

Check your comma use. Use the "search" command to locate the commas in your writing. Be sure that a comma rule justifies each use; check the position of the comma in relation to the items it separates or sets off from other sentence elements.

Add commas when necessary. Reread your final draft carefully, checking for places where needed commas are missing. Use the computer's ability to insert commas and automatically reformat the altered sentence. Check spacing and capitalization.

Commas help to establish meaning by separating elements in sentences. Thus, the use of commas where they are not needed confuses, distracts, and annoys readers and interferes with the communication of ideas.

Quick Reference

Unnecessary commas can be as confusing as too few necessary commas.

) *Do not place commas between subjects and verbs or between verbs and complements.*

) *Do not use a comma before a coordinating conjunction joining only two words, phrases, or clauses.*

) *Do not use commas to set off restrictive sentence elements.*

) *Do not use commas before quotations introduced by* that *or* if.

23a   **Do not use a comma between a subject and its verb or between a verb and its complement.**

In general, no punctuation should break the subject-verb or verb-complement pattern in a sentence. Insert commas only when they are necessary because of intervening elements, such as nonrestrictive phrases or clauses, appositives, coordinate modifiers, and transitional words.

Subject and Verb

Incorrect

Governments in many countries, control the prices of consumer goods.   (The comma interrupts the subject-verb pattern.)

Correct

Governments in many countries control the prices of consumer goods.

Correct

Governments in many countries, especially those in central Europe, control the prices of consumer goods.   (The pair of commas is required because a nonrestrictive phrase has been added.)

Verb and Complement

Incorrect

Black markets generally develop, in countries where consumer goods are scarce.   (The comma interrupts the verb-complement pattern.)

Correct

Black markets generally develop in countries where consumer goods are scarce.

| 23b | Do not use a comma before a coordinating conjunction that joins only two words, phrases, or dependent clauses. |

Words

Incorrect

The Federal Reserve controls the twelve Federal Reserve banks, and regulates the prime interest rate.   (The comma incorrectly separates the elements of a compound verb: controls *and* regulates.)

Correct

The Federal Reserve controls the twelve Federal Reserve banks and regulates the prime interest rate.

Phrases

Incorrect

The Federal Reserve's goals are to stabilize the national economy, and to help establish international monetary policies.   (The comma incorrectly separates two infinitive phrases joined by *and*.)

Correct

The Federal Reserve's goals are to stabilize the national economy and to help establish international monetary policies.

Clauses

Incorrect

Economists note that low interest rates encourage spending, but that they can also fuel inflation.   (The comma incorrectly separates two clauses, each beginning with *that*.)

Correct

Economists note that low interest rates encourage spending but that they also fuel inflation.

Remember that a comma is required between the independent clauses of a compound sentence.

Low interest rates encourage spending, but they also fuel inflation.

See Chapter 16 for more information and examples.

> | 23c | > | Do not use a comma before the first or after the
>   last item in a series.

Commas separate items in a series, but unless the series is part
of a nonrestrictive phrase, no commas should separate the
series as a unit from the rest of the sentence.

Incorrect

To earn extra money, to gain experience, and to make important
contacts, are reasons recent graduates in education often work as
substitute teachers.   (The infinitive phrases form a series that is the
subject of the sentence. The commas after *money* and *experience*
are appropriate, but the comma after *contacts* separates the compound subject from the verb.)

Correct

To earn extra money, to get more experience, and to make important contacts are reasons that recent graduates in education often
work as substitute teachers.

> | 23d | > | Do not use a comma with cumulative modifiers.

Cumulative modifiers—adjectives and adverbs that build upon
each other to create meaning—should not be separated by
commas. They differ from coordinate modifiers, which modify
words separately and require separation with commas.

Incorrect

The new, associate director is much younger than her predecessor.
(The comma separates cumulative adjectives: *associate* modifies
director, but *new* modifies the phrase *associate director.*)

Correct

The new associate director is much younger than her predecessor.

To test whether modifiers are cumulative, change their order. If the new order makes no sense, the modifiers are cumulative and no commas should be used. The example above would not make sense if it were written "The associate new director is much younger than her predecessor."

| 23e | Do not use commas to set off restrictive elements in sentences. |

Because restrictive elements—whether they are single words, phrases, or clauses—are essential to the meaning of a sentence, they should not be set off by commas.

Words

Incorrect
> The musical play, *West Side Story,* is based on Shakespeare's *Romeo and Juliet.* (The commas are incorrect because *West Side Story* is necessary to the meaning of the sentence.)

Correct
> The musical play *West Side Story* is based on Shakespeare's *Romeo and Juliet.*

Phrases

Incorrect
> Audience members continued to arrive, until well into the first act. (Because the phrase is essential to the meaning of the sentence, no comma should be used.)

Correct
> Audience members continued to arrive until well into the first act.

Clauses

Incorrect

Composers and lyricists, who adapt well-known plays, usually strive to maintain the spirit of the original works. (The commas are incorrect because the relative clause is essential; it identifies a particular group of composers and lyricists.)

Correct

Composers and lyricists who adapt well-known plays usually strive to maintain the spirit of the original works.

23f ⟩ **Do not use a comma before an indirect or a direct quotation introduced by *that* or *if.***

Because a quotation preceded by the word *that* or *if* functions as a complement, a comma would improperly separate verb and complement.

Incorrect

Mark Twain commented, that Wagner's music is more respected than it should be. (The subordinate clause following *commented* is the direct object of *commented*.)

Correct

Mark Twain commented that Wagner's music is more respected than it should be.

But:

Mark Twain commented, "Wagner's music is better than it sounds."

> **23g**   **Do not use a comma after *such as* or *like* or before *than*.**

Such as and *like* are prepositions that introduce examples in prepositional phrases; because these examples serve as objects, no comma is needed. *Than* signals a comparative construction, and it is illogical to separate with a comma the two items compared.

Incorrect

Some humanistic studies such as, philosophy, art history, and dramatic arts require a more scientific approach, than most people think. (The comma after *such as* inappropriately separates the preposition from its objects; the comma preceding *than* interrupts a comparative construction. The commas after *philosophy* and *art history* correctly separate items in a series.)

Correct

Some humanistic studies such as philosophy, art history, and dramatic arts require a more scientific approach than most people think.

EXERCISE 23.1 ❭ *Unnecessary commas*

 The following sentences contain far too many commas. Eliminate those that break the flow of the sentences or that obscure the logical connections between ideas.

1. Primary colors like, red, blue, and yellow are the most often used colors in national flags.

2. Interestingly enough, Libya's bright, green, flag is the only solid colored flag, in current use.

3. The small, Arab republic, Qatar, has a simple, black, and white flag.

4. Many countries—such as, Bahrain, Canada, Denmark, Indonesia, Japan, Monaco, Singapore, and Tunisia—use only red, and white, in their flags.

5. Most national flags use three, or four, bold colors, and use simple geometric shapes in their designs.

6. However, the ornate flag, of Sri Lanka, uses four colors, and black, and an elaborate design.

7. Only a few national flags, vary from the traditional, rectangular shape, including those of, Nepal and Switzerland.

8. The most frequently used colors, for flags, are red, white, and blue.

9. The U.S. flag, contains fifty, small, white stars on a blue field, and thirteen, alternating stripes of red and white.

10. As symbols of nations, flags serve, ideological, and political purposes—uniting citizens in times of peace, as well as in times of war.

EXERCISE 23.2   ⟩   Unnecessary commas

Delete the unnecessary commas from the following paragraph.

We went fishing, the first morning. I felt the same, damp, moss covering the worms, in the bait can, and saw the dragonfly alight on the tip of my rod, as it hovered a few inches from the surface of the water. It was the arrival of this fly, that convinced me, beyond any doubt, that everything was as it always had been, that the years were a mirage, and there had been no years. The small, waves were the same, chucking the rowboat under the chin as we fished at anchor, and the boat was the same boat, the same color green, and the ribs broken in the same places, and under the floor-boards the same fresh-water leavings and débris—the dead helgrammite, the wisps of moss, the rusty discarded fishhook, the dried blood from yesterday's catch. We stared, silently at the tips of our rods, at the dragonflies that came and went. I lowered the tip of mine into the water, tentatively, pensively dislodging the fly, which darted two feet away, poised, darted two, feet back, and came to rest again a little farther up the rod. There had been no years, between the ducking of this dragonfly and the other one—the one that was part of my memory. I looked at the boy, who was silently watching the fly, and it was my hands that held his rod, my eyes watching. I felt dizzy, and didn't know which rod, I was at the end of. —E. B. White, "Once More to the Lake"

Word processing and unnecessary commas

If you tend to use unnecessary commas, use the word processor to help you avoid this problem.

Check your comma use. Use the "search" command to locate the commas in your writing. Check each use, making sure that a comma rule justifies it.

Delete unnecessary commas. The word-processing program will automatically reformat sentences for you.

24 Semicolons and Colons

Semicolons perform various functions, sometimes acting as commas (separating items in a series) but more often acting as periods (separating closely related independent clauses).

A colon in effect says, "Notice what follows." Colons formally introduce lists, clarifications, and quotations.

Quick Reference

Use semicolons and colons selectively according to convention.

> *Use semicolons to join closely related independent clauses.*

> *Use colons to introduce lists, clarifications, and quotations.*

> *Do not allow colons to separate verbs from complements or prepositions from objects.*

24a ⟩ **Use a semicolon between closely related independent clauses not joined by a coordinating conjunction and before a conjunctive adverb that connects independent clauses.**

The use of a semicolon to link closely related independent clauses emphasizes the close relationship between the clauses.

Only a few hundred people in the United States know how to work with neon tubing; most of them are fifty years old or older.

The use of a conjunctive adverb in addition to a semicolon further stresses the interrelationship of the independent clauses.

Neon signs were once common at stores, restaurants, and gas stations across the country; however, in the sixties and seventies these sometimes garish advertisements fell into disfavor. (The conjunctive adverb *however* emphasizes the contrast.)

24b ⟩ **Use semicolons to separate equivalent sentence elements that contain commas.**

Items in a Series

When items in a series contain commas, use semicolons to separate them.

Sculptors creating works for outdoor display generally use native stone like sandstone, granite, or limestone; metals or alloys like bronze, cast iron, or steel; or imported stone like marble. (This use of semicolons helps readers identify the elements of the series.)

Heavily punctuated series can become awkward to read. If your sentence contains too many pauses, break it into briefer, smoother sentences.

Sculptors creating works for outdoor display generally use native stone like sandstone, granite, or limestone. Other frequently used materials include metals or alloys like bronze, cast iron, or steel or imported marble.

Independent Clauses

A semicolon effectively marks the break between independent clauses containing commas.

Much of the sculpture commissioned for public plazas is artistically innovative, visually exciting, and technically impressive; but often it does not appeal to the general public because they have grown accustomed to traditional, realistic statuary. (The semicolon clarifies the balance of the two-part sentence.)

Separate clauses into independent sentences if doing so would make reading them easier. Some rewording may be necessary.

Much of the sculpture commissioned for public plazas is artistically innovative, visually exciting, and technically impressive. Nevertheless, it often does not appeal to the general public because they have grown accustomed to traditional, realistic statuary.

24c ⟩ **Do not use a semicolon when other punctuation is required.**

With a Subordinate Clause

Use a comma, not a semicolon, after a subordinate clause at the beginning of a complex or compound-complex sentence.

Incorrect

Because it had a strong, centralized government; the Roman Empire was able to maintain relative stability, peace, and prosperity for nearly four centuries. (The semicolon obscures the relationship between the clauses; the opening, isolated clause is also a fragment.)

Correct

Because it had a strong, centralized government, the Roman Empire was able to maintain relative stability, peace, and prosperity for nearly four centuries.

To Introduce a List

Use a colon or a dash, not a semicolon or a comma, to introduce a list.

Incorrect

Historians cite several reasons for the decline of Rome; expanded citizenship, the deterioration of the army, barbarian invasions, economic decentralization, and inefficient agriculture.   (The closing list is a fragment.)

Correct

Historians cite several reasons for the decline of Rome: expanded citizenship, the deterioration of the army, barbarian invasions, economic decentralization, and inefficient agriculture.

24d	Use a colon to introduce elements formally or emphatically.

Selective use of colons adds clarity and emphasis to writing. Excessive use may be distracting.

To Introduce a Series

The part of the sentence that precedes a colon must be an independent clause, and the items in the series should never be direct objects, predicate nouns or adjectives, or objects of prepositions.

The names of six of the Seven Dwarfs reflect their personalities and habits: Bashful, Dopey, Grumpy, Happy, Sleepy, and Sneezy.   (The colon emphasizes the list; the words that precede the colon form a complete sentence.)

To Introduce an Independent Clause That Explains the Preceding Clause

When a complete sentence is needed to explain the meaning of the preceding sentence, use a colon to clarify the relationship. The first word following the colon usually begins with a lowercase letter, which identifies the clause as a clarification. However, the first word following the colon may begin with a capital letter.

> Good song lyrics are like good poetry: both express ideas in rhythmic, elliptical form.   (Without the second sentence, the meaning of the first would not be completely clear; the colon points to the explanatory relationship.)

To Introduce an Appositive at the End of a Sentence

Appositives (restatements of nouns or pronouns) are given special emphasis when they are introduced with colons. This use of the colon stresses the appositive as a necessary explanation of a key word in the main sentence.

> Early astronomers and astrologers assigning names to planets drew primarily on one source: mythology.

To Introduce a Direct Quotation

Direct quotations are formally introduced by colons. Both the introduction and the quotation must be independent clauses. The first word of the quotation is capitalized (see section 29a).

> The educational sentiment that Mark Twain articulated would shock many humorless educators: "It doesn't matter what you teach a boy, so long as he doesn't like it."   (The colon, preceded by a complete sentence, emphasizes Twain's comment.)

24e > **Use a colon to separate numerals in time references and Bible citations and to separate titles from subtitles.**

Hours and minutes given in numerals are separated by a colon. When the reference is to hours only, spell out the number.

The next flight to Tel Aviv leaves at 2:15 A.M.

We expect to be home by nine o'clock.

Chapter and verse in citations of books of the Bible are separated by a colon.

Genesis 3:23   Luke 12:27

Titles and subtitles are separated by a colon.

Nancy McPhee's *Book of Insults Ancient and Modern: An Amiable History of Insult, Invective, Imprecation, and Incivility (Literary, Political, and Historical) Hurled Through the Ages and Compiled as a Public Service* is a collection of amusing comments, criticisms, and rejoinders.

24f > **Do not use a colon between a verb and its complement or between a preposition and its object.**

Colons should not separate basic sentence elements. To test the accuracy of colon placement, change the colon to a period and drop the words that follow. If the remaining sentence is complete, the colon is correctly placed. If the remaining sentence is incomplete, delete or move the colon or rephrase the sentence.

Incorrect

The names of Enrico's cats are: Winston Churchill, T. S. Eliot, Eudora Welty, and Eleanor Roosevelt. (*The names of Enrico's cats are* is a fragment; the colon separates the verb from its complement.)

Correct

The names of Enrico's cats are Winston Churchill, T. S. Eliot, Eudora Welty, and Eleanor Roosevelt.

Incorrect

Enrico named his cats after: Winston Churchill, T. S. Eliot, Eudora Welty, and Eleanor Roosevelt. (The colon separates the preposition *after* from its objects, making the sentence incomplete.)

Correct

Enrico named his cats after Winston Churchill, T. S. Eliot, Eudora Welty, and Eleanor Roosevelt.

Correct

Enrico named his cats after historical figures and writers: Winston Churchill, T. S. Eliot, Eudora Welty, and Eleanor Roosevelt. (The prepositional phrase is complete, and the list of names adds clarification.)

EXERCISE 24.1 ❭ *Semicolons and colons*

Correct the errors in semicolon and colon usage in the following sentences.

1. The Mediterranean Sea is bordered to the south by: Egypt, Libya, Tunisia, Algeria, and Morocco.

2. The major ports on the Mediterranean Sea are: Barcelona; Spain, Marseille; France, Naples; Italy, Beirut; Lebanon, Alexandria; Egypt, and Tripoli; Libya.

3. Because the Bering Sea borders both the Soviet Union and the United States; it is often patrolled by military ships from each country.

4. In the Western Hemisphere, gulfs are more common than seas: however, several seas are located off the northernmost coasts of North America.

5. Four seas are named for colors; the Yellow Sea, the Red Sea, the White Sea, and the Black Sea.

EXERCISE 24.2) Semicolons and colons

The following paragraph uses the semicolon as its primary form of internal punctuation. Revise the punctuation, reserving the semicolon for places where it works better than any other mark of punctuation.

Ninety-six percent of Americans have eaten at one of the McDonald's restaurants in the last year; slightly more than half of the U.S. population lives within three minutes of a McDonald's; McDonald's has served more than 55 billion hamburgers; McDonald's commands 17% of all restaurant visits in the U.S. and gets 7.3% of all dollars Americans spend eating out; McDonald's sells 32% of all hamburgers and 26% of french fries; McDonald's is the country's largest beef buyer; it purchases 7.5% of the U.S. potato crop; McDonald's has employed about 8 million workers—which amounts to approximately 7% of the entire U.S. work force; and McDonald's has replaced the U.S. Army as America's largest job training organization. —John Love, *McDonald's: Behind the Arches*

Word processing and semicolons and colons

Because semicolons and colons must be used so infrequently and so carefully, you probably will want to check
each use. A word processor will help you do that easily.

Locate semicolons. Use the "search" command to
locate places where you have used semicolons. Make
sure that they separate independent clauses or items in
a series that contain commas.

Locate colons. Use the "search" command to locate
colons. Double-check their use, especially making sure
that they do not separate verbs from their complements
or prepositions from their objects.

25   **Apostrophes**

Apostrophes show possession (usually with an added *s*) and indicate the omission of letters or numbers from words or dates. Errors in the use of apostrophes are easily corrected.

Quick Reference

Apostrophes have two uses: to show possession and to indicate omission.

⟩ *Use an apostrophe and an s to form the possessive case of singular nouns and irregular plural nouns that do not end in* s.

⟩ *Use only an apostrophe to form the possessive of plural nouns ending in* s.

⟩ *Use an apostrophe to indicate the omission of letters in contractions and numbers in dates.*

⟩ *Do not use apostrophes with possessive pronouns* (yours, theirs); *do not confuse the possessive pronoun* its *with the contraction* it's ("it is").

| 25a ⟩ | **Use an apostrophe to form the possessive case.** |

Singular Nouns

Form the possessive of singular nouns, even those ending in *s*, by adding an apostrophe and an *s*.

Wyoming's state capitol   Braham's Requiem

Rockefeller's legacy   a week's wages

Saturday's game   Paris's night life

Plural Nouns

Form the possessive of plural nouns ending in *s* by adding an apostrophe only; an additional *s* is unnecessary. Irregular plural nouns that do not end in *s* (children, for example) form the possessive by adding an apostrophe and an *s*.

Teachers' lounge   a United Nations' task force

but:

children's theater   women's rights

To check whether the possessive form you have used is correct, mentally eliminate the apostrophe and *s* or the apostrophe. The word remaining should be the correct one for your meaning. For example, the phrase *earthquake's destruction* without the apostrophe and *s* refers to only one earthquake; the phrase *earthquakes' destruction* without the apostrophe refers to multiple earthquakes.

Compound Words and Joint Possession

Show possession in compound words or joint possession in a series by adding an apostrophe and *s* to the last noun only.

brother-in-law's objection

General Motors, Ford, and Chrysler's combined profits

the United States and Canada's trade agreement

If possession in a series is not joint but individual, each noun in the series must be possessive.

> Angela's, Bert's, and Lionel's fingerprints   (Each person has a separate set of fingerprints.)

| **25b** | Use an apostrophe to indicate the omission of letters from contractions and of numbers from dates. |

With apostrophe	*Complete form*
shouldn't	should not
I'll	I will *or* I shall
it's	it is
the '89 champions	the 1989 champions

Use contractions and dates with numbers omitted in informal writing only. In formal writing, present words and dates fully.

| **25c** | Do not use apostrophes with possessive pronouns. |

Possessive pronouns do not require the addition of an apostrophe. Do not be confused by those (*yours, ours, his,* and others) that end in *-s.*

Incorrect
   a belief of her's

Correct
   a belief of hers

EXERCISE 25.1 ❭ *Apostrophes*

Correct the use of apostrophes in the following sentences. Add needed apostrophes and delete unnecessary ones.

1. Even before people kept record's or conceived of science as a field of study, chemistry exerted its influence on their lives.

2. Early civilizations understanding of elements was primitive—the Greeks' and Romans' four elements were air, earth, fire, and water—but their applications of chemical principles were sophisticated.

3. Today, perhaps, its difficult to understand how much the development of the alloy bronze revolutionized human's lives.

4. During the Middle Ages, alchemists discovered how many chemical compounds work, even though trying to turn metals to gold was a chief preoccupation of their's.

5. By the seventeenth century, scientists studies were more methodical and practical, as was illustrated by Robert Boyles studies' of gases, for example.

6. Even before the development of sophisticated microscopes, John Daltons' theories of atomic elements explained chemical's reactions.

7. Dmitri Mendeleev, Russias foremost early chemist, explained the relationships among elements and devised the periodic tables that still appear on student's tests in classes' in introductory chemistry.

8. Marie Curie's and Pierre Curie's discovery of radium in 1898 further expanded scientist's understanding of chemistry.

9. Alfred B. Nobels' bequest of $9 million made possible awards in science and literature; one of the first five prizes in 1901 was an award for achievement in chemistry.

10. Chemist's work today is aided by sophisticated technology, but their search for knowledge has been shared by scientists' of generation's past.

26

Other Marks of Punctuation

Dashes, hyphens, parentheses, brackets, and ellipsis points serve specialized though important purposes in writing. Used effectively, these marks of punctuation help to create emphasis and establish meaning.

Quick Reference

Use specialized marks of punctuation carefully to emphasize elements of your sentences and to clarify your meaning.

⟩ *Use dashes to introduce parenthetical information, to set off material that contains commas, and to mark interruptions in thought, speech, or action.*

⟩ *Use hyphens to divide words, to form some compound words, and to join some prefixes and suffixes to root words.*

⟩ *Use parentheses in pairs to introduce parenthetical information and numbered or lettered sequences.*

⟩ *Use brackets to indicate alterations to direct quotations.*

⟩ *Use ellipsis points to indicate omissions in direct quotations and to indicate hesitation or suspended statements.*

26a ⟩ **Use the dash selectively to introduce parenthetical comments, to set off series, and to indicate breaks or shifts in thought, speech, or action.**

A dash, made by typing two hyphens with no space before or after, introduces parenthetical information emphatically and clearly, sets off a series at the beginning or end of a sentence, and marks interruptions in thought, speech, or action.

Parenthetical Comments

Parenthetical comments may be single words, phrases, or clauses inserted into a sentence to explain, amplify, or qualify the main idea. Parenthetical comments are grammatically independent of the rest of the sentence. They are frequently marked by parentheses, but those requiring special emphasis are set off with dashes.

> American military advisers did not acknowledge the strength and tenacity of the Viet Cong—a costly error.

> The reports of atrocities—in particular the My Lai Massacre—changed American attitudes about the war.

Appositives (phrases renaming nouns or pronouns) that contain commas may be set off by dashes (in place of commas) for greater clarity.

> Several presidents—Eisenhower, Kennedy, Johnson, and Nixon—were embroiled in political debates about the necessity of American involvement in Vietnam. (Because the appositive contains three commas, dashes mark the appositive more clearly than commas would mark it.)

A Series

A list of items placed at the beginning of a sentence for special emphasis is followed by a dash.

> The Tiger, the Mako, the Great White—these "man-eating" sharks deserve our respect more than our fear.

A dash may be used to introduce a list informally.

> *Jaws* portrayed most people's reactions to sharks—ignorance, fear, and irrationality. (In formal writing, use a colon to introduce a list.)

Shifts or Breaks in Thought, Speech, or Action

> Andrew Wyeth's monochromatic paintings—why does he avoid color?—are popular with the American public. (The dashes mark a shift in thought.)

> Because of cover stories and related articles in scholarly and popular magazines, interest in Wyeth's "Helga" paintings and drawings was intense for several months—and then suddenly subsided. (The dash marks a break in action.)

Selective Use

The use of dashes to show emphasis and discontinuity disrupts the rhythm of writing. Often, other punctuation serves as well—or better.

Too many dashes

The thunderstorm—coming from the southwest—looked threatening—with black and blue clouds and flashes of lightning. Within a matter of minutes—five to be exact—it was upon us. Around our house, the trees—delicate dogwoods, tall maples, and stout pines—bent in the heavy winds—their branches swaying violently. The black sky, the growing roar, the shaking house—all signaled the approach of a tornado—we headed for the basement. (Only two uses of the dash are required in this paragraph, with the appositive in the third sentence and with the introductory list in the last. The other uses are technically correct, but the use of fewer dashes would call less attention to the mechanics of the paragraph and allow readers to focus on the events described.)

Better

The thunderstorm coming from the southwest looked threatening, with black and blue clouds and flashes of lightning. Within five minutes, it was upon us. Around our house, the trees—delicate dogwoods, tall maples, and stout pines—bent in the heavy winds, their branches swaying violently. The black sky, the growing roar, the shaking house—all signaled the approach of a tornado. We headed for the basement.

EXERCISE 26.1 ❭ *Dashes*

Use dashes to combine each set of sentences into a single sentence.

1. The Distinguished Service Cross, the Navy Cross, the Silver Star, the Distinguished Flying Cross, the Bronze Star, and the Air Medal are awards given to members of the armed forces. These awards all recognize heroism.

2. Soldiers may be recognized for heroic behavior several times. They do not receive additional medals. Instead, they receive small emblems to pin on the first medal's ribbon.

3. Since 1932, the Purple Heart has been awarded to members of the armed forces who were wounded in combat. The medal is gold and purple, heart-shaped, and embossed with George Washington's image.

4. General George Washington established this military decoration in 1782. It was called the Badge of Military Merit. It wasn't given between 1800 and 1932.

5. The Congressional Medal of Honor is our nation's highest military award. The award was authorized in 1861 for the navy and in 1862 for the army.

<table>
<tr><td>26b</td><td>Use hyphens to divide words at the ends of lines, to form some compound nouns and adjectives, and to link some prefixes and suffixes to root words.</td></tr>
</table>

Word Division

Hyphens are used to divide words that do not fit in their entirety at the ends of typed or printed lines. Because hyphens must be placed between syllables, one-syllable words cannot be broken. Check your dictionary when you do not know where to divide a word. Other conventions of hyphenation dictate that one or two letters not be isolated on a line and that proper nouns not be divided. When it is not possible or acceptable to hyphenate a word, move the whole word to the next line.

Incorrect

Because of excavation difficulties, the archaeologist thought he'd quit the project.

Correct

Because of excavation difficulties, the archaeologist thought he'd quit the project.

Incorrect

Every year some natural disaster seems to strike Bolivia.   (Proper names should not be divided; two letters should not be isolated on a single line.)

Correct

> Every year some natural disaster seems to strike
> Bolivia.

 Many word processors can hyphenate words, providing an alternative to the sometimes awkward spacing that appears with justified right margins or the ragged edge that appears with unjustified margins. However, consider the workability of the word processor's hyphenation before using it.

■ *Check the hyphenation pattern.* Does the program introduce hyphens only between syllables? If it does not, do not use the "hyphenation" feature.

■ *Check proper names.* A word-processing program will not distinguish proper names from other words and will inappropriately hyphenate them. Check for hyphenated proper names and move any you find to the next line.

Compound Forms

A compound noun is a pair or group of words that together function as a single noun. Noun compounds may be open (*beer mug*), closed (*headache*), or hyphenated (*hurly-burly*). If you are unsure about how to present a compound noun, consult a dictionary. If the compound does not appear, it should be left open.

father figure	grandfather	mother-in-law
tomato soup	snowmobile	go-between
medical examiner	notebook	razzle-dazzle

When modifiers preceding a noun work together to create a single meaning, hyphens emphasize their unity. When the same modifiers follow the noun, hyphens usually are not needed.

Hyphens necessary	*Hyphens unnecessary*
out-of-the-way resort	a resort that is out of the way
long-term investment	an investment for the long term

When an adverb ending in *-ly* is the first word of a compound, omit the hyphen.

Margaret Atwood is a highly inventive writer.

When spelled out, fractions and cardinal and ordinal numbers from twenty-one through ninety-nine require hyphens. This rule applies whether the numbers are used as nouns, modifiers, or complements.

eighty-two recipes

forty-first president

two-thirds of the taxpayers

one hundred thirty-three CDs

Prefixes and Suffixes

Use hyphens to form words with the prefixes *all-, ex-,* and *self-* and with the suffix *-elect.* Other prefixes (*anti-, extra-, inter-, mid-, non-, over-, post-, pre-,* and *un-*) and suffixes (*-fold, -like,* and *-wide*) are generally spelled closed.

Hyphenate	*Spell closed*
all-consuming ambition	antibody
ex-department chairperson	extrasensory
self-restraint	midpoint
president-elect	statewide

When prefixes are joined to proper nouns or to compounds consisting of more than one word, hyphens are required. The proper nouns are capitalized.

un-American

post-World War II

non-native speakers

pre-Columbian

When a prefix has the same last letter as the first letter of the root word (or when a suffix has the same first letter as the last letter of the root word), hyphens are sometimes used for clarity.

anti-intellectual

bell-like

When the omission of a hyphen would result in ambiguity, a hyphen should be used.

release ("let go")	re-lease ("to lease again")
reform ("to improve")	re-form ("to form again")
unionized ("formed into a union")	un-ionized ("not ionized")

EXERCISE 26.2 ❯ Hyphens

Add or delete hyphens to correct the use of hyphens in the following sentences. (Some of the hyphens are used correctly.)

1. In the United States, senators are elected to six year terms, presidents (and their vice presidents) to four year terms, and members of Congress to two year terms.

2. Although these electoral guidelines are un-changed, little else about modern day elections has remained the way our national founders conceived them.

3. In pre-computer elections, hand-tabulated ballots were the norm, and results often were not certain for days.

4. Today, with computer-aided counting, officials post fully three fourths of election returns by mid-night of election day.

5. Television-networks quickly project the results of today's elections, usually on the basis of less than one fiftieth of the ballots cast.

6. Consequently, presidents elect now make victory speeches before mid-night on election day, rather than at mid-morning on the following day. Times have clearly changed.

| 26c | **Use parentheses selectively, always in pairs, to introduce parenthetical comments and numbered or lettered sequences.** |

Parenthetical Comments

Use parentheses to set off information that is only casually related to the flow of ideas in the rest of the sentence; essential information deserves direct presentation. Do not include long explanations parenthetically.

Joan of Arc (only seventeen at the time) led military troops to help return the rightful king of France to the throne.   (The information about Joan of Arc's age supplements the main idea; it is appropriately set off by parentheses.)

Parentheses are less emphatic and more disruptive than dashes, which are used for a similar purpose. The overuse of parentheses makes writing seem uneven, incoherent, or immature. To avoid such problems, use parentheses only when no other strategy or punctuation will serve your purpose.

Choppy

The compass (scratched and cracked) should have been replaced (years ago), but Joaquín (reluctant to spend the money) preferred to keep it as it was.   (The rhythm of the sentence is broken by the disruptive use of parenthetical details, some of which should be incorporated in the main sentence.)

Better

The scratched and cracked compass should have been replaced years ago, but Joaquín, reluctant to spend the money, preferred to keep it as it was.

Although you should use such complex patterns of punctuation sparingly, add clarifications of elements in parentheses using brackets, as in the following example:

HMS ("Her [or His] Majesty's Ship") *Reliant*

Numbered or Lettered Sequences

The numbering or lettering of steps can help clarify the steps of a complicated sequence of events or a process. Such lists, however, may be more distracting than helpful. Use them with care.

Freezing green beans involves six steps: (1) snap the ends off the beans; (2) wash the beans thoroughly in water; (3) blanch the beans for two to three minutes in boiling water; (4) cool them in ice water; (5) drain them for several minutes and then pack them into freezer containers; (6) seal the containers, label them, and put them in the freezer.

| 26d | **Use brackets selectively, always in pairs, to indicate alterations in a direct quotation.** |

Brackets indicate alterations in quoted material.

Clarification

When quotations out of context are not clear, use brackets to add clarifying information. Add only information that makes the original meaning clear; never add contradictory information or negative comments.

> Davies commented, "The army nurses' judgment in triage [where the medical staff decides which patients to treat first] is paramount, for they must determine a soldier's medical stability in a matter of seconds." (The bracketed material explains a key term, and the brackets indicate that the writer, not Davies, defined *triage.*)

> "If architectural preservationists are unsuccessful in their efforts, most [theaters built in the early 1900s] will probably be demolished by the end of the century," Walter Aspen noted. (In place of the bracketed material, the original read "of these fascinating buildings," an unclear reference outside of the original context.)

Alteration of Syntax

Use brackets to indicate changes in the syntax of a quoted passage. Make only minor changes—changes in verb tense, for instance—that allow you to insert a passage smoothly into the context of your writing. Do not alter the meaning of the original.

> Immigrants were sometimes confused or ambivalent about a new life in the United States. As a journalist noted in 1903, "Each day, thousands of immigrants [moved] through the turnstiles at Ellis Island, uncertain but hopeful." (The brackets show a change from the present tense *move,* which was appropriate in 1903, to the past tense *moved,* which is appropriate in current contexts.)

Notation of Error

When a direct quotation contains an error in grammar or fact, you must still transcribe the wording of the original exactly. However, to indicate for readers that you recognize the error and have not introduced it yourself, insert the word *sic* (Latin for "thus") in brackets following the faulty element.

> Adderson noted in her preface, "The taxpayers who [sic] the legislation will protect are the elderly, the handicapped, and those in low-income families." (*Sic* notes that the writer recognized Adderson's misuse of *who* for *whom.*)

To avoid seeming overly critical or pedantic, use *sic* only when necessary for clarity. The writer of the sentence above, for example, could have avoided using *[sic]* by being selective in how she used the quotation:

> Adderson noted in her preface that those protected by the legislation are "the elderly, the handicapped, and those in low-income families."

26e	Use ellipsis points to indicate omissions from quoted material and to indicate hesitating, trailing, or incomplete statements.

Ellipsis points are three *spaced* periods. Other marks of punctuation (periods, question marks, exclamation points, commas, and so on) are separated from ellipsis points by one space. Place ellipsis points either before or after the original punctuation, depending on the original sentence.

Omissions from Quoted Material

Use ellipsis points in quoted material to indicate where you have omitted extraneous information, parenthetical details, or unnecessary clarifications. Never omit words to change the original meaning of a source.

Original version

"The Ninth Street Station is a superb example of ornate woodworking and stonework. Typical of Steamboat-Gothic architecture, it was designed in 1867 by Fielding Smith. It is a landmark we should endeavor to preserve."

Acceptable shortened version

"The Ninth Street Station is a superb example of ornate woodworking and stonework. . . . It is a landmark we should endeavor to preserve." (Note the retention of the period at the end of the first sentence.)

Original version

"Theaters, such as the magnificent edifices built by the Lowe and Fox families, aging public buildings, and deteriorating commercial buildings in prime business locations are often demolished to provide space for new office buildings with little architectural interest."

Acceptable shortened version

"Theaters . . . , aging public buildings, and deteriorating commercial buildings in prime business locations are often demolished to provide space for new office buildings with little architectural interest." (The ellipsis points mark the omission of secondary material; the comma before *aging* is retained to separate the items in the series.)

Original version

"This is a great movie if you enjoy meaningless violence, gratuitous sex, inane dialogue, and poor acting. It is offensive by any standards."

Dishonest shortened version

"This is a great movie . . . by any standards." (This is clearly a misquotation.)

Hesitating, Trailing, or Incomplete Statements

More common in dialogue, especially in fiction, than in expository writing, the use of ellipsis points to indicate hesitating, trailing, or incomplete thoughts and statements can be effective if it is used sparingly.

Woody Allen's *Stardust Memories* was . . . boring.

From the back of the crowded elevator Chie shouted, "I have important news about. . . ." But the doors closed before she could finish.

EXERCISE 26.3 〉 *Parentheses, brackets, and ellipsis points*

Correct the faulty use of parentheses, brackets, and ellipsis points in the following sentences.

1. To install a cable converter, simply follow these directions: 1) remove the converter from the box; 2) attach the blue adapter wires to your television set; 3) plug the converter into an electrical outlet; 4) select a channel and test the equipment by turning it on.

2. "The benefits (to those who subscribe to cable services) are amazingly varied, from more programs to better programs," explained Ms. Abigail Fitzgerald, a cable network spokesperson.

3. Most cable subscribers would agree that they are offered more... but is it better?

4. Professor Martínez, media specialist at ASU, commented: "Much of what's offered is junk . . . When *Mr. Ed, Car 54,* and *The Munsters* make it to national rebroadcast, we have to question the uses to which cable is put. Of course, that's the long-standing issue (in television broadcasting)."

5. Then again, people (the American people in particular) have always enjoyed (really enjoyed) some mindless entertainment (*unchallenging* is, perhaps, a better word) to relieve the tension (and frustration) of the day.

EXERCISE 26.4 〉 *Punctuation review*

 Punctuate the following paragraph.

The Postal Reorganization Act signed into law by President Nixon on August 12 1970 created a government owned postal service operated under the executive branch of the government the new US Postal Service is run by an eleven member board with members appointed by the president of the Senate for nine year terms the Postmaster General who is no longer part of the president's cabinet is selected by the members of the board since 1971 when the system began operating four men have served as Postmaster General Winton M Blount E T Klassen Benjamin F Bailar and William F Bolger but has the postal system changed substantially since the PRA went into effect on July 1 1971 no not to any great extent first class second class third class and fourth class these still represent the most commonly used mailing rates however some services have been added for instance Express Mail which tries to rival Federal Express Purolator and other one day delivery services guarantees that packages will arrive at their destinations by 300 the day after mailing the prices are steep as one might expect in addition the Postal Service has instituted nine digit zip codes in some areas for all practical purposes however the business at 29990 post offices throughout the US continues in much the same way it did before the PRA

Word processing and specialized punctuation

Use a word processor to experiment with varied punctuation and to help you locate and check the correct use of specialized marks of punctuation.

Locate dashes, hyphens, parentheses, brackets, and ellipsis points in your writing. Use the "search" function to find each form of punctuation. Check sentences carefully to make sure that you have used these special punctuation marks correctly.

Experiment with varied punctuation. Because word-processing programs allow you to modify your work without completely retyping, experiment with alternative forms of punctuation to create various kinds of emphasis.

MECHANICS

27 Capitals

Capitals indicate the beginnings of sentences, signal proper nouns and proper adjectives, and identify important words in titles. Appropriate capitalization contributes to the clarity and correctness of your writing. Since unnecessary capitalization is confusing and annoying to readers, make sure when capitalizing a word that an uppercase letter is required.

Quick Reference

Capitals are used to create special emphasis.

⟩ *Capitalize the first word in every sentence.*

⟩ *Capitalize proper nouns and proper adjectives.*

⟩ *Capitalize first, last, and important words in titles.*

| 27a ⟩ | **Capitalize the first word in every sentence.**

Subtitles in foreign films can be as distracting as they are helpful.

Apply this rule when quoting a complete sentence.

The senator remarked, "*Initiating* dialogue among national leaders is an important step in solving problems in the Middle East."

In long, interrupted quotations, only words that begin sentences are capitalized.

"*Prospects* for peace in the Middle East exist," the senator reiterated, "only if leaders negotiate in good faith."

When a complete sentence follows a colon, capitalizing the first word is optional.

> The Declaration of Independence presents an idea we should remember: *All* people are created equal.

| 27b | > | **Capitalize proper nouns and proper adjectives.** |

Proper nouns and proper adjectives refer to specific people, places, and things and are therefore capitalized.

> In *August,* the *Benton Teachers' Association* voted to strike.   (specific name, capitals required)

But:

> In August, the teachers' union voted to strike.   (general noun, no capitals required)

Treat the pronoun *I* as a proper noun.

> *I* want to sail to the Bahamas, but I've got to earn some money first.

Names of specific individuals, races, ethnic groups, nationalities, languages, and places

Proper Nouns	*Proper Adjectives*
Samuel Johnson	Shakespearean sonnet
Caucasian	Egyptian border
Chicano	Hispanic traditions
New Yorker	German descent
Canadian	Portuguese trade
Kenya	Belgian lace

Southern Alps   Alpine village

Japanese-Americans   African-American organization

Registered trade names and trademarks, even those for common objects, must be capitalized.

Coke   Scotch tape   Kleenex   Xerox

Names of historical periods, events, and documents

the Age of Reason

the Battle of Bull Run

the Declaration of Independence

Names of days, months, and holidays

Monday   August   Presidents Day

Do not capitalize the names of seasons (*winter, spring, summer,* and *autumn*).

Names of organizations and government branches and departments

Phi Beta Kappa

National Wildlife Federation

the House of Representatives

the Department of Transportation

Names of educational institutions, departments, specific courses, and degrees

University of Chicago   Naperville High School

Department of Psychology   School of Business

Aviation Technology 421   Zoology 101

Bachelor of Arts   Doctor of Philosophy

General references to academic subjects do not require capitals unless they are languages (*English, Italian*) or use proper nouns or proper adjectives (*American history*). Course titles including numbers, however, require capitals.

Thomas earned an *A* in every speech course he took, but he was proudest of his *A* in *Speech 363*.

Religious names, terms, and writings

Islam	Christmas	God
Judaism	Torah	Allah
Christians	Koran	Krishna
Buddhists	Ramadan	the Resurrection

Titles used with proper names

Ms. Angélica Sánchez

Dr. Martin Luther King, Jr.

Professor Rebecca Shea

Secretary-Elect Andrus

President Roosevelt

but: my history professor

the former president

Abbreviations, acronyms, and call letters

100 B.C. (or b.c.)	7:30 P.M. (or p.m.)
NAACP	Schedule SE
WZZQ radio	KTVI-TV

Abbreviations and acronyms—including those for organizations, businesses, time designations, and documents—and radio and television station call letters are almost always capitalized.

> 27c ⟩ **Capitalize the first, last, and other important words in the titles and subtitles of books and other works.**

Words requiring capitals in titles and subtitles of books, plays, films, poems, articles, student papers, and so on are the first and last words and all nouns, verbs, adjectives, and adverbs. Nouns and adjectives in hyphenated compounds are also capitalized. Unless they appear as the first or last word, articles (*a, an,* and *the*), coordinating conjunctions, and prepositions of four or fewer letters are not normally capitalized.

Encyclopaedia Britannica   (a multivolume work)

The House of Mirth   (a novel)

Cat on a Hot Tin Roof   (a play)

Pulp Fiction   (a film)

"Sailing to Byzantium"   (a poem)

"The Book Burning"   (an article)

How to Make Yourself Miserable: Another Vital Training Manual (a book title and subtitle)

Seventeenth-Century English Poetry   (a hyphenated compound)

EXERCISE 27.1   ⟩   *Capitalization*

 Add the capital letters required in the following sentences.

1. art 426 (or english 426) is an interdisciplinary course that offers a survey of important artists and writers.

2. the course is team-taught by dr. nicholas bradford of the english department and ms. marlene jacobs of the art department.

3. during the fall of last year, i took the course to fulfill a humanities requirement.

4. we read a portion of dante's *divine comedy*—but not in italian—and saw slides of michelangelo's frescoes on the ceiling of the sistine chapel, both presenting perspectives on italian religious views.

5. we saw numerous paintings depicting the nativity, the crucifixion, and the ascension and read several religious poems.

6. turning our attention from europe, we saw *habuko landscape* by sesshu, a sixteenth-century japanese painter, and read samples of haiku poetry to learn of the spare but elegant images both create.

7. italian and flemish artists dominated the months of october and november.

8. we learned, however, that by the 1800s, neo-classicism had emerged and artistic dominance had shifted to france, where it remained for over a century; we read corneille's *phaedre* and saw representative paintings by david and ingres.

9. Over thanksgiving break, i took an optional field trip with ms. jacobs and several other students; we went to the art institute of chicago, her alma mater, to view their collection.

10. by the time we studied abstract art, national and artistic boundaries had been broken and painters like picasso and poets like t. s. eliot could be said to draw upon the same aesthetic traditions.

11. when ms. jacobs first said, "the fine arts are symbiotic, each reciprocally influencing the other," i wasn't sure i understood what she meant. now i think i know.

28 Italics

Italics distinguish titles of complete published works (except articles, essays, and short stories and poems, which require quotation marks): books; journals, magazines, and newspapers; works of art; the specific names of ships, trains, aircraft, and spacecraft; foreign words used in English sentences; and words or phrases requiring special emphasis.

In a printed text, italics are indicated with slanted type (*like this*), but in a typed or handwritten text, italics are indicated with underlining (like this). The meaning is the same.

Quick Reference

Use italics to create your intended meaning.

> Use italics to distinguish some titles, generally those of complete works.

> Italicize the specific names of ships, trains, aircraft, and spacecraft.

> Italicize unfamiliar foreign words and phrases.

> Italicize words used as words, letters as letters, and numbers as numbers.

> Italicize words to create special emphasis.

28a ▷ **Italicize the titles of most complete published works.**

The titles of books, journals, magazines, newspapers, pamphlets, plays, and long poems are italicized. Parts of long

386

works, such as chapter titles, and titles of articles, essays, and short stories and poems are presented in quotation marks. Titles of long musical compositions, albums, films, radio and television programs, paintings, statues, and other artworks are also italicized.

Books

Joseph Heller's *Catch-22*

Zora Neale Hurston's *Their Eyes Were Watching God*

The Bible, books of the Bible (Song of Solomon, Genesis), and legal documents (the Constitution) are not italicized, although they are capitalized.

Magazines and journals

Business Week

American Scholar

Charles Simic's essay "Reading Philosophy at Night" from *Antaeus*

Newspapers

the *Kansas City Star*

the *New York Times*

Long poems

John Milton's *Paradise Lost*

Walt Whitman's *Leaves of Grass*

but: Elizabeth Bishop's brief poem "In the Waiting Room"

Long musical compositions

Igor Stravinski's *Firebird Suite*

Giacomo Puccini's opera *Madame Butterfly*

Recordings

Kathleen Battle and Christopher Parkening's *Pleasures of Their Company*

the Beatles' *Abbey Road*

Seal's "Kiss from a Rose" from his album *Seal*

Plays

Sam Sheperd's *Buried Child*

Edward Albee's *Zoo Story*

Films

Sense and Sensibility

The Wizard of Oz

Radio and television programs

All Things Considered

Frasier

Although italic type is required for the name of a television series, the titles of episodes (daily, weekly, or monthly segments) are enclosed in quotation marks.

"Antarctica: Earth's Last Frontier" airs Tuesday at nine on *NOVA*.

Paintings

Pablo Picasso's *Three Musicians*

Georgia O'Keeffe's *Black Iris III*

Statues

Rodin's *The Thinker*

Michelangelo's *David*

Pamphlets

NCTE's *How to Help Your Child Become a Better Writer*

Roberta Greene's *'Til Divorce Do You Part*

28b	Italicize the specific names of ships, trains, aircraft, and spacecraft.

Only specific names are italicized and capitalized. The names of vehicle types and models are capitalized but not italicized. Abbreviations such as *SS* ("Steamship") and *HMS* ("Her [or His] Majesty's Ship") are not italicized.

Ships

Queen Elizabeth II

HMS *Wellington*

Andrea Doria

but: Starcraft Marlin, cruiser series XL

Trains

Orient Express

Stourbridge Lion

Aircraft

The Spirit of St. Louis

The Spruce Goose

but: Boeing 707

Spacecraft

Apollo XIII

Sputnik II

| 28c | Italicize unfamiliar foreign words and phrases in English sentences. |

If a foreign word or phrase is likely to be unfamiliar to your readers, italicize it.

> Andrea Palladio made frequent use of *trompe l'oeil* effects and murals in his villa designs.

The English language has borrowed extensively from the vocabularies of other languages. Some terms—such as *coffee, coupon, kasha, cliché,* and *kindergarten*—are fully assimilated into standard American usage and do not require italics. A standard college dictionary will help you to distinguish among unfamiliar, familiar, and assimilated foreign words. If a foreign word or phrase is not found in the dictionary (*cinéma vérité, perestroika*), it is likely to be recently imported or unfamiliar to your readers and should be italicized. If a foreign word or phrase is labeled in the dictionary as foreign (*adiós, coup de théâtre*), it may be unfamiliar to your readers; italics are optional. A word that is not labeled need not be italicized, even though the etymology indicates that it has been borrowed (*coup d'état, kibbutz*). When using any but the most common foreign terms, observe all conventions of spelling, including accents and other marks, found in the original language.

28d ⟩ **Italicize words used as words, letters used as letters, numbers used as numbers, and symbols used as symbols.**

"The *s* was put in *island,* for instance, in sheer pedantic ignorance."
—Bergen Evans

According to numerology, the numbers *5, 7, 12,* and *13* have occult significance.

28e ⟩ **Use italics selectively for emphasis.**

Italics may be used to call attention to words requiring emphasis, to signal a contrast, and to ensure close and careful examination of words by the reader.

"It makes a world of difference to a condemned man whether his reprieve is *upheld* or *held up.*" —Bergen Evans

Use italics very selectively to create emphasis. Emphasis should be created by effective diction and sentence structure. Overuse of italics dilutes emphasis and may distort the tone of your writing. By mimicking heavily stressed speech, overuse of italics may create an impression of irony or even cynicism that you do not intend. (See also section 29d.)

EXERCISE 28.1 **⟩** *Italics*

Supply italics where they are needed in the following sentences.

1. E. D. Hirsch's Cultural Literacy: What Every American Needs to Know—especially its appended list—has created a fascinating controversy since its publication.

2. For instance, Herman Melville's name is on the list, but his famous novel Moby Dick is not.

3. The statues David and the Pieta in St. Peter's Church in Vatican City are listed, but their creator Michelangelo does not appear.

4. Many of the foreign phrases—including ancien régime, bête noire, coup d'état, déjà vu, faux pas, fin de siècle, and tête-à-tête—are French, although a large number are Latin.

5. The Niña, Pinta, and Santa Maria do not appear, but the unfortunate Lusitania and Titanic do.

6. The maudlin poem Hiawatha and its author Henry Wadsworth Longfellow both appear, but Paradise Lost, the brilliant epic poem, appears without its author John Milton.

7. Birth of a Nation is the only film on the list not produced first as a book or play with the same name.

8. The absence of I Love Lucy, The Dick Van Dyke Show, The Mary Tyler Moore Show, All in the Family, and M*A*S*H makes it clear that popular television culture does not concern Hirsch.

9. Oddly enough, the ampersand (&) appears on the list.

10. Including the novel Tobacco Road on the list but not the play Who's Afraid of Virginia Woolf? seems arguable, but the enjoyment in lists is in disagreeing with them.

Word processing and italics

Word processors allow you to use italics easily, without extra typing.

Choose between slanted italic print and underlining. With some word processors and printers, italic automatically prints as underlining. Many, however, give you the choice of using slanted italic. Before you choose slanted italic, look at a sample printout. If the slanted type is difficult to read, choose underlining instead; the meaning will be the same.

Insert codes for slanted italic or underlining carefully. Once you enter a code, be sure to toggle out of the code; otherwise, your printer will continue the italics. If your word processor uses control marks in the text, rather than more visible contrasting bars, give this special attention.

Do not use codes for boldface in place of codes for italics. Many people enjoy experimenting with the typefaces made available by word processors and compatible printers, but boldface print is not an acceptable substitute for italics.

Accents and other diacritical marks are available on most word processors and printers. Learn how they work on yours and practice using them.

29 ` Quotation Marks

Quotation marks set off direct quotations and identify the titles of unpublished and short works and chapters and other sections of long works.

> ### Quick Reference
>
> *Use quotation marks in one of three ways:*
>
> ❭ *Use quotation marks to set off direct quotations.*
>
> ❭ *Use quotation marks with the titles of brief works, parts of longer works, and unpublished works.*
>
> ❭ *Use quotation marks to indicate ironic or special use of a word.*

| 29a | Use quotation marks with direct quotations and with dialogue. |

Direct Quotations

Direct quotations represent spoken or written words exactly; quotation marks indicate where the quoted material begins and ends. In contrast, indirect quotations—often introduced by *that* for statements or *if* for questions—report what people say or ask without using their exact words. Quotation marks are not needed with indirect quotations.

John Kenneth Galbraith commented, "In the affluent society no useful distinction can be made between luxuries and necessities." (The exact words are enclosed in quotation marks.)

But:

> Galbraith argues that the necessary and the desirable become inextricably mixed in a wealthy society.   (The paraphrase of Galbraith's comment needs no quotation marks, though it does require attribution and documentation.)

Dialogue

In dialogue, a record of a conversation between two or more people, quotation marks indicate the exact words used by each speaker in turn. By convention, each change of speaker begins a new paragraph.

> . . . I felt that I was getting a better sense of the language from novels than from grammars. I read hard, discarding a writer as soon as I felt I had grasped his point of view. At night the printed page stood before my eyes in sleep.
>
> Mrs. Moss, my landlady, asked me one Sunday morning:
>
> "Son, what is this you keep on reading?"
>
> "Oh, nothing. Just novels."
>
> "What you get out of 'em?"
>
> "I'm just killing time," I said.
>
> "I hope you know your own mind," she said in a tone that implied that she doubted if I had a mind. —Richard Wright, "The Library Card"

| 29b | Place punctuation marks with quotation marks according to convention. |

Periods and Commas

Periods and commas appear before closing quotation marks.

One of Flannery O'Connor's most haunting stories is "The River."

"The Circus Animals' Desertion," a late poem by William Butler Yeats, describes his growing frustration with poetry.

Semicolons and Colons

Semicolons and colons always follow closing quotation marks.

As a young poet, T. S. Eliot showed his brilliance in "The Love Song of J. Alfred Prufrock"; readers and critics responded to it enthusiastically.

One word describes Lewis Carroll's "Jabberwocky": nonsense.

Question Marks and Exclamation Points

Question marks and exclamation points must be placed to maintain the meaning of the sentence. If the material in quotation marks (whether a direct quotation or a title) ends with a question mark, then the closing quotation mark appears last. If your sentence is a question that contains material in quotation marks, then the question mark appears last. The same principles apply to the use of exclamation points with quotation marks.

Was it Archibald MacLeish who wrote "A world ends when its metaphor has died"? (The quotation is contained within the question.)

Have you read Ralph Ellison's "Did You Ever Dream Lucky?" (The question mark inside the quotation marks serves both the question in the title and the question posed by the sentence.)

If a quotation ends with a question mark or exclamation point, any other punctuation normally required by the sentence structure may be omitted.

I just read Ralph Ellison's "Did You Ever Dream Lucky?"

"Which is the right road?" he asked, but he received no reply.   (A comma is unnecessary following the question mark.)

| 29c | Use quotation marks with the titles of brief works, parts of long works, and unpublished works. |

Articles, short stories, short poems, essays, and songs are brief works whose titles should appear in quotation marks. Chapter or unit titles and episodes of television series require quotation marks because they are parts of long works. Titles of unpublished papers or dissertations of any length are placed in quotation marks.

Articles

"Good News Is No News" in *Esquire*

"The New World Through New Eyes" in *Smithsonian*

Short stories

Charles Baxter's "A Fire Story"

Isaac Bashevis Singer's "Gimpel the Fool"

Poems

Emily Dickinson's "Because I Could Not Stop for Death"

Theodore Roethke's "My Papa's Waltz"

Essays

Joan Didion's "Why I Write"

James Thurber's "University Days"

Songs

Sarah Vaughn's "How Long Has This Been Going On?"

George and Ira Gershwin's "Summertime"

Chapter or unit titles

"Theatre of the Orient" in O. G. Brockett's *History of the Theatre*

"Nightmare" in *The Autobiography of Malcolm X*

Episodes of television programs

"Chuckles Bites the Dust" from *The Mary Tyler Moore Show*

"Captain Tuttle" from *M*A*S*H*

Unpublished papers and dissertations

"Prohibition in the New England States"

"The Poetic Heritage of John Donne"

| 29d | Use quotation marks sparingly to indicate an ironic or other special use of a word. |

Words should be used according to their accepted meanings. The use of quotation marks to indicate irony may confuse and annoy readers. The use of quotation marks with nonstandard words—slang, regionalisms, or jargon—shows that you understand the words' potential inappropriateness in a sentence but does not justify their use. Either use the word with assurance or choose another word. (See also section 28e.)

Ironic use

Who needs enemies with "friends" like these? (Clearly *friends* is being used ironically. The phrase *so-called friends,* without quotation marks, would convey the same meaning more clearly.)

Disavowal

The negotiator asked for our "input." (Placing *input* in quotation marks suggests that the writer knows it is unacceptable jargon, but the disavowal does not make the word acceptable. Unless you are quoting directly, use a better word, such as *reactions, responses,* or *thoughts.*)

EXERCISE 29.1 ⟩ *Quotation marks*

Place the needed quotation marks in the following sentences. Pay attention to their positioning with other punctuation.

1. Running on Empty? an article in *National Wildlife,* stresses that water management should be a universal concern.

2. The opening chapter of *The Grapes of Wrath* contains this central image: The rain-heads [thunderclouds] dropped a little spattering and hurried on to some other country. Behind them the sky was pale again and the sun flared. In the dust there were drop craters where the rain had fallen, and there were clean splashes on the corn, and that was all.

3. Dry as Dust, a local documentary on the plight of the Depression farmers, had special meaning in 1994, when water shortages occurred throughout the midwestern states.

4. The very real fear of drought was softened during the Depression by ironic songs like What We Gonna Do When the Well Runs Dry?

5. Nadene Benchley's dissertation, Deluge or Drought: The Crisis in Water Management, ought to be published, for it contains information many people need to know.

> *Quick Reference*
>
> *Use numbers and abbreviations according to convention.*
>
> ❭ *In most instances, write out numbers expressible in one or two words.*
>
> ❭ *Use figures for exact numbers starting with 101.*
>
> ❭ *Use figures for measurements, technical numbers, and fractions.*
>
> ❭ *Use abbreviations sparingly in formal writing; if you use them, use standard abbreviations and forms.*

| 30a | In most writing contexts, use the written forms of numbers expressible in one or two words. |

Numbers Expressible in Words

Unless you are writing scientific or technical material, cardinal and ordinal numbers expressible in one or two words should be written out. This rule applies to numbers *one* through *one hundred* (*first* through *one hundredth*) and to large round numbers like *four thousand* (*four thousandth*) and *nine million* (*nine millionth*).

The Soviet Union has four cities—Moscow, Leningrad, Tashkent, and Kiev—with populations of more than two million.

Numbers from twenty-one through ninety-nine must be hyphenated.

Numbers at the beginning of a sentence must be spelled out—no matter how many words are needed. If the number is long and awkward, revise the sentence.

Incorrect

115 seniors attended graduation.

Correct

One hundred fifteen seniors attended graduation.

Better

We counted 115 seniors at graduation.

Numbers Expressible in Figures

Exact cardinal and ordinal numbers starting with 101 should be expressed in figures.

The Rogun Dam, the tallest in the world, stands 1,066 feet high.

Other Numbers Expressible in Figures

Addresses	316 Ridge Place; 1111 West 16th Street
Dates	24 December 1948 (*or* December 24, 1948); 150 B.C.; A.D. 1066
Divisions of books and plays	chapter 3; volume 9; act 2; scene 4
Exact dollar amounts	$3.12; $546 million; $7,279,000
Measurements	8 by 10
Identification numbers	332-44-7709; UTC 88 22495
Percentages	82 percent; 100 percent

Other Numbers Expressible in Figures

Fractions	3/4
Scores	101 to 94
Times	3:15 A.M.; 7:45 P.M. (*but* four-thirty in the morning; nine o'clock)

30b	Use abbreviations sparingly in formal writing and only in contexts in which their meaning is clear.

With few exceptions, abbreviations should not be used in formal writing. Commonly used personal titles such as *Ms., Mr.,* and *Dr.* are acceptable; also acceptable are some commonly used and easily recognizable abbreviations such as *JFK* and *AARP.* If you are unsure whether your readers will recognize an abbreviation, spell out the words.

If you choose to use a common abbreviation for a person or organization in formal writing, the first mention should include the full name, followed by the abbreviation in parentheses. Many common abbreviations may be written without periods. Check your dictionary for acceptable forms.

> The Potato Chip/Snack Food Association (PC/SFA) is an international trade association. Like other trade associations, the PC/SFA monitors government actions that affect the business of its members.

Certain specialized writing situations—technical directions, recipes, entries for works cited pages, résumés—use abbreviations to save space; but formal, academic writing should not. Instead, write the words out completely.

Acceptable Abbreviations

Well-known personal names	LBJ (Lyndon Baines Johnson); FDR (Franklin Delano Roosevelt)
Personal titles	John Walton, Jr.; Maria Santos, Ph.D.; Ms. Ella Beirbaum; Harold Blankenbaker, M.D.; Dr. Asha Mustapha; Rev. Joshua Felten; Gov. George Wallace (*but* Governor Wallace)
Names of countries	USA, US (*or* U.S.A., U.S.); UK (*or* U.K.); USSR (*or* U.S.S.R.)
Names of organizations and corporations	UNESCO; GE; FAA; AT&T
Words with figures	no. 133 (or No.)
Time of day	1:05 P.M. (*or* p.m.)
Dates	1200 B.C.; A.D. 476

Use the spell checker of your word-processing program to help you discover irregular abbreviations.

■ *Run the spelling program.* Because spelling programs include only a sampling of abbreviations—only the most common—most generally accepted ones are part of the dictionary. Reconsider your use of any abbreviations that the speller brings to your attention.

■ *Check a dictionary in special instances.* If you want to use the abbreviation anyway, check a dictionary to make sure that it is correct.

403

Unacceptable Abbreviations

	Not	*But*
Business designations	Co.	Company
	Inc.	Incorporated
Units of measurement	lb.	pound
	cm	centimeter
Names of days and months	Fri.	Friday
	Oct.	October
Academic subjects	psych.	psychology
	Eng.	English
Divisions of books and plays	p.	page
	chap.	chapter
	sc.	scene
	vol.	volume
Names of places	L.A.	Los Angeles
	Mass.	Massachusetts
Personal names	Wm.	William
	Robt.	Robert
Latin phrases	cf. *(confer)*	compare
	e.g. *(exempli gratia)*	for example
	et al. *(et alii)*	and others
	etc. *(et cetera)*	and so on, and others
	i.e. *(id est)*	that is

EXERCISE 30.1) *Numbers and abbreviations*

Correct the misuse of number forms and abbreviations in the following sentences.

1. Doctor Ruth Waller, an econ. prof. at UCLA, has written 26 articles and 2 books about Asian-American trade relations.

2. 1 of her books and 14 of her articles are on reserve at the ISU library—to be read by students in Econ. two-hundred and thirty-six.

3. Statistics in one article show that Japan's labor force is well diversified, with eleven percent in agriculture, thirty-four percent in manufacturing, and forty-eight percent in services.

4. Statistics also show that the Am. labor force is not as well diversified: we have seventy percent in services, with close to one-third of those in info. management.

5. By Fri., Dec. twelfth, each of us in the class must prepare a report on a US co. that is affected by Asian-American trade.

EXERCISE 30.2) *Numbers and abbreviations*

Correct the misuse of number forms and abbreviations in the following paragraph.

Walter E. Disney, better known as Walt, was born Dec. fifth, 1901, in Chicago. After early work at the Chicago Academy of fine arts and at a Commercial Art firm in MO, he moved to Hollywood in nineteen-twenty-three. It was there that he revolutionized US entertainment. 1928 was the year he produced "Steamboat Willie," a short cartoon that introduced Mickey Mouse, as well as the use of soundtracks with cartoons. 10 years later, his studio produced the 1st feature-length animated cartoon, *Snow White and the 7 Dwarfs,* and 2 years later, *Pinocchio.* The success of Disney's films stemmed from their innovations, i.e. their use of animated forms, color, music, voices, and story. After more than 12 successful films, Disney began work in television in 1950. In 55, Disneyland opened outside L.A., and Disney's theme parks created a new standard for amusement parks. Few would have suspected, in nineteen-twenty-six, that the man whose first cartoon creation was Oswald the Rabbit would change entertainment in the US of A.

Although familiar spelling rules (for example, *i* before *e*, except after *c*) can solve some spelling problems, spelling rules in English have many exceptions because English words derive from so many language groups. When you are uncertain of the spelling of a word, immediately consult a dictionary. Also develop practical strategies for overcoming spelling problems.

Quick Reference

Problems in spelling can be solved in a number of ways.

⟩ *Learn to use general spelling rules.*

⟩ *Use dictionaries to determine meaning and spelling.*

⟩ *Use correct pronunciation to guide spelling.*

⟩ *Check the spelling of technical terms carefully.*

31a ⟩ **Learn to use the general rules that guide spelling.**

Although rules for spelling in English have many exceptions, a few basic rules are helpful.

Forming Plurals

The letters that end a singular word dictate how its plural is formed.

Ending letters	Plural ending	Samples	
Consonant plus o	Add -*es*	potato	potatoes
		fresco	frescoes
Vowel plus o	Add -*s*	radio	radios
		stereo	stereos
Consonant plus y	Change *y* to *i* and add -*es*	victory	victories
		melody	melodies
Vowel plus y	Add -*s*	monkey	monkeys
		survey	surveys
s, ss, sh, ch, x, *or* z	Add -*es*	bonus	bonuses
		by-pass	by-passes
		dish	dishes
		catch	catches
		tax	taxes
		buzz	buzzes
Proper name with y	Add -*s*	Gary	Garys
		Germany	Germanys

Adding Prefixes

Some prefixes (*dis-, mis-, non-, pre-, re-, un-,* and others) do not change the spelling of the root word.

similar   dissimilar   restrictive   nonrestrictive

See pages 369–70 for exceptions to this rule.

Adding Suffixes

The pattern for adding suffixes depends on the letters that end the root word and those that begin the suffix.

Last letter of root word	First letter of suffix	Pattern	Examples
Silent e	Consonant	Retain the *e*	achievement, resolutely
Silent e	Vowel	Drop the *e*	grieving, sizable
Silent e *preceded by a "soft"* c *or* g	Vowel	Retain the *e*	noticeable, changeable
Single consonant in one-syllable word with one vowel	Vowel	Double the consonant	sitting, clipping

Distinguishing Between *ie* and *ei*

This familiar, useful poem explains the order of *i* and *e.*

> Write *i* before *e*
> Except after *c*
> Or when sounded like *ay*
> As in *neighbor* and *weigh*.

31b ▷ **Use dictionaries to determine meanings and spellings.**

Spelling Dictionaries

Spelling dictionaries provide the correct spellings of thousands of words. These specialized dictionaries dispense with pronunciation guides, notes on word origins, definitions, and synonyms. They generally indicate syllable breaks, however, which are helpful for hyphenating words at the ends of lines. People who have good vocabularies but spell poorly benefit from spelling dictionaries because they offer a quick way to confirm, for example, that *separate* is spelled with two *a*s and two *e*s and *develop* does not end with an *e*.

Standard Dictionaries

Words that sound alike, such as *mail* and *male,* may have very different meanings and spellings. Knowing which word has your intended meaning will lead you to the correct spelling. To determine that a word has your intended meaning and that you have spelled it correctly, use a standard dictionary. When reading a dictionary definition to select the proper word and spelling, be sure to read all the definitions to find the one you need.

The sample from *The American Heritage Dictionary, Second College Edition* (Boston: Houghton, 1985) shown in Figure 1 illustrates common features of a dictionary entry.

| 31c | Use correct pronunciation as a guide to correct spelling. |

The omission of letters in casual speech generally does not interfere with comprehension. Habitual mispronunciation, however, may lead to incorrect spelling. To ensure correct spelling when you write, sound out problem words, stressing all the letters—especially those omitted in speech. For instance, people often pronounce *accidentally* as if it were spelled "accident*ly*." Slowing down to sound out all the letters—*ac·ci·den·tal·ly*—will prevent this spelling problem.

Figure 1   A sample dictionary entry

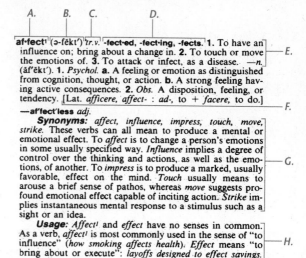

A. *Spelling and syllabification*
B. *Pronunciation (guide at bottom of dictionary page)*
C. *Part of speech*
D. *Spelling variations (past tense, present participle, plural)*
E. *Numbered definitions*
F. *Word origins*
G. *Synonyms and antonyms*
H. *Usage note*

31d ⟩ **Carefully check the spelling of technical words and British variants.**

Technical Words

If you use specialized words, check them individually. Their spellings are sometimes difficult to remember because we use such words infrequently. Keep a note card handy with a list of the correct spelling of any technical words that you use often.

British Variants

Dictionaries list alternative spellings for some common words, and many times any choice is acceptable if applied consistently. When alternatives are identified as *American (Am.)* and *British (Brit.)*, however, use the American spelling.

American Words with British Variants	
American	*British*
center	centre
color	colour
encyclopedia	encyclopaedia
judgment	judgement

However, when using a proper name, maintain the original spelling even if it is British.

Great Britain's *Labour Party* favors the nationalization of many industries. (Although the American spelling is *labor,* the proper name of the political party uses the British spelling.)

Word processing and spelling

If you use a word processor for writing, take advantage of its spelling program. A spelling program searches a manuscript for words not appearing in its dictionary and highlights them for your attention. Be aware, though, of several minor limitations of some spelling programs.

A spelling program cannot distinguish an error in the choice of homonyms (words that have the same sound but different meaning). As long as a word appears in the program's dictionary, the program will not highlight the word. For instance, the use of *pail* for *pale* and *blew* for *blue* would go unnoticed.

A spelling program cannot identify typing errors if they produce words that are in the dictionary of the program. For instance, the use of *quite* instead of *quiet* would go unnoticed because *quite* is a recognizable English word.

The dictionaries for spelling programs are necessarily general. Highly specialized words—proper names and technical terms, for instance—may not be included. In such cases, add these specialized words to the word list of the dictionary or check them individually.

Always proofread your writing carefully for spelling errors that are not identifiable by the spelling program.

32 ESL Writers: Working Beyond Mechanics

Writing in a foreign language is a challenge. Having worked to acquire a second language, you already understand some of the difficulties. Yet if you concentrate on only the smallest, most technical issues of language usage, your larger, more comprehensive language skills will not develop. As a result, most of the advice in this chapter concerns acclimating yourself to the contexts of writing within the American culture, even though it also addresses a number of important, technical issues related to the study of English as a Second Language (ESL).

Quick Reference

❭ *Recognize the contexts for writing in the American culture.*

❭ *Recognize special ESL needs when learning the writing process.*

❭ *Learn about the technical issues of writing from general discussions.*

❭ *Consider some special concerns for ESL students.*

32a ❭ **Recognize the unique contexts for writing in the American culture.**

Having arrived in the United States to study, you are well aware of the ways that American culture differs from your own. Where Americans live, what they eat, how they entertain themselves, where they shop, how they travel, and, perhaps more importantly for your studies, how they communicate no doubt vary from your experiences in your native country. That is not a surprise. Yet as a student in an American college, you will be expected to communicate—both in writing and in speaking—in an American fashion, and that will require practice. This chapter addresses a number of issues that may help you to write comfortably and fluently in American English.

As you begin to strengthen your writing through classroom experiences, consider the following ideas. They will give you insights into the contexts for your writing.

Individuality. In the United States, individuals assert their unique identities, even when they consider themselves to be members of groups. As a result, you may be expected to think of your individuality more than you have before. If you are from a culture that emphasizes group identity over individuality, expect some challenges as you think about yourself in this new way.

Personal experience. Because of the emphasis on individuality, personal experiences are highly valued in American culture, even while recognizing that those experiences are limited. The use of the first person (*I* paid for *my* education by working as a waiter) stresses how individuality and personal experience are emphasized in communication. If you are from a culture that deemphasizes personal matters in communication, expect some slight problems as you learn to share your personal experiences with people outside of your family and circle of friends.

Directness. American culture is, to a great extent, a direct one. To ensure that your ideas are understood, you will need to state your ideas in clearly expressed topic sentences and thesis statements. If you are from a culture that finds it rude or too obvious to state an important idea directly, learn to shift to this new, straightforward strategy.

Diversity. Because America includes many subcultures (immigrant groups have increased American diversity), you must realize the importance of differences among people. If you are from a homogeneous culture, you must learn to recognize the broadness of the American view and to acknowledge the importance of diversity.

Linear organization. Because Americans are generally direct people, you will need to develop organizational skills that present your ideas in a straightforward, uncluttered fashion. If you are from a culture that uses less direct organizational patterns, you will have some difficulty in adjusting to the "obviousness" required in American communication.

Explanations of unfamiliar material. Because students in American colleges and universities come from a broad spectrum of society, you will not be able to assume that they share the same kinds of experiences. As a result, you will need to explain your ideas, information, experiences, and insights with care. If you remember that readers must have detailed information to understand ideas, you will succeed in sharing your unique perspectives.

Growth and development. American education is, in large part, founded on the principles of growth and development, not finite results. Consequently, within a writing course, you will be judged on improvement: if your writing matures and your control of technical issues increases, teachers will recognize your development. Also, because development is central to the American educational experience, most schools have writing centers where tutors work with students to improve their skills.

Available tutoring. American colleges and universities are committed to providing help for their students to ensure that they receive additional help with writing instruction. Often affiliated with departments of English and composition or units with titles like Student Support Services, writing centers frequently provide free tutoring. Locate the tutoring center at your school and arrange for a tutoring time (generally one tutoring session each week); specially trained tutors will help you work to improve your skills.

Teachers. Unlike the teachers in some cultures, American teachers are, for the most part, willing to work with students on an individual basis. Do not feel embarrassed to ask for available help during teachers' scheduled office hours; they will help you isolate writing problems and discuss ways to solve those problems. Approach your teachers directly but politely, explaining your concerns about writing.

Computers. Computers are available on most college campuses in the United States, and they can provide you with special opportunities to improve your writing. After drafting a paper on a computer, you can use the word-processing program to check the spelling of words in the paper; be aware that some words that sound the same (homonyms) are spelled differently (*tale* and *tail,* for example) and that correctly spelled words—even if they are the wrong words for the sentence—will go unnoted (for example, if you use *their* instead of *there*). Computers also allow you to print copies of your paper to proofread and then make only the necessary revisions, without retyping the paper; this feature saves time and energy.

| 32b | Use the sections of this handbook to learn about general issues of writing, but recognize special ESL needs. |

The first five chapters of this handbook deal with the composing process—the strategies and techniques that help writers put their ideas into written form. The explanations included in those chapters are clear and direct; given sufficient time, you should be able to internalize the concepts those chapters contain. However, as an ESL writer, you may benefit from approaching those materials with these suggestions in mind.

Planning

Write about what you know. Although some international students hesitate to write about experiences in their native countries—feeling that such writing is predictable—or hesitate to write about their own experiences—feeling, perhaps, that it is immodest—use your unique experiences to your advantage. Teachers and classmates, who may know little about your culture, will be interested in the ideas and experiences you have to share.

Consider your readers carefully. Be aware that if you write about your experiences in another culture—or write about your new experiences in American culture—you will need to remember what your readers know and do not know. Provide details and clear explanations, rather than allowing readers to rely on stereotypes.

Solicit reactions to your work. Ask your teacher, a classmate, or a tutor to respond to your planning and outline. Seeking reactions at this early stage will help you to avoid problems later in the composing process.

Drafting

Outline your ideas fully. Outlines provide an excellent opportunity for you to see how comprehensive your paper will be. Arrange your information carefully and change the order of elements if you discover a better plan. Consider preparing your outline using full sentences to describe each element. Although such a strategy will take longer than creating an outline using words and phrases, you will discover appropriate ways of expressing your ideas while working in stages.

Concentrate on the ideas in your paper. Because you have spent so much time learning the technical issues of English, you may find it difficult to ignore them, even for a short while. However, you will compose more fluently if you concentrate first on explaining the ideas in your paper. During later stages of revision, you can concern yourself with technical matters.

Work in stages. Divide your writing into small blocks of time, working steadily but never too long at one sitting. You will be less frustrated—and more productive—if you relax between stages of writing.

Be patient and realistic. Remember that learning to write well is a difficult process for *all* writers; as a second-language student, you will discover that the task is even more challenging. Consequently, you must allow yourself some mistakes and recognize that you cannot solve all problems at once. In particular, remember that the more language skill you assimilate during your studies, the better your writing will become. Relax and allow yourself time to improve.

Solicit reactions to your work. Ask your teacher, a classmate, or a tutor to read through an early draft of one of your paragraphs. Explain that you will complete technical revisions later; have them respond only to the development of ideas within the paragraph. A response at this stage will indicate where you are succeeding with your writing and where you need more work.

Revising

Give special attention to content. Revise your draft by look-ing first at its content. Have you described the people, places, actions, and ideas with care? Could you explain them more fully? Have you provided useful explanations of your central ideas? Have you expressed them plainly? Is your material arranged in a logical order? At this stage, ignore technical matters to concentrate on the major ideas and examples in the paper.

Consider grammatical issues. Once you have reviewed the ideas of the paper, revise your sentences as needed. Make sure that your sentences are complete and that your verbs are in the proper tenses. Examine the order of adjectives and adverbs. Looking at these matters slowly and carefully—apart from your review of content—will allow you to concentrate on grammatical issues one sentence at a time.

Consider issues of usage. Once you have double-checked your sentences to ensure that they are grammatical, examine your word choices to determine whether they reflect current American usage. Have you included modifiers that are in the correct word form? Have you double-checked idiomatic structures? This is perhaps the most difficult kind of revision for ESL students, so attend to these matters with care.

Consider mistakes you frequently make. Based on responses to your earlier written work, give special attention to matters that have caused you problems before. If you have consis-tent difficulty with verb tense, examine your verb tenses in every sentence. If you sometimes confuse words, use the Glossary of Usage (654–71) to make sure that you have select-ed the appropriate word to convey your meaning.

Solicit reactions to your work. Ask your teacher, a classmate, or a tutor to review your work with you. In most instances, you cannot expect them to respond to every feature of your paper; they simply will not have time. However, select the feature (grammar or usage, for example) that has caused you the most consistent trouble and ask someone to respond only to that feature.

By dividing your work on a paper into stages, you will be able to concentrate on improvements one at a time. This pattern will make the work less demanding and more productive than it would be if you tried to revise all features at once. Remember, as well, that your papers will improve as you gain experience in composing in English. Patience, practice, and perseverance are qualities you will want to develop.

| 32c | Use the sections of this handbook to learn about technical issues of writing. |

Chapters 6–31 of this handbook discuss the technical issues of writing—from sentence development and word choice to grammar, punctuation, and mechanics. As an ESL student, you can use these discussions from the main portion of the handbook to find answers to many of your technical questions. This outline of topics, with brief descriptions, will help you to locate the sections that will be of most use to you:

Parts of Speech (Chapter 6). Turn to this chapter for a review of the parts of speech: nouns, pronouns, verbs, adjectives, adverbs, conjunctions, prepositions, and interjections. The discussion includes both explanations and example sentences. For brief definitions, also consult the Glossary of Grammatical Terms (672–90). Consult Chapter 6 and the Glossary of Grammatical Terms as you draft or revise the sentences in your papers.

Sentence Structures (Chapter 7). For a review of how sentences are formed in English, read this chapter. You will find discussions of parts of sentences (subject and predicate) and kinds of sentences (simple, compound, complex, and compound-complex). The Glossary of Grammatical Terms also includes brief definitions and samples. Consult Chapter 7 and the Glossary of Grammatical Terms as you draft or revise the sentences in your papers.

Sentence Elements (Chapters 8–12). For a review of the elements that will improve the effectiveness of your sentences (variety, emphasis, parallelism, pronoun reference, and positioning modifiers), read the discussions in these chapters. Although these issues are fairly sophisticated and will therefore be challenging, they are important elements to learn about as you work to improve your writing. Consult Chapters 8–12 as you draft or revise the sentences in your papers.

Word Choices (Chapters 13–14). To explore the possibilities for improving your individual word choices, review these chapters to learn about how your word choices affect the meaning of your sentences. Give particular attention to abstract and concrete words, idioms, jargon, and sexist language. The Glossary of Usage also contains discussions of frequently confused words and words used in special contexts. Consult Chapters 13–14 and the Glossary of Usage as you complete the stylistic revisions of your papers.

Grammar (Chapters 15–20). Because effective grammar is at the heart of effective writing, use these chapters to eliminate fragments, comma splices, and fused sentences from your writing; address issues of subject-verb and pronoun-antecedent agreement, pronoun case, and verb tense; follow the advice in these chapters to ensure that you use adjectives and adverbs in their proper forms. Consult Chapters 15–20 as you draft and revise the sentences in your papers.

Punctuation (Chapters 21–26). These six chapters include discussions of how to use three kinds of end punctuation (periods, question marks, and exclamation points) and a wide variety of in-sentence punctuation (commas, semicolons, colons, apostrophes, dashes, hyphens, parentheses, brackets, and ellipsis points). Consult Chapters 21–26 as you complete the technical revisions of your papers.

Mechanics (Chapters 27–31). These five chapters describe technical matters that relate to writing in American English: capitalization, italics (or underlining), quotation marks, number style, abbreviations, and spelling. Consult Chapters 27–31 as you complete the technical revisions of your papers.

Research (Chapters 33–35; Appendix B, pages 565–91). Offering advice on how to plan, research, write, and document a research paper, these chapters describe a wide variety of technical issues. The discussions pertain to the documentation style of the Modern Language Association, although Appendix B discusses the documentation style of the American Psychological Association. Consult Chapters 33–35 and Appendix B when you are required to research and document a paper.

Glossary of Usage (pages 654–71). Located at the back of the handbook, this glossary explains the usage of potentially confusing words and phrases. Many commonly confused word pairs (*accept/except, among/between, fewer/less,* and others) are included in this simple reference guide. Consult this appendix at any point during your work.

Glossary of Grammatical Terms (pages 672–90). Located at the back of the handbook, this glossary provides brief definitions of all grammatical terms used in the book. Sample sentences are included for easy reference. Consult this appendix at any point during your work.

Recognize some special concerns for ESL students.

As an ESL student, you will have some special concerns that develop because of the nature of the English language. These matters move beyond the issues of basic grammar—although some of them are grammatical—because they are concerned with either the irregularities of the language or with issues that native speakers develop intuitively and that are therefore discussed infrequently in textbooks for English speakers. Many of these matters are discussed in other sections of this handbook, but several unique issues are discussed below.

Articles (*a, an,* or *the*)

A and *an* are indefinite articles. Use *a* before a word that begins with a consonant sound; use *an* before a word with a vowel sound. For words beginning with *h,* use *a* when the *h* is voiced (sounded) and *an* when the *h* is unvoiced (unsounded). Uses of either *a* or *an* suggest that the noun or pronoun that follows is nonspecific and that it can be counted.

> *A* passport is required for travel in *a* foreign country. (In both instances, the use of *a* signals a nonspecific noun.)

> *An* honest person is not always *a* helpful one. (In the first instance, the *h* is unvoiced, so *an* is required; the voiced *h* in the second instance requires the use of *a.*)

When nonspecific nouns are plural, they do not require the use of an article, as the sample below illustrates:

> Chi Li and Miko took vacations three times a year.

But:

> Miguel took *a* vacation last year.

Use *the,* a definite article, with a noun that is specific and countable. The use of *the* suggests that readers are familiar with the specific noun or that other words in the sentence make it particular.

The travel agent whom Sasha recommended provided excellent help. (The use of *the* indicates that readers are able to identify the particular travel agent.)

But:

I prefer to consult *a* travel agent who is not too aggressive. (This general use requires the indefinite article *a,* since it is nonspecific.)

Modal Auxiliary Verbs

Modal auxiliaries are used along with the infinitive of a verb to create special meanings. By using modals, you can indicate ability, intention, permission, possibility, necessity, obligation, or speculation. The following examples illustrate the various meanings that modal auxiliaries create.

Meaning	Modals	Sample
Ability	can, could	You *can* pick up your tickets any time after 5:00 P.M.
Intention	will, would, shall	Jamal *will* study law next year.
Permission	can, could, may, might	Renters *may* keep small pets, so long as they are not noisy.
Possibility	may, might, can, could	Ian's family *can* afford to travel, but they don't.

Meaning	Modals	Sample
Necessity	must, have to	Nakia *must* work to help pay for her college expenses.
Obligation	should	Parents *should* read to their children on a regular basis.
Speculation	would	If we had a longer break, I *would* visit my family.

Idioms

In English, as in most other languages, some expressions create meaning collectively, even when the words do not make complete sense when considered individually. Consult the list below to ensure that you are conveying the meaning you want:

Idiom	*Meaning*
break down	stop functioning
break up	separate
call off	cancel
check into	investigate
figure out	understand
fill out	complete
find out	discover
get over	recover from
give up	stop trying

Idiom	*Meaning*
hand in	submit
hand out	distribute
leave out	omit
look after	take care of
look into	examine
look up	locate
look up to	admire
look forward to	anticipate
pick out	choose
point out	show
put off	postpone
run into	meet by chance
turn down	refuse

You can often avoid the potential confusion of using American idioms by using the single words or the descriptive phrases that convey the same meaning.

Order of Modifiers

In English, multiple words that modify a noun must appear in a specific sequence. When you include multiple modifiers, include them in this order:

1. Articles, possessives, and demonstratives (*the* computer, *her* apartment, *this* assignment)

2. Order (*third* speaker)

3. Number (*sixteen* candles)

4. Description (*beautiful* park)

5. Size (*enormous* lake)

6. Shape (*spiral* staircase)

7. Age (*middle-aged* teacher)

8. Color (*red* rose)

9. Origin (*Chinese* vase)

10. Material (*wooden* bowl)

The pattern for combining modifiers works in this way:

> the fourth white house (article, order, color)
> a dozen long-stemmed roses (article, number, shape)
> a talented young dancer (article, description, age)
> an ancient Egyptian statue (article, age, origin)

In most instances, restrict the number of modifiers used to describe a noun; more than three modifiers often makes a sentence seem overloaded with information. Use such terms selectively.

RESEARCH

33   Choosing and Researching a Topic and Taking Notes

To begin work on a research paper, you need to select a topic to research and write about. The possibilities are many, but some kinds of topics will have more value for you than others because of your interests and experiences. Explore alternative topics, keeping an open mind, and base your selection on a reasoned judgment. Consider topics related to your fields of study; consider topics related to your personal interests; consider topics that raise questions you would like to explore. Whatever your final choice, make sure you are committed to it because you will spend hours reading and thinking and writing about it.

Quick Reference

❭ Choose a general subject that is interesting, specific, and challenging.

❭ Narrow the subject to a specific topic by restricting its time period, its locale, or its special circumstances.

❭ Write a working thesis statement to guide your research.

❭ Compile a preliminary list of sources and evaluate their potential usefulness.

❭ Take clear, consistent, and complete notes.

❭ Avoid plagiarism by accurately identifying material quoted or paraphrased from any source.

Research papers can take two forms: factual, objective surveys of all the literature available on a topic, or interpretive analyses of selected evidence arrayed to support the writer's viewpoint and ideas. In psychology, sociology, economics, and some other courses, you may be required to write the first type of paper. Ask your instructor for guidelines and, if possible, for an example of a good paper of this type. Since most college research papers, particularly those for composition courses, are of the second type, this text focuses on interpretive research papers. An interpretive paper, though primarily concerned with the writer's own ideas and interpretations, cannot ignore contrary evidence. Writers of such papers must be thorough and fair even though they take a position on their material. Part of the challenge—and pleasure—of research is the constant need to reexamine your evidence in the light of new evidence and your ideas in the light of new ideas.

As you gather and read materials related to your topic, you will be taking notes to record information and ideas to use when you write the final paper. You will find the process of reading source materials and taking notes rewarding and enlightening if the topic intrigues and has value for you.

| 33a | Choose a subject and narrow it to a specific topic. |

Choosing a General Subject

Unless your instructor has assigned a general subject for your research paper, you must begin your work by selecting one. Your major or minor field of study or an academic subject that you enjoy or know well is a good broad subject to begin with. Any subject that you know well or have an interest in can lead you to a good topic. A student who worked for Eli Lilly during the summer, for example, might write about pharmaceutical testing or prescription pricing.

Guidelines for Assessing General Subjects

The subject should be interesting enough that you are willing to spend hours reading, thinking, and writing about it.

The subject should be of a scope broad or narrow enough to be treated adequately in the space recommended or required.

Enough material should be available to research the subject completely within the time available. (Very recent events sometimes do not make good subjects because adequate materials are not generally available.)

The subject should be challenging but should not require special knowledge that you do not have and do not have time to acquire.

The subject should not be overused; overused subjects are likely to be uninteresting to readers and difficult to research because of the high demand for the source materials.

When you have selected a general subject that meets the above requirements, you should consult with your instructor to be sure that it meets the requirements of the assignment.

Shingo, a music major, considered these general subjects:

The introduction of the compact disc

Music videos

The therapeutic value of music

He eliminated the first because it was potentially too technical, while the second seemed too broad. The therapeutic value of music was also broad, but it could be narrowed easily, and with strong music and psychology departments at his school, Shingo knew he could find a wide range of materials.

EXERCISE 33.1   )   *General subjects*

List five possible subjects for a research paper. Test them against the guidelines given on page 432. (If you have difficulty with this assignment, skim the index of a textbook in your major or minor field for interesting subjects.)

Example

1. Government subsidies

2. High-grossing films

3. The Federal Reserve Board

4. Museums

5. Child care

Narrowing a General Subject to a Specific Topic

With a general subject in mind, begin to narrow its focus. A focused topic will help you to determine your thesis. It will also help you to avoid wasting valuable research time reviewing and reading materials that will not fit into the final paper. An hour or two spent skimming reference books to narrow a subject often saves many hours later.

Begin by reading general sources in the library's reference room—various encyclopedias, specialized dictionaries, and fact books—to discover the scope and basic themes and details of your general subject. (See the selected list of general reference works on pages 438–43.) Use this information and the following strategies to narrow your subject to a specific topic:

Limit the scope of your paper to a specific, manageable time span. For example, restrict the topic *assembly-line automobile production* to the *1920s* or *1990s*.

Limit the scope of your topic to a single, specific location. For example, focus the topic *revitalization of cities* on *midwestern cities* or *St. Louis*.

Limit your topic to a specific set of circumstances. For example, the topic *the U.S. presidency* might focus on *the U.S. presidency in wartime*.

These strategies can be combined to achieve even greater focus. For example, a student might research *assembly-line automobile production in Japan in the 1990s* or *the U.S. presidency during the conflict in Vietnam*.

To obtain a general knowledge of music therapy and to find some themes or details to help him to narrow the general subject, Shingo skimmed some of the relevant reference books in the college library. He found that his general subject could be effectively narrowed by examining music therapy in particular periods, such as the nineteenth or twentieth centuries, or by discussing the uses of music therapy in the United States or in the treatment of individual disorders. Shingo also found many special circumstances that applied to his subject; for example, he noted that over time the uses of music therapy had changed. Narrowing the subject by limiting his focus to the United States in the twentieth century gave Shingo many additional topics. One of them was how music therapy has been used with autistic children.

Shingo was most interested, however, in what he read about the evolving uses of music therapy to treat varied disorders. He was unsure whether to treat the evolution or the disorders, but he decided to research all treatments, knowing that he could narrow his topic further if he found a great deal of information on one kind of therapy.

EXERCISE 33.2 ⟩ *Specific topics*

Select three subjects from your responses to Exercise 33.1 and write three focused topics by identifying a particular time, place, or special circumstance.

Example

1. Government subsidies for the dairy industry (special circumstance)

2. Museums and innovative programs in the last twenty years (special circumstance and time)

3. Child care in the inner city (place)

33b ⟩ **Write a working thesis statement.**

In the same way a working thesis statement guides your planning and drafting for other papers, it guides the planning and drafting for your research paper. For a research paper, which involves intensive reading and thinking, the working thesis statement also helps you to select and evaluate materials.

Your focused topic, presented as a complete statement or question and anchored with details derived from your preliminary research (see sections 33d and 33e), should yield an effective working thesis statement. A student working with the focused topic *the U.S. presidency during the conflict in Vietnam* might develop the following thesis:

> During the conflict in Vietnam, the presidency was forced to a new level of accountability by the peace movement and the media.

After writing your working thesis statement, evaluate its effectiveness. (For more information on thesis statements, see section 1e.) An effective thesis statement has three essential characteristics and may have three optional characteristics:

Essential Characteristics

Identify a specific, narrow topic.

Present a clear opinion on, not merely facts about, the topic.

Establish a tone appropriate to the topic, purpose, and audience.

Optional Characteristics

Qualify the topic as necessary, pointing out significant opposing opinions.

Clarify important points, indicating the organizational pattern.

Take account of readers' probable knowledge of the topic.

A thesis statement can make research seem a deductive process, one beginning with a general conclusion to support. But research should also be inductive, shaped by and building to a conclusion based on information discovered. When researching, allow new ideas and unexpected information to lead you in promising new directions. Keep an open mind by using your working thesis not as something to be proved but as a controlling idea to be confirmed, refuted, or modified on the basis of your reading in the weeks or months ahead.

From his general reading and discussions with other music students, Shingo decided to research the therapeutic uses of music. Before beginning his focused search for specific, relevant materials, he reviewed his preliminary research notes and formulated his working thesis statement:

Although most people know that music modifies moods, few recognize that because music has the power to influence people's behavior, it offers important treatment for the mentally and physically impaired.

Shingo planned to use this working thesis statement to guide him research; it would help him to eliminate sources that treated unrelated aspects of music therapy and direct him toward relevant sources. He kept in mind, however, that his thesis statement would likely change as he learned more about his topic.

A word processor allows you to revise your working thesis statement easily as you complete your research.

■ *Draft alternative working thesis statements.* Work freely and quickly, typing as many variations of your thesis statement as possible. In trying to express the thesis statement in alternative ways, you may discover different approaches to your work.

■ *Revise your working thesis statement as you learn more.* Because the computer allows you to add and delete freely, without retyping, review and revise your thesis statement frequently as you continue your research, acknowledging changes in your interpretation of the topic.

EXERCISE 33.3 ❭ *Working thesis statements*

Type three working thesis statements with which you might begin your research. Discuss them with other students or with your instructor to determine which one promises to lead to the most productive research and the best paper.

Example

1. Although the federal government first subsidized the dairy industry during the Great Depression to ensure its survival, the threat is long since past, and the time has come for the dairy industry to operate without subsidies.

2. Although museums have long been seen as formidable, formal institutions, today's curators challenge this assumption by hosting innovative exhibits.

3. Before government agencies can fairly expect parents on welfare to work, they must provide affordable, acceptable child care.

| 33c | Begin your research in the library. |

If you have not done so already, take a tour of your college library with a staff member. On your own, after a tour or using a map or guide to the library, locate and explore these areas of the library: the circulation area, where you will check out and return books; the card catalog area, which includes computerized, or card-based, catalogs; the reference area; the periodical and newspaper sections; the stacks; special collections; departmental libraries; the new-book area; the government documents area; the microform (microfilm, microfiche) and media area; and the reserve area. Locate the library's computer clusters, photocopy areas, and group study rooms. Talk to library staff members about other services offered by the library, such as interlibrary loans.

General Reference Works

The reference room in your library contains a number of useful general reference works: major encyclopedias, almanacs, atlases, dictionaries, and compendia of biographies, etymologies, and quotations. The following lists indicate the variety of material available.

General References

Contemporary Authors. Detroit: Gale, 1962 to date.

Current Biography. New York: Wilson, 1940 to date.

Facts on File: A Weekly World News Digest. New York: Facts on File, 1940 to date.

National Geographic Atlas of the World. 6th rev. ed. Washington, DC: Natl. Geographic, 1992.

The New York Times Atlas of the World. 2nd rev. ed. New York: Times, 1986.

Who's Who. London: Black, 1849 to date.

The World Almanac and Book of Facts. New York: Newspaper Enterprise, 1868 to date.

Encyclopedias

Academic American Encyclopedia. 21 vols. 1985 ed.

Collier's Encyclopedia. 24 vols. 1993 ed.

Concise Columbia Encyclopedia. 1989 ed.

Encyclopedia Americana. 30 vols. 1994 ed.

The New Encyclopaedia Britannica. 32 vols. 1993 ed.

Art and Music

Abraham, Gerald. *The Concise Oxford History of Music*. New York: Oxford UP, 1985.

Baker's Biographical Dictionary of Musicians. Ed. Nicholas Slonimsky. 8th ed. New York: Macmillan, 1992.

The Concise Oxford Dictionary of Art and Artists. Ed. Ian Chilvers. New York: Oxford UP, 1990.

New Grove Dictionary of Music and Musicians. Ed. Stanley Sadie. 20 vols. Washington, DC: Grove's, 1980.

The Pelican History of Art. 50 vols. in progress. East Rutherford, NJ: Penguin, 1953 to date.

Economics and Business

Concise Dictionary of Business. New York: Oxford UP, 1992.

Freeman, Michael J., and Derek Aldcroft. *Atlas of the World Economy.* New York: Simon, 1991.

The HarperCollins Dictionary of Economics. Ed. Christopher Pass et al. New York: Harper, 1991.

Rutherford, Donald. *Dictionary of Economics.* New York: Routledge, 1992.

Terry, John V. *Dictionary for Business and Finance.* 2nd ed. Fayetteville: U of Arkansas P, 1990.

History

The Almanac of American History. Ed. Arthur M. Schlesinger, Jr. New York: Putnam's, 1983.

Britannica Book of the Year. Chicago: Britannica, 1938 to date.

Brownstone, David M., and Irene M. Franck. *Dictionary of Twentieth Century History.* New York: Prentice, 1990.

Encyclopedia of American History. Ed. Richard B. Morris and Jeffrey B. Morris. 6th ed. New York: Harper, 1982.

Grum, Bernard. *The Timetables of History: A Horizontal Linkage of People and Events.* 3rd ed. New York: Simon, 1991.

Newsmakers: The People behind Today's Headlines. Ed. Louise Mooney Collins. New York: Gale, 1985 to date.

Rand McNally Atlas of World History. Rev. ed. Chicago: Rand, 1993.

The Times Atlas of World History. Ed. Geoffrey Barraclough. 3rd ed. Maplewood, NJ: Hammond, 1989.

Language and Literature

Cambridge Encyclopedia of Language. Ed. David Crystal. New York: Cambridge UP, 1987.

Cambridge Guide to Literature in English. Ed. Ian Ousby. New York: Cambridge UP, 1988.

Cambridge Handbook of American Literature. Ed. Jack Salzman. New York: Cambridge UP, 1986.

Crystal, David. *An Encyclopedic Dictionary of Language and Languages*. Oxford: Blackwell, 1992.

Holman, C. Hugh, and William Harmon. *Handbook to Literature*. 6th ed. New York: Macmillan, 1992.

The Oxford Companion to American Literature. Ed. James D. Hart. 5th ed. New York: Oxford UP, 1983.

The Oxford Companion to English Literature. Ed. Margaret Drabble. 5th ed. New York: Oxford UP, 1985.

Oxford English Dictionary. Ed. J. A. Simpson and E. S. C. Weiner. 2nd ed. 20 vols. New York: Oxford UP, 1989.

Philosophy and Religion

Cohn-Sherbok, Dan. *Dictionary of Judaism and Christianity*. Philadelphia: Trinity, 1991.

Contemporary Religions: A World Guide. Ed. Ian Harris et al. Harlow, Eng.: Longman, 1992.

Copleston, Frederick Charles. *A History of Philosophy*. Rev. ed. 9 vols. New York: Image, 1993.

Lacey, Alan R. *A Dictionary of Philosophy*. 2nd ed. London: Paul-Methuen, 1990.

Science and Math

American Men and Women of Science: Physical and Biological Sciences. 19th ed. 8 vols. New York: Bowker, 1995.

Ashworth, William. *Encyclopedia of Environmental Studies*. New York: Facts on File, 1991.

Cambridge Encyclopedia of Life Sciences. Ed. E. Adrian Faraday and David S. Ingram. Cambridge: Cambridge UP, 1985.

Concise Dictionary of Physics. New York: Oxford UP, 1990.

The Concise Oxford Dictionary of Earth Sciences. Ed. Ailsa Allaby and Michael Allaby. Oxford: Oxford UP, 1990.

The Concise Oxford Dictionary of Ecology. Ed. Michael Allaby. Oxford: Oxford UP, 1994.

Encyclopedia of Earth System Science. Ed. William A. Nierenberg. 4 vols. San Diego: Academic-Harcourt, 1992.

Encyclopedia of Mathematics and Its Applications. 31 vols. Reading, MA: Addison; Cambridge: Cambridge UP, 1976 to date. In progress.

The Encyclopedia of Physics. Ed. Robert Besancon. 3rd ed. New York: Van Nostrand, 1990.

Encyclopedic Dictionary of Mathematics. Ed. Kiyoshi Ito. 2nd ed. 2 vols. Cambridge, MA: MIT P, 1993.

Hale, W. G., and J. P. Margham. *The HarperCollins Dictionary of Biology*. New York: Harper, 1991.

McGraw-Hill Encyclopedia of Physics. Ed. Sybil P. Parker. 2nd ed. New York: McGraw, 1993.

Van Nostrand Reinhold Encyclopedia of Chemistry. Ed. Douglas M. Considine and Glenn D. Considine. 4th ed. New York: Van Nostrand, 1984.

Social Sciences

The Encyclopedia of the Peoples of the World. Ed. Amiram Gonen. New York: Holt, 1993.

Encyclopedia of Sociology. Ed. Edgar F. Borgatta and Marie L. Borgatta. 4 vols. New York: Macmillan, 1991.

Evans, Graham, and Jeffrey Newnham. *The Dictionary of World Politics: A Reference Guide to Concepts, Ideas, and Institutions*. New York: Simon, 1990.

Harvard Encyclopedia of American Ethnic Groups. Ed. Stephan Thernstrom, Ann Orlov, and Oscar Handlin. Cambridge, MA: Belknap-Harvard UP, 1980.

Jary, David, and Julia Jary. *The HarperCollins Dictionary of Sociology*. New York: Harper, 1991.

Multiculturalism in the United States: A Comparative Guide to Acculturation and Ethnicity. Ed. John D. Buenker and Lorman A. Ratner. New York: Greenwood, 1992.

Political Handbook of the New World. New York: McGraw, 1975 to date.

Winthrop, Robert H. *Dictionary of Concepts in Cultural Anthropology*. New York: Greenwood, 1991.

Catalog Search Systems

Computer and Card Systems

All search systems provide basic information about each book in the library's collection: author's name, title of the book, call number, publication information, technical information, subject classification, and cataloging information. These comprehensive, technical descriptions familiarize you with a source before you search for it in the collection.

Each book in the library's collection is cataloged in at least three ways, making your search for materials easier. For instance, if you know about a book by Carl Sagan but cannot remember the title, look under *Sagan* for a listing of the library's holdings of his books. Similarly, if you want a book titled *The Unheavenly City* but cannot remember the author's name, search under *Unheavenly City*. To locate books on a subject like "solar energy," search under the subject, name.

Computerized Catalogs (for Books)

Computer search systems have revolutionized research, increasing the efficiency of finding sources and providing mechanisms for searching selectively. Familiarize yourself with your library's computerized search system: take advantage of specialized training sessions or use the instructional handouts available near the computer terminals.

Most systems offer a variety of on-screen options to guide you through your search for materials, the most important ones included below:

Help Screens. These screens explain procedures, often explaining commands in detail and explaining options. They are frequently tailored to your library's system and collection.

No Entries Found. At times a search command will not produce a "match," meaning that the system cannot locate a corresponding entry. Most systems display a screen describing the common causes for failure: search procedures are inaccurate, the item is not in the library's collection, or the item is not included in the database.

Search Results. When your search retrieves records for sources in your library's collection, a screen will list the sources. If the number of sources is small, a *short list* will appear on the screen, with each item numbered (for example, 1–12). If the number of sources is large, a *long list* will appear, with items grouped (1–12, 13–24, 25–36) so that you can select from among the groups.

Short Record (Brief View). One of two kinds of listings, the short record includes the book's title, author, publishing information, description, subject classifications, location, call number, and status (whether checked out or not). (See Figure 1.)

Long Record (Long View). This listing includes all information in the short record but also includes edition numbers, descriptions of indexes, bibliographies (and their length), volumes, previous titles, series information, and selected information about the content. (See Figure 2.)

Computerized Indexes (for Periodicals)

Specialized systems using online services or CD-ROM technology provide information about **periodicals**—magazines, journals, and newspapers. Familiar indexes—such as *Readers' Guide to Periodical Literature, Education Index,* and others— now exist in electronic form.

Figure 1   Short record (brief view)

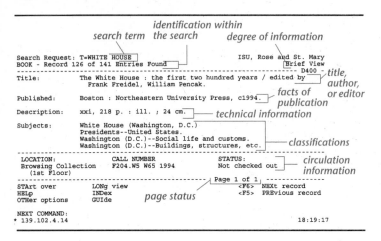

Most indexes to periodicals are organized by subject, not by author or title, but all entries will include article title, author, special information (about illustrations, bibliographies, maps, and other special features), and publication information. In addition, many computerized indexes also include abstracts, or brief summaries of articles. (See Figure 3.)

Because computerized indexes provide information on a much broader range of periodicals than most libraries subscribe to, you will need to determine whether the periodical is available to you. Some computer systems include "holdings" information; at other times, you may need to check a bound catalog or card catalog to verify the library's holdings.

Figure 2   Long record (long view)

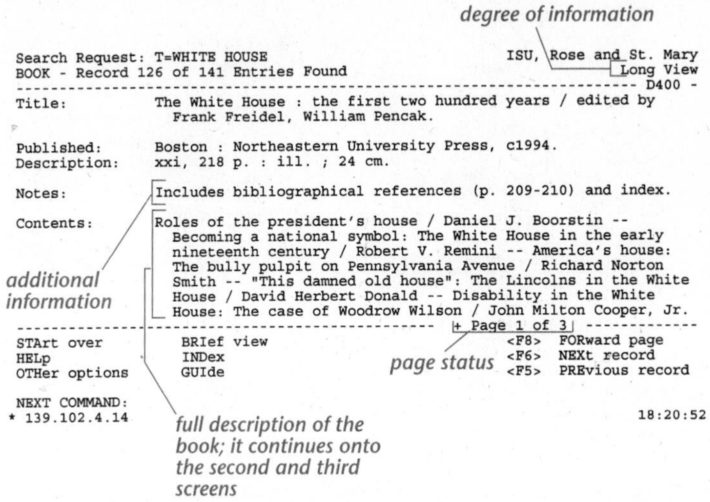

degree of information

```
Search Request: T=WHITE HOUSE                    ISU, \Rose and St. Mary
BOOK - Record 126 of 141 Entries Found                     └─Long View
------------------------------------------------------------------ D400 -
Title:         The White House : the first two hundred years / edited by
               Frank Freidel, William Pencak.

Published:     Boston : Northeastern University Press, c1994.
Description:   xxi, 218 p. : ill. ; 24 cm.

Notes:         Includes bibliographical references (p. 209-210) and index.

Contents:      Roles of the president's house / Daniel J. Boorstin --
               Becoming a national symbol: The White House in the early
               nineteenth century / Robert V. Remini -- America's house:
               The bully pulpit on Pennsylvania Avenue / Richard Norton
               Smith -- "This damned old house": The Lincolns in the White
               House / David Herbert Donald -- Disability in the White
               House: The case of Woodrow Wilson / John Milton Cooper, Jr.
------------------------------------------------- |+ Page 1 of 3| ------------
STArt over       BRIef view                     <F8>  FORward page
HELp             INDex               page status <F6>  NEXt record
OTHer options    GUIde                          <F5>  PREvious record

NEXT COMMAND:
* 139.102.4.14                                                  18:20:52
```

additional information (pointing to Contents)

full description of the book; it continues onto the second and third screens

Card Catalogs (for Books)

Card catalog entries list books in each of three formats: author, title, and subject. Depending on the size of the library's collection and the patterns established for organizing the collection, the catalog may be arranged in one of two ways:

Divided catalog. A divided catalog groups cards according to type: all author cards together, all title cards together, and all subject cards together. In a variation of the divided catalog, author and title cards are interfiled, and only subject cards are placed in a separate catalog.

Dictionary catalog. A dictionary catalog files author, title, and subject cards together.

Figure 3   Entries in periodical index

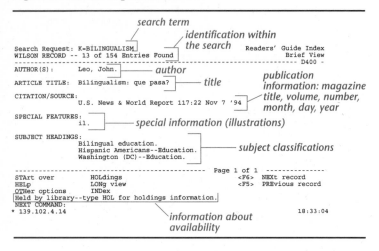

A clear description of the cataloging system and basic instructions on how to use it are generally available in the card catalog area.

Catalog Cards

Although the same information appears on all three source cards—the title, author, publishing information, description, subject classification, location, and call number—the first line of each card varies depending on the card's purpose: a title card begins with the book's title; a subject card begins with the book's subject classification; an author card begins with the book's author. As the samples in Figure 4 show, other information is the same.

Figure 4   Title, subject, and author cards

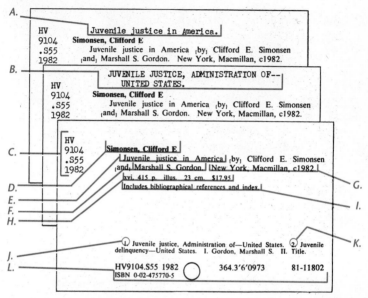

A. *Title card heading*
B. *Subject card heading*
C. *Library of Congress number*
D. *Author card heading*
E. *Title of book*
F. *Name of second author*
G. *Publication information: city, company, date*
H. *Technical information: number of pages in preface, number of textual pages, illustrations, book size, price*
I. *Additional infomation: textual apparatus*
J. *First subject classification*
K. *Second subject classification*
L. *Library of Congress number, ISBN number, Dewey Decimal number, On-line Computer Library Center number*

Periodical Indexes and Bibliographies

Because periodicals—magazines, journals, and newspapers—are important sources of current information, locate articles using specialized indexes and bibliographies.

A Guide to Magazine Articles

The *Readers' Guide to Periodical Literature* lists articles appearing in hundreds of popular magazines. Usually located in the reference or the periodical section, the *Readers' Guide* is printed regularly, is bound yearly, and covers most general-interest magazines (see pages 445–46).

The *Readers' Guide* alphabetically lists entries by author, title, and subject. Its condensed format uses many abbreviations, which are listed and explained in the front of each volume. (See Figure 5.)

Figure 5   Sample entries from the *Readers' Guide to Periodical Literature*

subject heading — FOREST CONSERVATION
article title
author
special information (illustrations)
cross reference
publication information: magazine title, volume number, page numbers, month, year

FOREST CONSERVATION
  Horticulture in hell [efforts to turn last remaining Haitian rain forest into protected botanical garden] R. Boling. il *American Forests* v101 p48-9 Aut 95
  Hot cars & hardwoods [forest restoration in New York City] W. Nixon. il *American Forests* v101 p28-9+ Aut '95
FOREST CROWN CANOPY
  The secret life of backyard trees [canopy research] K. Krajick. il *Discover* v16 p92-101 N '95
FOREST ECOLOGY
    See also
    Deforestation
    Forest crown canopy
  As the worm turns [earthworms and fungi in urban soil affect health of trees] W. Nixon il *American Forests* v101 p34-6 Aut '95
  Carnivores of the dry forest [Jalisco, Mexico] D. Tenenbaum. il *BioScience* v45 p587-8 O '95
FOREST FIRES
    See also
    Smokejumpers
    Prevention and control
      See also
      Airplanes in forest fire control

Guides to Journal Articles

To find articles in journals, use general and subject-specific indexes and bibliographies. Normally located in the reference area, these indexes and bibliographies list entries alphabetically by author, subject, and sometimes title. Indexes and bibliographies differ somewhat in format, but the excerpt from *Education Index* shown in Figure 6 is fairly representative.

Figure 6   Sample entries from the *Education Index*

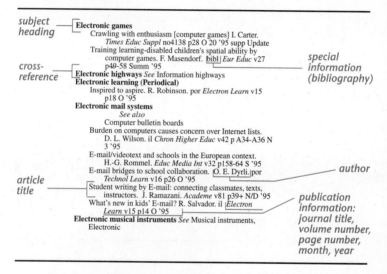

Guides to Newspaper Articles

The *New York Times Index, Wall Street Journal Index, London Times Index, Washington Post Index,* and other indexes list articles published in major newspapers. Often located in the reference or periodical area, these guides are compiled yearly and arranged alphabetically by subject. After finding a relevant reference in one index, check other indexes for related articles printed on the same day or a few days after or before. The section from the *New York Times Index* shown in Figure 7 is typical of newspaper indexes.

Figure 7   Sample entries from the *New York Times Index*

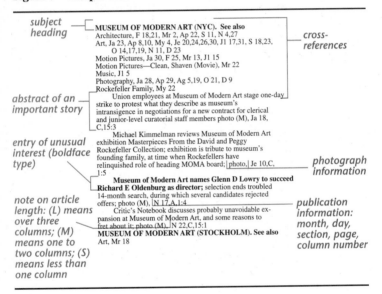

33d ▷ **Compile and evaluate a preliminary list of sources.**

Compiling a Preliminary List of Sources

A preliminary list of sources generally includes books and a variety of journal, magazine, and newspaper articles. However, you can expand the scope of your research by including non-print and electronic sources as well.

Nonprint Sources

Consider using the many nonprint sources that are available to you: use materials from radio and television; conduct interviews; administer questionnaires or surveys; use audiovisual sources such as films, television programs, recordings, visual art, or performances. These nonprint sources can provide unique perspectives when they are part of research.

Electronic Sources

Use a system-based computer on campus or a personal computer linked to an online service to gather information that is sometimes unavailable in traditional print forms. Use electronic mail to gather information through newsgroups and direct correspondence with individuals. Use discussion groups to gather ideas shared in on-going communication among people interested in a specific topic. Use bulletin boards to gather information that is "posted" about individual topics. Use Internet resources (Telnet, FTP, Gopher, World Wide Web, and others) to gather online information. Much of the information available through electronic sources is so new that it is unavailable in print forms. By taking advantage of electronic sources, you can ensure that your research is as current as possible.

On separate 3-by-5-inch note cards, jot down information about each potential source. Note its location. For books, note call number, author, and title. For articles, write down the complete index or bibliography entry. For interviews, documentaries, class notes, and so on, indicate date, title, speaker or producer, and any other relevant identifying information. For electronic sources, note author (when known), title, access information, and date. In addition to the information that is essential for locating or identifying a source, note any special features, such as maps or bibliographies, that might make the source especially useful.

Evaluating a Preliminary List of Sources

Review your preliminary list of sources, using the following guidelines to evaluate their potential usefulness:

Does the author have special credentials? An *M.D., M.A., Ph.D.,* or notice of an affiliation with a university or other organization following the author's name may indicate authority and expertise in the subject at hand.

Does the title of the work suggest a focus appropriate to your topic? The phrasing of a title or subtitle can indicate the author's subject and his or her attitude toward it. A title like *Latin American Civilization: Colonial Period* does not reveal its author's thesis or attitude, whereas *The Colonial Heritage of Latin America: Essays on Economic Dependence in Perspective* does reveal to an extent the book's approach to its subject.

Is the publishing company a reputable one? Most of the books you will use are published by university, academic, or trade presses. You will soon recognize the important publishers in your field.

Are the periodicals well respected by authorities in the field? You may not be able to evaluate a periodical thoroughly, but, depending on your subject and purpose, you will be able to determine the most reliable sources. For example, on issues of national and international importance, the *New York Times* or *Washington Post* are often more authoritative than local newspapers. You will learn which periodicals in your field are most respected by noting which are most frequently cited in the notes and bibliographies of the other works you consult. For academic research papers, the use of popular periodicals, such as *USA Today* and *Time,* should be kept to a minimum.

Is the publication date recent? For some topics, the current-ness of a source is unimportant, but for most topics, sources older than ten or fifteen years are of little value.

Using these guidelines, Shingo evaluated Juliette Alvin's *Music Therapy*. The title of the book suggested an appropriate focus, but the 1966 publication date troubled him: Was the book simply too old to use? Had its ideas been supplanted by newer ones? Shingo decided to use the book because its table of contents described the topic from many perspectives; he could, at least, use the book as a sample of early perspectives on music therapy. Later in his research, however, he discovered that Alvin's work was cited in many other sources, suggesting that, though somewhat dated, *Music Therapy* was still a well-respected source.

EXERCISE 33.4 ⟩ Preliminary list of sources

Prepare a preliminary list of sources for your paper. Using the card catalog, find at least four books on your topic, including one published within the last two years and one providing an overview of the topic. Using online or print versions of the Readers' Guide, *the appropriate subject index, and one or more newspaper indexes, find at least six articles on your topic. Using the nonprint resources of your library and other local resources—such as businesses, government agencies, and civic and cultural organizations—find two nonprint sources, including one potential interview.*

| 33e | ⟩ | **Evaluate your sources.** |

Before you begin to read your sources carefully, leaf through them quickly, noting their organization, content, and any tables, maps, photographs, or other illustrations. Do not read each source thoroughly or take notes at this stage; instead, follow the guidelines below for making a preliminary, general assessment of the usefulness of the materials you have gathered. Once you have a general sense of your sources, you can then read them carefully and take complete and consistent notes, following the guidelines given in section 33f.

Evaluating Books

Books will probably provide the most thorough treatment of your subject, but you should evaluate each one quickly to see if it meets the needs of your research before taking the time to read it closely. After considering the title and subtitle carefully and any information provided about the author's credentials and other writings, review the table of contents. Consider how material is divided and arranged and how much space is allotted to topics that relate to your paper.

Skim the preface, introduction, or first chapter to get a sense of the author's general approach and the context. Frequently, authors explain their reasons for writing, their strategies for presenting information, or their general interpretations of material here. These explanations can help you to assess the source's potential value for your paper.

Examine any special sections or appended materials: in-text illustrations, tables, charts, graphs, or diagrams; bibliographies; sections containing special supporting material, such as case studies or lists of additional readings. Reviewing these sections gives you a sense of the book's content and approach. Nontextual materials can be quite useful in providing details, illustrations, and leads to other sources.

Skim a portion of the text that specifically relates to your topic. Do not read it carefully yet, but instead note how the author has developed the content. For example, does the author use examples and facts or narration and description based on personal experience? Does the author explain and support assertions, document facts, and present balanced discussions? Also note the author's style. Is it varied, lively, and interesting? What technical and other vocabulary and tone does it employ? A quick analysis of content and style can reveal whether a source treats the topic seriously and in depth or superficially. (For more information about evaluating sources and forms of argument, see Chapter 5, "Critical Thinking and Writing.")

Evaluating Articles in Periodicals

Articles in magazines, journals, and newspapers can provide you with a great deal of information. To save time, you need to evaluate the potential usefulness of each article you might wish to use before you read it carefully and take notes.

First, read the title and subtitle carefully, assessing what they reveal about the author's content, approach, and tone. Check any note on the author (this may appear at the bottom of the first page or at the end of the article or in a separate section of the journal or magazine). These notes usually state the author's credentials and other publications, which may give you insight into the author's interests and attitudes.

Read any headings that are used to separate sections of the article. Note whether the headings indicate content specifically related to your topic.

Skim the article to assess its content and form of presentation. Without pausing over details, skim the article to see if it is specific, current, and complete, and if its style indicates an approach to the topic that will be useful to you.

Check for related materials in the same periodical. Sometimes lists of suggested readings or of people or organizations to contact appear with an article. Issues of periodicals are sometimes organized in whole or in part around a theme, so that a number of articles in the periodical may relate to your topic.

EXERCISE 33.5) *Evaluating a source*

Look briefly at four sources—two books and two articles from periodicals—and write a brief paragraph describing each. Note especially each source's potential usefulness for your paper.

| 33f | > | Take complete, consistent notes. |

Establish a uniform system for taking notes. Consider using 4-by-6-inch index cards because they are large enough to hold complete notes and easy to distinguish from 3-by-5-inch source cards. (For more on source cards, see section 33d.) Consider the generous space of legal pads or loose-leaf paper even though notes on paper are often more difficult to handle in later stages of planning and writing than those on cards. Consider taking notes on a computer to save time during later stages of typing.

If you use cards, use a new card for each new idea; during planning, this will make it easier for you to organize—and reorganize—your notes; if you use another format, leave several spaces between notes. At the top of each card or sheet of paper (or at the beginning of computer notes), record the following information to help you to identify sources easily and avoid plagiarism: the author of the source, title (if you are using more than one source by any given author), and the page number of the material you are noting. Make notes on one side of the card or paper only, so that later you do not overlook any information. Fit material on one card if possible; if additional cards are necessary, note the author's name, the number of each card, and the total number of cards at the top (for example, "Johnson, Card 2 of 3").

Keep your working thesis in mind as you take notes. Some researchers like to keep a rough outline handy, so that they can take notes with the overall structure of their argument in view and can mark cards with key words to indicate where information fits. Be alert as you take notes to unexpected information and ideas that alter or expand your working thesis in new and interesting ways. You will want to make note of relevant information (facts, examples, and details) and of ideas (the thoughts and conclusions offered by your sources to interpret or organize their information). You can take notes on both types of material in any of three ways: summaries, quotations, and paraphrases.

Summaries

Summaries present the substance of a passage in condensed form. They are a useful means of recording facts, best noted in list or other abbreviated form (see Figure 8); examples, perhaps noted as a sketch of the original (see Figure 9); or long arguments, perhaps noted in outline form. Summaries should be entirely in your own words. When taking notes, read the passage carefully, determine what information and ideas you want to record, and express them in lists of words, brief phrases, or short sentences. Do not use any of the original passage without enclosing it in quotation marks. Use quotation marks carefully at the note-taking stage to avoid inadvertently using others' words in your paper without giving proper credit.

Quotations

Quotations reproduce another's work word for word, with the original's exact spelling and punctuation. Quotations should not be overused in your writing and should be used sparingly in your notes. Assess the value of a quotation before you copy it. Ask yourself the following questions:

Figure 8   Summary note

Rubin, William B./<u>Faultline</u>   salaries

— 1990 figures: men with high school diploma
  (#28,911) and college diploma (#44,554);
  women with high school diploma (#18,954) and
  with college diploma (#28,043)//

— 1979-89: 2% increase in real earnings;
  1989-92: 1.6% decrease
                                    p. 128-29

Figure 9   Summary note

Larson/<u>Naked Consumer</u>   mailing lists

Equifax and TRW (major marketing firms) compile
lists—the book's example is people with credit cards
with spending limits over #5,000—and sell them
to direct-market retailers. That way retailers can
target people with, the assumption is, large
discretionary spending habits—the #5,000 figure
would generatate a list of several million people.
                                    p. 76

Is the author's style so distinctive that I could not say the same thing as well or as clearly in my own words?

Is the vocabulary technical and therefore difficult to translate into my own words?

Is the author so well known or so important that the quotation will lend authority to my argument?

Does the author's material raise doubts or questions or make points with which I disagree?

If you answer "yes" to any of these questions, then copy the quotation. If the material does not fulfill any of these criteria but is significant nonetheless, paraphrase it instead.

Always enclose quotations within quotation marks and double-check your note against the original. The copy must be *exact*. Figure 10 shows a sample quotation card.

Figure 10 Quotation note

Robinson/<u>Critics</u>   influence

"Freud has fundamentally altered the way we think. He has changed our intellectual manners, often without our even being aware of it. For most of us [,] Freud has become a habit of mind—a //bad habit, his critics would be quick to urge, but a habit now too deeply ingrained to be broken. He is the major source of our modern inclination to look for meanings beneath the surface of behavior—to be always on the alert for the 'real' (and probably hidden) significance of our actions."
                                                    p. 270-71

When a quotation continues from one page to the next in a source, indicate where the break occurs when you copy the quotation onto your note card (a double slash [//] is a useful indicator for this). This notation is important because when you use the quotation in your paper, you may use only part of it, and you must be able to cite the page reference accurately.

Because you can introduce errors each time you write or type a quotation, use a word-processing program to avoid extra recopying or retyping.

■ *Prepare a separate file for quotations.* Type each quotation into the file and double-check its accuracy against the original. Be sure to label each quotation completely with author, title, and page number.

■ *Copy quotations into the draft as needed.* Leave a copy in the quotation file in case you change your mind about where or how much of the quotation to use. The use of "copy" and "paste" functions to copy quotations avoids retyping, which saves time and prevents the introduction of errors.

Paraphrases

Paraphrases restate a passage in another form and in other words, but, unlike summaries, they contain approximately the same amount of detail and the same number of words as the original. If a passage contains an important idea but does not meet the requirements for quotation, restate the idea in your own words, sentence structure, and sequence. When you finish the paraphrase, check it against the original passage to be sure the idea has been completely restated. If you use any phrases or sentences from the original, place them in quotation marks. Intentional or not, unacknowledged borrowing from a source is plagiarism, and most schools impose severe penalties on students who plagiarize. (See section 33g.) Figure 11 shows a sample paraphrase card.

Figure 11   Paraphrase note

Mitford/<u>American Way</u>   c-sections

The rates of caesarian sections increase or decrease
depending on how doctors are paid and how patients
pay their bills. When doctors bill separately for
procedures and when patients have their own insurance,
the rates of caesarian sections increase to roughly one-
third of births (33-39%); hospitals with the lowest
c-section rates are those where doctors do not receiove
special fees and where bills are not itemized.

                                        p. 152

EXERCISE 33.6 ❯ *Taking notes*

*Using the books and articles that your evaluation of your prelimi-
nary list of sources determined would be useful, begin taking
notes. Summarize, paraphrase, and directly quote from your
sources, and make sure that each note card accurately reflects
the source and provides full identifying information.*

33g	❯	**Do not plagiarize.**

Plagiarism is the use of someone else's words, ideas, or line
of thought without acknowledgment. Even when, as is frequently the case, plagiarism is inadvertent—the result of careless note taking, punctuating, or documenting—the writer is
still at fault for dishonest work, and the paper will be unacceptable. You will remember the seriousness of the offense of
plagiarism, and work to avoid committing it, when you remember that the word *plagiarism* comes from the Latin for "kidnap-
ping." To avoid plagiarizing, learn to recognize distinctive

content and expression in source materials and to take accurate, carefully punctuated and documented notes.

Common Knowledge

Some kinds of information—facts and interpretations—are known by many people and are consequently described as **common knowledge.** That U.S. presidents are elected for four-year terms is commonly known, as is the more interpretative information that the U.S. government is a democracy with a system of checks and balances among the executive, legislative, and judicial branches of government. But common knowledge extends beyond these very general types of information to more specific information within a field of study. In English studies, for example, it is a commonly known fact that George Eliot is the pseudonym of Mary Ann Evans and a commonly acknowledged interpretation that drama evolved from a Greek religious festival honoring the god Dionysus. Documenting these facts in a paper would be unnecessary because they are commonly known in English studies, even though you might have just discovered them for the first time.

When you are researching an unfamiliar subject, distinguishing common knowledge that does not require documentation from special knowledge that does require documentation is sometimes difficult. The following guidelines may help.

What Constitutes Common Knowledge

Historical facts (names, dates, and general interpretations) that appear in many general reference books. For example, George Washington was the first president of the United States, and the Constitution was adopted in 1787.

Literature that cannot be attributed to a specific author. Two examples are *Beowulf* and the Bible; the use of specific editions or translations still may require acknowledgment.

General observations and opinions that are shared by many people. For example, it is a general observation that children learn by actively doing, not passively listening, and a commonly held opinion that reading, writing, and arithmetic are the basic skills to be learned by an elementary school child.

Unacknowledged information that appears in multiple sources. For example, it is common knowledge that the earth is approximately 93 million miles from the sun and that the *gross national product* is the market value of all goods and services produced by a nation in a given year.

If a piece of information does not meet these guidelines or if you are uncertain about whether it is common knowledge, always document the material.

EXERCISE 33.7 〉 *Common knowledge about your topic*

Make a list of ten facts, ideas, or interpretations that are commonly known or held about your topic. Beside each item, note into which category of common knowledge it falls.

Special Qualities of Source Materials

A more difficult problem than identifying common knowledge involves using an author's words and ideas improperly. Improper use is often the result of careless summarizing and paraphrasing. To use source materials without plagiarizing, learn to recognize their distinctive qualities:

Special Qualities of Sources

Distinctive prose style: the author's choices of words, phrases, and sentence patterns

Original facts: the result of the author's personal research

Personal interpretations of information: the author's individual evaluation of his or her information

Original ideas: those ideas that are unique to that author

As you work with sources, be aware of these distinguishing qualities and make certain that you do not appropriate the prose (word choices and sentence structures), original research, interpretations, or ideas of others without giving proper credit.

Look, for example, at these paragraphs from Joyce Appleby, Lynn Hunt, and Margaret Jacob's *Telling the Truth about History* (New York: Norton, 1994):

> Interest in this new research in social history can be partly explained by the personal backgrounds of the cohort of historians who undertook the task of writing history from the bottom up. They entered higher education with the post-Sputnik expansion of the 1950s and 1960s, when the number of new Ph.D.s in history nearly quadrupled. Since many of them were children and grandchildren of immigrants, they had a personal incentive for turning the writing of their dissertations into a movement of memory recovery. Others were black or female and similarly prompted to find ways to make the historically inarticulate speak. While the number of male Ph.D.s in history ebbed and flowed with the vicissitudes of the job market, the number of new female Ph.D.s in history steadily increased from 11 percent (29) in 1950 to 13 percent (137) in 1970 and finally to 37 percent (192) in 1989.
>
> Although ethnicity is harder to locate in the records, the GI Bill was clearly effective in bringing the children of working-class families into the middle-class educational mainstream. This was the thin end of a democratizing wedge prying open higher education in the United States. Never before had so many people in any society earned so many higher degrees. Important as their numbers were, the change in perspective these academics brought to their disciplines has made the qualitative changes even more impressive. Suddenly graduate students with strange, unpronounceable surnames, with Brooklyn accents and different skin colors, appeared in the venerable ivy-colored buildings that epitomized elite schooling.

Now look at the following examples of plagiarized and acceptable summaries and paraphrases.

Summaries

Plagiarized

—— *A historian's focus and interpretation are personal.*

—— *Because of their experiences, <u>they have a personal incentive</u> for looking at history in new ways.*

—— *Large numbers were important, but the change in viewpoint <u>made the qualitative changes even more impressive.</u>*

(The underlined phrases are clearly Appleby, Hunt, and Jacob's, even though the verb tenses are changed. To avoid plagiarism, place key words in quotation marks or rewrite them entirely in your own words and form of expression.)

Acceptable

—— *A historian's focus and interpretation are personal.*

—— *For personal reasons, not always stated, people examine the facts of history from different perspectives.*

—— *Large numbers were important, but the change in viewpoint "made the qualitative changes even more impressive."*

(Here the words and phrases are the writer's, not Appleby, Hunt, and Jacob's. Quotation marks enclose a selected phrase.)

Paraphrases

Plagiarized
Even though ethnic background is not easily found in the statistics, the GI Bill consistently helped students from low-income

families enter the middle-class educational system. This was how democracy started forcing open college education in America.

(Changing selected words, while retaining the basic phrasing and sentence structure of the original is not acceptable paraphrasing. Appleby, Hunt, and Jacob's thought pattern and prose style still mark the passage.)

Acceptable

Because of the GI Bill, college wasn't only for middle-class children anymore. Even poor children could attend college. For the first time, education was accessible to everyone, which is truly democracy in action. The GI Bill was "the thin end of a democratizing wedge prying open higher education."

(Here, the paraphrase presents Appleby, Hunt, and Jacob's idea but does not mimic their sentence structure; the quoted material records a single phrase for possible use later. Remember that summaries and paraphrases, as well as facts and quotations, require full citations.)

Avoiding plagiarism takes conscious effort, but by taking notes carefully and then documenting them completely, you can be sure your work is acceptable.

EXERCISE 33.8 ⟩ *Practice in note taking*

For practice, take notes on the following paragraphs as if you were researching their subjects. Include a summary, a quotation, and a paraphrase from each set. (Check your notes to confirm that you have not inadvertently plagiarized any part of the paragraphs.) Then in groups of three or four, discuss both your techniques for note taking and the ideas and information gleaned from these passages.

Collier, James Lincoln. *Jazz: The American Theme Song*. New York: Oxford UP, 1993. [The following paragraphs appear on pages 22 and 23; a double slash (//) indicates the page break.]

Furthermore, the feminism that was an integral part of the new spirit was critical to the acceptance of jazz. Until middle-class women were able to go out drinking and dancing, their boyfriends and husbands would not be able to do so either, more than occasionally. But now, by 1920, they could. So the middle class began visiting speakeasies, cabarets, roadhouses, and dance halls where the new music was played. Their financial support was critical, for it was only the middle class and the class above that could afford to patronize places // like the Cotton Club, where Duke Ellington developed his music and became celebrated; the Club Alabam, which provided the first home for the Fletcher Henderson Orchestra; Reisenweber's, where the Original Dixieland Jazz Band introduced jazz to mainstream America; the colleges where Beiderbecke, Oliver, and other groups got much of their employment in the early 1920s.

We have to understand, then, that while a substantial proportion of the American middle class did not like jazz—was indeed threatened by it—probably the majority at least tolerated it, and a large minority were excited by it. Conversely, a great many religious blacks, and religious working people in general, were as hostile to the music as was the middle-class opposition. Jazz was astonishingly democratic: both its friends and its foes came from the whole spectrum of the American class system.

Worster, Donald. *An Unsettled Country: Changing Landscapes of the American West*. Albuquerque: U of New Mexico P, 1994. [The following paragraphs appear on page 27.]

Westerners of many stripes want to lay claim to [John Wesley] Powell, because they sense that he shared their interest in, their loyalty toward, the West. He was, in a sense, the father of their country. But today he would be a most bewildered old fellow if he came back to look at the West we have been making: a West that is now the home of 77 million people, ranging from Korean shopowners in Los Angeles to African-American college students in Las Vegas, from Montana novelists and poets to Colorado trout fisherman and skiers, from Kansas buffalo ranchers to Utah prison guards. How to make a regional whole of all that? And how to turn the life and ideas of the nineteenth-century frontier dirt farmer become explorer-geologist become environmental reformer into a prophet for all those people today?

What those 77 million still have in common, despite the demographic and cultural changes, is the land itself. Even today questions about how that land ought to be used, exploited, or preserved continue to dominate western conversations and public-policy debates. Much of that land is still in public title, despite all the access that has been allowed to private users. Perhaps the most distinctive feature of the West, after aridity, is the fact of extensive public ownership of that land, hundreds of millions of acres in all, a feature that ties the past to the present. In New Mexico the federal government owns 33 percent of the state, in Utah 64 percent, in Nevada 82 percent, though in my own state of Kansas it owns about 1 percent.

The research process is painstaking, especially when it comes to recording complete and accurate information about sources for use in documenting the final paper. Careful documentation and a complete works cited list provide readers with full information on sources cited in the paper. (See section 35d for information on in-text citations.)

To be useful to readers, citations must be clear and consistent. Therefore, very specific rules of documentation have been devised and must be applied.

Quick Reference

Begin preparing your works cited entries, using the formats shown below, as soon as you begin taking notes. Use a new 3-by-5-inch card for each entry and keep them current and in a safe place or create a works cited file on your word processor.

> *A book by one author*

   Author's last name, first name. Book title. Additional information. City of publication: Publishing company, publication date.

> *An article by one author*

   Author's last name, first name. "Article title." Periodical title Date: inclusive pages.

Guidelines for preparing entries for other types of sources appear on the pages that follow.

34a > **Follow the standard citation format required by your subject.**

Most writing in English and other humanities courses uses the documentation format described in Joseph Gibaldi's *MLA [Modern Language Association] Handbook for Writers of Research Papers,* fourth edition (New York: MLA, 1995). This documentation format, known as MLA style, is simple, clear, and widely accepted. Some subjects, however, require other styles of documentation, so always ask instructors, especially in nonhumanities courses, whether MLA style is acceptable. In addition to the *MLA Handbook,* a number of other style guides are frequently used.

Frequently Used Style Guides

The Chicago Manual of Style. 14th ed. Chicago: U of Chicago P, 1993.

Publication Manual of the American Psychological Association. 4th ed. Washington, DC: APA, 1994.

Scientific Style and Format: The CBE [Council of Biology Editors] Manual for Authors, Editors, and Publishers. 6th ed. Chicago: Cambridge UP, 1994.

Turabian, Kate. *A Manual for Writers of Term Papers, Theses, and Dissertations.* 5th ed. Chicago: U of Chicago P, 1987.

The most widely used of these alternate styles is that of the American Psychological Association (APA), often the preferred style for writing in the social sciences. Guidelines for using APA style appear in Appendix B.

34b > **Prepare accurate and complete works cited entries.**

Because works cited entries direct readers to sources used in researched writing, these entries must be as complete as possible and presented in a consistent and recognizable format. If the following guidelines do not cover a source you want to use, consult the *MLA Handbook.*

To complete a citation, leaf through the sample citations until you find the one that most closely corresponds to your source, remembering that some citations combine information according to the guidelines noted below. Prepare your citations using 3-by-5 index cards (one citation per card), sheets of paper, or a computer. If you prepare citations on a computer, use a separate file with an easily recognizable name (for example, *paper2.cit, research.cit,* or *aviation.cit*). Since a citation file will remain comparatively small, you can retrieve it quickly, add to it and delete from it, and then append the complete works cited file to the final draft of your paper.

Whichever pattern you choose—index card, paper, or computer—record complete and accurate citations. Forgetting to record full information when you first use a source requires you to return to it at a later—and potentially less convenient—time to supply missing information.

Information for MLA Citations

MLA citations present information in an established order. When combining forms (to list a translation of a second edition, for example), follow these guidelines to determine the order of information:

1. *Author(s).* Use the name or names with the spelling and order shown on the title page of books or on the first page of articles, without degrees, titles, or affiliations. If no author

(individual or organization) is named, list the work by title in the works cited entry.

2. *Title*. List titles from part to whole: the title of an essay (the part) before the book (the whole), the title of an article before the periodical title, an episode before the program, or a song before the compact disc. Use complete titles, including subtitles, no matter how long they are (use a colon and one space to separate the title from the subtitle).

3. *Additional information*. In the order noted below, include any of the following information listed on the title page of the book or on the first page of an article: editor, translator, compiler, edition number, volume number, or name of series.

4. *Facts of publication*. For books, find the publisher's name and the place of publication on the title page and the date of publication on the copyright page (immediately following the title page); use the publisher's name in abbreviated form (see samples in sections 34c–34f), use the first city listed if more than one is given, and use the most recent date shown. When a city is unfamiliar, abbreviate the state using two capital letters without a period. For periodicals, find the volume number, issue number, and date on the masthead (at the top of the first page of newspapers or within the first few pages in journals and magazines, often in combination with the table of contents).

5. *Page numbers*. When citing a part of a book or an article, provide inclusive page numbers without page abbreviations. Record inclusive page numbers from one to ninety-nine in full form (8–12, 33–39, 68–73); inclusive numbers of one-hundred or higher require at least the last two digits and any other digits needed for clarity (100–02, 120–36, 193–206).

Format for MLA Citations

MLA citations follow general formatting guidelines, to ensure that they are consistent:

Begin the first line of each entry at the left margin, and indent subsequent lines five spaces.

Invert the author's name so that it appears with the last name first (to alphabetize easily). If sources are coauthored, list additional authors' names in normal, first-then-last order.

Italicize or underline titles of full-length works; the meaning is the same. Be consistent throughout the paper.

Separate major sections of entries (author, title, and publication information) with periods and one space, not two. When other forms of end punctuation are used (when titles end with question marks or exclamation points, for example), the period may be omitted.

Double-space all entries.

Using a word processor to prepare citations is especially helpful because entries can easily be added, changed, or deleted as your research continues, and programs have features that simplify typing.

■ *Block-indent second and subsequent lines of each entry.* Use the program's "block-indent" feature (also called a *hanging paragraph*), instead of using a five-space tab to indent each second and subsequent line individually.

■ *Revise entries to adjust the spacing, punctuation, and position of information.* Word processors allow you to insert, delete, and rearrange information without retyping.

■ *Prepare entries in a separate file.* You can later use the "cut" and "paste" commands to correct alphabetization and then to append the complete file to your research paper.

34c > **Follow the appropriate citation forms for books.**

A Book by One Author

```
Freemuth, John C. Islands Under Siege: National Parks

    and the Politics of External Threats. Lawrence: UP

    of Kansas, 1991.
```

(The period with the author's middle initial substitutes for the period that normally follows the author's name. The letters *UP*, without periods or a space, abbreviate *University Press*.)

A Book by Two or More Authors

Authors' names appear in the order presented on the title page, which may or may not be in alphabetical order. A comma follows the initial author's first name; second and third authors' names appear in normal order.

```
Scott, John Paul, and John L. Fuller. Genetics and the

    Social Behavior of the Dog. Chicago: U of Chicago

    P, 1965.
```

When a book has four or more authors, include the first author's name in full form, but substitute *et al.* (meaning "and others," not italicized or underlined) for the names of additional authors.

```
Gershey, Edward L., et al. Low-Level Radioactive Waste:

    From Cradle to Grave. New York: Van Nostrand, 1990.
```

A Book with No Author

When no author is named, list the work by title. Alphabetize books listed by title using the first important word of the title, not the articles *a, an,* or *the.*

<u>United Press International Stylebook: The Authoritative</u>

    <u>Handbook for Writers, Editors, and News Directors</u>.

    3rd ed. Lincolnwood, IL: Natl. Textbook, 1992.

(Because the city of Lincolnwood is not commonly recognized, the state abbreviation is required. Note that *national* is abbreviated when it is part of a publisher's name.)

Multiple Works by the Same Author

When citing multiple works by the same author, present the first citation completely. Subsequent entries, alphabetized by title, are introduced by three hyphens and a period and alphabetized by title. Coauthored works require full names and are alphabetized after those with single authors.

Ehrenreich, Barbara. "Battered Welfare Syndrome." <u>Time</u>

    3 Apr. 1995: 82.

---. <u>Fear of Falling: The Inner Life of the Middle</u>

    <u>Class</u>. New York: Pantheon, 1989.

Ehrenreich, Barbara, Elizabeth Hess, and Gloria Jacobs.

    <u>Re-Making Love: The Feminization of Sex</u>. Garden

    City, NY: Anchor-Doubleday, 1986.

(Notice that the publisher of the last selection includes a two-part name: the imprint and the major publisher [see Imprints, page 482, for an additional sample].)

A Book with an Organization as Author

When an organization is both the author and the publisher, present the name completely in the author position and use an abbreviation in the publisher position.

Gemological Institute of America. The Diamond

   Dictionary. Santa Monica, CA: GIA, 1977.

An Edition Other than the First

The edition number, noted on the title page, follows the title of the book. When a book also has an editor, translator, or compiler, the edition number follows that information. Edition numbers are presented in numeral-abbreviation form (2nd, 3rd, 4th).

Mano, M. Morris. Digital Design. 2nd ed. Englewood

   Cliffs, NJ: Prentice, 1991.

A Reprint

A reprint, a newly printed but unaltered version of a book, is identified as such on the title page or copyright page. The original publication date precedes the facts of publication, and the date of the reprinted edition follows the publisher's name.

Palmer, John. The Comedy of Manners. 1913. New York:

   Russell, 1962.

A Multivolume Work

A multivolume work may have one title, or it may have a comprehensive title for the complete work and separate titles for each volume. When you use the entire set of volumes, use the collective title and note the number of volumes.

Perspectives on Western Art: Source Documents and

   Readings from the Renaissance to the 1970s. Ed.

   Linnea H. Wren. 2 vols. New York: Icon-Harper,

   1994.

To emphasize a single volume, first cite the volume as a separate book. Then add the volume number, the collection title, and the total number of volumes.

```
Direct Solar Energy. Ed. T. Nejat Veziroglu. New York:

    Nova, 1991. Vol. A of Energy and Environmental

    Progress. 7 vols.
```

(Volumes identified by letters should be presented that way in the citation.)

A Work in a Collection

To cite a work in a collection, include the name of the selection's author, the title of the specific selection (appropriately punctuated), the collection title, publication facts, and the inclusive page numbers for the selection (without page abbreviations). To cite more than one selection from the collection, prepare separate citations (see Multiple Selections from the Same Collection, page 480).

```
Modelski, George, and William R. Thompson. "Long Cycles

    and Global War." Handbook of War Studies. Ed. Manus

    I. Midlarsky. Ann Arbor: U Michigan P, 1993. 23-54.
```

A Previously Published Work in a Collection

To indicate that a selection has been previously published, begin the citation with original facts of publication. *Rpt.,* meaning "reprinted," begins the second part of the citation, which includes information about the source you have used.

```
Wallace, Mike. "Mickey Mouse History: Portraying the

     Past at Disney World." Radical History Review 32

     (1985): 33-55. Rpt. in Customs in Conflict: The

     Anthology of a Changing World. Ed. Frank Manning

     and Jean-Marc Philbert. Peterborough, ON:

     Broadview, 1990. 304-32.
```

Multiple Selections from the Same Collection

To cite several selections from the same collection, prepare a citation for the complete work—beginning either with the editor's name or with the collection title. Additional references begin with the author of the selection and its title; however, instead of providing full publication information, include the editor's name or a shortened version of the title; provide inclusive page numbers for the selection. Notice that all citations are alphabetized.

```
Gilbert, Sandra, and Susan Gubar. "The Parable of the

     Cave." Richter 1119-26.

James, Henry. "The Art of Fiction." Richter 420-33.

Richter, David H., ed. The Critical Tradition: Classic

     Texts and Contemporary Trends. New York: Bedford,

     1989.
```

An Article in an Encyclopedia or Other Reference Work

Use an author's name when it is available. If only initials are listed with the article, match them with the name from the list of contributors. Well-known reference books require no information other than the title, edition number (if any), and date.

Citations for less well-known or recently published reference works include full publication information. Page numbers are not needed when a reference work is arranged alphabetically.

Angermüller, Rudolph. "Salieri, Antonio." The New Grove

Dictionary of Music and Musicians. 1980 ed.

(This twenty-volume set is extremely well known and consequently needs no publication information.)

Gietschier, Steven. "Paige, Satchel." The Ballplayers:

Baseball's Ultimate Biographical Reference. Ed.

Mike Shatzkin. New York: Arbour, 1990.

(Since this source is relatively new, full publishing information is required.)

When no author's name or initials appear with an article, begin with the title, reproduced to match the pattern in the reference book. Other principles remain the same.

"Glenn, John Hershel, Jr." Who's Who in Aviation and

Aerospace. US ed. Boston: Natl. Aeronautical

Inst., 1983.

A Work in a Series

Names of series (collections of books related to the same subject, genre, time period, and so on) are typically found on a book's title page and should be included just before the publishing information. Abbreviate the word *Series* if it is part of the series title.

Morley, Carolyn. Transformation, Miracles, and Mischief:

The Mountain Priest Plays of Kyogen. Cornell East

Asia Ser. Ithaca, NY: Cornell UP, 1993.

When volumes in a series are numbered, include both the series name and number, followed by a period.

Forster, E. M. <u>Passage to India</u>. Everyman's Library 29.

New York: Knopf, 1992.

An Imprint

An imprint is a specialized division of a larger publishing company. When an imprint name and a publisher name both appear on the title page, list them together (imprint name first), separated by a hyphen and no additional spaces.

<u>African Rhapsody: Short Stories of the Contemporary</u>

<u>African Experience</u>. Ed. Nadezda Obradovic. New

York: Anchor-Doubleday, 1994.

(Anchor is the imprint; Doubleday is the publisher.)

A Translation

A translator's name must always be included in a citation for a translated work because he or she prepared the version that you read. To emphasize the original work (the most common pattern), place the abbreviation *Trans.* (for "translated by," not italicized) and the translator's name after the title (but following editors' names, if appropriate).

Esquivel, Laura. <u>Like Water for Chocolate: A Novel in</u>

<u>Monthly Installments, with Recipes, Romances, and</u>

<u>Home Remedies</u>. Trans. Carol Christensen and Thomas

Christensen. New York: Doubleday, 1992.

If selections within a collection are translated by different people, then the translator's name should follow the selection.

Placing the translator's name after the book title indicates that he or she translated *all* selections in the collection.

```
Salamun, Tomaz. "Clumsy Guys." Trans. Sonja Kravanja. The
     Pushcart Prize XVII: Best of the Small Presses. Ed.
     Bill Henderson et al. New York: Pushcart, 1993. 443.
```

A Government Document

Congressional Record

Citations for *Congressional Record* are exceedingly brief: the italicized and abbreviated title, *Cong. Rec.,* the date (presented in day-month-year order), and the page number. Page numbers used alone indicate Senate records; page numbers preceded by an *H* indicate records from the House of Representatives.

```
Cong. Rec. 15 June 1993: 7276+.
```

(This simple citation is for a Senate record. The plus sign (+) following the page number indicates that the discussion continues on several pages.)

```
Cong. Rec. 7 Oct. 1994: H11251.
```

(Note the page reference, with the *H* indicating that this citation is for a House record.)

Committee, Commission, Department

Information to describe government documents is generally presented in this order: (1) country, state, province, or county; (2) government official, governing body, sponsoring department, commission, center, ministry, or agency; (3) office, bureau, or committee; (4) the title of the publication, italicized; (5) if appropriate, the author of the document, the number and session of Congress, the kind and number of the document; (6) the city of publication, the publisher, and the date.

When citing more than one work from the same government or agency, use three hyphens and a period to substitute for identical elements.

```
United States. Commission on Migrant Education. Invisible

     Children: A Portrait of Migrant Education in the

     United States. Washington: GPO, 1992.
```

(The Government Printing Office, the publisher of most federal documents, is abbreviated to save space.)

```
---. Cong. Budget Office. An Analysis of the Managed

     Competition Act. Washington: GPO, 1994.

---. ---. ---. Federal Financial Support for High-

     Technology Industries. Washington: GPO, 1985.
```

(The three sets of three hyphens indicate that this source also was prepared by the United States Congressional Budget Office.)

```
---. ---. Senate. Committee on Aging. Hearings. 101st

     Cong., 1st sess. 1989. Washington: GPO, 1990.
```

(The use of only two sets of hyphens indicates that only the first two elements correspond to the preceding citation: this source was prepared by the United States Congress, but the Senate affiliation requires the introduction of new, clarifying information in the third position.)

A Preface, Introduction, Foreword, Epilogue, or Afterword

To cite material that is separate from the primary text of a book, begin with name of the person who wrote the separate material, an assigned title (if applicable) in quotation marks, a descriptive title for the part used (capitalized but not punctuated), the title of the book, the name of the book's author (introduced with *By,* not italicized), publication facts, and inclusive page numbers for the separate material. Note that most prefatory or introductory material is paged using lowercase roman numerals.

```
Dabney, Lewis M. "Edmund Wilson and The Sixties."

     Introduction. The Sixties: The Last Journal, 1960-

     1972. By Edmund Wilson. New York: Farrar, 1993.

     xxi-xlvii.

Finnegan, William. Epilogue. Crossing the Line: A Year

     in the Land of Apartheid. New York: Harper, 1986.

     401-09.
```

A Pamphlet

When pamphlets contain clear and complete information, they are cited like books. When information is missing, use these abbreviations: *N.p.* for "No place of publication," *n.p.* for "no publisher," *n.d.* for "no date," and *N. pag.* (with a space between the abbreviations) for "no page."

```
Adams, Andrew B. Hospice Care. New York: American

     Cancer Soc., 1984. 9-16.

America's Cup? The Sober Truth about Alcohol and

     Boating. Alexandria, VA: Boat/U. S., n.d.
```

A Dissertation

A citation for an unpublished dissertation begins with the author's name, the dissertation title in quotation marks, the abbreviation *Diss.,* the name of the degree-granting school (with *University* abbreviated as *U*), and the date.

```
Stevenson, David Stacey. "Heat Transfer in Active

     Volcanoes: Models of Crater Lake Systems." Diss.

     Open U, UK, 1994.
```

(When the university's location is unfamiliar, include the state,
province, or country.)

A published dissertation is a book and should be presented
as such. However, include dissertation information between the
title and the facts of publication.

```
Salmon, Jaslin U. Black Executives in White Businesses.

     Diss. U of Illinois-Chicago, 1977. Washington, DC:

     UP of America, 1979.
```

Sacred Writings

Citations for sacred writing follow patterns similar to those of
other books, with several notable variations. First, titles of
sacred writings (the parts or the whole) are neither placed in
quotation marks nor italicized; they are capitalized only.
Second, full facts of publication are not required for traditional
editions. When appropriate, include additional information
according to the guidelines for the element.

```
The Bhagavad Gita. Trans. Juan Mascaró. New York:

     Penguin, 1962.
```

(Include translators when appropriate.)

```
The Holy Bible.
```

(This citation is for the King James version of the Bible, the traditional
edition.)

The New Oxford Annotated Bible. Rev. Standard Version.

    Ed. Herbert G. May and Bruce M. Metzger. New York:

    Oxford UP, 1973.

(This citation provides full information, highlighting a version other than the King James and the editorial work that it includes.)

| 34d | Follow the appropriate citation forms for periodicals. |

An Article in a Monthly Magazine

To cite an article in a monthly magazine, include the author's name, the article's title in quotation marks, the magazine's name (italicized), the month (abbreviated) and year, and the inclusive pages of the article (without page abbreviations).

Hosford, William F., and John L. Duncan. "The Aluminum

    Beverage Can." Scientific American Sept. 1994:

    48-53.

(Note that the period comes before the closing quotation marks of the article's title, that one space [but no punctuation] separates the periodical title and the date, and that a colon separates the date and the pages.)

An Article in a Weekly Magazine

Citations for articles in weekly magazines are identical to those for monthly magazines, with one exception: the publication date is presented in more detailed form, in day-month-year order (with the month abbreviated).

```
Auster, Bruce B., Stephen Budiansky, and Steven V.

     Roberts. "The Pentagon under the Gun." U. S. News

     and World Report 22 Mar. 1993: 24-26.
```

(Even though magazines often use special typography [as in *U. S. News & World Report*], such material is standardized in citations.)

An Article in a Journal with Continuous Paging

Journals with continuous paging number the issues sequentially for the entire year. For this kind of journal, place the volume number after the journal title, identify the year in parentheses, follow it with a colon, and then list page numbers.

```
Nussbaum, Jon F., and Lorraine M. Bettini. "Shared

     Stories of the Grandparent-Grandchild

     Relationship." The International Journal of Aging

     and Human Development 39 (1994): 67-80.
```

An Article from a Journal with Separate Paging

For journals that page each issue separately, follow the volume number with a period and the issue number (without spaces).

```
Felix, Judith Walker de, and Richard T. Johnson.

     "Learning from Video Games." Computers in the

     Schools 9.2-3 (1993): 119-34.
```

(When issues are combined, list both numbers, separated by a hyphen without additional spaces.)

An Article in a Newspaper

Citations for newspapers resemble those for magazines: they include the author's name, article title (in quotation marks), newspaper title (italicized), the date (in day-month-year order, followed by a colon), and inclusive pages.

However, when newspapers have editions (*morning, evening, national*), they must be identified; after the year, place a comma and describe the edition, using abbreviations of common words.

When sections of newspapers are designated by letters, place the section letter with the page number, without a space (*A22, C3, F11*); if sections are indicated by numerals, place a comma after the date or edition (rather than a colon), include the abbreviation *sec.*, the section number, a colon, a space, and the page number (*sec. 1: 22, sec. 3: 2, sec. 5: 17*).

When an article continues in a later part of the paper, indicate the initial page, use a comma, and then add the subsequent page. If the article appears on more than three separated pages, list the initial page, followed by a plus sign (*22+, A17+, sec. 2: 9+*).

Weekly newspapers are cited just like daily newspapers.

```
Hershey, Robert D., Jr. "How to Preserve Buying Power

        over Time." New York Times 15 Oct. 1994, natl.

        ed., sec. 1: 29.

Nuhn, Roy. "Collectors Go Ape over King Kong Movie

        Memorabilia." Antique Week 17 Oct. 1994: A2, 48.
```

An Editorial

The citation for an editorial resembles that for a magazine or newspaper article, with one exception: the word *Editorial* (not italicized), with a period, follows the title of the essay.

```
Hall, Virginia. "When Do Schools Own a Student's Work?"

        Editorial. St. Louis Post-Dispatch 19 Oct. 1994: B7.
```

A Letter to the Editor

Letters to the editor follow a very simple format. Include the author's name, the word *Letter* (not italicized), the name of the publication (magazine, journal, or newspaper), and appropriate facts of publication. Do not record descriptive, attention-getting titles that publications, not authors, supply.

```
Mogavero, Michael A. Letter. Business Week 16 Jan.

    1995: 11.
```

(The quotation "Cutting Kuttner to the Quick on Capital Gains" served as the functional title of this letter to the editor. It is not used in the citation.)

A Review

A citation for a review begins with the author's name and the title of the review (if one is provided). The abbreviation *Rev. of* (not italicized) follows, with the name of the book, film, recording, performance, product, or whatever is being reviewed, followed by clarifying information. Publication information ends the citation, incorporating elements required for different kinds of sources.

```
Cushman, Kathleen. "Addicted to 'Getting Normal.'" Rev.

    of Smoking: The Artificial Passion, by David Krogh.

    Atlantic Oct. 1991: 131-34.
```

| 34e | Follow the appropriate citation forms for nonprint sources. |

Finding documentation information for nonprint sources is usually easy but sometimes requires ingenuity. Compact disc booklets provide the manufacturers' catalog numbers and copyright dates. Printed programs for speeches or syllabuses for course lectures provide names, titles, locations, and dates. Information about films or television programs can be obtained from opening or closing credits or from reference books such as *Facts on File* or *American Film Record.* If you have difficulty finding the information to document nonprint sources clearly, ask your instructor or a librarian for help.

A Lecture or Speech

A citation for a formal lecture or speech includes the speaker's name, the title of the presentation (in quotation marks), the name of the lecture or speaker series (if applicable), the location of the speech (convention, meeting, university, library, meeting hall), the city (and state if necessary), and the date in day-month-year order.

    Branch, Tayler. "Democracy in an Age of Denial."

        Humanities on the Hill Ser. Washington, DC, 7 May

        1992.

    Mitten, David M. "Greek Art and Architecture in the

        West: Southern Italy, Sicily, and Campania." Class

        lecture. Harvard University. Cambridge, 15 May 1989.

(For class lectures, provide as much of this information as possible: speaker, title of lecture [in quotation marks], a descriptive title, the school, the city [and state if necessary], and the date.)

    Quayle, J. Danforth. "The Most Litigious Society in the

        World." American Bar Assn. Annual Meeting.

        Atlanta, 13 Aug. 1991.

A Work of Art

When artists title their own work, include this information: artist's name; the title (italicized); the museum, gallery, or collection where the work of art is housed; and the city (and state, province, or country if needed for clarity).

Cézanne, Paul. Houses along a Road. The Hermitage, St.

    Petersburg, Russia.

When artists have not titled their work, use the title that art historians have given to it (but do not place it in quotation marks), followed by a brief description of the work. The rest of the citation is the same as that for other works of art.

Amateis, Edmond Romulus. Jonas Edward Salk. Sculpture

    in bronze. Natl. Portrait Gallery, Washington, DC.

(*Jonas Edward Salk* is the attributed title of the statue of this famous scientist.)

A Map, Graph, Table, or Chart

Maps, graphs, tables, and charts are treated like books. If known, include the name of the author, artist, designer, scientist, or person or group responsible for the map, graph, table, or chart. Then include the title (italicized), followed by a separately punctuated descriptive title. Include other necessary information.

Lewis, R. J. [Noninteractive and Interactive]

    Telecommunication Technologies. Table. Meeting

    Learners' Needs Through Telecommunication: A

    Directory and Guide to Programs. Washington, DC:

    American Assn. for Higher Education, 1983. 75.

(Clarifying information can be added within brackets.)

A Cartoon

Begin with the cartoonist's name, the title of the cartoon in quotation marks, and the word *Cartoon* (not italicized), followed by a period. Then include the citation information required for the source.

```
Davis, Jack, and Stan Hart. "Groan with the Wind."

     Cartoon. Mad Jan. 1991: 42-47.
```

(This cartoon appeared in a monthly magazine.)

A Film

To cite a film as a complete work, include the title (italicized), the director (noted by the abbreviation *Dir.,* not italicized), the studio, and the date of release. If you include other people's contributions, do so after the director's name, using brief phrases (*Screenplay by, Original score by*) or abbreviations (*Perf.* for "performed by," *Prod.* for "produced by") to clarify their roles.

```
On the Waterfront. Dir. Elia Kazan. Perf. Marlon Brando

     and Eva Marie Saint. Horizon-Columbia, 1954.
```

To emphasize the contribution of an individual (rather than the film as a whole), place the person's name first, followed by a comma and a descriptive title (beginning with a lowercase letter). The rest of the citation follows normal patterns.

```
Coppola, Francis Ford, dir. Apocalypse Now. Perf.

     Martin Sheen, Marlon Brando, and Robert Duvall.

     United Artists, 1979. Suggested by Joseph Conrad's

     Heart of Darkness.
```

A Television Broadcast

List regular programs by title (italicized), the network (CBS, CNN, FOX), the local station (including both the call letters and the city, separated by a comma), and the broadcast date (in day-month-year order).

Include other people's contributions after the program title, using brief phrases (*Written by, Hosted by*) or abbreviations (*Perf.* for "performed by," Prod. for "produced by") to clarify their roles.

> M*A*S*H. Perf. Alan Alda, Loretta Swit, Harry Morgan,
>
>   and David Ogden-Stiers. CBS. WTHI, Terre Haute,
>
>   IN. 12 Mar. 1996.

To cite a single episode of an ongoing program, include the name of the episode, in quotation marks, before the program's title. Other elements are presented in the same order as used for a regular program.

> "The Understudy." Seinfeld. Perf. Bette Midler. NBC.
>
>   WTHR, Indianapolis. 18 May 1995.

List special programs by title, followed by traditional descriptive information. If a special program is part of a series (for example, Hallmark Hall of Fame, Great Performances, or American Playhouse), include the series name without quotation marks or italics immediately preceding the name of the network.

> The Sleeping Beauty. Composed by Peter Ilich Tchaikovsky.
>
>   Choreographed by Marius Petipa. Perf. Viviana
>
>   Durante and Zoltan Solymosi. Great Performances.
>
>   PBS. WFYI, Indianapolis. 24 Dec. 1995.

A Radio Broadcast

A citation for a radio broadcast follows the same guidelines as for a television broadcast.

The War of the Worlds. WCBS, New York. 30 Oct. 1938.

A Recording

Citations for recordings usually begin with the performer or composer, followed by the title of the recording (italicized except for titles using numbers for musical form, key, or number), the recording company, the catalog number, and the copyright date.

List other contributors after the title, using brief phrases or abbreviations (*Cond.,* the abbreviation for conductor, *Perf.* for "performed by," *Composed by*) to clarify their roles; orchestras (abbreviated *orch.*) and other large musical groups are listed without clarifying phrases, usually following the conductor's name.

When appropriate, include recording dates immediately following the title. Compact discs (CDs) are now the standard recording format; indicate other formats, when necessary, after the title.

Notation of multidisc sets, similar to the pattern for multivolume books, appears immediately preceding the record company.

The Beatles. Live at the BBC. 2 discs. Capital,

     C2-31796-2, 1994.

Mahler, Gustav. Symphony no. 1 in D major. Record.

     Cond. Georg Solti. Chicago Symphony Orch. London,

     411731-2, 1984.

(Since this selection is titled by musical form and key, it is not italicized. As noted after the title, this is a record, not a CD.)

To cite a single selection from a recording, include the selection title in quotation marks just before the title of the complete recording. All else remains the same.

```
Clapton, Eric. "Tears in Heaven." Eric Clapton

    Unplugged. Reprise, 9 45024-2, 1992.
```

To cite liner notes, the printed material that comes with many recordings, list the name of the writer and the description *Liner notes* (not italicized), followed by a period. The rest of the citation follows normal patterns.

```
McClintick, David, and William Kennedy. Liner notes.

    Frank Sinatra: The Reprise Collection. 4 discs.

    Reprise, 020373, 1990.
```

An Interview

Citations for personally conducted interviews include the name of the person interviewed, the type of interview (personal or telephone), and the interview date.

```
Otwell, Stephen. Personal interview. 11 Nov. 1996.
```

Citations for broadcast or printed interviews include the name of the person interviewed, the descriptive title *Interview* (not italicized), and necessary information to describe the source.

```
Stewart, Jimmy. Interview. Reflections on the Silver

    Screen. Arts and Entertainment. 5 Nov. 1994.
```

A Transcript

Transcripts of programs are presented according to the source of the original broadcast, with clarifying information provided. The entry ends with information about availability.

```
Watkins, Terri, et al. "McVeigh Said to Have Mentioned

     Other Bombings in Letter." Transcript. Daybreak.

     CNN. 28 Apr. 1995. Available: Journal Graphics

     Online.
```

34f	**Follow the appropriate citation forms for electronic sources.**

Because electronic sources are available from such a wide variety of sources, only a general format is established at present. Provide as much information as possible, being aware that all sources will not provide all kinds of identifying information.

A CD-ROM Source

If a CD-ROM source reproduces print material, include full print information: the author's name, the title, and facts of publication; follow this information about the print source with the title of the database (italicized), the description *CD-ROM* (not italicized), the city and name of the company that produced the CD-ROM (if available), and the electronic publication date (if known).

```
"On the Brink: An Interview with Yitzhak Rabin."

     Jerusalem Post 23 Apr. 1994: 16. PAIS [Public

     Affairs Information Service] International. CD-

     ROM. Silverplatter, 1995. Access no.: 94-0504485.
```

(The information in brackets and the access number are optional, but they add clarity.)

If a CD-ROM presents material unavailable in print form, include the author's name (if given), the title of the material in quotation marks, the date of the material (if appropriate), the title of the database (italicized), the description *CD-ROM* (not italicized), the city and name of the company that produced the CD-ROM (if available), and the electronic publication date (if known).

"National Rifle Association of America (NRA)."

Encyclopedia of Associations. CD-ROM. Detroit:

Gale, 1994.

If the CD-ROM is not regularly revised or updated, the citation follows a pattern similar to that for a book, with one exception: the description *CD-ROM* (not italicized) precedes the electronic publication date.

Welmers, William E. "African Languages." The New

Grolier Multimedia Encyclopedia. 1994 ed. CD-ROM.

New York: Grolier, 1994.

An Online Database or Other Source

Because online databases are part of a computer network, identify the means to gain access to information. The order in which information is presented is the same as for CD-ROM sources, but with several important changes: use the description *Online* (presented as one word, not italicized), name the computer service, and provide the date on which you gained access to the material. In addition, provide the electronic address used to retrieve the material, introduced by the word *Available* (not italicized) and a colon.

With other electronic sources available online (electronic newsletters, journals, correspondence), provide as much clarifying information as possible, in the order described for other electronic sources.

Americans with Disabilities Act. S. 933. Government

    Publication, McHenry Library, University of

    California, Santa Cruz. Federal Government

    Resources. Online. Gopher. 17 Apr. 1995.

(This online government document is cited by title; the clarifying information about the location of a print version of the document is optional. The date indicates when the information was retrieved.)

Davis, Roger. E-mail Interview. 1 June 1995.

    ejdavis.root.indstate.edu.

(Citations for electronic sources resemble those for print corollaries while, at the same time, providing clarifying information. The inclusion of the interviewee's electronic mail address is optional.)

"La Mosquitia, Honduras." NASA Shuttle Photos. Earth

    Observation Images Database. Online. Netscape.

    World Wide Web. 2 May 1995. Available: http://www.

    clearlake.ibm.con/ERC.

(Provide additional information when helpful, as in "NASA Shuttle Photos.")

Ladew, Jennie. "Re: Hyperlexia, Autism, and Language."

    29 May 1995. Online posting. Newsgroup

    bit.listserv.autism. Internet. 30 May 1995.

(Provide a descriptive title if the author has not provided one, placed in quotation marks and including the abbreviation *Re* (not italicized), which means "regarding." The date on which Ladew's information was posted on the newsgroup follows the title; the date on which the material was retrieved ends the citation.)

EXERCISE 34.1) *Compiling a works cited page*

From the following sets of scrambled information on sources related to secondary education, produce correct sample works cited entries and arrange them alphabetically.

1. pages 25–30; Winter 1984; "The Blackboard Bumble: Popular Culture and the Recent Challenges of the American High School"; Steven A. Hilsabeck; volume 18; *Journal of Popular Culture.*

2. Order number AAC 9540951; James Sweeney, advisor; "An Examination of the Student Culture of a Comprehensive High School"; Iowa State University; Jan Westerman-Beatty; dissertation; 1995; 199 pages.

3. "Shaking Up the Schools"; May 3, 1994; section A; *New York Times;* page 22; late edition.

4. Todd Barrett; illustrated; volume 121; "Be Careful What You Ask For"; page 74; February 15, 1993; *Newsweek.*

5. *Fast Times at Ridgemont High;* with Sean Penn, Jennifer Jason Leigh, Judge Reinhold, Phoebe Cates, Forest Whitaker, Eric Stoltz, Nicholas Cage, and Anthony Edwards; written by Cameron Crowe; 1982; 92 minutes; color; directed by Amy Heckering; Universal-Refugee.

6. 1995 edition; "High School Enrollments"; *Facts on File.*

7. *The Learning Gap: Why Our Schools Are Failing and What We Can Learn from Japanese and Chinese Education;* Summit Books; Harold Stevenson and James Stigler; New York; 1992.

8. October 1992; pages 157–159; *Phi Delta Kappan;* volume 76; Larry Cuban; "The Corporate Myth of Reforming Public Schools."

9. E-mail interview with C. Mitchell Chávez, principal; Wednesday, March 20, 1996; North Jackson High School; 9:30–10:30 A.M.; cmchavez@jhs.ind.edu.

10. Andrew Nikiforuk; Toronto, Canada; Macfarlane Walter & Ross, Inc.; 1993; *School's Out: The Catastrophe in Public Education and What We Can Do About It.*

11. *Encyclopedia of Associations;* 1994; CD-ROM; Gale Publishers; Detroit; "National Parent-Teacher Organization (NPTO)."

12. Leslie Freemont; Internet; online posting; posted April 25, 1996; Newsgroup; retrieved April 28, 1996; bit.listserv.education; regarding school standards.

13. WXIN; Fox; Indianapolis, Indiana; *Party of Five;* March 27, 1996; with Matthew Fox, Neve Campbell, and Scott Wolf.

14. Harper & Row, Publishers; 1983; Ernest L. Boyer; New York; *High School: A Report on Secondary Education in America;* prepared for the Carnegie Foundation.

35 Organizing, Writing, and Documenting the Research Paper

After weeks of gathering information, organizing and writing the research paper may seem an enormous undertaking. It is. It is also an exciting stage in your work because you now are ready to bring your information and your ideas together in a clear and convincing paper.

> ### Quick Reference
>
> ❭ Reread your notes and organize them into groups that correspond to logical divisions of your topic.
>
> ❭ Write a rough draft based on this organization, working with one group of notes at a time.
>
> ❭ Integrate source material smoothly with your ideas.
>
> ❭ Use parenthetical notes to provide readers with information about your sources.
>
> ❭ Revise the rough draft to clarify organization and content, to improve style, and to correct technical errors. (See Chapter 3, "Revising," for revision checklists.)
>
> ❭ Prepare and submit the final copy according to your instructor's or other standard guidelines.

35a ❭ Organize your notes.

The basic patterns of organizing a research paper resemble patterns used for other papers. (See Chapter 4, "Paragraphs," to review patterns of organization.) Your note taking has given you a wealth of material; now you need to arrange that material in the way that will best present your thesis to your readers.

Reread Your Notes

To begin, review your notes. Though time consuming, rereading all notes will help you to see the scope of your materials and the connections among ideas distilled from sources. A complete grasp of your materials is crucial as you revise the thesis statement, prepare an outline, and sort materials.

Revise Your Thesis Statement

Examine your working thesis statement. Based on the information gathered during research, test the validity of your thesis statement:

Does it identify the topic clearly?

Does it present a valid judgment?

Does it incorporate necessary qualifications and limitations?

Does it state or imply that you have acknowledged opposing views?

Is it worded effectively?

If you cannot respond "yes" to these questions, revise your thesis statement.

Use the Revised Thesis to Develop a Rough Outline

Once the thesis statement is clearly and effectively worded, print or type a clean copy and use it to help you to construct a rough outline for your paper. What major categories does the

thesis statement imply? Use them as the basis of a rough outline with which to sort your note cards into meaningful groups
dictated by your thesis and ideas.

Shingo reviewed his working thesis statement:

> *Although most people know that music modifies moods, few rec-
> ognize that because music possesses a power to influence peo-
> ple's behavior, it offers important treatment for the mentally and
> physically impaired.*

He was satisfied with his qualification—about general perceptions—and felt that the working thesis statement identified the
related areas of emphasis for his paper: the influence of music
and its use as a therapy. Knowing that he could refine the thesis statement further if necessary, Shingo felt that he could
move forward with organizing the paper.

Allowing for an introduction and conclusion, Shingo created
this rough outline to arrange the ideas of his paper:

> *Introductory paragraph (Thesis statement: Although most people
> know that music modifies moods, few recognize that because
> music possesses a power to influence people's behavior, it offers
> important treatment for the mentally and physically impaired.)*

> *History of music therapy*
>   *—Ancient cultures: Egypt and Greece*
>   *—Modern cultures: U.S.*
> *Recent uses of music therapy*
>   *—Recreational use*
>   *Stimulus (Oliver Sacks,* Awakenings)
>   *Programs (orchestras, etc.)*
>   *—Therapeutic use*
>   *expression*
>   *communication*
>   *remembrance*

Music's appeal
   —*Rhythm*
   —*Pitch and melody*
   —*Harmony*
   —*Nonverbal communication*
Concluding paragraphs/where are we heading?

Remember that you can revise your outline if you discover a better way to arrange materials as you write the rough draft.

Although you are only sketching your research paper when you are composing a rough outline, preparing it on a word processor has advantages.

- *Type the rough outline on your word processor and then take a break.* Return to the outline and print it out, examine it, and then make any necessary changes. Revise it and print a new copy. It will be much easier to evaluate the outline if it is typed rather than handwritten.
- *Write alternative versions.* Prepare different versions of the rough outline, experimenting with the arrangement of information and ideas. Print two versions side by side and compare their clarity, balance, and emphasis.
- *Save the rough outline.* The structure of the rough outline—and even some of its phrasing—can be used later in devising a formal outline.

Sort Your Notes

Using the major headings of the rough outline, sort your notes. First, find a roomy place—a large table in the library, the floor in your family room, your bed. Make label cards using the major topics from your rough outline. Spread them out and then sort your note cards into the appropriate major topic groups.

If a note fits in more than one group, place the card in the most appropriate group and place a cross-reference card (for example, "See Parker quotation, p. 219—in *childhood*") in each of the other appropriate groups. Expect to have a stack of notes that do not logically fit into any group. Label them *miscellaneous* and set them aside. You may see where they fit as you continue working. Use paper clips, binder clips, rubber bands, or envelopes to keep groups of notes together.

Allow a few days to organize and perhaps reorganize your notes. Sorting cards involves analyzing, reconsidering, and rearranging. Expect temporary chaos.

Prepare a Formal Outline

After sorting your cards into major topics, use the topics to decide on the arrangement of information within sections of your paper. Take each group of cards and organize them into a clear, logical sequence. Creating a formal outline is generally the most useful way to accomplish this. (To review outlining, see section 2b.)

Through a formal, detailed outline derived from his notes, Shingo evolved the structure of his paper, including chronological organization of material on music therapy and topical organization of material on specific treatments. His formal outline appears on pages 531–35.

Using the word processor, expand your rough outline to produce the formal outline of your paper.

■ *Introduce the elements of a formal outline:* roman numerals, uppercase letters, arabic numerals, and lowercase letters to indicate levels of detail.

■ *Add clarifying information.* Insert details that will guide you in writing the rough draft.

■ *Insert your revised thesis statement.* Using the "cut" and "paste" commands, copy your thesis statement into the file that contains your formal outline and place it at the top, below the title.

■ *Use the "outline" feature of your word processor* to arrange material easily into the correct format.

| 35b | Write the rough draft. |

With notes, revised thesis, and formal outline in hand, you are ready to begin writing the rough draft. The rough draft of a research paper, like the rough draft of any paper, will be messy and inconsistent, sketchy in some places and repetitive in others. That is to be expected. In fact, writing the draft of a research paper may present even more problems than writing other papers because of its greater length and complexity. To help with the process of drafting the research paper, remember the drafting strategies that you developed in writing other kinds of papers. (For a complete discussion, see section 2c.)

General Drafting Strategies

Gather all your materials together.

Work from your outline.

Remember the purpose of your paper.

Use only ideas and details that support your thesis statement.

Remember your readers' needs.

Do not worry about technical matters.

Rethink and modify troublesome sections.

Reread sections as you write.

Write alternative versions of troublesome sections.

Periodically give yourself a break from writing.

Beyond these general principles, which apply to all writing, the following specific principles apply to writing a research paper and take into account its special requirements and demands.

Drafting Strategies for Research Papers

Allow ample time to write. Begin writing as soon as you can and write something every day.

Work on one section at a time. Work steadily, section by section. When you come to a section that is difficult to write or for which you need more information, leave it for later and move on to the next section. Remember to look for necessary new material as soon as possible.

Give special attention to introductory and concluding paragraphs. Ideas for introductory and concluding paragraphs may occur at any time during the writing process. Consider several strategies and select the one most clearly matched to the tone and purpose of your paper.

Give special attention to technical language. Define carefully any technical language required in your paper. Thoughtful definition and use of important technical terms will help you to clarify your ideas as you draft your paper.

Think of your paper by section, not by paragraph. Because of the complexity of material in a research paper, discussions of most topics will require more than one paragraph. Keep that in mind and use new paragraphs to present subtopics.

Use transitions to signal major shifts within your work. The multiparagraph explanations required for key points can make it difficult for readers to know when you have moved from one key point to another. Consequently, emphasize transitions in your draft; you can refine them during revision if they are too obvious.

Incorporate your research notes smoothly so that they are an integral part of your paper. Material from sources should support, not dominate, your ideas. Incorporate source material as needed to support your thesis; do not simply string notes together with sentences. (For a complete discussion of incorporating research notes, see section 35c.)

As you write, remember that a research paper should present your views on a subject, based on outside reading and interpretation; it should not just show that you can collect and compile what others have said about the subject. Develop your own ideas fully. Be a part of the paper: add comments on sources and disagree with them when necessary. Be a thinker and a writer.

If possible, compose at the computer. The "add," "delete," "move," and "reformat" features will give you flexibility as you prepare your rough draft. You will also be able to print "clean" pages to review and revise later. Drafting a research paper is a complex process, but a few suggestions may simplify your work.

■ *Create a file for your draft and copy your thesis statement into it.*

■ *Copy quotations from your quotation file into the paper as you need them.* By copying quotations into the file rather than retyping them, you will save time and avoid introducing new errors.

■ *Keep in mind the kinds of changes that you can easily make during revision.* You will be able to move or change words, phrases, sentences, paragraphs, or whole sections; check spelling; change format and spacing; use "search and replace" procedures; and add full documentation.

35c   **Incorporate notes smoothly into the research paper.**

The information from your note taking—summaries, quotations, and paraphrases—must be incorporated smoothly into your research paper, providing clarifications, explanations, and illustrations of important ideas. Use your notes selectively to substantiate your points, not simply to show that you have gathered materials, and provide your own commentary on the central ideas. Your readers should know why you have included the source material you did.

Facts and Summaries

Incorporate facts and summaries into your own sentences. Sentences containing facts and summarized ideas require parenthetical notes (see section 35d) to identify the sources of the information, as in this example:

```
Unlike productions from earlier generations, current

musicals are extravaganzas, developed by multination-

al groups and presented in multiple venues. Les

Misérables--produced in France, England, and the

United States in 1989--had eighteen companies touring

world wide, bringing in $450 million (Rosenberg and

Harburg 65).
```

[Rosenberg, Bernard, and Ernest Harburg. *The Broadway Musical: Collaboration in Commerce and Art.* New York: New York UP, 1993.]

Commonly known information, however, does not require an identifying note; that *Les Misérables* is based on the novel by Victor Hugo is generally known and consequently does not require a note (see section 33g for a discussion of common knowledge).

Paraphrases

Include paraphrased materials wherever they fit into the paper. A one-sentence paraphrase should be followed immediately by a parenthetical note. Longer paraphrases, especially background information taken from a single source, should be placed in a separate paragraph with parenthetical documentation at the end; identify the author and source at the beginning of the paragraph. For example:

In <u>School Choice: The Struggle for the Soul of</u>

<u>American Education</u>, Peter W. Cookson, Jr., provides a

useful summary of why people have come to question

the government's monopoly in public education.

According to Cookson, high drop-out rates, in-school

violence, disintegrating facilities, low educational

standards, and cultural fragmentation have all con-

tributed to education's decline. However, he con-

tends that it was media attention to these troubles,

coupled with the conservative backlash of the Reagan

years, that gave the school choice movement its

momentum. (2-7)

[Cookson, Peter W., Jr. *School Choice: The Struggle for the Soul of American Education*. New Haven, CT: Yale UP, 1994.]

Quotations

Use quotations selectively to add clarity, emphasis, or interest to a research paper, not to pad its length. Overquoting reduces the effectiveness of a paper because it suggests an overdependence on other people's ideas.

Never include a quotation without introducing or commenting on it, expecting readers to know why it is worth quoting. Instead, frame the quotation with your own ideas and provide evaluative comments, no matter how brief. Numerous verbs may be used to introduce quotations.

Some verbs used to introduce quotations

add	explain	reply
answer	mention	respond
claim	note	restate
comment	observe	say
declare	reiterate	stress
emphasize	remark	summarize

The examples given on pages 512–16 demonstrate an effective pattern for introducing quotations: identify the author and source and explain the quotation's relevance to the discussion. Quotations of prose or poetry can be either brief and included within the text or long and set off from the text.

Brief Prose or Verse Quotations

Include prose quotations of fewer than forty-five words (four or fewer typed lines) within the paragraph text. Enclose the words in quotation marks. For example:

```
No community is free from the effects of news as

business.  As Doug Underwood observes in When MBAs

Rule the Newsroom: How the Marketers and Managers Are

Reshaping Today's Media: "In this era of conglomer-

ates and concentrated ownership, the tentacles of the

big media companies are reaching everywhere, connect-

ing with their electronic competitors and entertain-

ment combines, plugging up the remaining independent
```

```
media outlets, and extending their hold even into our

smallest communities" (181).
```

For variety, place identifying material at the end of the quoted material or, if not disruptive, in the middle of it. For example:

```
No community is free from the effects of news as

business.  "In this era of conglomerates and concen-

trated ownership," Doug Underwood observes in When

MBAs Rule the Newsroom, "the tentacles of the big

media companies are reaching everywhere, connecting

with their electronic competitors and entertainment

combines, plugging up the remaining independent media

outlets, and extending their hold even into our

smallest communities" (181).
```

To use only a phrase or part of a sentence from a source, incorporate the material into your own sentence structure. Although derived from the same passage as the quotation used above, this example uses only a small portion of the original:

```
No community is free from the effects of news as

business.  In When MBAs Rule the Newsroom: How the

Marketers and Managers Are Reshaping Today's Media,

Doug Underwood suggests that national and interna-

tional media companies are "plugging up the remaining

independent media outlets, and extending their hold

even into our smallest communities" (181).
```

[Underwood, Doug. *When MBAs Rule the Newsroom: How the Marketers and Managers Are Reshaping Today's Media.* New York: Columbia UP, 1993.]

Punctuate such quotations according to the requirements of the entire sentence. Do not set such quotations apart with commas unless the sentence structure requires commas.

Incorporate verse quotations of one or two lines within the paragraph text. Use quotation marks, indicate line divisions with a slash (/) preceded and followed by one space, and retain the poem's capitalization. Cite poetry using line numbers, not pages.

In "Morning at the Window," T. S. Eliot offers a familiar, foggy image, the distant musings of a person who observes life but does not seem to live it: "The brown waves of fog toss up to me / Twisted faces from the bottom of the street" (5-6).

[Eliot, T. S. "Morning at the Window." *The Complete Poems and Plays: 1909–1950.* New York: Harcourt, 1971. 16.]

Long Prose or Verse Quotations

Incorporate prose quotations of forty-five words or more (five or more typed lines) by setting the quotation off from the body of the paragraph. Indent the quotation ten spaces from the left margin. Double-space the material but do not enclose it within quotation marks. If a clause introduces the quotation, follow it with a colon, as in this example:

Anthropologists and social scientists are now realizing that a broader range of information must be col-

lected in order for us to understand the diversity of
ethnic and social groups. Rhoda H. Halperin offers
this rationale in "Appalachians in Cities: Issues and
Challenges for Research":

> Family histories that reveal the dynamics
> of intergenerational relationships in all
> of their dimensions (education, economic,
> psychological)--the constant mentoring and
> tutoring, the patience of grandmothers with
> grandbabies--must be collected. We need as
> researchers to collect data that avoid the
> patronizing "we" (urban professionals) who
> know what is best for "you" or "them" (the
> poor people). (196)

[Halperin, Rhoda H. "Appalachians in Cities: Issues and Challenges for Research." *From Mountains to Metropolis: Appalachian Migrants in American Cities.* Ed. Kathryn M. Borman and Phillip J. Obermiller. Westport, CT: Bergin, 1994. 181–97.]

To quote three or more lines of poetry, follow the pattern for long prose quotations: indent ten spaces, double-space the lines, and omit quotation marks. Follow the poet's line spacing as closely as possible, as in this example:

In "Poem [1]," Langston Hughes offers a spare, critical assessment of western culture:

```
        I am afraid of this civilization--

            So hard,

                So strong,

                    So cold.  (4-7)
```

[Hughes, Langston. "Poem [1]." *The Collected Poems of Langston Hughes*. Ed. Arnold Rampersad and David Roessel. New York: Knopf, 1994.]

Punctuation with Quotations

Single Quotation Marks. To indicate an author's use of quotations within a passage, follow one of two patterns. In a brief passage, enclose the full quotation in double quotation marks (" ") and change the source's punctuation to single quotation marks (' '), as in this example:

```
In Tribes: How Race, Religion, and Identity Determine

Success in the New Global Economy, Joel Kotkin empha-

sizes the influence of immigrants in American culture

and business: "Even blue denim jeans, the 'uniform'

of the gold rush--and indeed, the American West--owe

their origination and popular name to Levi Strauss, a

gold rush-era immigrant to San Francisco" (57).
```

[Kotkin, Joel. *Tribes: How Race, Religion, and Identity Determine Success in the New Global Economy*. New York: Random, 1993.]

In a long quotation—indented ten spaces and therefore not enclosed within quotation marks—the author's quotation marks remain double, as in this example:

James Sellers, in <u>Essays in American Ethics</u>, suggests

that self-identify is often inextricably linked to

one's nationality:

> National identity need not always be in the
>
> forefront of one's awareness of who he [or
>
> she] is. But in America, it is. The United
>
> States is the "oldest new nation," we are
>
> often told by political scientists; and the
>
> national heritage, while it has certainly
>
> not turned out to be a "melting pot," has
>
> become a powerful background influence upon
>
> the identity of Americans, reshaping even
>
> the ways in which they express their eth-
>
> nicity or their religion. (97)

[Sellers, James. *Essays in American Ethics*. Ed. Barry Arnold. New York: Lang, 1991.]

Brackets. Use brackets to clarify words or phrases in a quotation. For example, in the passage below, the bracketed phrase "value-destroying industries" (a commonly understood phrase in economic studies) substitutes for the words "one of these firms," which has no clear referent in the quotation or its introduction.

In "The Disintegration of the Russian Economy,"

Michael Spagat explains a major industrial dilemma:

"Workers in these industries are receiving more wages

than the wealth they are creating for society. So if

```
[value-destroying industries] were closed down, money

would be saved but the savings would not be enough to

pay full unemployment compensation" (52).
```

[Spagat, Michael. "The Disintegration of the Russian Economy." *Russia's Future: Consolidation or Disintegration?* Ed. Douglas W. Blum. Boulder, CO: Westview, 1994. 47–67.]

Bracketed information can substitute for the original wording, as in the example above, or appear in addition to the original material: "she [Eleanor Roosevelt]" or "he [or she]." If a quotation requires extensive use of brackets, use another quotation or express the information in your own words.

Ellipses. Use ellipsis points (three spaced periods) to show where words are omitted from a quotation. Omissions from the middle of a sentence do not require any punctuation other than the ellipses. To indicate an omission from the end of a sentence, retain the sentence's end punctuation, followed by the ellipsis points (producing four spaced periods).

```
Robert I. Williams stresses the social dimensions of

comedy in Comic Practice: Comic Response: "Humor is a

guide.  It is largely culture bound. Chinese

Communist jokes do not do well here, just as ours

tend to be duds in Beijing. . . . Yet there is a

range of humor that works for a broad, variegated

audience. The very existence of comic films is

testimony" (56-57).
```

[Omitted: "The humor of a Chicago street gang will not work in a retirement home, even one in Chicago. Regional, age, gender, and social differences all enter in."]

[Williams, Robert I. *Comic Practice: Comic Response*. Newark: U of Delaware P, 1993.]

Ellipsis points are unnecessary at the beginning or end of a quotation because readers know that quotations come from more complete sources.

| 35d | Use parenthetical notes to document research. |

Internal documentation identifies materials from sources and indicates where facts, quotations, or ideas appear in original sources. In the past, note numbers (one half-space above the line) at the end of sentences indicated when information, ideas, and quotations came from source materials. Those note numbers corresponded to full citations placed either at the bottom of the page (footnotes) or gathered at the end of the paper (endnotes). Numbered notes are still used in University of Chicago and Turabian style (see page 472) and can be seen in most older books and articles. However, simplified, less repetitive methods of citation are more commonly used today.

Acknowledging the repetitive nature of full note citations, the Modern Language Association (MLA), following the lead of the American Psychological Association (APA), now briefly identifies sources in the paper in parentheses. See section 34a for a discussion of MLA and other style guides.

Consistency of Reference

Parenthetical references must correspond to entries in the list of works cited. If a works cited entry begins with an author's name, then the parenthetical reference in the text must also cite the author's name, not the title, editor, translator, or some other element. Readers then match the information within the parenthetical references with the information in works cited entries.

Basic Forms of Parenthetical Notes

To avoid disrupting the text, parenthetical notes use the briefest possible form to identify the relevant source: the name of the author (or in some instances the title) and, for print sources, a page number (without a page abbreviation). For example:

```
Soon after Johnson was inaugurated in 1965, Operation

Rolling Thunder began; ultimately American planes

dropped 643,000 tons of explosives on North Vietnam

(Brownmiller 20).
```

In the interests of clarity and economy, you may incorporate some of the necessary information into your sentences.

```
Brownmiller notes that soon after Johnson was inaugu-

rated in 1965, Operation Rolling Thunder began; ulti-

mately American planes dropped 630,000 tons of explo-

sives on North Vietnam (20).
```

[Brownmiller, Susan. *Seeing Vietnam: Encounters of the Road and Heart*. New York: Harper, 1994.]

In special cases, however, the rule of using the author's last name and the page reference is superseded:

Special circumstance	Rule and sample
Two authors with the same last name	Include first and last name: (John Barratt 31), distinct from (Jessica Barratt 2–4)

Special circumstance	*Rule and sample*
Two works by the same author	Include the title or a shortened version of the title, separated from the author's name by a comma: (Morrison, *Beloved* 116), distinct from (Morrison, *Solomon* 13)
Two authors	Include both last names: (Scott and Fuller 213–14)
Three authors	Include all last names, separated by commas: (Jarnow, Judelle, and Guerreiro 58)
Four or more authors	Include the first author's last name and *et al.,* not italicized: (Gershey et al. 22)
Corporate author	Include the organization as the author: (AMA 117)
Multivolume works	Include the volume number after the author's name, followed by a colon: (Tebbel 4:89–91)
Reference works	Include the author's name or a shortened form of the title, depending on how the work appears in the works cited list; no page numbers are required for alphabetically arranged sources: (Angermüller) or ("Manhattan Project")
Poetry or drama in verse	Include the author's name, a short title (if necessary), and line (not page) numbers: (Eliot, "Waste Land" 173–181)

Nonprint Sources

Cite nonprint sources, for which no page numbers can be given, by "author" (lecturer, director, writer, producer, performer, or interview respondent) or title, as they appear in the list of works cited.

> The isolation and despair of patients with AIDS are
>
> captured in these haunting images:
>
>> I walked the avenue till my legs felt like
>>
>> stone
>>
>> I heard the voices of friends vanished and
>>
>> gone
>>
>> At night I could hear the blood in my veins
>>
>> Black and whispering as the rain.
>>
>> (Springsteen, "Streets")

Such citations, however, are often clearer if incorporated into the text of the paper.

> The isolation and despair of patients with AIDS are
>
> captured in these haunting images from Bruce
>
> Springsteen's "Streets of Philadelphia":
>
>> I walked the avenue till my legs felt like
>>
>> stone
>>
>> I heard the voices of friends vanished and
>>
>> gone
>>
>> At night I could hear the blood in my veins
>>
>> Black and whispering as the rain.

[Springsteen, Bruce. "Streets of Philadelphia." *Philadelphia*. Soundtrack. Epic, 7464-57624-2.]

Because nonprint sources require limited information in parenthetical notes, incorporate all needed information in the written text when possible.

Positioning Parenthetical Notes

Without disrupting the text, place parenthetical notes as close as possible to the material they identify—usually at the end of the sentence but before the end punctuation. Allow one space before the opening parenthesis.

Facts, Summaries, and Paraphrases

```
Congressionally approved military assistance to for-
eign nations gradually increased from $2 billion per
year during Kennedy's administration to $7 billion a
year during the Reagan administration (Hinckley
122-23).
```

[Hinckley, Barbara. *Less than Meets the Eye: Foreign Policy Making and the Myth of the Assertive Congress*. Chicago: Twentieth Century-U of Chicago P, 1994.]

Brief Quotations

For brief quotations, place the notes *outside* the quotation marks but *before* the end punctuation, a change in the usual pattern of placing end punctuation before closing quotation marks.

```
Economic and political power are intertwined because
"together, the politically strong and our legislators
```

devise measures to limit [economic] competition from

those who are politically weaker" (Adams and Brock

118).

[Adams, Walter, and James W. Brock. *Antitrust Economics on Trial: A Dialogue on the New Laissez-Faire.* Princeton: Princeton UP, 1991.]

Long Quotations

For long, set-off quotations (indented ten spaces and not enclosed by quotation marks), place a period at the end of the quotation. Then add the parenthetical note without additional punctuation.

Unlike the traditional "hard" sciences, the study of

past cultures must, by nature, be somewhat intuitive.

As Rachel Harry suggests in "Archaeology as Art":

> Objectivity in archaeology is at once both
>
> an easy and an impossible target to shoot
>
> down because it simply does not exist.
>
> Archaeologists cannot <u>choose</u> objectivity.
>
> We will find what we look for, and are left
>
> with what by chance is revealed to us. (133)

[Harry, Rachel. "Archaeology as Art." *Archaeological Theory: Progress or Posture?* Ed. Iain M. Mackenzie. Worldwide Archaeological Ser. Brookfield, VT: Avebury, 1994. 131-39.]

| 35e | Revise the rough draft into a final draft. |

After writing the draft of the paper, set it aside for at least two or three days, and longer if possible. Then reread it carefully.

Consider the paper's organization, content, and style. Your ideas should be clearly expressed, logically organized, and effectively supported with appropriate and illuminating facts, quotations, and paraphrases smoothly and accurately incorporated. Leave time in your schedule to rework your paper, strengthening undeveloped sections by expanding them, clarifying confusing sections by rewriting them, and focusing overly long sections by cutting unnecessary material. For more information on this stage of the writing process, see Chapter 3, "Revising."

Evaluate the Rough Draft

Using the guidelines given below, assess your rough draft or consider having a peer editing session with someone in your class. Make revisions according to your assessment of the paper's strengths and weaknesses.

Introduction

Is the title interesting, accurate, and appropriate?

Is the introductory strategy interesting and appropriate to the tone and subject of the paper?

Is the thesis statement clear?

Is the length of the introduction proportionate to its importance and to the length of the entire paper?

Organization

Is the organizational pattern appropriate to the subject?

Are topics and subtopics clearly related to the thesis?

Is background information complete and well integrated?

Are interpretations of and conclusions from research clearly stated?

Content

Is the thesis statement clearly developed throughout?

Are topics adequately supported by facts, ideas, and research?

Are quotations and paraphrases well chosen to support the thesis?

Is material from sources smoothly and accurately incorporated?

Style

Is the tone of the paper consistently serious and appropriate for a college paper?

Are sentences clear and logical?

Are sentences in the active voice when possible?

Are sentences varied in length and type?

Is the diction appropriate and consistent?

Are unfamiliar terms clearly explained?

Mechanics

Is correct grammar used throughout?

Is spelling correct throughout?

Are capitals, italics, and punctuation used correctly throughout?

Are parenthetical notes correctly placed and punctuated?

Conclusion

Does the conclusion restate the main ideas of the paper or offer a final interpretation or illustration of them, without repetition?

Does the concluding strategy leave the reader with the impression of a thorough, thoughtful paper on a meaningful subject?

Prepare the List of Works Cited

Separate the source cards containing the works cited entries for *sources used in the paper* and alphabetize them. Double-check the form of the entries (see section 34b) and then type the list of works cited, starting on a new page. (See pages 555–57 for an illustration of the correct format.)

If you have prepared your citations on the computer, your job will be simple: all you will need to do is add the heading "Works Cited," alphabetize the entries, and double-check the form of each entry. (See the sample on pages 555–57.)

| 35f | Prepare and submit the final manuscript. |

The manuscript format for the research paper varies only slightly from that for other papers. (See Appendix A, Manuscript Form.) The margins, the heading, and the paging are the same, and double-spacing is still required throughout. Because the research paper has additional parts and because parenthetical notes complicate typing, however, allow extra time to prepare the final copy. Do not assume that typing and proofreading a research paper is a one-night process.

Typing

Type at an unhurried pace, proofreading and correcting pages as you work. Type the list of works cited, if you have not already done so, using the guidelines given on page 527. When the final copy is complete, proofread it carefully for typing errors and make any small corrections neatly in black ink.

If you have prepared your paper using a word processor, you will be able to make final changes quickly and easily.
- *Create a "header."* The "header" should include your last name and consecutive page numbers.
- *Print a draft copy.* Examine this copy to check the general presentation and format. If you need to alter anything—move a list so that it all appears on the same page, for example—do so now.
- *Print a high-quality copy to submit.* Use a laser or letter-quality printer, if possible, to produce the final manuscript.

Submitting the Paper

Submit manuscripts according to your instructor's directions. If you receive no specific guidelines, secure the pages with a paper clip in the upper-left corner. Place lengthy papers in a 9-by-12-inch manila envelope with your name and course information typed or written on the outside. Always keep a photocopy of the paper before submitting it.

Be aware that instructors may ask for a disk copy of the paper. In that case, submit a copy of the final paper on a separate disk, clearly labeled with your name and course information. Keep a disk version for yourself.

35g >   **A sample research paper.**

The following paper, written for a freshman composition class, demonstrates many important aspects of writing and documenting a research paper.

An Optional Outline

Not all instructors will expect an outline with the final copy of the research paper, but some will. On those occasions when you must submit an outline, place it at the beginning of the paper.

Examine Shingo Endo's outline for his paper on music therapy, considering especially these important features:

1. On each page, the student's last name and the page number are given in the upper-right corner.

2. A standard heading is provided, with the student's name, instructor's name, course number, and date.

3. The complete title of the paper is given.

4. The introduction (and conclusion), separated from the outline, appear without roman numerals.

5. The full thesis statement is presented.

6. A traditional outline format is used. Roman numerals indicate major divisions; uppercase letters, arabic numerals, and lowercase letters indicate subdivisions.

1.

2. Shingo Endo

   Dr. Robert Perrin

   English 105

   7 July 1996

3.   Music Therapy: An Art of Communication

4. INTRODUCTION

5. <u>Thesis Statement</u>: Although most people know that
   music modifies moods, few recognize that because
   music possesses a power to influence people's behavior, it offers important treatment for the mentally
   and physically impaired.

6. I. History of music therapy

      A. Ancient cultures

         1. Egypt

         2. Greece

      B. United States

         1. Veterans' hospitals

            a. After World War II

            b. Concerts

         2. Dentists

            a. 1959 and later

            b. Music and less medication

7. Shingo used topic-outline form for both roman numeral divisions and subdivisions. To provide additional clarity, he could have used complete sentences for roman numeral divisions, with subdivisions in topic-outline form.

An outline of a research paper serves as a "table of contents" and clearly and completely describes the information presented in the paper.

7. II. Recent uses of music therapy

    A. Recreational use

        1. Stimulus

           a. <u>Awakenings</u>

           b. Oliver Sacks

           c. Special music

        2. Programs

           a. Mental hospitals

           b. Varied activities

        3. Discontinued programs

           a. Closed institutions

           b. Changes in treatment

    B. Therapeutic use

        1.Expression

           a. Schizophrenics

           b. Improvisation

           c. Rhythm instruments

        2. Communication

           a. Autistic children

           b. Improvisation

           c. Recorded music

        3. Remembrance

           a. Alzheimer's patients

           b. Listening

           c. Popular songs

III. Music's appeal

    A. Rhythm

        1. Energy

        2. Structure

    B. Pitch and melody

        1. Emotion

        2. Pleasure

    C. Harmony

        1. Regularization

        2. Emotion

    D. Nonverbal communication

        1. Feelings

        2. Language barrier

        3. Stress

CONCLUSION

1. Begin page numbering on the first page. In the upper-right corner, one-half inch from the top of the paper, type your last name, followed by one space, and then the page number. Position the page number flush against the one-inch margin on the right. (Or use your word processor's "header" feature.)

2. Use the same heading for the research paper that you use for other papers: your name, the instructor's name, course number, and date. Double-space the heading and place it within the normal one-inch margins in the upper-left corner.

3. Double-space down from the heading and center the title. If the title runs to a second line, center both lines. Double-space down from the title to the first paragraph of the paper.

4. Shingo begins his paper with a general introduction, drawing upon people's common perceptions of music.

5. Shingo's thesis statement comes at the end of his introductory paragraphs. It is presented in one sentence but establishes the qualified opinion that will focus his paper.

1.   Endo 1

2. Shingo Endo

   Dr. Robert Perrin

   English 105

   7 July 1996

3.   Music Therapy: An Art of Communication

4.   For many people, listening to their favorite
   music at the end of a busy day or going to a concert
   on a weekend is an essential aspect of their lives.
   Most people know that being involved with music,
   either playing or listening, is a rewarding and pleasurable experience because music relieves stress
   effectively.

        However, it is often forgotten, or not known,
   that beyond its entertainment value music has a salutary effect on people with illness and distress, a
   fact once underestimated by mainstream medicine
   (Weiss WH11). In the United States, so many people
   think of music as a mood modifier that this view
   overshadows the medical effects of music (Weiss

5. WH11). Yet because music possesses a power to reach
   a level of awareness that goes beyond verbal and
   physical communication, it offers important treatment
   for mentally or physically impaired people.

6. Shingo begins the body of his paper by describing the historical context for his larger discussion, noting that music was used as therapy in ancient cultures.

7. Shingo creates a transition to his later discussions by including his first extended example of music therapy.

8. To include a phrase that he found appropriate—from a source whose style did not justify a lengthier quotation—Shingo incorporates a few words into his own sentence.

6.   Music therapy, though itself a rather new medical discipline, can be traced back to 1500 BC in Egypt, where magicians used sound and music to communicate directly with what they believed to be the evil spirits in a patient's body (Alvin, <u>Music Therapy</u> 21-23). Later, the Greeks developed a systematic use of music to alleviate disorder, and now they are most often regarded as the founders of music therapy (Bunt 10). However, it was not until after World War II that doctors began sustained and rigorous experimentation in music therapy (Bunt 11).

7.   Two early, successful examples of music therapy in the United States are worth noting. One is the result of concerts by community music groups. When groups performed in hospitals for injured veterans of World War II, staff noted that many patients respond-

8. ed to the music and "perked up and got better" (Weiss WH11). And in 1959, dentists first used music as a way to minimize pain during surgery--a technique that allowed them to use lower dosages of nitrous oxide when treating their patients (Scofield and Teich 70). Since then, hundreds of research studies have demonstrated the positive effects of music on a wider

9. Using a brief transition paragraph, Shingo moves into his primary discussion of the alternative uses of music therapy.

10. To draw his readers into his discussion, Shingo uses an example from a popular contemporary film, *Awakenings*.

11. Knowing that some readers might be unfamiliar with the film, or may not have seen it recently, Shingo includes an extended description.

range of symptoms, and research has helped to establish music therapy as a behavioral science (Bunt 11).

9.   Yet a central question remains: What, then, is
music therapy? It is self-explanatory that therapists use music to heal people--but how? In what
situations? And how effective is it? These factors
are less known.

10.   _Awakenings_, a popular film based on the writings
of neurologist Oliver Sacks, presents the lives of
post-encephalitic patients, who were catatonic as
well as partially paralyzed, in a mental ward in the

11. 1960s. In one scene, an elderly female patient, who
is otherwise immobile, reacts to a recording of an
aria from _La Bohème_. At first, her eyes are unfocused, but gradually they narrow, and as the melody
reaches its familiar climax, the patient appears to
be in a state of catharsis. As a further experiment
with music therapy, a male nurse plays big-band music
for elderly patients as an accompaniment to their
meals. The music provides a stimulus for the
patients and somehow prompts them to begin eating on
their own. The charge nurse later reports to the
doctor: "It's not just any music; it has to be music
that's right for them" (_Awakenings_). These examples,

12. Rather than quote extensively from Juliette Alvin's work at this point, Shingo summarizes several important ideas. Note that he attributes the ideas to Alvin and provides clear documentation.

13. To convey the impact of Tyson's description, Shingo includes her language in a moderately long quotation; however, because the quotation is briefer than four lines (or 45 words), it is merged with the paragraph.

14. To provide a broad range of details (about the variety of programs available) in a limited amount of space, Shingo quotes from Tyson's book. Notice that the quotation is introduced with a colon and that it is indented ten spaces from the left margin and double-spaced.

from a well-known film, only hint at the uses of
music therapy.

12.   Juliette Alvin, a renowned British music therapist, explains that severely regressed patients, with
whom contact is difficult, sometimes react when they
hear music that was recorded when they were young
(Alvin, Introduction 7). And Florence Tyson, in

13. Psychiatric Music Therapy: Origins and Development,
says that music is "especially effective as a psychological stimulus in a total hospital environment when
used as an accompaniment to meals, calisthenics, and
remedial exercises" (8).

During the years from 1950 to 1970, many state
mental hospitals had full-scale music programs, incorporating activities such as these:

14.   small orchestra, band, chamber music, chorus;
music-listening appreciation; ward and audi-
torium concerts; musical quiz, variety and
talent shows; staging of Broadway-type musicals; individual music study, including creative musical writing; folk and square
dancing, religious choir, holiday pageants;
maintenance of musical instruments, construction of simple instruments; maintenance of
representative library records. (Tyson 12)

15. To draw attention to a particular author, Shingo introduces this quotation with the author's name and the title of her book.

16. Notice that second references to an author use only his or her last name: in this case *Tyson* is used instead of *Florence Tyson* (which was used the first time she was mentioned in the paper).

17. To show the changes in music therapy, Shingo discusses the treatments that have been replaced by newer ones, explaining briefly why the older treatments are used less often than they once were.

15.   Larol Merle-Fishman, a New York music therapist,
states in <u>The Music Within You</u>, that "either playing
an instrument or joining a singing group builds confidence, nurtures creative self-expression, and helps
you to understand who you are" (Scofield and Teich

16. 76). Tyson describes a range of patients' responses
to those activities: "clapping hands, sudden smiling,
humming, singing or dancing, which often provided the
opening toward contact with reality and resocialization" (9).

Early activities in music therapy, with their
considerable emphasis on the pleasurable and recre-
ational aspects of music, were mainly conducted by
large institutions for mentally ill people. However,

17. they have virtually disappeared today, partly because
of increasing costs, and have been replaced by music
therapy with more focus on the cognitive, emotional,
and spiritual areas of patients' lives (Bunt 160-61).
These new areas of treatment, importantly, are compatible with the community-based day centers, small
hospital units, and hostels where treatment usually
occurs (Bunt 160). Now music therapists have to work
outside of the security of a hospital department
because the way that society deals with people with
serious illness or disabilities has changed.

18. Because Shingo felt that most readers were familiar with the use of musical improvisation as a therapeutic technique, he considered it common knowledge and consequently did not supply a source note.

19. Shingo includes an extended example related to the treatment of autistic children, to illustrate the use of music therapy with young people.

In these new settings, the practices and techniques used in music therapy change according to the
individual needs of patients. As Donald E. Michel
points out in Music Therapy, therapy is about bringing about "changed behavior," and it is also an
"individualized procedure" (6). Music can be used in
various ways to accomplish these goals.

One of the important new developments in music
therapy is the use of improvisation. This spontaneous
activity can be done by using any instruments--from
African percussion to the grand piano. With their
instruments, patients can develop feelings of self-
identification through music-making; they may express
their feelings through the instruments instead of
18. through speech. Many music therapists employ improvisation to initiate a nonverbal conversation with
patients. The goal is not to achieve musical perfection, but to express the self, and it often evokes
feelings patients have not even recognized. Improvisation is a widely used procedure today for treating
schizophrenic, as well as brain-injured, patients.

19.   Music is no less effective for helping children
with disabilities or behavior disorders. The treatment of autistic children is perhaps the best known

20. To provide balance, Shingo also includes another extend-
    ed example, this one related to the treatment of patients
    with Alzheimer's disease—providing balance by addressing
    treatment of the elderly.

21. Having discussed individual treatment patterns, Shingo
    shifts directions to describe and analyze music's appeal.

among them, providing many successful cases. Through frequent music sessions, autistic children often show responses and curiosity in recorded or improvised music or simple rhythm instruments, and the interest in music can often be used to draw these children into contact with their therapists (Michel 49). Through active associations with music--improvising and singing, for example--autistic children improve responsiveness and behavior (Nordoff and Robbins 192-93).

20.   Music is often the last thing that is destroyed from memories in people with Alzheimer's disease and other forms of dementia. These older adults often remember the words to songs, even when they cannot remember whether they've eaten lunch (Hardie E1). And what is even more striking is that music, at least for a short time, often helps patients to stay organized for a time afterward (Weiss WH12). The scientific reason why music brings a brief lucidity to Alzheimer's patients is not yet known, but it certainly reveals the power of music to evoke deep-seated memories.

21.   What parts of music do these patients react to? Music has many elements such as tone, color, loudness,

22. Shingo quotes from an alphabetized reference book for which no page numbers are required. Since he has identified the author in his text, no additional information is required in a parenthetical note.

23. Shingo summarizes technical information from a source whose style did not justify a quotation.

duration, rhythm, pitch, melody, and so on. Each element seems to have its own therapeutic power. For
example, Natasha Spender observes that rhythm has "a
power to focus energy and to bring structure into the
22. perception of temporal order." In addition, Juliette
Alvin notes that rhythm "expresses an alternation of
tension and relaxation through stresses, accentua-
tion, breathing spaces, strong and weak beats" (Music
Therapy 67).

23.   Pitch and the melodic interval between notes certainly evokes emotional responses in people. Much of
the folk music from America, Scotland, and Ireland is
based on the pentatonic scale, which consists of C,D,E,
G,A--a melodic scale popular in music therapy group work
because of its pleasing non-Western sound (Bunt 67).

Harmony may also appeal to emotions. The propor-
tionally spaced harmonies of major chords soothe,
strengthen, and regularize while minor chords may
ease sorrow or yearning (Priestly 214).

Yet, we usually do not separate these elements
when we listen to music. Music provokes feelings, but
as we all know, these feelings cannot always be
translated into words. Indeed, that is what makes
music unique and effective when used in therapeutic

24. Notice that within the set-in quotation, the word *true* appeared in quotation marks in the original; because there are no surrounding quotes, the punctuation follows the original pattern.

25. To move from general discussions of music's appeal to specific applications, Shingo introduces his last example, this one relating to prison inmates. His choices of examples helps to establish the broad context of his discussion.

26. In a few well-chosen words, Shingo draws together the central ideas of his paper and then visualizes the future as his concluding strategy.

Endo 9

ways; music does not fall into the trap of intrusive language. Philosopher Suzanne Langer elaborates:

24.
> The real power of music lies in the fact that it can be "true" to the life of feeling in a way that language cannot; for its significant forms have the <u>ambivalence</u> of content which words cannot have. (Bunt 73)

25. Music also helps to assist inmates of correctional institutions, who need to learn skills in order to adapt to society. Jeff Mayers, who teaches music therapy at a correctional facility in Washington, DC, uses harp music to relieve inmates' stress. Some of the inmates say that their bodies, minds, and souls are in balance after listening to Mayers' harp sound, and it even causes a desire in them to reach out and help others (Milloy C3).

26. Music therapy is itself very versatile because of its variety and accessibility. Medical research, along with psychological and biological study, will continue to explore the effects of music therapy, and new clinical uses of music therapy will expand its potential in the future. And through these advancements we will be reminded of something we often forget in the flow of commercial music--the indispensable power and the humanizing quality of music.

27. Continue page numbering, using last name and page number, through the works cited list.

28. Center the title "Works Cited." Include in the list only sources providing material actually incorporated in the paper. (A works *consulted* page would include not only sources cited in the paper itself but also any sources read during the process of research.)

29. Alphabetize the list of sources by the first word of each entry, not including *a, an,* and *the.* Provide complete information for each entry, following exact patterns of organization and punctuation (see pages 476–87). Begin the first line of each entry at the normal left margin and indent second and subsequent lines five spaces. Double-space the entire list.

27.

28.   Works Cited

29. Alvin, Juliette. Music Therapy. New York: Basic, 1966.

---. Introduction to Music Therapy. Papers read at the
    Two Day Course Given at the University of London
    Institute of Education April 13th-14th, 1961.
    London: The Society for Music and Remedial Music.

Awakenings. Dir. Penny Marshall. Written by Oliver
    Sacks. Perf. Robin Williams and Robert De Niro.
    Columbia, 1990.

Bunt, Leslie. Music Therapy: An Art Beyond Words.
    London: Routledge, 1994.

Hardie, Ann. "Old Songs Strike Right Note." Atlanta
    Journal and Atlanta Constitution 12 Mar.
    1994: El.

Michel, Donald E. Music Therapy: An Introduction to
    Therapy and Special Education Through Music.
    Springfield, IL: Thomas, 1976.

Milloy, Courtland. "A Healing Force in London Prison."
    Washington Post 9 Feb. 1992: C3.

Nordoff, Paul, and Clive Robbins. "Improvised Music as
    Therapy for Autistic Children." Music Therapy.
    Ed. E. Thayer Gaston. New York: Macmillan, 1968.
    191-93.

Priestley, Mary. _Music Therapy in Action_. New York:
    St. Martin's, 1975.

Scofield, Michael, and Mark Teich. "Mind-Bending
    Music." _Health_ 19 (1987): 69-76.

Spender, Natasha. "Music Therapy." _The New Grove
    Dictionary of Music and Musicians_. Ed. Stanley
    Sadie. 1980 ed.

Tyson, Florence. _Psychiatric Music Therapy: Origins
    and Development_. New York: Creative Arts
    Rehabilitation Center, 1981.

Weiss, Rick. "Music Therapy: Doctors Explore the
    Healing Potential of Rhythm and Song."
    Washington Post 5 July 1994: WH 11-12.

APPENDIXES

Appendix A
Manuscript Form

Writers in language-related disciplines follow these guidelines for preparing and presenting manuscripts. Although there are some slight variations depending on the type and length of the paper, follow these guidelines unless your instructor advises you to follow a different pattern.

Paper

When using a printer with a word processor, use letter-quality (not draft-quality or bar-graphed) paper or submit a photocopy on medium-weight paper. Laser-perforated paper is preferable to standard-perforation paper, and single-sheet paper is preferable to continuous-feed, perforated paper.

When typing, use white, medium-weight, 8-1/2-by-11-inch paper. If you must use onion-skin or erasable paper, submit a high-quality photocopy on medium-weight paper.

Printing Formats

Use a letter-quality printer or use the correspondence-quality mode on a dot-matrix printer (which double-strikes each letter for enhanced clarity). When possible, use a laser or ink-jet printer for the clearest, most readable manuscript.

With a typewriter, use a black ribbon. A carbon ribbon (with its accompanying correction tape) produces the sharpest, clearest typed manuscript and is therefore the best choice.

Use only the most generally accepted fonts: Courier, Helvetica, Times Roman, Palatino, or another similar font; do not use script or another decorative style. Do not justify (line up in a straight vertical line) the right margin of the paper unless you are using a printer (all lasers and most ink-jets) that uses proportional spacing.

Because italics and underlining mean the same thing (identifying titles of books, periodicals, albums, paintings), either form is acceptable. However, be consistent throughout the paper.

Spacing

Double-space everything: the heading, the text, set-in quotations, notes, the works cited page, and any appended materials. When using a word processor, set the line spacing to 2 at the beginning of the document (the default setting will be single-spaced).

Margins

Leave one-inch margins on the left, right, and bottom of the main text; paging (which appears at the top) determines the top margin (example on page 562). If the preestablished or default margins for a word processing program are not wide enough, reset them. Indent paragraphs five spaces (these tabs are also preset in most word-processing programs); indent long quotations ten spaces from the left but maintain the normal right margin.

Paging

In the upper-right corner of each page, one-half inch from the top, type your last name, a space, and the page number (without a page abbreviation). Two spaces below, the text of the paper continues (one inch from the top of the page).

Word-processing programs usually have default patterns for placing page numbers (often centered at the bottom of the page). In that case, change the page numbering format. Using the command for "headers and footers" (lines that will run at the top or bottom of every page in the manuscript), set a header at the beginning of the document, make sure that it is flush

½" Davis 1

1"

Ronald Davis

Dr. L. C. Nichols

1"

English 231

10 September 1997

Title of the Paper

_____

_____

_____

_____

_____

_____

_____

_____

_____

_____

_____

1"

½" Davis 2

1"

_____

1"

_____

with the right margin, and include your last name and the command to number pages automatically. Once set, headers usually do not appear on the screen, but they will appear in the printed text.

Headings and Title

In MLA style, a paper has no separate title page. Instead, in the upper-left corner of the first page, two spaces down from the header, type on separate lines your name, your instructor's name, the course number, and the date. If instructors require, section numbers for courses follow the course name, and assignment numbers or descriptions are placed between the course name and the date. Two lines below, center the paper's title. Capitalize all important words in the title but do not italicize it or place it in quotation marks. Two lines below, begin the first paragraph.

Tables, Graphs, Charts, Maps, and Illustrations

Place tables, graphs, charts, and illustrations within the text of the paper, as close as possible to the appropriate discussion.

Introduce a table with the word *Table* (unitalicized but flush with the left margin) and an arabic numeral. On the next line, also flush left, include a caption or descriptive phrase, capitalized like a title. Use horizontal lines to indicate the beginning and end of the table itself; after the closing line, include the source of the table, introduced by the word *Source* (unitalicized) and a colon.

Graphs, charts, maps, and illustrations appear within the text. Immediately below the illustration, flush with the left margin, include the abbreviation *Fig.* (unitalicized) for *Figure,* an arabic numeral, and a title, caption, or descriptive phrase. Follow this information with a comma and the name (and publication facts) of the source, with elements separated by commas, not periods.

Submitting the Paper

Submit manuscripts according to your instructor's directions. If you receive no specific guidelines, secure the pages with a paper clip in the upper-left corner. Place lengthy papers in a 9-by-12-inch manila envelope with your name and course information typed or written on the outside. Always keep a photocopy of the paper before submitting it.

Be aware that instructors may ask for a disk copy of the paper. In that case, submit a copy of the final paper on a separate disk, clearly labeled with your name and course information. Keep a disk version for yourself.

Appendix B
APA Documentation Style

In fields such as psychology, education, public health, and criminology, researchers follow the guidelines given in the *Publication Manual of the American Psychological Association,* fourth edition (Washington, DC: APA, 1994), to document their work. Like MLA style (see Chapters 34 and 35), APA style encourages brevity in documentation, uses in-text parenthetical citations of sources, and limits the use of numbered notes and appended materials. The two styles, however, vary in their requirements for the organization of manuscripts and the forms for some notes.

The information that follows is an overview of APA style. If your major or minor requires APA style, you should acquire the APA manual, study it thoroughly, and follow its guidelines carefully.

Paper Format

MLA	*APA*
No separate title page: Identification and title placed on the first page of the paper.	*Separate title page:* Includes a descriptive title, author's name, and affiliation with two spaces between elements (centered left to right and top to bottom). In the upper-right corner, put the first few words of the paper's title, followed by five spaces and the page number (without a page abbreviation). Two lines below, typing from the left margin, include the words *Running head* (not italicized and followed by a colon) and a brief version of the title (no more than fifty letters). The title page is always page 1.

MLA	*APA*
No abstract.	*Abstract:* On a separate page following the title page, type the label *Abstract* (capitalized but not italicized). Two lines below, include a paragraph describing the major ideas in the paper; it can contain no more than 960 characters (including punctuation and spaces).
Introduction: A paragraph or series of paragraphs used to present the topic of the paper and interest readers.	*Introduction:* A paragraph or series of paragraphs used to define the topic, present the hypothesis (or thesis), explain the method of investigation, and state the theoretical implications (or context.)
Body: A series of logically connected paragraphs that explore the main idea through various patterns of description, illustration, and argument.	*Body:* A series of paragraphs that describe study procedures, results obtained, and interpretations of the findings.
In-text parenthetical documentation: Author and page number, unless title is necessary to distinguish among multiple works by one author.	*In-text parenthetical documentation:* Author and date for summaries and paraphrases; author, date, and page number for quotations.
List of sources: Cited sources fully identified in a listing titled "Works Cited."	*List of sources:* Cited sources fully identified in a listing titled "References."
Appendix: Seldom included.	*Appendix:* Included when related materials (charts, graphs, illustrations, and so on) cannot be incorporated into the body of the paper.

Manuscript Format

MLA

Type: Any standard font—printer or typewriter. Underlining or italics may be used.

Spacing: All elements of the paper are double-spaced.

Margins: One-inch margins at top and bottom and on left and right. Right-justified margins are acceptable. Indent paragraphs five spaces; indent long quotations ten spaces.

Paging: Author's last name and page number placed in the upper-right corner.

In-text headings: Not recommended except in very long papers.

Number style: Express numbers one through one hundred in words, as well as larger numbers that can be expressed in two words. Numbers that require more than two words are included in numeral form.

APA

Type: Any standard font with serifs (cross lines on individual letters)—printer or typewriter. Sans serif fonts like Helvetica are used only for labeling illustrations, not for text. Underlining is used instead of italics.

Spacing: All elements of the paper are double-spaced.

Margins: One-inch margins at top and bottom and on left and right. Indent paragraphs five to seven spaces; indent long quotations five spaces.

Paging: Put the first two or three words of the title (no more than fifty letters) in the upper-right corner; after five spaces, include the page number without a page abbreviation. The author's name is not included.

Headings: Recommended for divisions and subdivisions of the paper.

Number style: Express numbers one through nine in words and all other numbers in numeral form. When numbers are used for comparisons, all appear in numeral form.

Citation Format

APA format for citations in lists of references and in the text differs from MLA format. Below are listed several basic APA forms. Differences from MLA format are noted, and cross-references to the MLA model in Chapter 34 are provided.

Reference List Format

A Book by One Author

> Freemuth, J. C. (1991). <u>Islands under siege:</u>
>
> <u>National parks and the politics of external threats.</u>
>
> Lawrence: University Press of Kansas.

(Use initials for the author's first name. After the author's name, place the publication date in parentheses, followed by a period. Capitalize only the first word of the title and of the subtitle and any proper nouns and proper adjectives. Spell out the names of university presses. For MLA form, see page 476.)

A Book by Two or More Authors

> Freedman, D., Pisani, R., Purves, R., & Adhikari, A.
>
> (1991). <u>Statistics</u> (2nd ed.). New York: Norton.

(Invert the names of all authors. Insert an ampersand [&] before the last author. For MLA form, see page 476.)

A Book with an Organization as Author

> American Psychological Association. (1994).
>
> <u>Publication manual of the American Psychological</u>
>
> <u>Association</u> (4th ed.). Washington, DC: Author.

(When the organization is also the publisher, use the word *Author* (not italicized) in the publisher position. For MLA form, see pages 477–78.)

A Work in a Collection

> Graham, B. J. (1988). Tall buildings as symbols. In
>
> L. S. Beedle (Ed.), <u>Second century of the skyscraper</u>
>
> (pp. 117-147). New York: Van Nostrand.

(Do not enclose the title of a short work in quotation marks. *In* introduces its source. The editor's name, the abbreviation *Ed.* [capitalized and placed in parentheses] followed by a comma, the collection title, and inclusive page numbers for the short work [given in parentheses] are provided. Abbreviate *pages*. For MLA form, see page 479.)

An Article in a Monthly Magazine

> Gould, S. J. (1989, March). The wheel of fortune and
>
> the wedge of progress. <u>Natural History, 98,</u> 14-21.

(Give the year of publication followed by a comma and the month and day [if any]. When appropriate, follow the title with a comma, one space, the volume number, and another comma [all underlined]. Do not use a page abbreviation. For MLA form, see page 487.)

An Article in a Journal with Separate Paging

> Felix, J. W., & Johnson, R. T. (1993). Learning from
>
> video games. <u>Computers in the Schools,</u> 9(2-3), 119-134.

(Underline the name of the journal, the comma that follows it, and the volume number. The issue number [or numbers] in parentheses immediately follows the volume number; no space separates them. No abbreviation for pages accompanies the inclusive page numbers. For MLA form, see page 488.)

An Article in a Newspaper

Leatherman, C. (1994, September 28). Free speech or

harassment? <u>The Chronicle of Higher Education</u>, p. A22.

(Invert the date. Do not include information on the edition or section. When sections are indicated by letters, they are presented along with the page numbers with no intervening space. For MLA form, see pages 488–89.)

A Lecture or Speech

Branch, T. (1992, May 7). <u>Democracy in an age of</u>

<u>denial.</u> Speech presented for the Humanities on the Hill

lecture series, Washington, DC.

(Underline the title of the speech. Follow the title with the name of the sponsoring organization and the location, separated by commas. For MLA form, see page 491.)

Nonprint Materials

Apted, M. (Director). (1994). <u>Nell</u> [Film]. Beverly

Hills: 20th Century-Fox.

(List entries by the name of the most important contributor [director, producer, speaker, and so on]; note the specific role in full in parentheses following the name. Identify the medium [film, filmstrip, slide show, tape recording] in brackets after the title. The place of production precedes the name of the production company. For MLA form, see pages 490–91.)

Electronic Sources

National Rifle Association of America (NRA). (1994).

<u>Encyclopedia of associations.</u> [CD-ROM]. Available:

Gale: Encyclopedia of Associations.

(This citation is for a CD-ROM source that is prepared independently from a printed version. Since the materials are arranged in alphabetical order and can be accessed from an electronic index, no item number is required—but a closing period is. For MLA form, see pages 497–98.)

Ladew, J. (1995, May 29). Hyperlexia, autism, and

language [Discussion], [On-line]. Available: Internet

Newsgroup bit.listserv.autism

(The descriptive title is taken from the "message" line of the electronic correspondence; the date indicates when Ladew's information was posted on the newsgroup. For MLA form, see pages 497–98.)

Text Citation Format

One Author

Greybowski (1985) noted that . . .

Or:

In a recent study at USC (Greybowski, 1985), partici-

pants were asked to . . .

Multiple Authors: First Citation

Calendrillo, Thurgood, Johnson, and Lawrence (1967) found in their evaluation . . .

Multiple Authors: Subsequent Citations

Calendrillo et al. (1967) also discovered . . .

Corporate Authors: First Citation

. . . a close connection between political interests and environmental issues (Council on Environmental Quality [CEQ], 1981).

Corporate Authors: Subsequent Citations

. . . in their additional work (CEQ, 1981).

Quotations Within the Text

First Option

She stated, "The cultural awareness of a student depends, by implication, on the cultural awareness of the parents" (Hermann, 1984, p. 219).

Second Option

Hermann (1984) added that "enrichment in our schools
is costly and has little bearing on the later lives
of the students" (pp. 230-231).

Third Option

"A school's responsibility rests with providing solid
educational skills, not with supplementing the cultural education of the uninterested," stated Hermann
(1984) in her summary (p. 236).

1. APA form requires a separate title page. (For MLA form, see page 531.)

2. In the upper right corner of every page, APA style requires a short title consisting of the first two or three words of the paper's title. The short title (which must have the same wording as the running head, see item 3 below) identifies each page in the event that any pages go astray. The page number, without a page abbreviation, appears on the same line as the short title, following five spaces. (For MLA form, see page 531.)

3. At the top of the page, beginning at the left margin, include the phrase *Running head* (not italicized and followed by a colon) and the shortened form of the title, capitalized.

4. The title, subtitle (if any), and the author's name and affiliation are centered on the page (both from the top and bottom and from the right and left). If a title runs over to a second line, the runover line is also centered. (For MLA form, see page 537.)

1., 2.   Music Therapy   1

3. Running head: MUSIC THERAPY

4.   Music Therapy: An Art of Communication
                        Shingo Endo
                   Indiana State University

5. The second page of a manuscript prepared in APA style is an abstract, a paragraph of no more than 960 characters (including punctuation and spacing) describing the major ideas presented in the paper. The page begins with the heading *Abstract,* not italicized. (In MLA form, there is no equivalent to the abstract.)

5.   Abstract

Although many people realize that music alters moods,
they do not realize that it provides useful treatment
for mentally and physically impaired people.
Beginning in ancient times, music has been used for
therapy. In the twentieth century--especially in the
United States--music has been used to alter moods and
influence behavior. Currently, music therapy is used
to treat patients with schizophrenia, Alzheimer's
disease, autism, and asocial behaviors. Studies
indicate that further uses will be found for music
therapy in treating various disorders.

6. The text of the paper begins on page 3. (For MLA form, see page 537.)

7. Repeat the title and subtitle at the top of the third page, centered and worded as on the title page. Double-space and begin the body of the paper. (For MLA form, see page 537.)

8. When an author's name is not given in the text, include the author's name, the publication date of the source, and a page citation (if needed) in parentheses. (For MLA form, see page 539.)

6.   Music Therapy   3

7.   Music Therapy: An Art of Communication

For many people, listening to their favorite music at the end of a busy day or going to a concert on a weekend is an essential aspect of their lives. Most people know that being involved with music, either playing or listening, is a rewarding and pleasurable experience because music relieves stress effectively.

However, it is often forgotten, or not known, that beyond its entertainment value music has a salutary effect on people with illness and distress, a fact once underestimated by mainstream medicine

8. (Weiss, 1994, p. WH11). In the United States, so many people think of music as a mood modifier that this view overshadows the medical effects of music (Weiss, 1994, p. WH11). Yet because music possesses a power to reach a level of awareness that goes beyond verbal and physical communication, it offers important treatment for mentally or physically impaired people.

Music therapy, though itself a rather new medical discipline, can be traced back to 1500 BC in

9. Because Alvin wrote more than one source used in this paper, a shortened version of the title must be included for clarity. (For MLA form, see page 539.)

10. Both authors' names are included in citations for coauthored sources. Notice that the names are joined by an ampersand (&), not the word *and*. (For MLA form, see page 539.)

Egypt, where magicians used sound and music to communicate directly with what they believed to be the
9. evil spirits in a patient's body (Alvin, 1966, <u>Music
Therapy,</u> pp. 21-23). Later, the Greeks developed a
systematic use of music to alleviate disorder, and
now they are most often regarded as the founders of
music therapy (Bunt, 1994, p. 10). However, it was
not until after World War II that doctors began sustained and rigorous experimentation in music therapy
(Bunt, 1994, p. 11).

Two early, successful examples of music therapy
in the United States are worth noting. One is the
result of concerts by community music groups. When
groups performed in hospitals for injured veterans of
World War II, staff noted that many patients responded
to the music and "perked up and got better" (Weiss,
1994, p. WH11). And in 1959, dentists first used
music as a way to minimize pain during surgery--a
technique that allowed them to use lower dosages of
10. nitrous oxide when treating their patients (Scofield &
Teich, 1987, p. 70). Since then, hundreds of
research studies have demonstrated the positive

11. Notice that titles are underlined, not italicized. (For MLA
    form, see page 543.)

effects of music on a wider range of symptoms, and
research has helped to establish music therapy as a
behavioral science (Bunt, 1994, p. 11).

   Yet a central question remains: What, then, is
music therapy? It is self-explanatory that therapists use music to heal people--but how? In what
situations? And how effective is it? These factors
are less known.

11.   <u>Awakenings,</u> a popular film based on the writings
of neurologist Oliver Sacks, presents the lives of
post-encephalitic patients, who were catatonic as
well as partially paralyzed, in a mental ward in the
1960s. In one scene, an elderly female patient, who
is otherwise immobile, reacts to a recording of an
aria from <u>La Bohème.</u> At first, her eyes are unfocused, but gradually they narrow, and as the melody
reaches its familiar climax, the patient appears to
be in a state of catharsis. As a further experiment
with music therapy, a male nurse plays big-band music
for elderly patients as an accompaniment to their
meals. The music provides a stimulus for the
patients and somehow prompts them to begin eating on

12. A film is cited by its director and the date. Because a film is a nonprint source, no page references can be provided. (For MLA form, see page 541.)

13. If an author's name is mentioned in the text (with the publication date of the source), only the page number is required. (For MLA form, see page 543.)

14. Double-space and indent long quotations five spaces from the left margin. (For MLA form, see page 543.)

their own. The charge nurse later reports to the doctor: "It's not just any music; it has to be music
12. that's right for them" (Marshall, 1990). These examples, from a well-known film, only hint at the uses of music therapy.

Juliette Alvin, a renowned British music therapist, explains that severely regressed patients, with whom contact is difficult, sometimes react when they hear music that was recorded when they were young (Alvin, 1961, <u>Introduction,</u> p. 7). And Florence Tyson (1981), in <u>Psychiatric Music Therapy:</u> <u>Origins and Development,</u> says that music is "espe-cially effective as a psychological stimulus in a total hospital environment when used as an accompani-
13. ment to meals, calisthenics, and remedial exercises" (p. 8).

During the years from 1950 to 1970, many state mental hospitals had full-scale music programs, incorporating activities such as these:

14.   small orchestra, band, chamber music, chorus; music-listening appreciation; ward and auditorium concerts; musical quiz, variety and talent shows;

15. Parenthetical notes for long quotations follow the closing
    punctuation. (For MLA form, see page 543.)

staging of Broadway-type musicals; individual

music study, including creative musical writing;

folk and square dancing, religious choir, holiday

pageants; maintenance of musical instruments,

construction of simple instruments; maintenance

15.   of representative library records. (Tyson,

1981, p. 12)

Larol Merle-Fishman, a New York music therapist,

states in The Music Within You, that "either playing

an instrument or joining a singing group builds con-

fidence, nurtures creative self-expression, and helps

you to understand who you are" (Scofield & Teich,

1987, p. 76). Tyson (1981) describes a range of

patients' responses to those activities: "clapping

hands, sudden smiling, humming, singing or dancing,

which often provided the opening toward contact with

reality and resocialization" (p. 9).

16. The short title and page number appear on all pages of the reference list and on any appendix pages. (For MLA form, see page 555.)

17. Center and type the title *References* (not italicized) at the beginning of the list of sources. APA requires that all sources included on the reference list be cited in the text. (For MLA form, see page 555.)

18. For a book by a single author, list the author's name first, inverted and followed by a period. Use only an initial for the author's first name. Include the publication date in parentheses, followed by a period. Underline book titles but capitalize only the first word of the title and of the subtitle and any proper nouns or proper adjectives. (For MLA form, see page 555.)

19. Titles for newspaper articles appear without quotation marks. The title of the newspaper appears in complete form, with all major words capitalized. (For MLA form, see page 555.)

20. Films are listed by director, with the word *Director* (not italicized) enclosed in parentheses after the person's name. After the title of the film, the word *Film* (not italicized) appears in brackets, followed by the city (and state if necessary for clarity) and company. (For MLA form, see page 555.)

21. When a source has more than one author, invert the names of all the authors, not just the first. Use commas to separate the names, and place an ampersand (&) before the name of the last author. A citation for an article in a book begins with the author's name (in this case two authors), followed by the publication date in parentheses. (If an article has no author, begin the entry with the article title, not enclosed in quotation marks, followed by the publication date in parentheses.) Use the word *In* (not ital-

16.

17. References

18.   Alvin, J. (1961). Introduction to music therapy. London: The Society for Music and Remedial Music.

Alvin, J. (1966). Music therapy. New York: Basic Books.

Bunt, L. (1994). Music therapy: an art beyond words. London: Routledge.

19.   Hardie, A. (1994, March 12). Old songs strike right note. The Atlanta Journal and Atlanta Constitution, p. El.

20.   Marshall, P. (Director). (1990). Awakenings. [Film]. Burbank, CA: Columbia.

Michel, D. (1976). Music therapy: an introduction to therapy and special education through music. Springfield, IL: Thomas.

Milloy, C. (1992, February 9). "A healing force in London prison." The Washington Post, p. C3.

21.   Nordoff, P., & Robbins, C. (1968). Improvised music as therapy for autistic children. In E. Gaston (Ed.), Music therapy (pp. 191-193). New York: Macmillan.

Priestley, M. (1975). Music therapy in action. New York: St. Martin's.

icized) followed by the editor's name, the abbreviation *Ed.* (not italicized) in parentheses, and a comma. The title of the book follows, with inclusive page numbers enclosed in parentheses. (For MLA form, see page 555.)

22. For an article in a periodical, the author's name (in this case two authors) is followed by the year, month and day (if any) of publication. The article title is not placed in quotation marks, and only the first word of the title, proper nouns, and proper adjectives are capitalized. The name of the periodical is both underlined and capitalized, followed by the volume number (also underlined). Inclusive page numbers are listed without page abbreviation. (For MLA form, see page 557.)

23. Articles from well-know reference sources do not require facts of publication, and sources that are alphabetized do not require inclusive pages.

22.   Scofield, M., & Teich, M. (1987). Mind-bending music. Health, 19, 69-76.

23.   Spender, N. (1980). Music therapy. In S. Sadie (Ed.), The New Grove dictionary of music and musicians.

Tyson, F. (1981). Psychiatric music therapy: origins and development. New York: Creative Arts Rehabilitation Center.

Weiss, R. (1994, July 5). Music therapy: doctors explore the healing potential of rhythm and song. The Washington Post, pp. WH11-12.

Appendix C
Writing Essay Exams

To study for an essay exam, reread course materials (books, articles, classroom notes), review important concepts, and memorize specific information related to major topics. This work is best done over a period of days or weeks.

When confronted by the exam, consider the following strategies for writing effective responses.

Point Values

Apportion your writing on each question according to its point value. For instance, if a question is worth ten points out of a possible one hundred, devote no more than ten percent of the total exam time to your response; if a question is worth fifty points out of one hundred, spend approximately half of the exam time writing your response. Spending disproportionate time on one question may leave you with little time for other parts of the exam.

Multiple Questions

To respond to two or more essay questions, pace your writing. Decide, on the basis of point values, how much time each question deserves and write accordingly. An extended response to one question worth ten points and a brief, superficial response to another worth ten points may yield only fifteen points, whereas balanced discussions of both questions would probably yield more points.

Optional Topics

When given alternative questions, construct a brief topic outline for each choice, to see which essay would be most substantial. A few moments spent outlining will help you to select the questions to which you can respond most completely and effectively.

Careful Reading

Many essay questions provide an implied topic sentence for a paragraph-length essay or a thesis statement for a longer essay. Focus your work by developing the idea presented in the question. Follow instructions carefully. Describe, illustrate, compare, contrast, evaluate, analyze, and so on according to instructions.

Style and Technical Matters

To guarantee that responses are grammatically correct, well worded, complete, and free from errors in punctuation and mechanics, adjust your writing strategies. Either write slowly, to make your sentences clear, complete, and free from errors in a first draft, or allow time to make corrections and revisions after you have written your response. For either approach, pacing is crucial.

Organization and Development

A response to an essay question is like a brief paper: It requires an introduction, a body, and a conclusion, although the development and length of each part will depend on the type of question and its point value. A ten-point and a fifty-point essay on the same question will require very different degrees of development, but the structure of each response will be similar. Before an essay exam, quickly review the patterns of development in Chapter 4 (description, examples, facts, comparison and contrast, analogy, cause and effect, process analysis, classification, and definition); you will then be able to organize your responses appropriately according to the pattern explicitly or implicitly required by the question.

Varied Organization

For an illustration of how the organizational pattern of an essay question response varies with the form of the question, examine the topic outlines below, which clearly show the differences in structure required by the two questions. The first question implicitly requires a comparison and contrast structure. The second explicitly requires an analysis structure. The full essay responses would also require appropriate support.

Question

Which is more effective: the impromptu or the extemporaneous speech?

Introduction (thesis): Though both impromptu and extemporaneous speeches are flexible, the planning required for extemporaneous speeches makes them more coherent, more fully developed, and more effective.

I. Impromptu

   A. No written manuscript

   B. Words chosen while speaking

   C. Minimal preparation

   D. Unrehearsed

II. Extemporaneous

   A. No written manuscript

   B. Words chosen while speaking

   C. Substantial preparation

   D. Rehearsed

Conclusion: Extemporaneous speeches are generally more effective because they are more organized and substantive than impromptu speeches.

Question

Of the four speech-making techniques, choose the one you believe is the most useful and analyze the factors contributing to its effectiveness.

Introduction (thesis): Because they are at once organized but flexible, extemporaneous speeches are the most effective.

I. Preparation

   A. Reading

   B. Thinking

   C. Selecting

   D. Organizing

II. Presentation

   A. Flexible

      1. Change examples

      2. Adjust to audience

      3. Add or drop material

   B. Personal

      1. Suited to audience's needs

      2. Suited to speaker's needs

      3. Not manuscript bound

      4. Better contact with audience

Conclusion: Because of advantages in planning and presentation, extemporaneous speaking is generally the most effective.

Degree of Development

For an illustration of the similar structures but different degree of development of essay responses with different point values, examine the samples below, prepared as part of an hour-long exam.

Question

What are the four speech-making strategies and how do they differ?

Ten-point response

There are four basic speech-making strategies. Impromptu speeches are presented on the "spur of the moment"; the speaker has no time to organize or rehearse. Extemporaneous speeches are organized in outline form but are not written word for word. Manuscript speeches are written in advance and then read from a written or typed copy. Memorized speeches are written in advance and then learned word for word, to be presented without a written copy. These four strategies allow speakers to suit their presentations to their speaking situations.

Fifty-point response

Situations for speech making vary, and speakers, as a result, choose among four different speech-making strategies to present their ideas most effectively.

Impromptu speeches are given on the "spur of the moment"; the speaker has no chance to organize or rehearse. These highly informal speeches are often unfocused (because they are unplanned) and ineffective (because they were not rehearsed), but they are the usual kinds of speeches given at organization meetings and in class discussions.

Extemporaneous speeches are given from prepared outlines, but they are not completely written. Rather, speakers decide what to discuss and what details or examples to use, and then they choose words as they speak. Extemporaneous speeches have the advantage of being organized but at the same time flexible, allowing speakers to modify what they say to suit the needs of their audiences. For this reason, they are often the most effective speeches at informal meetings.

Manuscript speeches are written in complete form and then read, much like a newscast. Because they are prepared in advance, manuscript speeches are well organized and carefully worded. If they are also well rehearsed, manuscript speeches are effective in formal speaking situations because they present an exact, well-worded version of the speaker's ideas.

Memorized speeches are written in complete form and then committed to memory. Because they are carefully prepared, they often present solid content, but few speakers can memorize a lengthy speech and deliver it well. In addition, memorized speeches are not flexible and work only in highly formal circumstances, like awards ceremonies and formal banquets.

Because of the differences among these four speech-making strategies—in organization, presentation, and flexibility—they provide speakers with a number of ways to share ideas with audiences.

Timed Practice

Before writing an essay exam, practice composing under time pressure. Using notes from class, write and respond to sample essay questions. Use a timer and write several practice responses over several days' time. If necessary, allow yourself extra time to respond to a question, gradually reducing the time until it approximates the time available for the exam. Practice will quicken your writing pace while helping you to study for the exam.

Appendix D
Business Writing

Business Letters

Like a good paper, a business letter should be clearly organized and carefully written in support of a stated or implied thesis. Business letters differ from papers, however, in format and purpose.

When writing business letters, be sensitive to tone. In most instances, you will be writing to solve a problem or to ask for help. A moderate tone, formal but friendly, will work best. Do not be harsh or demanding in an initial letter, but if a problem continues, use a firmer tone in later correspondence.

The following guidelines and example (see page 602) describe a block-form letter, which is appropriate for most purposes.

General Guidelines

Use high-quality, white 8-1/2-by-11-inch paper.

Use a laser or letter-quality printer or type using a clean black ribbon.

Maintain at least one-inch margins on all sides.

Single-space within paragraphs; double-space between paragraphs. Do not indent the first words of paragraphs; position them flush with the left margin.

Proofread the final copy carefully for spelling, punctuation, mechanics, grammar, and typing errors.

Fold the letter in thirds and place in a legal-size envelope.

Letter Format

Your Address.   Use the address at which you wish to receive follow-up correspondence. Do not include your name with the address; type it beneath your signature at the end of the letter.

The Date.   Use the date on which you plan to mail the letter.

Inside Address.   Name the person to whom you are writing and include his or her title if you know it. If the letter is addressed to a company, begin this section with the name of the company and then use the complete business address.

Salutation.   This greeting should be specific rather than general. Begin with *Dear,* followed by the name of the person and a colon (not a comma). Use general titles (*Mr., Ms.,* or *Dr.*) with the person's name. Use *Mrs.* or *Miss* only when you know that a woman prefers to be addressed in one of those ways. When you do not know the name of the person to whom you are writing, use "Dear Madam or Sir"; avoid "To Whom It May Concern."

Introductory Paragraph.   Like a paper, a business letter needs an introductory paragraph. The first paragraph should establish the context for the letter. Be concise but specific. Include answers to the important questions that your correspondent might ask: What do you want to discuss? When did it take place?

Body Paragraph or Paragraphs.   The middle paragraphs should provide a description of the problem. They should be clearly written, with careful word choices and specific details. Essentially, these paragraphs give you a chance to present your case, and they must therefore be precise and convincing. If you have tried to solve a problem, describe the strategies you have used, again supplying detailed information and descriptions.

Request for Action.   The closing paragraph should ask for help in solving the problem. Be reasonable. If alternative solutions are acceptable, explain them.

Closing.   Use a reasonably formal, standard closing, such as *Sincerely, Sincerely yours,* or *Yours truly.* Position the closing at the left margin.

Signature.   Sign your name in ink in a space that is at least four lines deep, so that it does not look cramped.

Typed Name.   At the left margin, type your name as you wish it to appear in return correspondence.

Envelope Format

Return Address.   Include your full return address, including your name, in the upper-left corner of the envelope.

Mailing Address.   Address the envelope fully. Include the person's name and title (if applicable) and the full business address, including zip code.

Postage.   Be sure to use sufficient postage.

```
Alicia Hudson                                          ┌──────┐
1627 Lafayette Avenue                                  │Stamp │
Topeka, KS  66603                                      └──────┘



                Aaron Steinmann, Service Director
                Museum Reproductions, Incorporated
                392 Hazelwood Drive
                Chicago, IL  60607
```

1627 Lafayette Avenue
Topeka, KS 66603
September 25, 1996

Aaron Steinmann, Service Director
Museum Reproductions, Incorporated
392 Hazelwood Drive
Chicago, IL 60607

Dear Mr. Steinmann:

On June 26, 1996, I ordered several small pieces of statuary
from your Spring 1996 sale catalog: Child with Rabbit
(#097444), Sleeping Cat (#097118), and Swan (#097203).

On July 17, 1996, my insured package was delivered by UPS,
and I excitedly opened the cartons to examine my newest
collector's items. Two of the statues were in excellent
condition, but the third, Child with Rabbit, was not. The
glaze on the rabbit and the base was streaked and irregularly
colored. These flaws in the finish disappointed me greatly,
especially since that piece alone had cost $54.

I immediately called the service number listed on the
invoice. Your representative instructed me to repack the
statue and return it for a replacement. I did so the next
day--July 18, 1996--enclosing a photocopy of the invoice
(#1784229). More than two months have passed, and I have yet
to receive my new Child with Rabbit statue.

I would appreciate receiving my statue soon (since I have
already paid for it), or I would like to know the reason for
the delay. If you are unable to send me the statue, I would
appreciate your crediting my account for $54. Thank you for
your help in solving my problem.

Sincerely,

Alicia Hudson

Alicia Hudson

The Résumé

A résumé is a brief listing of important information about your academic credentials, work experience, and personal achievements. The title *Résumé, Curriculum Vitae,* or simply *Vitae* in academic work, or the general designation *Data Sheet* in almost any context, sometimes appears as a heading at the top of the page. Such a title is probably unnecessary, however, because employers are familiar with this form. A résumé is commonly submitted with a job application letter to obtain an interview and sometimes submitted with admissions or scholarship applications, funding requests, project proposals, and annual personnel reports, and in other situations when you need to document your accomplishments.

Because a résumé must make a strong, favorable impression—suggesting the caliber of employee or student you are—you should prepare it carefully. Start by analyzing your goals and background; then gather pertinent information. Consider the following discussion and modify the format and content of the samples shown in Figures 1 and 2 to emphasize your individual strengths and fit your own needs. Do not be too "creative" or "artistic" with your résumé unless your job objective is in a field like advertising, graphic design, or art education.

Sections

Heading.   Center your name at the top of the page. Use capitals, underlining, italics, boldface, or special lettering to make your name stand out.

Address.   List your current mailing address in standard postal form, including zip code, and your full phone number, including area code. If available, also include an electronic-mail address. If you expect to change addresses soon, or if you spend time in two places (such as at college and at home), include both addresses, and indicate when you use each.

Personal Information.   Include information on age, marital status, health, height, weight, and so on *only* if it in some way is pertinent to your objective (for example, if the job has requirements about physical size, such as for a police officer or flight attendant). Employers and agencies can no longer request such information and may not legally use it when assessing applications. Provide a photograph only if you are required to do so.

Statement of Objectives.   If you are applying for a specific position or purpose, state your immediate objectives and long-range goals. This statement is important because it serves as the controlling thesis for the description of your qualifications. Everything in the résumé should be relevant to your objective. Your statement of objectives should include the job title(s) of the position(s) you are seeking, the types of skills you possess or the types of duties you can perform, and your career goals. If the résumé is a general data sheet and its purpose is simply to list information, the statement of your career objective may be omitted.

Education.   Students or recent students who have little work experience generally describe education before work experience. Specify degrees, majors, minors, names and locations of schools, month and year of graduation (your anticipated date of graduation is acceptable), and grade point average (overall, major, or junior/senior). If specific schoolwork—important courses, term projects, or research papers—is relevant to your objective, briefly note it. If you have a college degree, you need not mention high school unless you did exceptionally well (such as being class valedictorian) or the school is prestigious or might interest the employer for some other reason (because it is in the same city, for instance). List honors and awards with education, or list them in a separate section for emphasis if they are numerous and impressive. Extracurricular activities are sometimes included here, but they too can be developed into another section if they warrant such treatment. Internships, co-op training, observation programs, conference workshops, and so on might be described as part of your education or considered as professional experience and listed in that section. The latter is a good idea if you have little relevant work experience.

Work Experience.   Work experience may appear after education, if it is not impressive or extensive, or before education, if it is impressive or recent. Arrange work experience either chronologically (to show progress or promotion) or in descending order of importance, and list job titles, names of businesses or organizations (including the military), locations (not necessarily full addresses), dates of employment, and duties. Using active verb phrases, provide specific details about relevant skills employed—including technical skills, such as methods (double-entry accounting) and equipment (computers) used—and note improvements or suggestions that you contributed. If your work experience is not directly relevant to the objective of your application, mention responsibilities and accomplishments involving such general skills as communication, leadership, organization, problem solving, and money handling. Mention volunteer work, internships, and other non-paying experience if appropriate.

Activities, Interests, and Hobbies.   List activities specifically related to your objective, such as memberships in professional, fraternal, and community organizations. Mention special participation, contributions, and official positions. Other interesting activities (such as participation in organized sports, challenging hobbies, reading preferences, and cultural interests) may be included to show your habits and character.

References.   List two to four recent employers and teachers who are willing to describe your qualifications and recommend your work. Supply their full names, titles, work addresses and

605

phone numbers, and electronic-mail addresses. Be sure to contact them for permission before using them as references.

If you do not want to list your references on the résumé (perhaps because of limited space), note that references are available upon request. Use your college's career development and placement service, which will maintain a placement file that includes your letters of reference, transcripts, and résumé. If you use your school's placement service, list the full address and phone number of the office at the bottom of your résumé; if your file is designated by a number (rather than your name), include that information.

Format

Length.   Unless you have an exceptional amount of experience and education, limit your résumé to one page. If you must go to a second page, arrange the information so that you have two full and evenly balanced pages, not a full first page and half of a second page. Do not split a major section between pages.

General Appearance.   Make the résumé attractive, balanced, and scannable. Do not cramp information in dense blocks. Rather, divide information into discrete, parallel sections. Be consistent in your use of indentation, alignment, capitalization, boldface, underlining, parentheses, and other devices that identify similar kinds and levels of information. Use lists and columns, but make minimal use of patterns that create obvious vertical lines. Leave at least one-inch margins and double-space between sections, but avoid blocks of "white space" (large, unused areas).

Headings.   Use headings that clearly describe the information in each section. Position the main headings at the left margin or center them. Headings positioned at the left margin are very noticeable, but they can create a wide strip of white space down the side and make the résumé look imbalanced. Centered headings create a better balanced design and allow more efficient use of space, and they show up clearly if they are set off in some way (underlined, boldfaced) and if adequate space is left between sections. Subheadings can further indicate and emphasize areas of special interest, but too many levels of headings will make the résumé look choppy.

Arrangement. Arrange the sections and the items within each section so that the information flows in a logical and emphatic order. One way is to start with the most relevant and impressive accomplishments and follow a descending order of importance throughout. Chronological order is appropriate when you have only a few items to mention (two part-time jobs, for instance). Reverse chronological order is effective when you have many degrees, experiences, and activities to present—especially if the most recent ones are the most important. Alphabetical order might be useful for listing references, organizations, and courses, but usually even these are best presented in order of importance.

Style. Abbreviate sparingly, using only standard abbreviations (such as two-letter abbreviations for state names in addresses) and acronyms (such as professional organizations). Avoid first-person pronouns and complete sentences. Use active verb phrases. Instead of saying, "I was responsible for training new crew members," you need write only, "Trained new crew members."

Typing

Print Quality. Use a word processor if possible and print the final résumé on a laser printer; if a laser printer is not available, use a letter-quality (not a dot-matrix) printer. Use a standard font (Times Roman or Helvetica) in 10–12 point size. If you type the résumé, use the pica or elite size of a standard type style. Single-space within and double-space between sections.

Corrections. When using a word processor, make corrections and additions and print new copies to send. If you must type your résumé, make corrections using correction fluid or tape. When you make photocopies to submit, these corrections will not show on the copy, whereas smudges on erasable paper will.

Proofreading. Proofread carefully to make sure that your résumé is free of spelling and typing errors. It represents you, so it must be "letter perfect."

Photocopying

Have high-quality photocopies made at a reliable copy shop. Consider having your résumé copied on fluorescent white bond paper, "parchment" paper, or some other special-purpose paper so that it will be distinctive. Spending a little extra money might be worth the investment.

Figure 1.   Standard Résumé Format

SANDRA K. BOYER

<u>Present Address</u>   <u>After May 15, 1996</u>
363 Maehling Terrace   431 N. Seventh St.
Alton, IL 62002   Waterloo, IL 62298
(618) 465-7061   (618) 686-2324
e-mail: sboyer@coral.freemont.edu

CAREER OBJECTIVE

Music teacher and orchestra director, eventually leading to work as a Music
Program Coordinator for a school district.

EDUCATION

<u>Bachelor of Science in Education</u>: May 1996. Freemont College, Alton, IL.
<u>Major</u>: Music education. <u>Minors</u>: Music theory and business. <u>G.P.A.</u>: 3.87 on a
4.0 scale. Alpha Alpha Alpha, music honorary society (secretary, 1995-1996).
<u>Division 1 Ratings</u>: violin, viola, clarinet; <u>Division 2 Ratings</u>: cello, oboe

MUSICAL EXPERIENCE

<u>Waterloo Community Orchestra</u> (1990-1992): first violin, 1992; 10-17
performances each year, Waterloo Arts Festival; classical and popular music
<u>Waterloo Community String Ensemble</u> (1992): coordinator; 8 performances each
year, Waterloo Arts Festival; classical music
<u>Freemont College Orchestra</u> (1993-present): second violin, 1993-1994; first
violin, 1994-present; student conductor, 1996; 10-20 performances each year;
conducted 3 concerts; classical and popular music

WORK EXPERIENCE

Appointment secretary and sales clerk. Carter's Music Shop, Waterloo, IL
(1992-1993): coordinated 65 lessons each week; demonstrated and sold
instruments and music Sales clerk. Hampton Music, Alton, IL (1993-present):
demonstrated and sold instruments and music

REFERENCES

Available upon request from the Placement Center, Freemont College, Alton,
IL 62002, (618) 461-6299, extension 1164; file #39261

Figure 2.   Alternate Résumé Format

RÉSUMÉ

<u>Sandra K. Boyer</u>

<u>ADDRESS</u>

School: 363 Maehling Terrace   Home: 431 N. Seventh St.
        Alton, IL 62002   Waterloo, IL 62298
School phone: (618) 465-7061   Home phone: (618) 686-2324
e-mail: sboyer@coral.freemont.edu

<u>EDUCATION</u>

1988-1992: Benjamin Thomas High School, Waterloo, IL
1992-1996 :Freemont College, Alton, IL
           Major: Music education. Minors: Music theory and business

<u>EXTRACURRICULAR ACTIVITIES</u>

1988-1992: Benjamin Thomas High School Orchestra (1st violin, 1990-1992)
           Benjamin Thomas High School String Ensemble (student
           coordinator, 1990-1992)
1992-1996: Freemont College Orchestra (2nd violin, 1993-1994; 1st violin,
           1994-present; student conductor, 1996) Alpha Alpha Alpha, music
           honorary society (secretary, 1995-1996)

<u>WORK EXPERIENCE</u>

1992-1993: Carter's Music Shop, Waterloo, IL 62298; part-time appointment
           secretary and sales clerk
1993-   : Hampton Music, Alton, IL 62002 (837 Telegraph and Alton Square
           shops); sales clerk

<u>REFERENCES</u>

Dr. Glendora Kramer, Professor of Music and Orchestra Director, Freemont
   College, Alton, IL 62002, (618) 461-6299, extension 2110,
   gkramer@music.freemont.edu
Mr. Philip Sheldon, Manager, Hampton Music, 837 Telegraph, Alton, IL
   62002, (618) 466-6311
Mrs. Rhonda Travis, Music Instructor, Benjamin Thomas High School,
   Waterloo, IL 62298, (618) 686-5534

Appendix E

by Deborah Barberousse
Horry-Georgetown Technical College

Writing About Literature

Preparing to Write

Preparing to write can be just as important as actually writing the paper. Good preparation will simplify the entire writing process and help you write a better paper.

Choosing What to Write About

Not everyone responds to every literary work in the same way. Some pieces you will like, others you will not, and some works will leave you ambivalent, just as certain authors will strike a chord with you and others will not. Most teachers, recognizing that writing about literature reflects individual reactions and interpretations, will allow you some freedom in selecting authors, literary works, and topics. Whenever possible, you should write about a work that appeals to you on some level.

However, even when you have been assigned a specific author or literary work, certain aspects of that author's writing or certain elements within the work are likely to appeal to you. For example, Ernest Hemingway's short story "Hills Like White Elephants" may not be one of your favorites in terms of theme, but you may be fascinated with the way in which Hemingway uses simple prose, allowing emotion to be communicated almost entirely by the direct actions of the characters. If so, you have the basis for a well-focused paper about literature.

Reading Critically

Once you have chosen an author or a literary work about which to write, you need to read critically, looking for anything that seems especially meaningful or significant.

Marking Passages.   One of the best ways to read critically is to mark passages with a pencil, underlining and making margin notes as you proceed. This method is effective because it keeps the work and your notations about it directly linked. But use it only if the book you are marking is your own.

Using Index Cards.   Another good method of critical reading involves using index cards to note meaningful and significant details. When using index cards, be sure to put page or line number notations on each card so that you can easily find passages if you need to review them later in the context of the entire work.

Index cards work well because as you begin to write your paper, you can arrange the cards to reflect the organization of your paper, thus ensuring that your notes are used effectively and at the appropriate place in your paper.

Photocopying.   You may photocopy specific passages of a work (not an entire work) for reference, according to copyright laws. Then, as you begin writing your paper, you may choose to make notes on the photocopied sheets rather than in the book itself.

What should you note as you read? The list depends on where you plan to go with your paper. You may have an idea about your thesis before you begin reading critically and marking, or one may begin to form as you look at the work critically.

Your notations might identify particular uses of these elements:

- language
- symbolism
- irony
- structure

- tone
- dialogue
- character
- description

- plot movement
- imagery
- foreshadowing
- epiphany
- theme development

You should note anything that strikes you as significant. It is better to mark a passage when you first read it than to hunt later for something that you vaguely remember. Also, through your notations, you may find the way to proceed with your paper. After you have developed a clear and focused thesis, you can review the work and disregard notations that are not relevant.

Approaches

Once you have chosen a literary work and have read it critically, it is important to determine the approach you will take in writing about it. Most literary essays fall into one of three categories: explication, analysis, and comparison/contrast.

Although the approaches differ to a great extent, all have one element in common: the intent of each is to show how the author has carried out or furthered the theme, or message, of the work.

Asking yourself a series of questions about specific literary elements in the work(s) under consideration will help you discover which elements to discuss in your paper and what approach to take:

1. Are there any **allusions** that seem significant?

2. Are there any **symbols** in the work? How has the author used **symbolism**? Can any of the symbols be interpreted in different ways?

3. What **images** are particularly strong?

4. Is there any **irony** in the work? How has the author used irony to express his or her meaning?

5. How has the author used language (**connotation, figures of speech**) to express his or her meaning?

6. What is the **tone** of the work? How is the tone significant to the reader's understanding of the message?

7. Is the **plot** of the work significant?

8. If the work is **poetry,** is the overall structure of the poem significant?

9. Has the author used **foreshadowing**? How is the foreshadowing significant?

10. How has the author used sound to express his or her thoughts?

11. What is especially significant about the **characters** and **characterization**? Are any minor characters significant to the development of the theme? Have any of the characters experienced an **epiphany**?

12. How is **setting** used in the work?

13. Does the **point of view** of the **narrator** play an important role in the reader's understanding of the work?

14. How is **dialogue** used to express the action or meaning?

15. What is the **theme** of the work? Is there more than one major theme?

16. How do any or all of these elements work together to create the meaning?

Explication

To **explicate** means to explain. An **explication essay** requires the writer to explain a meaning or meanings in a work of literature. An essay based on this approach moves carefully through a work of literature, or sometimes through a single passage, calling attention to details and noting every element that furthers the author's theme.

Explication works best with poetry. An explication of a poem moves through the work, sometimes line by line, sometimes passage by passage, noting its complexities.

Because explication involves such attention to detail, it generally is not the best approach to use when writing about entire short stories, novels, or plays. Yet such works of literature can benefit from explication when the writer's focus is limited to selected passages or scenes. In dealing with these works, the writer should identify and explain a particular descriptive passage, a key scene, a conversation, or a **monologue.** Explication used in this way is an excellent strategy to show how minute details contribute dramatically to the whole.

The organization of an explication essay is the most obvious and simple of the three approaches. Because explication involves explaining, it is best simply to begin at the beginning of the work or passage and proceed to the end. The organization of the essay essentially reflects the organization of the work.

One final but important note about explication must be made. Explication does not mean paraphrasing, or rewording. A paper that simply restates the author's words, line by line or passage by passage, will be not only boring to the reader but also insulting to the author. Although sometimes it may be necessary to paraphrase in order to clarify, a **paraphrase** should not be the basis of the paper.

Analysis

To **analyze** means to separate a subject into its elements as a means to understanding the whole. An **analysis essay,** therefore, looks not at the entire work but rather at how the author has used one or several elements to carry out or further a theme.

A well-written analysis paper has a specific focus on the element or elements under discussion and clear organization. Two basic methods of organization work well and can be easily modified to suit the purpose of the paper.

One-Element Organization.   The writer first identifies one element or technique that the author uses to advance the theme of the work. The writer then discusses the various ways in which that element is used.

Several-Elements Organization.   The writer first identifies several elements or techniques that the author uses to advance the theme of the work. The writer then discusses each element individually.

Comparison/Contrast

To **compare** means to show how two subjects are alike, to **contrast** means to show how two subjects are different, and to **compare and contrast** means to show how two subjects are both alike and different. A **comparison/contrast essay** may involve any one of three approaches: it may compare, it may contrast, or it may do both.

An essay based on this approach may deal with two subjects within one literary work, two or more works that have the same subject or the same basic theme, two or more works by the same author, two authors and their works, or one work compared to or contrasted with a particular style of writing.

The approach works well whether you are writing about short stories, novels, poetry, or drama.

As with analysis, the key to a well-written comparison/contrast essay lies in organization. It is important not only to identify the two subjects to be discussed but also to determine the basis of the comparison/contrast.

Generally, it is best to identify several ways in which the subjects can be compared/contrasted. Finding a basis for comparison/contrast isn't as hard as you might think. You do this sort of thing all the time. For example, if you were considering which of two colleges to attend, you would establish a basis of comparison/contrast to help yourself make the decision. You might compare/contrast the two schools on the basis of cost, programs offered, and location. You will use the same type of thinking when you write a comparison/contrast essay.

It is important to identify clearly the manner in which the subjects will be compared/contrasted. Otherwise, your discussion may go in too many directions and be confusing to the reader.

A comparison/contrast essay may be organized in one of two basic patterns. The patterns limit and direct the focus of your essay, resulting in a clearly stated, logically organized paper.

Whole-to-Whole Method.   Using this organization, the writer first discusses one of the subjects under consideration according to the identified bases of comparison/contrast and then discusses the second subject according to the same bases.

Part-to-Part Method.   Using this organization, the writer discusses each basis of comparison/contrast, giving examples from the two subjects.

Just as you have preferences in reading literature, you will find that you also have preferences in approaches to writing about literature. Although your paper should follow one basic approach, it is certainly possible for you to use one or both of the other approaches within your paper. A comparison/contrast paper may include some explication as well as some analysis, and an analysis paper may include some explication and some comparison/contrast.

Although approach is important, it should not dictate your choice of literature. Instead, the literature under discussion should dictate your choice of approach. Critical reading of the work you intend to write about can lead you to ask pertinent general questions, besides the questions you ask about individual literary elements. For example:

1. How have the author's life experiences affected the work?

2. Is there some particular historical significance to the work? Does it reveal something about a specific time or place?

3. Can we compare the work of one author with that of another author writing on the same subject? Can we find a basis of comparison or contrast for two or more works by the same author?

4. Does the work set forth some universal theme of love, death, or human nature?

Your answers may point to the approach you should take. But neither the questions nor the approaches they lead to are intended to constrict your creativity and imagination. Rather, they serve as guides and patterns that you can and should modify to suit your purpose and the literary work under discussion.

The Structure

A paper about literature is no different in form from any other type of essay. Most essays have a three-part structure:

- an introduction with a thesis statement

- a body made up of several supporting paragraphs

- a conclusion

By asking yourself a series of questions about each part of your essay, you can ensure that your paper will have a clear and effective organization.

The Introduction and Thesis Statement

1. Have I started my discussion of the topic in fairly broad terms rather than leading with my thesis statement?

2. Does my introduction identify the work of literature to be discussed and the author?

3. Does my introduction narrow the focus more and more, directing the reader's attention to a clear and narrow thesis statement?

4. Does my thesis statement express the controlling idea of the essay?

5. Is my thesis stated in one tightly focused sentence, and is that sentence located near the end of the introductory paragraph?

The Body

1. Have I selected an appropriate number of main points to support my thesis effectively, and have I developed one point per paragraph?

2. Have I developed clear support for my thesis in each body paragraph?

3. Have I adhered to the standards of good paragraph writing in each paragraph, and does each have a clearly focused topic sentence?

4. Has each body paragraph explained (explication), analyzed (analysis), or compared/contrasted (comparison/contrast) the work(s) or author(s) under discussion, according to the approach I have selected?

5. If I am using explication, does the body of my paper reflect the organization of the work or passage itself?

6. If I am using analysis or comparison/contrast, have I saved my strongest point for the last body paragraph?

7. Have I supported the topic of each paragraph with material from the work(s) under discussion?

8. Does the body of my paper have continuity, and does it flow logically from one point to the next, employing clear transition?

The Conclusion

1. Have I started the concluding paragraph with the general idea of my thesis?

2. Have I avoided simply restating the thesis?

3. Have I used the concluding paragraph to summarize or to draw a conclusion based on my thesis and on the body paragraphs?

4. Have I worked toward a more generalized discussion of the topic near the end of my conclusion?

In addition to ensuring a clear organization, these checklists can help you maintain the focus of your essay and enable you to create an effective, logical discussion.

Quotation and Documentation

A subject that greatly concerns student writers is how to use and document quotations from the work(s) they are writing about. Although documentation is not a difficult process, it is a critical part of writing and must be handled according to accepted standards.

Most teachers prefer that literary papers use **MLA documentation style,** which is universally accepted within the humanities. Many composition and literature textbooks contain a section on MLA documentation, and most college bookstores sell manuscript documentation booklets. If you do not have a copy of the MLA documentation guidelines, you need to obtain one before writing a literary paper. See Chapters 34 and 35 for a fuller discussion of MLA requirements.

Use of Quotations and Paraphrasing

Although MLA guidelines are quite specific and complete, a few points are especially important to remember:

You must cite (give credit to) all sources you use, including the work(s) under discussion, by using parenthetical documentation within the paper and including a Works Cited page at the end.

You should integrate paraphrases and quotations with your own discussion and interpretation.

You should use direct quotations when it is important to reproduce the words exactly as they are written so as not to lose something vital. Otherwise, you should paraphrase.

Quotations of fewer than four typed lines should be enclosed in quotation marks and worked into your paragraph like any other sentence. Parenthetical documentation of the source goes at the end of the sentence. Be sure to use quotation marks to indicate directly quoted material.

Quotations longer than four typed lines should be set off by indenting them ten spaces from the left margin. Such quotations should be double-spaced like the rest of the paper. They should not be enclosed in quotation marks. Parenthetical documentation follows the quotation.

Parenthetical Documentation

The MLA guidelines include instruction in how to use **parenthetical documentation** to cite references within the paper. Parenthetical documentation is simply a set of parentheses containing identification of the source; it follows the cited material.

Each literary form—fiction, poetry, and drama—uses a different form of parenthetical reference. It is important that you recognize and use the appropriate form.

When citing a passage from a short story or novel, indicate the page number.

> "It is impossible to say how first the idea entered my brain; but once conceived, it haunted me day and night" (37).

When citing a part of a poem, indicate the line number(s).

> "The only other sound's the sweep / Of easy wind and downy flake" (11–12).

When quoting lines from poetry, use a slash (/) to indicate the end of a line as it is printed in your source.

When citing a part of a classic play, indicate the act, scene, and line numbers.

> "There are more things in heaven and earth, Horatio, / Than are dreamt of in your philosophy" (1.5.166–67).

If the play you are citing is a verse play, use a slash (/) to indicate the end of a line. Otherwise, use no slashes.

When citing a part of a modern play, indicate the act and page number.

"I am not a dime a dozen! I am Willy Loman, and you are Biff Loman" (2.1421).

If you are using more than one source for your paper, such as two poems, you will need to provide more detailed parenthetical information, according to MLA guidelines, or you will need to indicate in the text of your paper which source you are referring to in order to avoid confusion.

In "Stopping by Woods on a Snowy Evening," Frost describes the quiet of an evening in the country by explaining "The only other sound's the sweep / Of easy wind and downy flake" (11–12). In contrast, the city nights speak more loudly. Frost explains in "Acquainted with the Night" that he has ". . . stood still and stopped the sound of feet / When far away an interrupted cry / Came over houses from another street" (7–9).

Works Cited Page

Also included in the MLA guidelines is instruction in how to document your sources on a Works Cited page. The Works Cited page comes at the end of your paper and lists all the sources you have used.

Strictly speaking, your essay should conclude with a Works Cited page listing in MLA style all the sources you have used. However, if you have used only one source, such as your textbook, your teacher may prefer that you use simple parenthetical references as described above and omit the Works Cited page. If in doubt, you should ask your teacher which method he or she prefers.

Smooth Use of Quotations

Quotations from the literature under discussion should be worked into your paper smoothly. You can best accomplish this by weaving a quotation into your own sentence. When you do so, you may need to omit words from the work you are quoting in order to write a sentence with correct verb or pronoun agreement. Use ellipsis points—three spaced periods—to indicate the omission of words from a quotation (as in the correct example below).

It is not a good idea simply to quote a passage and then add a sentence telling what the passage means. Instead, try to present the quotation and explanation in the same sentence.

Incorrect

"I put my forehead down to the damp, seaweed-smelling sand" (2). This is an example of Robert Bly's metaphorical language in his poem "In Rainy September."

Correct

Robert Bly uses metaphorical language in his poem "In Rainy September" when he describes how he put his forehead ". . . down to the damp, seaweed-smelling sand" (2).

Correct documentation is an integral part of writing about literature. Careful attention must be paid to documentation in order to avoid plagiarism and to avoid confusing the reader.

Writing About Stories or Novels

If you plan to write about a short story or novel, read the work thoroughly and carefully, all the while noting your overall reaction and trying to determine the author's message. Critical reading will help you determine the point you want to make in your paper and, in turn, the approach you will take.

Because of the length of most short stories and novels, explication may not be the best approach, unless you plan to explicate selected passages in order to make your point. Analysis and comparison/contrast, however, usually work quite well. No matter which approach you choose, here are some key elements for you to consider:

- plot
- characters
- setting
- point of view

- symbolism
- irony
- theme
- tone

Sample Student Essay

The following student essay is based on Jose Donoso's short story "Paseo" and uses analysis. The writer takes into account how one element of the story, symbolism, is used in several ways in order to create the whole.

The writer organized the essay so that each body paragraph analyzes a different interpretation of a single symbol:

1. Introduction and thesis: Jose Donoso's short story "Paseo" uses multiple interpretations of a single symbol, the dog.

2. The dog representing emotion

3. The dog representing disorder

4. The dog representing madness

5. Conclusion

Jane Perry

Ms. Barberousse

English 102, Section 1

11 December 1996

                    The Object of Her Affections

        The use of symbolism has long been a technique

by which an author can present far more than the lit-

eral meaning of a story. However, symbols are not

always easily defined; indeed, it is sometimes possi-

ble that one symbol in a story may be endowed with

multiple meanings, all of which lead the reader to a

greater understanding of the author's message. Such

is the case in Jose Donoso's short story "Paseo."

The story is told from the point of view of a grown

man looking back on the isolated, frightened child he

was. As the boy's jealousy focuses on the attention

gained by a nondescript but persistent dog, Donoso

leads us into the realm of multiple symbolism.

        Perhaps most obviously, the dog represents emo-

tion. The boy in the story grows up with cold people

in a house that is "not happy" (316) and that

expresses "an absence, a lack, which because it was

unacknowledged was irremediable" (316). The boy
wishes that his family's "confined feeling might
overflow and express itself in a fit of rage . . . or
with some bit of foolery" (317). Of course, he knows
it is not to be. The dog that his Aunt Mathilda
adopts, however, represents the opposite of
repressed, or perhaps nonexistent, emotion: "Her
whole body, from her quivering snout to her tail
ready to waggle, was full of an abundant capacity for
fun" (323). It is the dog's expression of emotion
that permeates Aunt Mathilda's cold exterior and provokes her to express emotion of her own. Yet the boy
is still isolated, perhaps more so, as his jealousy
takes hold. As he watches his aunt stroke the dog
sleeping on her lap, he realizes the extent of his
own isolation and feels the loss of any hope that he,
too, might be the recipient of her affection:

>   On seeing that expressionless hand reposing
>   there, I noticed that the tension which had
>   kept my aunt's features clenched before,
>   relented, and that a certain peace was now
>   softening her face. I could not resist. I
>   drew closer to her on the sofa, as if to a
>   newly kindled fire. I hoped that she would

> reach out to me with a look or include me
> with a smile. But she did not. (324)

In addition to emotion, the dog also represents
disorder and its effect on constrained order.
Dedicated to her brothers, one of whom is the father
of the boy in the story, Aunt Mathilda is the creator
of order in the house, one whose focus is frightening
in its rigidity and in her insistence on perfection.
Defects cannot be tolerated and, as the boy relates,
"When she saw affliction about her she took immediate
steps to remedy what, without doubt, were errors in a
world that should be, that had to be, perfect" (317).
Yet, the dog itself is a walking representation of
disorder:

> It was small and white, with legs which
> were too short for its size and an ugly
> pointed snout that proclaimed an entire
> genealogy of misalliances: the sum of
> unevenly matched breeds which for genera-
> tions had been scouring the city, searching
> for food in the garbage cans and among the
> refuse of the port. (320)

Mathilda, surprisingly, grows more and more attached to the dog, and with her attachment comes the beginning of chaos. The chaos starts with simple things, such as Mathilda losing at billiards and no longer remembering the order of the shooters, but it progresses to the point that she loses "the thread of order" (323) that has been the thread of her life. Eventually, the disorder so dissolves the very core of Mathilda that her midnight strolls extend to her disappearance.

In retrospect, the dog also represents madness, a madness that results when the spontaneity of the dog disrupts the rigid world of the adults. The boy speculates on the first look that passes between the dog and his aunt and feels that look "contained some secret commitment" (320). When the dog first makes Mathilda laugh, the boy is surprised, but not amused, because he "may have felt the dark thing that had stirred it up" (324). It is that unnamed dark thing that permeates the boy's jealousy and causes him to imagine a sinister influence in the dog. When he perceives in his aunt "an animation in her eyes, an excited restlessness like that in the eyes of the

animal" (326) after one of her evening walks with the
dog, the boy begins to feel concern rather than jealousy. His aunt, formerly a fortress of routine and
order, has become a mystery of the night: "Those two
were accomplices. The night protected them. They
belonged to the murmuring sound of the city, to the
sirens of the ships which . . . reached my ears"
(326).

   One night upon hearing his aunt come in, the boy
recognizes the final influence the dog and the madness it represents are to have on his aunt: "I went
to bed terrified, knowing this was the end. I was
not mistaken. Because one night . . . Aunt Mathilda
took the dog out for a walk after dinner, and did not
return" (327).

   Who is to say whether the aunt's disappearance
is a manifestation of her madness or simply a rebel-
lion on her part, an affirmation of the life she has
never before experienced? Yet, in the boy's mind,
she is dead, and her death has been brought about by
the dog and all it symbolizes. The repression of
emotion in his aunt has been freed by something not
human, and in doing so, it has brought disorder to
order and madness to composure.

Works Cited

Donoso, Jose. "Paseo." The Riverside Anthology of

Literature. Ed. Douglas Hunt. 2nd ed. Boston:

Houghton, 1991. 315-27.

Writing About Poetry

Poetry is perhaps the oldest form of literature. It has been used throughout the ages as a form of history, an expression of religion, and a presentation of images and emotions. Whatever its form, poetry is intended to create in us the experience that is being expressed.

Because poetry is so rich in language and its subtleties, it lends itself to all three literary approaches. Explication provides an excellent opportunity to explore the artistry and talent involved in employing a wide range of elements and techniques to create the whole. Analysis, too, is an excellent approach for a paper based on poetry, where the discussion is narrowed to just one or several basic elements or techniques. Also, poetry is often the basis of comparison/contrast papers in terms of subject, theme, and authors. Whether you are explicating, analyzing, or comparing/contrasting, key elements to consider when writing about poetry include these:

- speaker
- sound
- imagery
- figures of speech
- connotations

- symbolism
- irony
- structure
- tone
- theme

Sample Student Essay

The following student essay is based on Louise Bogan's poem "The Dream" and uses explication. The organization of the essay is simple, following the organization of the poem itself. The writer takes into account how all the elements of the poem work toward carrying out the poet's theme.

The essay examines the four stanzas of the poem and its overall structure:

1. Introduction and thesis: Louise Bogan's poem "The Dream" is about fear, and Bogan's message—the message of the dream, in fact—is that fear can be tamed through trust.

2. First stanza

3. Second stanza

4. Third stanza

5. Fourth stanza

6. Overall technical structure

7. Conclusion

Marvin Poplin

Ms. Barberousse

English 102, Section 1

4 December 1996

Taming the Beast

Dreams have long been the basis for extensive
analysis, their meanings interpreted and reinterpret-
ed. Some people believe that dreams reflect our
repressed emotions, providing a necessary outlet for
the negative aspects of our reality. Others find
answers through dreams, believing that dreams provide
simple solutions to seemingly complex issues in our
lives. Louise Bogan, in her poem "The Dream,"
describes a dream that expresses both repression and
solution. It is a poem about fear, and Bogan's mes-
sage--the message of the dream, in fact--is that fear
can be tamed through trust.

In the first stanza of the poem the speaker
describes the fearful dream she had. Bogan introduces
the symbol of a mighty horse that embodies the fear
and retribution carried from the speaker's childhood,
fear and retribution that have been "kept for thirty-
five years" (3). Bogan effectively uses metaphorical
language as she describes the fear personified in

Poplin 2

the horse as it "poured through his mane" (3) and the
retribution as it "breathed through his nose" (4).
The source of her fear is unclear, but it may be that
the horse is a symbol of life that can be both beautiful and terrifying. The imagery created when the
speaker tells us, "the terrible horse began / To paw
at the air, and make for me with his blows" (1-2)
describes a sense of entrapment as life corners her
and spews forth repressed fear and retribution, emotions that must be faced.

The speaker's shame at her cowardice is clear in
the second stanza as she describes how she "lay on
the ground and wept" (5). It is at this point that
Bogan introduces another symbol in the poem, a woman
who "leapt for the rein" (6). The stranger's
strength and courage seem so alien to the speaker
that she refers to her as a "creature" (6), something
not shackled by human fears. Perhaps this other
woman represents the speaker's alter ego, a side of
her yet to be set free. Nonetheless, Bogan creates a
dramatic contrast between the speaker's inability to
respond to her fear as she "lay half in a swound"
(7) and the other woman's determination as she

"Leapt in the air, and clutched at the leather and chain" (8).

In the third stanza, the other woman advises the speaker to give the horse a token as a gesture of peace: "Throw him, she said, some poor thing you alone claim" (9). In effect, she tells the speaker to surrender to her fate and to approach life with love. The speaker's long-held sense of hopelessness and fear is further contrasted to the possibility of a fresh approach to life as she tells the stranger, "No, no . . . he hates me; he's out for harm, / And whether I yield or not, it is all the same" (11-12).

Yet, face to face with her fears, perhaps shamed by the courage of the other woman, the speaker yields at last in the final stanza of the poem. The imagery created is one of coldness, the coldness that resides in the heart of fear. She describes her act of courage and the fear still inherent in that act when she explains, "I flung the glove / Pulled from my sweating, my cold right hand" (14-15). With that act, the imagery changes from cold to warmth as suddenly as does the beast who, like life that "no one may understand" (15), came to her side and "put down his head in love" (16). After thirty-five years, the beast is tamed.

Like dreams so often are, Bogan's poem is a simple one, not only in the narration of the dream, but also in the metrical pattern and the rhyme scheme of the poem. Rarely is a regular iambic beat achieved in the poem, thus reinforcing the theme of confusion. Yet, at the end of the poem, when the meaning is clear, the last line contains three successive iambs in "put down his head in love." Also, after a routine rhyme scheme of abab in the first three stanzas, Bogan introduces new tension in the last stanza with an abba rhyme scheme. The word "love" comes fresh and unexpectedly to rhyme with "glove," just as Bogan's poem points out that with trust comes peace, often just as fresh and unexpectedly.

Louise Bogan points out in her poem that life is rarely as predictable as we might like, but it must be faced, regardless of our fears. Like the speaker, we may be surprised by the gentleness and peace we find when we face life head on, offer it our love, and surrender to its power--just as it surrenders to ours.

Works Cited

Bogan, Louise. "The Dream." The Riverside Anthology of

   Literature. Ed. Douglas Hunt. 2nd ed. Boston:

   Houghton, 1991. 730.

Writing About Drama

Since its ancient beginnings, drama has been used as a literary vehicle to express the condition of humankind. Through the unfolding of events in a play, human existence is played out through a cause and effect relationship. The biggest difference between drama and other forms of literature is that drama is intended to be seen as it is acted on a stage, a fact that is critical to interpretation as a play is read.

Explication may not be the best approach for a paper about drama unless you plan to explicate a key scene, a conversation, or a monologue. Used in this way, explication can be an excellent way to show how details in a play contribute dramatically to the whole. Analysis works quite well as an approach to writing about drama because it is possible to analyze how a playwright uses a single element or several elements to set forth a specific theme. Theme also serves as an excellent starting point for the comparison/contrast approach to drama, whether expressed historically or through character. An essay based on drama typically includes a discussion of one or more of these basic elements:

- dialogue
- plot
- characters
- conflict

- setting
- symbolism
- dramatic conventions
- theme

Sample Student Essay

The following student essay is based on Aristotle's definition of tragedy and Arthur Miller's play *Death of a Salesman*. The writer uses comparison. Although Miller's play is a modern one, the writer shows that it can be viewed as an Aristotelian tragedy.

The essay uses the part-to-part method of organization. Each of Aristotle's defining points of tragedy is a basis of comparison:

1. Introduction and thesis: In spite of its modernity, Arthur Miller's great twentieth-century tragedy, *Death of a Salesman,* can be successfully compared to the Aristotelian description of traditional tragedy.

2. The tragic hero

3. The hero's tragic flaw

4. The hero's recognition of the truth about himself

5. Redemption

6. Conclusion

Della Smith

Ms. Barberousse

English 102, Section 1

2 December 1996

<u>Death of a Salesman</u>: A Modern Tragedy

In the fourth century B.C., Aristotle set forth
his description of dramatic tragedy, and for centuries after, tragedy continued to be defined by his
basic observations. It was not until the modern age
that playwrights began to deviate somewhat from the
basic tenets of Aristotelian tragedy and, in doing
so, began to create plays more recognizable to the
common people and, thereby, less traditional. Even
so, upon examination, the basic plot structure of
some modern tragedies actually differs very little
from that of the ancient classics. In spite of its
modernity, Arthur Miller's great twentieth-century
tragedy, <u>Death of a Salesman</u>, can be successfully
compared to the Aristotelian description of traditional tragedy.

According to Aristotle, the protagonist, or tragic
hero, of a tragedy is a person of great virtue and of
high estate, usually a member of a royal family. The

tragedy then carries the protagonist from his position of esteem and happiness to one of misery.
Although Miller's protagonist, Willy Loman, is not of
high estate, he is the head of his household. His
wife, Linda, aware though she is of his failings,
sees him as "the dearest man in the world" (1.1373).
Furthermore, he is a man whose intentions to be the
best salesman possible are honorable, although mis-
guided. It must not be overlooked that prior to the
twentieth century, almost all literature had as its
protagonist someone of high estate. The typical protagonist of the modern age, however, is one whose
main conflict is survival, and that conflict is certainly true of Willy Loman. Linda summarizes the
plight of the modern tragic hero when she says, "A
small man can be just as exhausted as a great man"
(1.1374).

Aristotelian tragedy further defines the tragic
hero as one who has a tragic flaw or frailty that is
very often the error of pride. It is this tragic flaw
that causes the hero's downfall. Willy Loman's tragic flaw is certainly bound by his pride, a pride that
will not allow him to recognize that he is not the

salesman he has always dreamed of being. As a result, he becomes further and further detached from reality, believing more in his dreams than in reality. When Linda tries to get Willy to slow down his travels and work in New York, he tells her, "I'm the New England man. I'm vital in New England" (1.1347). Yet, Willy has just returned from another unsuccessful New England sales trip. His pride will also not allow him to recognize that he is no longer respected by his sons, nor have they achieved the great successes he has dreamed of for them. When Biff, Willy's older son, momentarily falls for his brother's sporting goods business scheme, Willy tells them, "I see great things for you kids, I think your troubles are over. But remember, start big and you'll end big" (1.1379).

The Aristotelian hero eventually recognizes the dark truth to his life. With this recognition comes, both for the hero and the audience, further recognition that the downfall has resulted from acts for which he is responsible. After all, the hero is capable of making choices. Willy, too, is capable of making choices, but as Biff states in the Requiem, "He

had the wrong dreams. All, all wrong" (2.1425). As
Willy seems to slip further and further from reality
toward the end of the play, he actually comes closer
to the truth about himself than ever before. In his
delusionary discussion with his brother Ben, Willy
plans his suicide, and Ben mentions that it might be
seen as cowardly. Willy replies, "Why? Does it take
more guts to stand here the rest of my life ringing
up a zero" (2.1417)? Even though he quickly slips
back to his destructive pride, the mirror has been
faced and Willy has seen a zero. His very act of
suicide indicates that he knows he cannot regain the
respect of Biff nor can he provide for his family, as
he has pretended for so long. It is only through his
death that he can make something of himself for them.

Traditional tragic heroes find a form of redemption
in their suffering, and through that suffering the
audience learns moral lessons and experiences a
catharsis. Perhaps Willy is most notably a true
tragic hero in that his tragic flaw, his battle to be
what he is not, is one that is carried out wrongly
but for all the right reasons, as is typical of the
traditional tragic hero. Traditional heroes are also

victims to some degree, victims of their own flaw and
victims of a force greater than themselves. In
Willy's case, his destructive pride in being what he
is not comes about, at least in part, because of mis-
guided definitions of success. Biff tries to stop
Willy's spiraling fall as he pleads with his father
to "take that phony dream and burn it before something happens" (2.1422). However, Willy's definition
of success has been too wrapped up in money for too
long. As audience members of traditional tragedies
experience a catharsis, so does Biff, as he learns
from his father's mistakes and realizes that the key
to success lies in knowing who he is. Perhaps it is
only through Biff's recognition of the truth that
Willy is redeemed, though not as he planned. Biff
asks Willy, "Why am I trying to become what I don't
want to be . . . when all I want is out there, waiting for me the minute I say I know who I am"
(2.1421)?

Tragedy did not end with the modern age.
Instead, it has found new form and is perhaps more
recognizable with the common man as its protagonist.
Traditional tragedy is intended to create in the

Smith 6

audience pity and terror for the tragic hero's condition. Most of us see enough of ourselves in Willy
that we sympathize with him, even when we disagree
with him. Furthermore, it is difficult for late-
twentieth-century Americans not to feel terror when
considering how the forces that destroyed Willy might
destroy us as well. Perhaps that fear is, indeed,
the very heart of the tragedy Arthur Miller created.

Works Cited

Miller, Arthur. <u>Death of a Salesman</u>, <u>The Riverside</u>
    <u>Anthology of Literature</u>. Ed. Douglas Hunt. 2nd ed.
    Boston: Houghton, 1991. 1345-1426.

Getting It Right

Although writing about literature is just like any other form of expository writing, certain conventions, or standards, must be considered. These conventions ensure that you make your point clearly with appropriate references to sources and with adherence to specific style guidelines (MLA).

Literary Essay Conventions

Use the present tense when discussing works of literature and events within those works.

Use the past tense only when discussing events that happened in the past, whether in the author's life or in the story itself.

Work quotations into your paper smoothly, conforming to correct sentence structure and grammatical form. Quotations should not be overlong, nor should they intrude on the text of your paper; instead, they should become part of the text, acting as support for your points.

Use parenthetical documentation for all quotations, and include a Works Cited page following MLA documentation style.

Identify works of literature correctly: titles of novels and plays should be italicized or underlined: titles of short stories and poems should be enclosed within quotation marks, although titles of some extremely long poems are italicized.

Avoid contractions and colloquialisms.

Write objectively, avoiding reference to yourself. Expressions such as "I think," "In my opinion," and "I believe" tend to weaken your point. Your essay is, by its very nature, an expression of your opinion, supported with specific and concrete references to the work.

Once you are sure that you have adhered to the conventions of literary essays in your paper, it is important that you proofread and edit for clarity and correctness.

Editing Guidelines

Review your essay to determine if your thesis is narrow enough and states something other than the obvious.

Make sure that your basic organization allows you to develop your thesis fully and logically.

Make sure that you have supported each of your main points with specific and concrete references from the work(s) under discussion.

Check your documentation style against MLA standards.

Edit for grammar, spelling, and typing errors.

Manuscript Form

Correct manuscript form is another important consideration. MLA format is usually acceptable. However, it is always a good idea to ask your instructor how he or she prefers you to handle issues such as typing, whether to have a title page, and whether to include a Works Cited page (see Appendix A).

Literary Terms

Allusion   An indirect reference to another work of art, a person, or an event.

Analysis A method by which a subject is separated into its elements as a means to understanding the whole. An analysis essay approaches a work of literature by examining one or several key elements.

Character An imagined person appearing in a work of fiction, poetry, or drama.

Characterization The method by which characters in a work of literature are made known to the reader.

Comparison A discussion concerning how two or more persons or things are alike.

Conflict A struggle among opposing forces in a literary work.

Connotation The set of implications and associations that a word carries in addition to its literal meaning.

Contrast A discussion concerning how two or more persons or things are different.

Dialogue Conversation between characters.

Drama A play.

Dramatic Conventions Customary methods of presenting an action by means of devices that an audience is willing to accept.

Epiphany A moment of insight when a character suddenly realizes something previously unrecognized about life or about himself or herself.

Explication   A method of explaining. An explication essay explains the meaning or meanings in a work of literature.

Fiction   Stories that are at least partially imagined and not factual.

Figures of Speech   Words that mean, in a particular context, something more than the dictionary definitions.

Foreshadowing   An indication or hint of something yet to come.

Imagery   The use of words or groups of words that refer to the senses and sensory experiences.

Irony   An effect created when statements or situations seem at odds with how things truly are.

Metaphor   An implicit comparison of a feeling or object with another unlike it. *Example:* He is a snake in the grass.

Metaphorical language   Language that draws comparisons between things that are essentially dissimilar. Metaphorical language is most often created through the use of metaphor, simile, and personification.

MLA documentation style   The standardization of references to sources established by the Modern Language Association of America. Although other documentation styles exist, MLA is universally accepted within the humanities.

Monologue   An extended speech by one character in a literary work.

Narrator   The person telling the story in a work of literature.

Novel A long fictional narrative.

Paraphrase A restatement in your own words of what you understand a poem or some other passage to say.

Parenthetical documentation A set of parentheses containing identification of the source of cited material.

Personification A figure of speech in which nonhuman things are said to have human characteristics. Example: The car died on the hill.

Plot The sequence of events in a literary work.

Poetry A form of writing in which the author writes in lines using either a metrical pattern or free verse.

Point of view The position of the narrator in relation to the events that occur.

Prose Any form of writing that is not poetry.

Setting The background in which a literary work takes place. Time, place, historical era, geography, and culture are all part of the setting.

Short story A brief fictional narrative.

Simile A comparison of a feeling or object with another unlike it, using the term "like" or "as." *Example:* He eats like a horse.

Summary A brief restatement in your own words of the main idea of a literary work.

Symbol   Something concrete representing something abstract.

Symbolism   The use of symbols to give a literary work a message greater than its literal meaning.

Theme   The message, or main idea, of a literary work.

Tone   The expression of a writer's attitude toward a subject in a literary work and the creation of a mood for that work.

Glossary of Usage

This brief glossary explains the usage of potentially confusing words and phrases. Samples illustrate how the words and phrases are used. To check words or phrases not included here, consult a dictionary.

A, An Use *a* before a consonant sound; use *an* before a vowel sound. For words beginning with *h*, use *a* when the *h* is voiced and *an* when it is unvoiced. (Sound out the following examples carefully.)

a locket   **a** historical novel

an oration   **an** honest mistake

Accept, Except *Accept* means "willing to receive"; *except* means "all but."

Hoover rightfully would not **accept** the blame for the Stock Market Crash of 1929.

No elected official in the United States earns more than $200,000, **except** the president.

Accidentally, Accidently Use *accidentally,* the correct word form. The root word is *accidental,* not *accident.*

The curator **accidentally** mislabeled the painting.

Advice, Advise *Advice,* a noun, means "a suggestion or suggestions"; *advise,* a verb, means "to offer ideas" or "to recommend."

Lord Chesterfield's **advice** to his son, though written in 1747, retains its value today.

Physicians frequently **advise** their cardiac patients to get moderate exercise and eat wisely.

Affect, Effect *Affect,* a verb, means "to influence"; *effect,* a noun, means "the product or result of an action;" *effect,* a verb, means "to bring about, to cause to occur."

The smallness of the audience did not **affect** the speaker's presentation.

One **effect** of decontrol will be stronger competition.

To **effect** behavioral changes in some house pets is no small task.

Agree to, Agree with *Agree to* means "to accept" a plan or proposal; *agree with* means "to share beliefs" with a person or group.

Members of the Writer's Guild would not **agree to** the contract's terms.

Although I **agree with** the protesters' position, I cannot approve of their methods.

All ready, Already *All ready* means "all prepared"; *already* means "pre-existing" or "previous."

Ten minutes before curtain time, the performers were **all ready.**

Volumes A through M of the *Middle English Dictionary* are **already** in print.

All right, Alright Use *all right,* the correct form.

The Roosevelts clearly felt that it was **all right** for their children to be heard as well as seen.

All together, Altogether *All together* means "all acting in unison"; *altogether* means "totally" or "entirely."

Synchronized swimming requires participants to swim **all together.**

Life in a small town is **altogether** too peaceful for some city dwellers.

Alot, A lot   Use *a lot*, the correct form. Generally, however, use more specific words: *a great deal, many,* or *much.*

The senator's inflammatory comments shocked **a lot** of his constituents.

The senator's inflammatory comments shocked **many** of his constituents.

Among, Between   Use *among* to describe the relationship of three or more people or things; use *between* for two.

Disagreements **among** the lawyers disrupted the proceedings.

Zoning laws usually require at least forty feet **between** houses.

Amount, Number   Use *amount* for quantities that cannot be counted separately; use *number* for items that can be counted. Some concepts, like time, use both forms, depending on how elements are described.

The **amount** of money needed to restore Ellis Island was surprising.

The contractor could not estimate the **amount** of time needed to complete the renovations.

We will need a **number** of hours to coordinate our presentations.

In the 1960s, a large **number** of American elm trees were killed by Dutch elm disease.

An   See **A.**

And/or   Generally, avoid this construction. Instead, use either *and* or *or.*

Anxious, Eager   *Anxious* means "apprehensive" or "worried" and consequently describes negative feelings; *eager* means "to anticipate enthusiastically" and consequently describes positive feelings.

For four weeks, Angie was **anxious** about her qualifying exams.

Lew was **eager** to see the restaging of *La Bohème.*

As, As if, Like   Use *as* or *as if,* subordinating conjunctions, to introduce a clause; use *like,* a preposition, to introduce a noun or phrase.

Walt talked to his cocker spaniel **as if** the dog understood every word.

Virginia Woolf's prose style is a great deal **like** that of Leslie Stephens, her father.

As, Because, Since   *As,* a subordinating conjunction, establishes a time relationship; it is interchangeable with *when* or *while. Because* and *since* describe causes and effects.

As the train pulled out of the station, it began to rain.

Because (Since) the population density is high, housing is difficult to find in Tokyo.

Awful   Generally avoid using this word, which really means "full of awe," as a negative description. Instead, use *bad, terrible, unfortunate,* or other similar, more precise words.

Bad, Badly   Use *bad,* an adjective, to modify a noun; use *badly,* an adverb, to modify a verb.

Napoleon's winter assault on Russia was, quite simply, a **bad** plan.

Although Grandma Moses painted **badly** by conventional standards, her work had charm and innocence.

Because, Due to the fact that, Since   Use *because* or *since; due to the fact that* is merely a wordier way of saying the same thing.

Beef prices will rise **because** ranchers have reduced the size of their herds.

Before, Prior to   Use *before* in almost all cases. Use *prior to* only when the sequence of events is drawn out, important, and legalistic.

Always check your appointment book **before** scheduling a meeting.

Prior to receiving the cash settlement, the Jacobsons had filed four complaints with the Better Business Bureau.

Being as, Being that, Seeing as   Use *because* or *since* instead of these nonstandard forms.

Beside, Besides   *Beside* means "next to"; *besides* means "except."

In Congress, the vice president sits **beside** the Speaker of the House.

Few of Georgia O'Keeffe's paintings are well known **besides** those of flowers.

Between   See **Among.**

Borrow, Lend, Loan   *Borrow* means "to take something for temporary use"; *lend* means "to give something for temporary use"; *loan* is primarily a noun and refers to the thing lent or borrowed.

People seldom **borrow** expensive items like cars, furs, or electronic equipment.

Many public libraries now **lend** compact discs and video tapes.

The **loan** of $5,000 was never repaid.

Bring, Take   *Bring* means "to transport from a distant to a nearby location"; *take* reverses the pattern and means "to transport from a nearby location to a distant one."

Soviet dissidents **bring** to the United States tales of harsh treatment and inequity.

American scholars working in central Europe must **take** computers with them because the machines are not readily available at many European universities.

Can, May   *Can* means "is able to"; *may* means "has permission to." *May* is also used with a verb to suggest a possible or conditional action.

Almost anyone **can** learn to cook well.

Foreign diplomats **may** travel freely in the United States.

I **may** learn to like escargot, but I doubt it.

Can't help but   Avoid this phrase, which contains two negatives, *can't* and *but;* instead rewrite the sentence, omitting *but.*

We **can't help** wondering whether the new curriculum will help or hinder students.

Center around, Center on   Use *center on. Center around* is contradictory because *center* identifies one position and *around* suggests many possible positions.

If we can **center** our discussions **on** one topic at a time, we will use our time productively.

Compare to, Compare with   *Compare to* stresses similarities; *compare with* stresses both similarities and differences.

Jean Toomer's novel *Cane* has been **compared to** free verse.

In reviews, most critics **compared** the film version of *Amadeus* **with** the original play by Peter Shaffer.

Complement, Compliment   *Complement,* normally a noun, means "that which completes"; *compliment,* either a noun or a verb, means "a statement of praise" or "to praise."

A direct object is one kind of **complement.**

One of the highest forms of **compliment** is imitation.

The renovators of the Washington, D.C., train station should be **complimented** for their restraint, good taste, and attention to detail.

Continual, Continuous   *Continual* means "repeated often"; *continuous* means "without stopping."

In most industries, orienting new workers is a **continual** activity.

A **continuous** stream of water rushed down the slope.

Could of, Should of, Would of   Use the correct forms: *could have, should have,* and *would have.*

The athletic director **should have** taken a firm stand against drug use by athletes.

Council, Counsel   *Council,* a noun, means "a group of people who consult and offer advice"; *counsel,* a noun or a verb, means "advice" or "to advise."

The members of the **council** met in the conference room of the city hall.

Following the meeting, they offered their **counsel** to the mayor.

Ms. Reichmann **counsels** the unemployed at the Eighth Avenue Shelter.

Different from, Different than   Use *different from* with single complements and clauses; use *different than* only with clauses.

Most people's life styles are **different from** those of their parents.

Our stay in New Orleans was **different than** we had expected.

Disinterested, Uninterested *Disinterested* means "impartial" or "unbiased"; *uninterested* means "indifferent" or "unconcerned about."

Olympic judges are supposed to be **disinterested** evaluators, but most are not.

Unfortunately, many people are **uninterested** in classical music.

Due to the fact that See **Because.**

Each and every Generally, avoid this repetitious usage. Use *each* or *every,* not both.

Eager See **Anxious.**

Effect See **Affect.**

Enthusiastic, Enthused Use *enthusiastic,* the preferred form.

William was **enthusiastic** about his volunteer work for the Special Olympics.

Etc. Except in rare instances, avoid the use of *etc.,* which means "and so forth." Normally, either continue a discussion or stop.

Every day, Everyday *Every day,* an adjective-and-noun combination, means "each day"; *everyday,* an adjective, means "typical" or "ordinary."

Nutritionists suggest that people eat three balanced meals **every day.**

Congested traffic is an **everyday** problem in major cities.

Exam, Examination *Exam,* a conversational form, and *examination,* a formal variation, are interchangeable.

The CPA **exam (examination)** is given three times a year.

Except See **Accept.**

Farther, Further   *Farther* describes physical distances; *further* describes degree, quality, or time.

Most people know that it is **farther** to Mars than to Venus.

The subject of teenage pregnancy needs **further** study if we intend to solve the financial and social problems that it creates.

Fewer, Less   Use *fewer* to describe physically separate units; use *less* for things that cannot be counted.

Fewer than ten American companies have more than one million shareholders.

Because the cost-of-living raise was **less** than we had anticipated, we had to revise our budget.

Finalize, Finish   Generally, use *finish* or *complete,* less pretentious ways of expressing the same idea.

Fun   As an adjective, *fun* should be used in the predicate-adjective position, not before a noun.

White-water rafting is dangerous but **fun.**

Further   See **Farther.**

Good, Well   Use the adjective *good* to describe someone or something; use the adverb *well* to describe an action or condition.

A **good** debator must be knowledgeable, logical, and forceful.

We work **well** together because we think alike.

Has got, Have got   Simply use *has* or *have.*

Major networks **have** to rethink their programming, especially with the challenge of cable networks.

He or she, Him or her, His or hers, Himself or herself
Use these paired pronouns with indefinite but singular antecedents; avoid awkward constructions like *he/she* or *s/he.*

Generally, however, use plurals or specific nouns and pronouns when possible.

Each person is responsible for **his or her** own actions.

People are responsible for **their** own actions.

President Clinton is responsible for **his** and **his staff's** actions.

Hopefully, I Hope Use *hopefully,* an adverb, to describe the *hopeful* way in which something is done; use *I hope* to describe wishes.

Marsha **hopefully** opened the envelope, expecting to find a letter of acceptance.

I hope the EPA takes stronger steps to preserve our wildlife.

Imply, Infer *Imply* means "to suggest without stating"; *infer* means "to reach a conclusion based on unstated evidence." They describe two sides of a process.

Chancellor Michaelson's awkward movements and tentative comments **implied** that he was uncomfortable during the interview.

We **infer,** from your tone of voice, that you are displeased.

In, Into *In* means "positioned within"; *into* means "moving from the outside to the inside." Avoid using *into* to mean "enjoys," an especially nonsensical colloquialism.

Investments **in** the bond market are often safer than those **in** the stock market.

As the tenor walked **into** the reception room, he was greeted by a chorus of "bravos."

Infer See **Imply.**

Irregardless, Regardless Use *regardless,* the accepted form.

Child custody is usually awarded to the mother, **regardless** of the father's competence.

Its, It's, Its'   *Its,* a possessive pronoun, means "belonging to it"; *it's,* a contraction, means "it is"; *its'* is nonstandard.

After the accident, the quarter horse favored **its** right front leg.

It's unlikely that the government will increase educational spending.

Kind of, Sort of   Use *rather, somewhat,* or *to some extent* instead.

Lay, Lie   *Lay* means "to place something"; *lie* means "to recline." Some confusion is typical because *lay* is also the past tense of *lie.*

In hand-treating leather, a tanner will **lay** the skins on a large, flat surface.

People with migraine headaches generally **lie** down and stoically wait for the pain to subside.

Nina **lay** awake all night worrying about her interview.

Lead, Led   *Lead* is the present-tense verb; *led* is the past-tense form.

The clergy used to **lead** quiet lives.

Montresor **led** the unsuspecting Fortunato into the catacombs.

Learn, Teach   *Learn* means to "acquire knowledge"; *teach* means "to give instruction." These are two sides of the same process.

Children **learn** best in enriched environments.

Experience **teaches** us that hard work is often the key to success.

Less   See **Fewer.**

Lie   See **Lay.**

Like   See **As.**

Loan   See **Borrow.**

Loose, Lose   *Loose,* an adjective, means "not tight or binding"; *lose,* a verb, means "to misplace."

In tropical climates, people typically wear **loose,** lightweight garments.

Overcooked vegetables **lose** vitamins, minerals, texture, and color.

May   See **Can.**

May be, Maybe   *May be,* a verb, means "could be"; *maybe* means "perhaps."

The use of animals in research **may be** legal, but it raises ethical questions.

Maybe Van Gogh was mad; if so, his work is the result of an inspired madness.

Number   See **Amount.**

Off of   Use *off* by itself; it is perfectly clear.

During re-entry, a number of tiles came **off** the first space shuttle.

On account of   Use *because* or *since,* briefer ways of saying the same thing.

Passed, Past   Use *passed* as a verb; use *past* as a noun, adjective, or preposition.

Malcolm X **passed** through a period of pessimism to reach a time of optimism in his last months.

The **past,** as the saying goes, helps to determine the present.

Thoughtful people often reflect on their **past** actions and inactions.

The ambulance raced **past** the cars, hurrying from the site of the fire to the hospital.

People, Persons   Use *people* when referring to a group, emphasizing anonymity; use *persons* to emphasize unnamed individuals within the group.

People who lobby for special-interest groups must register their affiliations with Congress.

Several **persons** at the hearing criticized the company's environmental record.

Percent, Percentage   Use *percent* with a number; use *percentage* with a modifier.

More than fifty **percent** of the government's money is spent on Social Security and defense.

A large **percentage** of divorced people remarry.

Persons   See **People.**

Pretty   *Pretty* means "attractive" or "pleasant looking"; do not use it to mean "rather" or "somewhat."

Principal, Principle   *Principal,* an adjective, means "main" or "highest in importance"; *principal,* a noun, means "the head of a school"; *principle,* a noun, means "a fundamental truth or law."

The **principal** difficulty of reading the novels of Henry James is sorting out his syntax.

The **principal** in the satiric novel *Up the Down Staircase* seems oblivious to the needs of his students.

The **principle** of free speech is vital to American interests.

Prior to   See **Before.**

Quotation, Quote   *Quotation,* the noun, means "someone else's material used word for word"; *quote,* the verb, means "to use a quotation." In conversation, *quote* is often used as a noun; in formal writing, however, distinguish between these two forms.

In his speeches and essays, Martin Luther King, Jr., frequently incorporated **quotations** from the Bible.

In his poem "The Hollow Men," T. S. Eliot **quotes** from *The Heart of Darkness,* a brief novel by Joseph Conrad.

Reason, Reason why, Reason that, Reason is because
Reason, used by itself, is sometimes unclear; *reason why* or *reason that,* more complete expressions, are generally preferred. *Reason is because* is repetitive, because *reason* itself implies a connection.

Literature about AIDS often explores the **reasons why** the general public reacts so irrationally to the disease.

Respectfully, Respectively   *Respectfully* means "showing respect" or "full of respect"; *respectively* means "in the given order."

George Washington **respectfully** declined to be named king of the newly independent colonies.

These cited passages were submitted by Joshua Blaney, Andreas Church, and Joanna Meredith, **respectively.**

Seeing as   See **Being as.**

Set, Sit   *Set* means "to place or position something"; *sit* means "to be seated."

The photographer **set** the shutter speed at 1/100th of a second.

Many civil rights demonstrators refused to **sit** in segregated sections of buses, theaters, and government buildings.

Shall, Will   *Shall,* which indicates determination in the future tense, was once clearly distinguished from *will,* which merely describes future actions or conditions. Past distinctions

667

between these forms are disappearing, and *will* is used in almost all cases. *Shall* remains standard, however, for questions using the first person.

Many animals raised in captivity **will** die if released into the wild.

"Shall I compare thee to a summer's day?" —Sonnet 18, William Shakespeare

Should, Would   Use *should* to explain a condition or obligation; use *would* to explain a customary action or wish.

Universities **should** not invest funds in companies whose policies conflict with their own.

When asked a pointed question, John Kennedy **would** often begin his response with a humorous remark to ease the tension.

Should of   See **Could of.**

Since   See **As, Because.**

Sit   See **Set.**

Sort of   See **Kind of.**

Suppose to, Supposed to   Use *supposed to,* the standard form.

Affirmative action policies are **supposed to** ensure fair hiring practices nationwide.

Take   See **Bring.**

Teach   See **Learn.**

That, Which, Who   Use *that* to refer to people or things, but usually to things; use *which* to refer to things; use *who* to refer to people.

The musical work **that** set the standard for CD size was Beethoven's Ninth Symphony.

O'Neill's *Long Day's Journey into Night,* **which** won the 1957 Pulitzer Prize, was published posthumously.

People **who** cannot control their tempers are irritating and sometimes dangerous.

Their, There, They're   *Their,* a possessive pronoun, means "belonging to them"; *there,* usually an adverb, indicates placement; *they're,* a contraction, means "they are."

Legislation is pending to give artists royalties whenever **their** work is sold for profit.

Put the boxes over **there,** and I will open them later.

Let them sit wherever **they're** comfortable.

Theirself, Theirselves   Use *themselves*, the standard form.

The members of Congress did not hesitate to vote **themselves** a raise.

There   See **Their.**

They're   See **Their.**

Threw, Through, Thru   *Threw,* the past tense of the verb *throw,* means "hurled an object"; *through* means "by way of" or "to reach an end"; *thru* is a nonstandard spelling of *through.*

In a pivotal scene in *Hedda Gabler,* Hedda **threw** Lovborg's manuscript into the fire.

Blue Highways is a picaresque account of William Least Heat-Moon's travels **through** the United States.

Till, Until, 'Til   Both *till* and *until* are acceptable; *'til,* though slightly archaic, is also admissible; watch spelling and punctuation.

There will be no peace in the Middle East **till (until)** religious groups there become more tolerant of each other.

To, Too, Two   *To* is a preposition or part of an infinitive; *too* is a modifier meaning "in extreme" or "also"; *two* is the number.

In Cold Blood was Truman Capote's attempt **to** create what he called a nonfiction novel.

James Joyce's *Finnegan's Wake* is **too** idiosyncratic for many readers.

China gave the Washington Zoo **two** pandas who were promptly named Yin and Yang.

Try and   Use *try to,* the accepted form.

Producers of music videos **try to** recreate the essence of a song in visual form, with mixed success.

Uninterested   See **Disinterested.**

Until   See **Till.**

Use to, Used to   Use *used to,* the standard form.

Painters **used to** mix their own paints from pigments, oils, and bonding agents.

Utilize, Utilization   Generally use *use,* a shorter, simpler way of expressing the same idea.

Wait for, Wait on   *Wait for* means "to stay and expect"; *wait on* means "to serve."

In Beckett's famous play, Vladimir and Estragon **wait for** Godot.

Because of severe bouts of asthma and allergies, Marcel Proust was frequently bedridden and had to be **waited on** most of his life.

Weather, Whether   *Weather* means "conditions of the climate"; *whether* means "if."

In the South, rapid changes in the **weather** can often be attributed to shifts in the Gulf Stream.

Citizens must pay taxes **whether** they like it or not.

Well   See **Good.**

Whether   See **Weather.**

Which   See **That.**

Who   See **That.**

Who/Whom, Whoever/Whomever   Use *who* and *whoever* as subjects; use *whom* and *whomever* as objects.

Doctors **who** cannot relate well to patients should go into research work.

Whoever designed the conference program did a splendid job.

To **whom** should we submit our report?

Contact **whomever** you wish. I doubt that you will get a clear response.

Who's, Whose   *Who's,* a contraction, means "who is" or "who has"; *whose,* a possessive pronoun, means "belonging to someone unknown."

We need to find out **who's** scribbling graffiti on the walls.

A spelunker is someone **whose** hobby is exploring caves.

Will   See **Shall.**

Would   See **Should.**

Would of   See **Could of.**

Glossary of Grammatical Terms

Absolute Phrase   See **Phrase.**

Abstract Noun   See **Noun.**

Active Voice   See **Voice.**

Adjective   A word that modifies or limits a noun or pronoun by answering one of these questions: *what kind, which one, how many, whose.*

> **Distilled** water makes the best ice cubes.

A **regular adjective** precedes the word it modifies:

> The **velvet** dress cost two hundred dollars.

A **predicate adjective** follows a linking verb but modifies the subject of the sentence or clause:

> Ladders should be **sturdy** and **lightweight.**

An **article** (*a, an, the*) is considered an adjective:

> **A** good friend is **a** good listener.

A **demonstrative adjective** can show closeness (*this, these*) or distance (*that, those*) and singularity (*this, that*) or plurality (*these, those*):

> All of **these** books will not fit in **that** bookcase.

A **pronoun-adjective** is a pronoun that modifies a noun:

> **Somebody's** car is parked in **my** space.

Adjective Clause   See **Clause.**

Adjective Phrase   See **Phrase.**

Adverb   A word that modifies a verb, adjective, adverb, clause, phrase, or whole sentence by answering one of these questions: *how, when, where, how often, to what extent.*

Roberto enunciates **carefully.**   (*Carefully* modifies *enunciates,* telling how.)

He is **usually** soft-spoken.   (*Usually* modifies *is,* telling when.)

He sometimes speaks **too** softly.   (*Too* modifies *softly,* telling to what extent.)

Frequently, he has to repeat comments.   (*Frequently* modifies the whole sentence, telling how often.)

Adverb Clause   See **Clause.**

Adverbial Conjunction   See **Conjunctive Adverb.**

Agreement   The matching of words according to number (singular and plural) and gender (masculine, feminine, and neuter). A verb takes a singular or plural form depending on whether its subject is singular or plural. A pronoun must match its antecedent (the word it refers to) in gender as well as number. A demonstrative adjective must match the number of the word it modifies (*this* and *that* for singular, *these* and *those* for plural).

Antecedent   The word to which a pronoun refers.

Debra changed the tire herself.   (*Debra* is the antecedent of the reflexive pronoun *herself.*)

Appositive   A word or group of words that restates or defines a noun or pronoun. An appositive is positioned immediately after the word it explains.

Nonrestrictive appositives clarify proper nouns and are set off by commas:

Crest, **the best-selling toothpaste,** is recommended by many dentists.

Restrictive appositives are themselves proper nouns and require no commas:

The toothpaste **Crest** is advertised heavily on television.

Article   See **Adjective.**

Auxiliary Verb   Same as Helping Verb. See **Verb.**

Balanced Sentence   See **Sentence.**

Case   The form that a noun or pronoun takes according to its grammatical role in a sentence.

Subjective case describes a word used as a subject or predicate noun:

She drives a Honda Civic LX.

Objective case describes a word used as a direct object, indirect object, or object of a preposition:

The small size is just right for **her.**

Possessive case describes a word used to show ownership:

Her Civic is cherry red.

Most nouns and pronouns change only to form the possessive case (by adding an apostrophe and *s: cat's, someone's*). Personal, relative, and interrogative pronouns, however, change form for all three cases.

Clause   A group of words that has a subject and predicate.

An **independent clause** is grammatically complete; when used separately, it is indistinguishable from a simple sentence:

Dinosaurs had small brains.

An independent clause can be joined to another clause with a coordinating conjunction, a subordinating conjunction, or a semicolon.

A **subordinate clause** also has a subject and predicate, but it is not grammatically complete; it must be joined to an independent clause:

> **Although dinosaurs had enormous bodies,** they had small brains.

A subordinate clause can function as an adjective, an adverb, or a noun.

An **adjective clause** modifies a noun or pronoun:

> We want a television **that has surround-sound.**

An **adverb clause** modifies a verb, an adjective, another adverb, a clause, a phrase, or a whole sentence:

> Adam gets up earlier **than I usually do.**

A **noun clause** functions as a noun:

> **Whoever finds the wallet** will probably return it.

Collective Noun   See **Noun.**

Comma Fault   See **Comma Splice.**

Comma Splice   Independent clauses incorrectly joined by a comma:

> Einstein's brain has been preserved since his death, the formaldehyde has damaged the tissue.

Common Noun   See **Noun.**

Comparative Degree   See **Degree.**

Complement   Words or groups of words that complete the meaning of a sentence.

A **direct object** follows a transitive verb and answers these questions: *what, whom:*

> Jason rented some **skis.**

An **indirect object** follows a transitive verb, is used with a direct object, and answers these questions: *to what, to whom:*

Jason gave **me** skiing lessons.

A **predicate noun** follows a linking verb and restates the subject of the sentence or clause:

Jason is a patient **instructor.**

A **predicate adjective** follows a linking verb and modifies the subject of the sentence or clause:

Nevertheless, the lessons were **frustrating.**

Complete Predicate   See **Predicate.**

Complete Subject   See **Subject.**

Complex Sentence   See **Sentence.**

Compound   Two or more words, phrases, or clauses that work together as one unit. **Compound words:** *dining room, razzle dazzle.* **Compound subject: Shimita** and **Amir** were married on Tuesday. **Compound predicate:** We **attended** the wedding but **skipped** the reception.

Compound-Complex Sentence   See **Sentence.**

Compound Predicate   See **Compound.**

Compound Sentence   See **Sentence.**

Compound Subject   See **Compound.**

Concrete Noun   See **Noun.**

Conjunction   Words that join words, phrases, and clauses. Conjunctions link compound words, explain alternatives, show contrast, clarify chronology, and explain causal relationships.

A **coordinating conjunction** (*and, but, for, nor, or, so,* or *yet*) links equivalent sentence parts:

Stenographic **and** typing skills are required for the job.

A **subordinate conjunction** (*although, because, until,* and others) introduces a subordinate clause in a sentence:

Although Todd could type, he could not take shorthand.

A **correlative conjunction** (*either . . . or, neither . . . nor,* and others) links equivalent sentence parts and provides additional emphasis:

He will **either** learn shorthand **or** look for other work.

Conjunctive Adverb   Though used to link ideas logically, a conjunctive adverb does not make a grammatical connection as a traditional conjunction does and must therefore be used in an independent clause:

The experiment lasted two years; **however,** the results were inconclusive.

Coordinating Conjunction   See **Conjunction.**

Correlative Conjunction   See **Conjunction.**

Dangling Modifier   An introductory modifier that does not logically modify the subject of the sentence:

Charred from overcooking, we could not eat the steaks.

Degree   The form that adjectives and adverbs take to show degrees of comparison. **Positive degree** is a direct form, with no comparison: *simple.* **Comparative degree** compares two items: *simpler.* **Superlative degree** compares three or more items: *simplest.*

Demonstrative Adjective   See **Adjective.**

Demonstrative Pronoun   See **Pronoun.**

Dependent Clause   Same as Subordinate Clause. See **Clause.**

Direct Address   The use of a noun to identify the person or people spoken to; the noun is set off by commas and restricted to speech or writing that approximates speech:

> **Friends,** it is time for us to voice our opinions.

Direct Object   See **Complement.**

Direct Quotation   Using someone's exact words, taken from speech or writing, in speech or writing. Quotation marks indicate where the quoted material begins and ends:

> Professor Mullican often says, **"Writing is never finished; it is only abandoned."**

An **indirect quotation** reports what people say without using direct wording; an indirect quotation is often introduced with *that* for statements and *if* for questions:

> Professor Mullican asked **if I understood what he meant.**

Double Negative   Nonstandard use of two negative words within one construction. See also **Can't help but** in the Glossary of Usage.

> He **didn't** do **no** work on the project.

Elliptical Construction   A construction that omits words (usually verbs and modifiers) that are considered understood:

> Gorillas are more intelligent than chimpanzees [are].

Expletive Construction   A construction (*here is, it is, there are,* and *there is*) that functions as the subject and verb of a sentence or clause but depends on a complement to create meaning:

> **There are** too many desks in this office.

Fragment   A group of words improperly presented as a sentence, with a capital letter at the beginning and with end punctuation. A fragment can lack a subject or a verb:

> Left her baggage in the terminal.

It can be an unattached subordinate clause:

> Although the clerk had said the bags were ready.

It can be an unattached phrase:

> Stood at the baggage claim area for ten minutes.

Fused Sentence   Two or more independent clauses placed one after the other with no separating punctuation:

> The vegetables at Trotski's Market are always fresh those at Wilkerson's are not.

Future Perfect Tense   See **Tense.**

Future Tense   See **Tense.**

Gender   Three classes of nouns and pronouns based on sex: masculine (*Roger, he*), feminine (*Martha, she),* and neuter (*tractor, it*).

Gerund   See **Verbal.**

Gerund Phrase   See **Phrase.**

Helping Verb   Same as Auxiliary Verb. See **Verb.**

Imperative Mood   See **Mood.**

Indefinite Pronoun   See **Pronoun.**

Independent Clause   Same as Main Clause. See **Clause.**

Indicative Mood   See **Mood.**

Indirect Object   See **Complement.**

Indirect Quotation   See **Direct Quotation.**

Infinitive   See **Verbal.**

Infinitive Phrase   See **Phrase.**

Intensive Pronoun   Same as Reflexive Pronoun. See
   Pronoun.

Interjection   A word that expresses surprise or emotion or
   that provides a conversational transition:

>   **Well,** I don't want to go either.

Interrogative Pronoun   See **Pronoun.**

Intransitive Verb   See **Verb.**

Irregular Verb   See **Verb.**

Linking Verb   See **Verb.**

Loose Sentence   See **Sentence.**

Main Clause   Same as Independent Clause. See **Clause.**

Misplaced Modifier   A modifier incorrectly placed in a sentence; the word, phrase, or clause it modifies is not clear:

>   Anthony said before midnight he would have his paper done.

Modifier   A word, phrase, or clause used as an adjective or
   adverb to limit, clarify, qualify, or in some way restrict the
   meaning of another part of the sentence.

Mood   A verb form that allows writers to present ideas with
   proper meaning.

Indicative mood presents a fact, offers an opinion, or asks
   a question:

>   The baby **has** a fever.

Imperative mood presents commands or directions:

>   **Call** the doctor.

Subjunctive mood presents a conditional situation or one contrary to fact:

I wish she **were feeling** better.

Nominative Case   Same as Subjective Case. See **Case.**

Nonrestrictive Element   An appositive, phrase, or clause that supplies information that is not essential to the meaning of a sentence. A nonrestrictive element is separated from the rest of the sentence by commas:

Cabaret, **my favorite film,** is on Cinemax next week. (appositive)

Michael York, **with charm and humor,** played the leading male role.   (phrase)

Marisa Berenson, **who was better known for her modeling than for her acting,** played the wealthy Jewish woman who came for English lessons.   (clause)

Noun   A word that names a person, place, thing, idea, quality, or condition. A **proper noun** names a specific person, place, or thing: *Elijah P. Lovejoy, Versailles, the Hope Diamond*. A **common noun** names a person, place, or thing by general type: *abolitionist, palace, jewel*. A **collective noun** names a group of people or things: *team, herd*. A **concrete noun,** either common or proper, names something tangible: *Mrs. Mastrioni, clinic, credit card*. An **abstract noun** names an intangible quality or condition: *honesty, nervousness*.

Noun Clause   See **Clause.**

Noun Marker   Same as Article. See **Adjective.**

Number   Two classes of nouns, pronouns, and verbs: singular (one) and plural (two or more). A noun in the plural form usually ends with *s: problem* (singular), *problems* (plural); a verb in the third-person singular form ends with *s: she cares* (singular), *they care* (plural); a demonstrative pronoun in the plural form ends with *se: this rabbit* (singular), *these rabbits* (plural).

Objective Case   See **Case.**

Object of a Preposition   A noun or pronoun that a preposition links to the rest of the sentence:

> The electrical outlet is behind the **couch.**   (*Couch* is linked to *is,* telling *where.*)

Parallelism   The use of the same form for equivalent verbs in the same tense, a series of similar verbals or predicate nouns, and so on:

> Congressman Abernathe **denied** the charges, **questioned** the evidence, **produced** full records, and **received** a formal apology. (all past-tense verbs)

Parenthetical Expression   A word or group of words that interrupts the pattern of a sentence, separating elements and adding secondary information. Such expressions are separated by parentheses or dashes:

> Seeing *Arcadia* in New York was expensive—**the tickets were fifty-five dollars each**—but worthwhile.

Participial Phrase   See **Phrase.**

Participle   See **Verbal.**

Parts of Speech   The classification of words into eight categories according to their use in sentences: noun, pronoun, verb, adjective, adverb, conjunction, preposition, and interjection. Each part of speech is separately defined in this glossary.

Passive Voice   See **Voice.**

Past Participle See **Verbal.**

Past Perfect Tense See **Tense.**

Perfect Tenses See **Tense.**

Periodic Sentence See **Sentence.**

Person Three classes of nouns, pronouns, and verbs that indicate the relationship between the writer and the subject. **First person** (*I am, we are*) indicates that the writer writes about himself or herself; **second person** indicates that the writer writes about and to the same people (*you are*); **third person** indicates that the writer is writing to an audience *about* someone else (*she is, they are, Mitch is, the researchers are*).

Personal Pronoun See **Pronoun.**

Phrase A group of words that cannot function independently as a sentence but must be part of a sentence. A whole phrase often functions as a noun, adjective, or adverb.

A **prepositional phrase** consists of a preposition (*above, during, under,* and others), its object, and any modifiers: *above the front doorway, during the thunder storm, under the subject heading.* A prepositional phrase can function as an adjective or adverb:

The woman **next to me** read **during the entire flight.** (*Next to me* is adjectival, modifying *woman; during the entire flight* is adverbial, modifying *read.*)

A **gerund phrase** combines a gerund and its complements and modifiers; it functions as a noun:

Conducting an orchestra requires skill, patience, and inspiration. (*Conducting an orchestra* is the subject of the sentence.)

A **participial phrase** combines a participle and its modifiers; it functions as an adjective:

> From her window, Mrs. Bradshaw watched the children **playing under her maple tree.**   (*Playing under her maple tree* modifies *children*.)

An **infinitive phrase** combines an infinitive and its complements and modifiers; it functions as a noun, an adjective, or an adverb:

> **To succeed as a freelance artist** is difficult.   (noun)

> Supplies **to use in art classes** are costly unless I get them wholesale.   (adverb).

> **To make ends meet,** I work part time at a bank.   (adjective)

An **absolute phrase** modifies a whole sentence or clause. It contains a noun and a participle and is separated from the rest of the sentence by a comma:

> **All things considered,** the recital was a success.

Positive Degree   See **Degree.**

Possessive Case   See **Case.**

Predicate   A word or group of words that expresses action or state of being in sentences; it consists of one or more verbs, plus any complements or modifiers.

A **simple predicate** is the single verb and its auxiliaries, if any:

> Iago mercilessly **destroyed** the lives of Othello and Desdemona.

A **complete predicate** is the simple predicate, plus any complements or modifiers:

> Iago **mercilessly destroyed the lives of Othello and Desdemona.**

Predicate Adjective   See **Complement.**

Predicate Noun   See **Complement.**

Preposition   A word that establishes a relationship between a noun or pronoun (the object of the preposition) and some other word in the sentence:

> **After** his term **in** office, Jimmy Carter returned **to** Plains, Georgia. (*Term* is linked to *Carter; office* is linked to *term; Plains, Georgia* is linked to *returned.*)

Prepositional Phrase   See **Phrase.**

Present Participle   See **Verbal.**

Present Perfect Tense   See **Tense.**

Present Tense   See **Tense.**

Progressive Tense   See **Tense.**

Pronoun   A word that substitutes for a noun (its antecedent). A **personal pronoun** refers to people or things: *I, me, you, he, him, she, her, it, we, us, they, them.* A **possessive pronoun** shows ownership. Some possessive pronouns function independently: *mine, yours, his, hers, its, ours, theirs;* some (known as adjective-pronouns) must be used with nouns: *my, your, his, her, our, their.* A **reflexive pronoun** shows that someone or something is acting for itself or on itself: *myself, yourself, himself, herself, itself, ourselves, yourselves, themselves.* An **interrogative pronoun** is used to ask a question: *who, whom, whoever, whomever, what, which, whose.* A **demonstrative pronoun** is used alone: *this, that, these, those.* An **indefinite pronoun** has no particular antecedent but serves as a general subject or object in a sentence: *another, everything, most, somebody,* and others. A

relative pronoun introduces an adjective or noun clause: *that, what, which, who, whom, whoever, whomever, whose.*

Proper Adjective   An adjective derived from a proper noun: *Belgian lace, Elizabethan sonnet.*

Proper Noun   See **Noun.**

Quotation   See **Direct Quotation.**

Reflexive Pronoun   Same as Intensive Pronoun. See **Pronoun.**

Regular Verb   See **Verb.**

Relative Pronoun   See **Pronoun.**

Restrictive Element   An appositive, phrase, or clause that supplies information necessary to the meaning of a sentence. A restrictive element is not set off by commas:

> The dramatic show *Party of Five* was critically successful but only moderately popular. The problems **that four parentless siblings might face** were dealt with honestly.

Run-on Sentence   See **Fused Sentence.**

Sentence   An independent group of words with a subject and predicate, with a capital at the beginning, and with end punctuation. It expresses a grammatically complete thought. For most purposes, sentences are classified by their structure.

A **simple sentence** contains one independent clause and expresses one relationship between a subject and predicate:

> The test flight was a success.

A **compound sentence** contains two or more independent clauses joined by a comma and a coordinating conjunction or by a semicolon:

> The test flight was a success, and we began production on the jet.

A **complex sentence** contains one independent clause and one or more subordinate clauses:

Although there were some problems, the test flight was a success.

A **compound-complex sentence** contains at least two independent clauses and one or more subordinate clauses:

Although there were some problems, the test flight was a success, and we began production on the jet.

In addition, a sentence can be classified by the arrangement of its ideas. A **loose sentence** presents major ideas first and then adds clarifications:

The bus was crowded with students, shoppers, and commuters.

A **periodic sentence** places the major idea or some part of it at the end:

Although we wanted a car with power steering, power brakes, power windows, automatic transmission, air conditioning, and quadraphonic sound, we couldn't afford one.

A **balanced sentence** contains parallel words, phrases, or clauses:

Lawrence was irresponsible, undisciplined, and rowdy, but his brother Jerod was responsible, disciplined, and reserved.

Sentence Fragment   See **Fragment.**

Simple Predicate   See **Predicate.**

Simple Sentence   See **Sentence.**

Simple Subject   See **Subject.**

Simple Tenses   See **Tense.**

Subject   The people, places, things, ideas, qualities, or conditions that act or are described in an active sentence or that are acted upon in a passive sentence.

A **simple subject** is the single word or essential group of words that controls the focus of the sentence:

> **Oppenheimer and Teller,** participants in the Manhattan Project, disagreed about the development of the hydrogen bomb.

A **complete subject** is the simple subject plus all related modifiers, phrases, and clauses:

> **Oppenheimer and Teller, participants in the Manhattan Project,** disagreed about the development of the hydrogen bomb.

Subjective Case   Same as Nominative Case. See **Case.**

Subjunctive Mood   See **Mood.**

Subordinate Clause   See **Clause.**

Subordinating Conjunction   See **Conjunction.**

Superlative Degree   See **Degree.**

Tense   The modification of main verbs to indicate when an action occurred or when a state of being existed. **Simple tenses** include the **present** (*he plans, they plan*), **past** (*he planned, they planned*), and **future** (*he will plan, they will plan*). **Perfect tenses** include the **present perfect** (*he has planned, they have planned*), **past perfect** (*he had planned, they had planned*), and **future perfect** (*he will have planned, they will have planned*). The **progressive tenses** indicate habitual or future action (*he is planning, he was planning, he will be planning, he had been planning, they are planning, they were planning, they had been planning, they will have been planning*).

Transitive Verb   See **Verb.**

Verb A word or group of words that expresses action or a state of being. For most purposes, verbs are classified by their function. An **action verb** expresses physical or mental action:

The cat **pounced** on the mouse. I **thought** it was cruel.

A **linking verb** expresses a state of being or condition and joins the subject with a complement:

The cat **seemed** indifferent to my reaction. Cats **are** skillful predators.

An **auxiliary verb** is used with a main verb to form a verb phrase, commonly used to clarify time references, explain states of being, or ask questions:

We **will** stay on schedule.

Things **could** be worse.

Can you play the harpsichord?

All verbs are classified by the way they form basic verb parts. A **regular verb** forms the past tense by adding *-ed* or *-d* and maintains that form for the past participle: *talk, talked, had talked; close, closed, has closed.* An **irregular verb** follows varied patterns and may change for each form: *go, went, has gone; sing, sang, had sung.*

Verbal A verb form used as a noun, adjective, or adverb. A **gerund** is an *-ing* verb form that functions as a noun; the form of a gerund is the same as the present participle:

Hiking is my favorite sport.

An **infinitive** is a verb form that uses *to;* it functions as a noun or adverb:

To open his own shop is Gerhardt's dream.   (noun)

Gerhardt is too committed **to give up.**   (adverb)

A **participle** is a verb form that uses *-ing, -ed, -d, -n,* or *-t;* it functions as an adjective or adverb. A **present participle** ends in *-ing:*

Beaming, Clancey accepted the first-place trophy.

A **past participle** ends in *-ed, -d, -n,* or *-t;* a past participle can also help form a verb phrase:

The window pane, **broken** by a baseball, must be replaced. (adjective)

We have **broken** that window many times.   (part of main verb)

See also **Phrase.**

Verb Phrase   See **Phrase.**

Voice   The form of a transitive verb that illustrates whether the subject *does* something or has something *done to it.*

Active voice indicates that the subject acts:

Roy Hobbs **wrote** the feature article.

Passive voice indicates that the subject completes no action but is instead acted upon:

The feature article **was written** by Roy Hobbs.

Credits

Credits

Word-Processing Index

General Index

Boldface numbers refer to section numbers; other numbers refer to pages.

REVISION CHECKLISTS

Content

Are the title and the introductory strategy interesting, clear, and appropriate in tone?

Does the thesis statement clearly present the topic and your opinion about it?

Do the topics of the paragraphs support the thesis statement? Are they clearly stated?

Are the topics presented in a clear, emphatic order?

Are the paragraphs adequately developed? Is there enough detail? Are there enough examples? Does information in each paragraph relate to the thesis statement?

Are the summary and concluding strategy effective?

Style

Do the lengths and types of sentences vary?

Do sentences clearly and concisely express their meaning?

Are word choices vivid, accurate, and appropriate?

Do most sentences use the active voice?

Do transitions adequately relate ideas?

Technical Errors and Inconsistencies

Are all words correctly spelled? (When in doubt, always look up the correct spelling in your dictionary.)

Are any necessary words omitted? Are any words unnecessarily repeated?

Is punctuation accurate? (See "Punctuation," starting on page 320.)

Are elements of mechanics properly used? (See "Mechanics," starting on page 379.)

Are all sentences complete?

Do nouns and pronouns and subjects and verbs agree in number and gender as appropriate?

Are all pronoun antecedents clear?

Are all modifiers logically positioned?